Grandmasters of
Educational Thought

Grandmasters of Educational Thought

Adolphe E. Meyer, Ph.D.

Emeritus Professor of Educational History
New York University

Member of the Authors League of America

McGraw-Hill Book Company

New York   St. Louis   San Francisco   Auckland   Düsseldorf
Johannesburg   Kuala Lumpur   London   Mexico
Montreal   New Delhi   Panama   Paris
São Paulo   Singapore   Sydney   Tokyo   Toronto

Library of Congress Cataloging in Publication Data

Meyer, Adolphe Erich, date
    Grandmasters of educational thought.

    Bibliography: p.
    1. Education—Philosophy—History. 2. Educators.
I. Title.
LA21.M47   370.1'092'2   74-18397
ISBN 0-07-041737-7
ISBN 0-07-041750-4 (pbk.)

GRANDMASTERS OF EDUCATIONAL THOUGHT

  2 3 4 5 6 7 8 9 0 DODO 7 9 8 7 6 5

This book was set in Times Roman by National ShareGraphics, Inc.
The editors were Stephen D. Dragin and James R. Belser;
the cover was designed by Nicholas Krenitsky;
the production supervisor was Judi Frey.
R. R. Donnelley & Sons Company was printer and binder.

THIS BOOK IS AFFECTIONATELY INSCRIBED
TO THE MEMORY OF
WILLIAM DOUGLAS BRYANT, MY BROTHER-IN-LAW,
AND ADOLPH E. MEYER, JR., MY SON.

Contents

Preface

This book is, in a sense, of the same breed as my earlier one, *An Educational History of the American People,* and its sister volume, *An Educational History of the Western World.* Unlike them, however, it concerns itself only incidentally with institutions and directs its chief attention instead to the doctrines of a limited number of selected educators, the grandmasters, as it were, of pedagogy. To this purpose it turns the spotlight upon educational ideas as their holders exposed them to the public eye and, more important, as they strove to infuse them with the breath of life in practice. Designed in the beginning to serve the needs of my graduate students at New York University in a course concentrating on the educational classics, the material laid bare in the pages that follow grew with the passing years, and, considerably altered and reworked, it assumed the role of giving a helping hand to my students as they made their way through the thickets of the foundational courses in educational theory, both at N.Y.U. and other institutions of higher learning. What I tried to accomplish is, by the power of the written word, to make them hear and feel, and above all, to appreciate the vast and impressive effort that has been expended through the centuries in the making of modern education.

Adolphe E. Meyer

Chapter 1

Socrates and the Sophists

THE COMING OF THE NEW THOUGHT

In the journals of the Western world the year 490 B.C. is one that should be circled in scarlet. For in that year at Marathon a small force of Athenians, aided by a handful of Plataeans, not only stayed the inrush of an immensely larger horde of fighting Persians and assorted allies, including engineers, horses, elephants, slaves, and professional strumpets, but trounced them so convincingly that the intruders decided then and there that there was no place like home. So amazing was the Hellenic feat that it staggered the common imagination, and from the Pillars of Hercules to the Syrian backwaters and beyond, as the news began to trickle down to the public it became the object of prodigious parley. For the Greeks in general, hitherto known all too well for their acrimonious dissensions and strifes, the triumph was an exhilarating shot in the arm, but it was especially so for the Athenians whose verve and enterprise galvanized them to forge, as the years ran on, a new and thoroughly cosmopolitan civilization.

As Athenian trade and commerce zoomed higher and higher, outlanders, seduced by the city's sudden glamor and its marvelous opportunities, poured in from all directions in ever-swelling numbers. Not a few of them, doubtless, were self-seekers, fevering, like the gold-rushers of '49 in our own republic, to make their fortune. But among the chaff there was also some good, sound grain—men of insatiable curiosity, and often of abundant talent, destined to be among the great of the world. For example, there was Hippocrates, the father of medicine, and an émigré from Asia Minor; there was Thales of Miletus, saluted by historians as the founder of Greek philosophy; and there was the incomparable Aristotle from Stageirus, a town on the Aegean's northwestern littoral.

Whatever their estate, whether they were men of learning, of the marketplace, or mere soldiers of fortune, the newcomers brought with them a cargo of novel ideas of which the Athenians were for the most part happily innocent. Vivified by a sprightly freshness, often rakish, some of them were also provocative, and like so many new things, intellectual or otherwise, they began to be talked about. But as everyone knows, trafficking in strange ideas can be risky, for sometimes their precepts, however charming, run head-on into the cherished values of the elders. Thus it was with the New Thought in Athens. Alluring though some of its propositions were, especially in the minds of the Athenian youth, at bottom many of them were also in plain defiance of the established tradition. The result of this threat of the new to the venerable old was a rise in skepticism which, invading both the sacred and secular domains, showed itself at every turn, from the pointed queries of the homely Socrates to the hilarious lampooneries of Aristophanes. Under the glare of skepticism even the gods were reduced to mere figments of human fancy. Morality, set loose from the convention that had anchored it for uncounted generations, found itself adrift with no support save reason. In matters of statecraft, the one-time respect for blood and breeding, the prime requisite for the fulfillment of political ambitions, succumbed to the power of wealth, with a consequent surge in the number of opulent politicos and their footlings. In the meantime, young Athenians, smitten by the New Thought's promise of personal gain and advancement, chafed at the state's hoary ideal of public service and finally turned their backs on the old order—or, to use the current term, the Establishment—with its restraining tradition. The young, as the elderly well know, are naturally restive over and impatient with things as they are. Indeed, it seems that the only way they can form their minds is to stand up against the reigning opinion. Hence, when a new education began to emerge, the youth of Athens were ready to give it attention.

THE SOPHISTS—HIPPIAS, GORGIAS, PRODICUS, PROTAGORAS

The most audible, and very likely the most spectacular skeptics of the time were the Sophists, so called because they specialized in the teaching of wisdom that in Greek parlance was spoken of as *sophia*. But the word, endowed with a double meaning, could also stand for cleverness, a fact the anti-Sophists, led by Plato, were quick to note. The new teachers came almost entirely from foreign lands, a circumstance which outraged the ideals of the defenders of things as they used to be. Even more unspeakable was the Sophists' insistence on being paid for their instruction, a practice which in conservative eyes put them on a level not of worthy Athenians but of the nethermost tradesfolk. Appearing in Athens during the 400s B.C., these vendors of *sophia* taught only a few students at a time. They maintained no schools and thereby spared themselves the bother of having to pay a landlord. Instead, they dispensed their instruction wherever convenience suggested, in the coolness, say, of some shadowed grove during the heat of summer, or in the sanctuary of some friendly snuggery when the rainy season struck. Not being shackled to any particular school, the Sophists were free to set up their stand not only in Athens itself, but anywhere they chose. One might liken them to traveling salesmen, peripatetic drummers of knowledge, offering to teach their specialties wherever they could find a paying clientele.

The information we have of these men is extremely spare. Even their names have for the most part vanished into oblivion, as has the overwhelming bulk of their writings. Until not so long ago, moreover, they suffered from the critical slings and arrows of their adversaries, chiefly Plato and Isocrates. Some Sophists, doubtless, were more clever than wise, slippery phrasemakers, and sometimes shameless mountebanks, whose chief interest lay in self-enrichment rather than in the illumination of the young. Indeed, for a fee some of them gave instruction in anything at all.

But for every such quack there were others at the opposite pole. Among the handful whose names still linger, not a few were first-rate scholars. The most erudite, and also the most vain, was Hippias. A veritable Sorbonne on legs, he came to Athens from Elis, wasting no time on his arrival in letting it be known that there was nothing that he did not know, and for a fee would teach. Rhetorician, lyricist, and musician, he also discoursed at great length on politics, morals, and letters. In addition, he taught astronomy and mathematics. By assembling and arranging a list of Olympic victors, he laid the groundwork of Greek chronology. He took a fling at history and the art and industry of practical diplomacy, besides acting in his spare time as his own clothier. Laws and social usages he ignored as man-made inventions that were in collision with human nature. He was, on a small scale, an early incarnation of Rousseau, that romantic bubbler for a return to nature as the one sure way to human happiness.

Less cocky than the self-important Hippias, although also less learned, was Gorgias, a Sicilian from Leontini. A virtuoso of rhetoric and politics, he represented his country for awhile as its Athenian ambassador. But it was in speech-making that he threw off his brightest sparks, and whenever he was to perform in public, his admirers came from miles about to hear him. To young Greeks his great talent was a powerful magnet, and they came to beseech him to give them lessons in the secrets of his art. It was an invitation which, for a respectable compensation, he accepted with alacrity.

Gorgias was under no compulsion to publish or perish, as are so many of his academic successors today, yet before he went to his grave, a centenarian, he put his main thoughts into several books. Of these *On Nature* was by all odds the boldest. Certainty, he maintained therein, is unattainable. Nothing, he went on, exists beyond the senses. And even assuming that it did, its existence would be unknowable since what we know is attainable only through the senses. Finally, even it were knowable, there would be no way to disseminate our knowledge, since all communication depends upon the senses. Gorgias's epistemological agnosticism extended even to the Hellenic divinities, for never having perceived them, he was unwilling to ratify their existence. Of Gorgias's numerous compositions, the aforementioned ideas are the sole survivors in our possession—a mere speck, as it were, on the cosmic flywheel. Nevertheless, they are not lightly to be dismissed. For in the intellectual's warfare on a priori assumptions—assumptions not grounded on human experience—they have proved to be a sharp and terrible sword.

The Sophists' outstanding moral scientist was Prodicus of Cios, who specialized in trying to make his students upright and decent by teaching them ethics, natural philosophy, religious history, and the language to make such mysteries understandable. To help his learners, he prepared a handbook, *On Correct Language.* Antagonistic to the ethical dogmatism of the Old Guard Athenians, he expressed grave doubts about the possibility of such a thing as absolute virtue, for, at bottom, the quality of good and evil is variable. Like the pragmatists of our own times, Prodicus held that the only reliable test of good conduct is how it works in human experience. Rather noteworthy, particularly in the light of certain Sophists' appetite for lush fees, is Prodicus's almost abstemious tuition levy of one to fifty drachmas per course. But, as the saying is, you get what you pay for, and Prodicus saw to it that the one-drachma student got substantially less than the fifty-drachma customer.

Supreme among the Sophists—their architect of thought—was Protagoras of Abdera. Not only was he a violator of all the accepted canons, but he was the highest-paid Sophist practitioner. Thus, where Prodicus was willing to settle for fifty drachmas or less, Protagoras demanded and got two hundred times as much. But though this may come under the heading of avarice, yet it is not meant to impugn the man's integrity as either a gentleman or scholar. Even Plato, with all his disrelish for the Sophists, praised Protagoras as a man of the highest rectitude. The inventor, very likely, of what came to be known as the Socratic dialogue, he was also one of the world's first philologists. A creative grammarian, he gained fame as a solver of linguistic problems. He gladdened our humdrum existence by conjuring up three genders of nouns, besides unearthing a number of tenses, and discovering that verbs entertained moods. Like Gorgias, who for a spell was his contemporary, Protagoras insisted that our only means of attaining new knowledge are the five senses, a view which after all these centuries still commands a ponderable backing. Protagoras brushed aside philosophical absolutes, so highly regarded by Plato and the latter-day idealists, as so much humbug. Perfect and forever fixed, as Plato would have it, absolute justice, virtue, beauty, happiness, even truth, are a metaphysician's dream. In actuality they are relative and ephemeral. Like man, their maker, they are here today and gone tomorrow. "Man," Protagoras gave notice, "is the measure of all things." The generality of men, Protagoras was convinced, have a sense of justice as well as a sense of shame. The exceptions he likened to wild beasts who, to safeguard the rest of us, called for extinction.

Protagoras's bold thinking, like that of Gorgias, his fellow sinner, drew his attention to the holy pantheon. "As for the gods," he was heard to say, "I know not whether they exist . . . or what they are like. Many things prevent our knowing; the subject is obscure; and brief is the span of our mortal life." His irreverence so enraged right-feeling Athenians that their assembly promptly banished him and ordered the seizure of all his writings, including his works on education and even his grammar, *On Good Speech*, for public incineration in the marketplace.

THE SOPHISTS SUMMARIZED

Among Sophists, as has been said, there were charlatans, but there were also lustrous and original thinkers. Their purpose at its best was to teach; at its worst simply to make money. Their movement was ethical no less than intellectual, and its foremost exemplars were evangelists no less than pedagogues. There is no gainsaying that some of them left their mark on learning. To fill the growing void between the dying Athenian city-state of old and its emerging cosmopolitan successor, the Sophists attacked the conventional education, adequate and even praiseworthy in its time but now exhausted and sterile, and in place of moral absolutes they introduced the doctrine of ethical relativity, which is to say that right and wrong are not static and immovable, but that, on the contrary, they are ever changing. Addressing themselves to the individual rather than the mass, the Sophists put a high stress on clear and forceful speaking, coupled with the essential tools of grammar, rhetoric, and logic, which, as the years proceeded, put a tight hammerlock on Western learning, and which are with us still today. Crafting their curriculum to suit their trade, the Sophists were ready to give instruction in philology, geometry, and astronomy, even in the melodrama of applied politics, not to mention military tactics and household management. By their stress on practical and useful learning, the Sophists broke through the barbed wires of tradition, but their enterprise, though jubilantly welcomed by the young, brought them only derision from intrenched Old Believers.

Living today in the American republic, the Sophists would find much to put music in their hearts. There is, for one thing, the common philosophic renunciation of unalterable absolutes, and the correlative confidence in the relativity of moral values. There is, for another, the national affinity for the utilitarian. Finally, there is the ever-lurking accent on success and money making, as witness such bread-and-butter courses as scientific salesmanship, cafeteria management and radio and TV play acting. Even for the unadulterated Sophist frauds there are plums aplenty, such gaudy mountebankery, for example, as offering to teach even the simple person how to be a "mental wizard" without really trying; or how to read 5,312 words in 5½ seconds flat; or how to astound one's friends by producing exotic arpeggios from a piano after only ten easy lessons.

Altogether, however, the Sophists did education a good turn. Not only did they slip outside the pale of established practice, but in doing so they also drenched it with an unsparing iconoclasm. Often irreverent, their skepticism successfully defied the time-honored Athenian values, probing them under the white light of reason. Though the light was to dim in the passing years, it was never to waste completely. Without the Sophists, one may say, in truth, there might have been no Socrates.

SOCRATES, THE MAN

A maker of talk rather than a literatus, Socrates left no written legacy. What we know of him, therefore, flows from the portrayals of others; from Plato, his student and friend; from Xenophon, his idolizer; and from Aristophanes, his critic. How trustworthy these verbal pictures are we do not know, for inevitably they are suffused with their author's bias. Plato, for example, was prone to take off in flights of literary fancy; Xenophon was a concocter of historical fiction; and Aristophanes was a successful crafter of comedy and devastating satire. Taking them together, their profile of Socrates becomes somewhat unclear, and the only certainty we have is that he was an extraordinary man, adored and despised probably more heartily than anyone else of his era.

Socrates was born in Athens in 496 B.C. or thereabouts. His father was a stonecutter and his mother a midwife, both estimable callings. Though humbly circumstanced, Socrates's father put his son upon his studies, which is to say that, like the general pack of Athenian boys, he was made literate, besides being made to cultivate his body and soul by means of gymnastics, dancing, and music. In time he became proficient in mathematics and astronomy, but as he grew older he gave them less and less thought. It is reported that in his salad days he was something of an athlete, but if a laurel ever bedecked his brow, the record of it is hidden in darkness. We do know that he participated actively in politics and that for a fleeting moment he held high office, though he entertained an outspoken hostility toward democracy. "It is absurd," Xenophon has him saying, "to choose magistrates by lot, whereas nobody would dream of drawing lots for a pilot, a mason, a flute-player, or any craftsman whatsoever, though the shortcomings of such men are far less harmful than those who disorder our government."

Socrates was an excellent soldier, and in battle he distinguished himself. His main strength, however, lay not in the might of his spear, but in the power of his mind which, when he grew to manhood, he used with great agility. Wed to Xanthippe, a shrew and a scold (not without provocation, however, for living with a loafer rather than a provider can be galling), Socrates nevertheless found the connubial condition pleasurable enough. At all events, when, because of an alarming shortage of males, Athens gave a transient legality to polygamy, Socrates is said to have contributed his services by taking to his couch an additional spouse. Yet he was not a handsome man. "You will not deny, Socrates," the young and beloved Alcibiades reminded him, "that your face is that of a satyr." Bug-eyed, thick-lipped, and barrel-bellied, Socrates was one of the homeliest men in Athens. So ugly was he that, reportedly, at the battle of Delium he transfixed the onrushing Spartans simply by glowering at them, thereby managing to escape with his life.

His personal wants were slight. Not heated by any passion to see the world, he spent the greater part of his three score and ten years in Athens, leaving it only when he was summoned to wield arms in war, or when he chose to make a pilgrimage to some outlying oracle. Whenever he worked, which was only in the last extremity, he cut stone, as had his father before him. Although he was a diligent bather, and rarely skipped his daily splashing, for his sartorial tidiness he cared not a tinker's damn. His covering was shabby, often patched and messy, and when he trod the city's streets he usually left his sandals at home. He ate and drank discreetly, though he had the taste buds of an epicure; whenever men of means issued him an invitation to drink and dine, he usually accepted with enthusiasm.

THE SOCRATIC METHOD

A man of nimble wit and a consuming interest in ideas, Socrates turned to philosophy as naturally as a mouse noses its way to cheese. He was still a youth when he encountered the Sophists, and at some time he made the acquaintance of their leading wizards, Protagoras, Gorgias, Hippias, and a number of others. It is likely that he got some of his basic intellectual weapons from them, such as his skepticism, his trust in the miracle-working possibilities of logic, and his shiftiness in disputation, although he shrugged off as fatuous their proclivity for rhetoric; and he vouchsafed no interest in the natural sciences. But from the Sophists he also derived his logical tactic, the so-called "dialectic," or as it is sometimes known, because of his masterful adroitness with it, the Socratic method. It became his custom to bring into question other men's opinions, divesting them jot by jot of their substance, until they were exposed in all their shortcomings, inappropriateness, or even stark absurdity.

To illustrate: "Do you believe," Socrates would ask an unsuspecting victim, "that Zeus leads a stainless life?"

"Of course I do," comes the swift retort.

"And do you believe," Socrates leads on, "that Zeus had intercourse with certain mortal women?"

The man can but affirm, for long ago his elders had told him tales of the god's amorous adventures with mundane females, and the resultant increase in the Hellenic population.

"Is it your belief then," Socrates drives on, "that Zeus is an adulterer?"

The hard-pressed respondent begins to fidget, for he knows full well that Zeus is a married god, and so, whether he likes it or not, he emits a doleful affirmation.

The implications are obvious. If Zeus committed adultery, then his life is not without stain, and his divinity must be suspect. But remark how different the business would have been had Socrates accosted the stranger with the blunt query, "Do you believe that Zeus is a god?" The very question breeds alarm and, maybe, even a call for the police.

SOCRATES AS TEACHER

So Socrates piloted himself about Athens, making the rounds of its shops and groggeries, the gymnasiums and the marketplace, in hopes of ferreting out a likely prospect, a soldier, say, like Lachis, a politician like Critias, or even a call girl like Theodote, to quiz about the nature of honor, truth, courage, justice, piety, and so on down the ethical track to human goodness. So he aspired to keep going even in the afterworld, to discern "who is wise, who pretends to be, and who is not." It was his mission—his demon, he said—to x-ray and elucidate ideas, first by exposing false and malformed opinions, and then by reforging them on the anvil of reason. His dialectic method, it pleased him to say, was simply the art of making careful distinctions—or, to put it another way, the science of precise definition.

Unhappily, his adversaries, particularly those who had felt the prick of his rapier, were of a different mind. He had, they said, a clever tongue. Bent on discrediting their keepsake beliefs, he left them no replacement. There is something to be said for this accusation, for, like the Sophists, Socrates took recourse in the logician's sleight of hand. Unsuspected by his prey, he would cunningly alter the meaning of terms in midstream. He would obfuscate his opponent with an avalanche of counterfeit analogies and, when caught, equivocate like a child. Worst of all, when asked to answer his own questions, he flatly refused. "By Zeus!" roared Hippias, surely no novice in the use of the smooth and narcotic phrase, "you shall not hear another word from me till you yourself state what justice is." To such reproaches Socrates blithely retorted that he knew nothing. He was, he said, a god-appointed midwife, assisting to deliver knowledge into the world, but forbidden to be its maker.

A mediator, like Plato and Aristotle, between the supporters of a dying Athens on the one hand and their radical challengers on the other, Socrates put the latter's dictum that "man is the measure of all things" under the glass and found it needed qualification. If a man is to be the measure of all things, then, asserted the philosopher, he must know his inner strengths and weaknesses, for only thus is wisdom within his reach. The wise man, Socrates was convinced, can do no wrong—by which he probably meant that it is psychologically reprehensible for him to commit evil. Whether the Athenian thinker was right or wrong does not greatly matter at this point. What does matter is that he was convinced that knowledge is the indispensable basis of truth, the truth not of any one person, for such truth leads into the Sophist moral wilderness, but the truth on which all men regardless of their personal disparities and diversities, could agree.

Does this hunter of verity differ from the Sophists in the weight they placed on the individual? Then he is also at odds with them for their accent on rhetoric, which he denounced. As a teacher, moreover, he did not venture, as did the Sophists, to give instruction in almost everything. His was the mission to promote morality, and it was to this end that he directed his skill of turning ideas inside out. Finally, though Athenians persisted in pigeonholing him as a Sophist, he at all times refused payment for his instruction on the ground that he had taught nothing.

A moralist rather than a metaphysician, Socrates addressed his thinking not to scaling some transcendental utopian alp, but rather to the making of a good society. Alive to the virtues and the shortcomings of his people, he undertook to persuade them to make themselves upright and decent by getting them to think straight. Such capacity, he believed—unlike his student Plato—is native to all. To give tomorrow's citizens the knowledge they needed, Socrates drew no grandiose educational blueprint for an imaginary perfect state; instead, he put his stress on preparing them for the concrete realities they would have to face in everyday living. To give them guidance, Socrates recommended much the same things he himself had studied when he was a boy, namely, the inevitable ABC's to make them literate, and physical culture to keep them fit both as civilians and as soldiers. To enhance poise and grace—in short, to give at least the air of good breeding—Socrates pleaded for instruction in the dance, the tonal art, and their ever-present partner, poetry. In addition he invited the students' attention to arithmetic, geometry, and astronomy insofar as they bore on the common daily experience. Overlying it all—the frosting on the cake, so to speak—was ethics; not, however, the bloodless sermonizing favored by many dons of moral science, but rather the groundwork for a happy and satisfactory relationship with others.

THE END

For all his good intentions, Socrates made more enemies than friends. It may have been, as the Delphic oracle is reported to have said ex cathedra, that no wiser man than Socrates had ever lived. At the same time his genius did not seem to apprehend that for the common person thinking is unpleasant, and sometimes even painful. To imbed the most elemental ideas is a staggering job, and all too frequently the effort is of no avail. The philosopher's students, oblivious to his homeliness, knew only the warmth of his heart. They loved him dearly; yet, sad to say, they numbered only a handful. But Socrates upset the vast mass of folk. By indulging in tearing down without building up he seemed bent on making light of their values, most of them heirlooms from their forebears, and hence deeply felt—such homely values, for example, as matrimony and democracy, and above all, religion. As one who had publicly confessed that he knew nothing, it should astonish no one that, like Protagoras and Hippias, Socrates extended his know-nothingness to the gods, an act which was to do him irreparable damage. At the same time Socrates, as the wisest man who ever lived, was sufficiently wise to make no statement which might be construed, even remotely, as an affront to the Olympian deities, or even to the established religious practice—in truth, he put great store in dreams as bulletins issuing from on high, and like all good and true Hellenes he frequented oracles and gravely attended to their cryptic counsel.

Even so, the years saw the current of public feeling against him grow ever stronger. Where once he had been tolerated as a nuisance, he came to be regarded as an inflammatory fellow, a sinister subversive, and finally a public enemy. When the state served notice on him to answer its charges, its indictment credited him with corrupting youth to disrespect its elders; with discomposing the established moral code; and with being contumacious to the gods. Found guilty by a majority of 60 votes out of 502, the old man was condemned. He was offered exile, but he spurned it and chose death instead. "He was," mourned Plato, "truly the wisest and justest and best of all the men I have ever known."

Socrates did not live nor die in vain. The ray of wisdom and virtue he shone on the folly and ugliness of the world was kept alive by his successors, especially by Plato, and subsequently by Aristotle. In their hands the effort to illuminate man's enveloping darkness was to receive still further cultivation, more systematic and more sophisticated, though, unfortunately, far from sufficient.

Chapter 2

Isocrates

THE BEGINNING

Isocrates (436–338 B.C.) was born in Athens in 436 B.C., and there he expired some ninety-eight years later. His era, like ours, was heavily beset by distress and upheaval. Wars among Greek states were unpleasantly plentiful, and one of them, the Pelopponesian War, a life-and-death grapple between Sparta and Athens, worked its evil for almost thirty years, leaving ruin in its wake for all concerned. The son of Theodorus, a wealthy flute maker, Isocrates received an education befitting his station in life, which is to say the best attainable. He studied under such renowned and expensive Sophists as Prodicus and Gorgias, the latter then living in Thessaly, and for a brief spell he came into contact with the incisive dialogue of Socrates. From the first two he adopted a few ideas, notably their insistence on the importance of knowing how to speak well and persuasively, but for the common run of the Sophist clan he professed an acute disrelish. Indeed, though he was deferential enough to his mentors, in later years, in a speech, *Against the Sophists*, he made sport of their general ideas and practice.

The long and grueling Pelopponesian War devoured the family purse, so that presently Isocrates found it necessary to work for a living. He found his forte not in flute making, but in ghostwriting speeches for litigants waging their feuds in the courts of law. Although he maintained a consuming interest in public affairs, especially those concerned with economics and politics, he never actually engaged in them himself, and he never held public office. The ironic fact is that nature had afflicted him with failings of which he was all too conscious. Not only was he of an almost blushful bashfulness; he was also handicapped by a frail voice, a liability, if ever, to chill the cockles of an aspiring politician's heart—although one that, had its victim been living in this day of microphones, loudspeakers, doctors of the subconscious, and specialists in vocal pathology, could doubtless have been at least greatly alleviated, if not cured.

AS TEACHER

In his early thirties Isocrates went to Chios, where, for a year or so, he gave instruction in rhetoric, after which he returned to his native haunt to resume his speechwriting. He worked at it resolutely for a decade or so when the itch to teach overcame him and he opened a school not far from the spot where, on a later day, Aristotle was to operate his Lyceum. The man doubtless had a natural gift for the tutorial art, and though he extracted 1,000 drachmas, cash in advance, from each of his learners, he was never known to suffer from a lack of clients. For over half-a-hundred years they made tracks to his grove from every part of the Hellenic world, and even though he was at pains to hold down the size of his classes—to, say, preferably a clutch of five or six, but in any case never more than nine—over the years he became a man not only of colossal reputation, but also of stupendous wealth, an accomplishment which, among teachers, is so rare as to be almost unique.

AS WRITER

During the long pageant of his years on earth, besides discharging his regular pedagogic duties, Isocrates compounded some five dozen speeches, or rather essays, draped, as it were, in oratorical dress, none of which, as has been hinted, did he present vocally. Time has inflicted a heavy casualty upon his literary output, and of his sixty pieces less than half remain, and many of these have suffered from loss and deterioration. Two of the survivors, one, *Against the Sophists,* the other, *On the Antidosis,* present the author's pedagogical credo. The rest are concerned in large part with his thoughts on the affairs of state and of the world, a lament for a departed celebrity, a few lofty homilies to help prod the imagination of certain ruling princes, and, finally, the fulfillment of his dream, the formation of a Panhellenic league to bring unity and peace to the fratricidal Hellenes.

Although the Sophists laid great store in the magic of proficient speaking to advance a youth to the pinnacle of success, yet it remained for the minivoiced Isocrates to conceive the oration not only as a means to purify the polluted waters of public thinking and thereupon provoke some appropriate and responsive civic action, but also as a high form of literary art, a thing of beauty, as full of music as the stateliest dithyramb. To perfect his art, Isocrates drove himself unsparingly, writing and rewriting a single piece for years—on his *Panegyric,* for example, it is believed that he spent close to a decade and a half, a long exercise, indeed, even in the life of one destined to become an advanced nonagenarian. Yet through his writing and his teaching he not only raised oratory to a place of dignity and high distinction in his own world, but as the centuries unwound his torch passed into the hands of the Romans, whereafter it was picked up to illuminate, however pallidly, the medieval Seven Liberal Arts, and then, far more vividly, the learning of the Renaissance, and from then on the liberal education of later times.

AS CRITIC

When Isocrates opened his center of culture in 392 B.C., Greek education, especially in its higher reaches, was riven, like the Greeks themselves, with dispute. What he could surely count on, therefore, as he took the field against his rivals, was not only their sullen looks, but in all likelihood some nasty words as well. On the one hand he had to contend with the claims of the heirs of the Sophists, lesser illuminates, to be sure, than his own incandescent mentors, but still alluring. On the other hand he confronted the minor Socratics, emulators of the martyred philosopher—in the glare of that man's grandeur only a pale and passing shadow, but even so, not without a sizable following. To reinforce himself against the predictable antagonism of his academic critics, Isocrates prepared a brief monograph, *Against the Sophists,* wherein he not only laid bare the faults and shortcomings of the pedagogical doctrines and practices then in currency, but also undertook to explain and defend his own. Unluckily, only the first part of his discourse has come down to us, and were it not for another work, *On the Antidosis,* which he wrote some two score years following, in 353 B.C., our knowledge of his educational views and practices would in truth be sadly impaired.

What complaints does Isocrates lodge against some of the leading purveyors of the higher learning of his time? There were, first of all, he said, those "false masters" who would teach their students virtue and perfect knowledge to enable them to comport themselves correctly at all times and places. Actually, he said, these fellows seek to gull their customers with bogus promises, for it should be clear to anybody that "foreknowledge of events to come is not vouchsafed to our human nature." Next, there are the professors of "political discourse," specialists in practical oratory, which they claimed lay within the grasp of anyone, including the most dim-witted. To such an end all the would-be haranguer needed to know was the mechanics of stringing words beguilingly together, besides a few of the tricks of dissimulation found in the working kit of every professional speechifier, and presto! he would soon be saying thanks at the altar of fame and riches. Such pedagogues, declared Isocrates, were mere pretenders. They cared not for decency and honor, but only for success, however tawdry. The speeches they fancied rested on artificiality and bore neither on life nor on the good, the true, and the beautiful. To become a good speaker, Isocrates went on, mere training is not enough. Of the utmost importance, he believed —doubtless holding the glass up to his own deficiencies of a weak voice and almost pathological shyness—is the possession of a natural talent. Add to this proper instruction and the student's willingness to suffer the grind of endless practice, and he might some day be able to bring an audience leaping to its feet.

Was Isocrates adept in knocking down the dubious theories and practices of his rivals? Then he was also at pains to replace what he attacked with a positive canon of his own which, presumably, for all his timorousness, he was confident enough to pronounce correct. It was to this dogma that he devoted his *Antidosis*. He was convinced that what Greece needed above all else was a competent and reliable leadership. What he accordingly sought, he tells us in the *Antidosis,* was to transmute his students into "good men in their relations to the state, to their friends, and to their households." To bring this about he addressed his teaching to the cultivation of the whole person, a person integrated in body, mind, and spirit, and able, therefore, when his day arrived, to lead the people.

HIS COURSE OF STUDY

Concerned in large part with the theory and practice of the higher learning, Isocrates left no words on the education which preceded it. Presumably, he accepted the existing seminaries of lower learning as sufficient unto their purpose, and so he neither hymned nor damned them. What was of supreme importance, however, was that his students have a firm grip on their native tongue. Consequently, every one of his charges, whatever Everest of ambition they hoped someday to conquer, was put upon learning how to speak well. Speech alone, their professor told them, is what separates man from all other living creatures. Clear and forceful speaking is the "basis of all progress in law, art, and mechanical invention"—as well, he added, as justice, civilization, and culture.

Once the student was on familiar terms with good speech, he was set upon the study of philosophy, by which, however, Isocrates had in mind not the windblown balloonings of the metaphysicians, which he dismissed not only as buncombe but also for the most part as irrelevant to living in the everyday world—as did also the great Roman rhetorician Quintilian during the first of the Christian centuries, and also the Messrs. Franklin and Jefferson many hundreds of years later. What Isocrates called philosophy was at bottom a general culture, with extra attention to its efficacious use in discourse. Beginning with a dissection of the classics, it embraced not only the lyrical flights of the poets, but also ethics and politics as well as a study of past events and their consequences as these were encapsulated in the works of the historians Herodotus and Thucydides. As in much later times, poesy was studied for the mental training it supposedly offered in the unraveling of its complex syntax, but even more for the lessons it afforded on right and wrong, good and evil. The notion that a meritorious literary work may be totally void of anything conducive to moral elevation, that it may, indeed, be simply beautiful, is fairly modern.

Although Isocrates declared for a general culture, such subjects as geometry and astronomy did not sit well with him. In the main he found them of no practical value, a charge which, remembering that they were then generally taught as theory, carries water. This is not to say, however, that the professor heaved them recklessly over the rail. For all its alleged lack of practical use, the study of mathematics, he conceded, helps to mold the young and tender mind—it is, he volunteered, "a gymnastic of the mind." Known to later pedagogues as the doctrine of formal discipline, the idea that the operations of the medulla oblongata can be strengthened by taxing it with formidable subjects, such as formal grammar and mathematics, held sway until the early twentieth century, when the scientific psychologists, sweating in their labs, succeeded in doing it in.

RHETORIC REIGNS

It hardly needs to be said that in his school, dedicated as it was to the production of superlative speakers, Isocrates put his primary accent on rhetoric. He ushers his novices into its mystery as per the familiar custom of teaching them the elemental rules of composition and elocution. But in so doing he took care to slice off every ounce of adipose theory, not to say pedantry. He thereby not only spared his charges needless grief, but also saved them valuable time, which, he allowed, they could turn to better account by putting the principles they had studied in class into actual practice—in short, they were to learn by doing. Soon, in fact, we find them at work, turning their abstract knowledge into actual rhetorical utterance. Like most earnest merchants of words, Isocrates made his budding orators study the best available models, among which, interestingly, the master gave a high priority to works of his own. For this practice his critics chided him. How comes it, some of them openly wondered, that this shrinking violet disports himself like a bumptious dahlia? The bald fact is, of course, that he was doing what enterprising professors have been doing ever since.

If Isocrates favored his own discourse over the conventional outlines for his protégés, this is by no means to suggest that he expected them to imitate his style. Immensely better than the lot of handbooks compiled by his academic competitors, his speeches represented the living reality of the principles their holder had expounded in the classroom. In his speeches, although no one had ever heard their author publicly speak them, was a splendid, melodious prose, inspiring and at times not a little awesome, an utterance of substance as well as form, flowing like the tempered wind, tarrying for a detail here, an explanation there, but making its relentless journey, rhythmically and harmoniously, to its appointed end.

Among the host of students who passed part of their nonage in the master's teaching chamber, the bulk, as usual, have long since faded into anonymity. But not all. Some became the old man's friends, and among them not a few rose to fame and glory, as witness—to mention but a handful—Timotheus, a general; Lycurgus, an orator; Ephorus, a historian, standing cheek to jowl with the eminent Herodotus; and Theophilus, the first cataloguer of recent events of whom we have any historical remembrance.

ISOCRATES AND PLATO

Five years after Isocrates had founded his school Plato opened his Academy. There is not much to be gained by a microscopic comparison of these two illuminati. Both were masters of a radiant prose, and both devoted their pens to the advancement of the art and science of statecraft—Plato in his *Republic* and the *Laws,* Isocrates in the sheaves of his oratorical essays. Both men had high confidence in the power of education to renew a rapidly deteriorating society. But in the means they chose to bring this about they differed. For Plato the consummation of the highest culture lay in philosophy, particularly in the realm of pure ideas, a profound and elusive mystery which could be fathomed only by those of the highest powers of ratiocination, the so-called "intellectual élite"—a minority among mankind, as everybody, save the majority, well knows. For Isocrates the endless concentration on philosophy with its quest for pure ideas made no sense, and though he did not outlaw the subject in his grove, he eschewed its metaphysical juggling—in fact, he even let fall some tart remarks about grown adults engaged in blowing metaphysical soap bubbles.

If Isocrates reduced the study of philosophy, in the Platonic sense, to a role of minor consequence in the curriculum of subjects, then Plato, for his part, downgraded Isocrates's darling of rhetoric. It was, he scoffed, scarcely more than a kind of applied dialectics, and hence unworthy of higher cultural consideration. Nevertheless, in spite of Plato's great, and at times even inordinate, intellectuality—or maybe because of it—the distinction of being the foremost educator of the pre-Christian fourth century Greeks fell not to the philosopher but the rhetorician. It was Isocrates who transported oratory into an art form, and it was Isocrates who, for good or ill, invested the upper learning with its literary orchestration. Thenceforward, until the coming of Darwin and his comrade evolutionists Spencer and Huxley, such was to remain the immutable tradition.

Chapter 3

Plato

EARLY DAYS

Plato (ca. 427–347 B.C.) was not, like Socrates, rooted in the middle class. In him, in contrast, flowed the blood of the peerage, of royalty, even, we are told, the divine juices of Poseidon, the god of the sea. His actual name was Aristocles, but because of his tremendous heft and beam his friends got to calling him Plato—literally, "the broad-shouldered one"—an appellation which has stuck ever since. As good-looking as Socrates was homely, this human Parthenon evoked no end of oohs and ahs from certain ladies and not a few, in those days of homosexual tolerance, from smitten males. So powerfully built, Plato relished physical activity, especially wrestling, wherein he gained an impressive reputation. He did his turn at soldiering, and on three occasions his valor brought him gauds of honor. A *bon viveur* of the first order, he splurged in life's pleasures. He was a horseman and a yachtsman. Good fellowship gladdened him, and to his very end he was something of an epicure, with a cultivated palate for the finest food and drink. And yet, in this same frame there resided a being of spacious mind, a connoisseur not merely of men and women and horses, but of mathematics and music as well as rhetoric, and, in the passing years, philosophy. When he was still in the early springtime of his long and fruitful life he courted the Muses, wooing them assiduously as a composer of classical tragedy and some florid poesy.

Plato had scarcely cleared the frontier of twenty when he ran into the phenomenon of Socrates. So enthralled was the youth by the master's spell that presently he renounced his sporting life, including women, and fed his dramas and verses to the flames, to devote his main energies from that time forward to the pursuit of wisdom.

FLIGHT FROM GREECE—AND RESCUE

In 404 B.C.—the broad-shouldered one was then twenty-three—the discord which had been smoldering in Athens blew up into insurrection. Supported and directed by, among others, Plato's aristocratic kinsmen, the revolution pursued its bloody end, routing the old order and replacing it with a despotism more to its leaders' reactionary liking, only in turn to be done in by a counterrevolution and the return of an embittered and vengeful democracy, its enemies slain or in flight. As the curtain fell, Socrates was tried and executed in 399 B.C., a fatality of his assault on the public's cherished credulities, but a casualty as well to politics.

Shattered by the dreadful turn of events, the bereaved Plato took flight from his bedeviled city. For a while he just knocked about, groping from one place to another. We sight him now at Megara, now at Cyrene. He passed some time in Egypt pondering its mathematical and historical learning. In 395 B.C., or thereabouts, he returned to his native city, fighting in one of its perennial wars, whereupon, the gory business done, he took sail again, grappling with the philosophy of Pythagoras along the way, taking a look at the volcanic Etna in Sicily, and stopping at Syracuse, where he made acquaintance with its reigning tyrant, Dionysius the Elder, who in later years was to commission him to give instruction to his son and heir, Dionysius the Younger.

But the willful Fates continued to dog the philosopher. He fell into unfriendly hands and was sold into slavery. Yet, as things turned out, his ill fortune was to become both his own and Athens's good, for when friends found out about his misfortune they not only rounded up the 3,000 drachmas to reimburse his ransomer, which, it is pleasant to report, the good man refused to accept, but with a rare skill and delicacy they also prevailed upon Plato to come back to Athens. Thereupon, on the city's northern outskirt at Colonus, they acquired for him a tract of land where he organized his renowned Academy, the archsire and name-giver of all academies ever since. Today the site is reachable by rapid transit, but in Plato's time, it lay far off in the stillness of a placid, bucolic solitude. The land itself, we are told, was offensive to good health, but its lack of fitness as a health resort was more than offset by its religious aura. It was, indeed, something of a holy ground, sanctified by the presence of crypts and monuments to the dead, as well as shrines to the immortal deities, including such active and high executives in the Hellenic pantheon as the gay and goatish Dionysus, the giver of the vine and its fermented offspring, and Poseidon, the lord of the sea, its killifish and its whales, and even more striking, as we are asked to believe, one of Plato's ancestors.

THE ACADEMY

The Academy itself was but one of several buildings, all stoutly constructed. Set among the shadowy trees, it was consecrated to the Muses, and in particular to the honor of Academus, the local head divinity, and, after the founder's passing, as was only meet, to Plato. Although the Academy served as a gymnasium for higher cerebration, in its organization it was actually something of a religious brotherhood, a loosely knit monastic community, as it were, without any vowed abnegations, however, and, better still, with sisters in its midst—in short, a religious cult whose participants were linked in amity, sometimes erotic, but generally in mere camaraderie.

Despite their cloistered mode of living and the mementos to the dead, the students of the Academy were strangers to austerity. Confectors of comedy, in fact, lampooned them frequently for their preciosity, their foppish and ceremonious manners no less than their sartorial splash. Far from being awed by their fearsome quest for the highest truth, they indulged their egos with fancy caps and walking sticks, and even the scholar's flowing plumage—so ancient are some of our current academic trappings.

Unlike Isocrates's rhetorical plant, the Academy tilted its nose at such materialities as tuition fees, relying in their place on the altruism of its friends and admirers. Altogether, the practice proved to be a success. Not only did fathers dig freely into their coffers—most of them were of the well-heeled upper class and could easily afford it—but, then as now, a big wind would occasionally fall, spilling upon the Academy some welcome manna, a legacy, say, or an outright donation. We are told, for example, that King Dionysius II of Syracuse favored Plato with a gift of a round half a million dollars. As a result, unlike so many other groves of serious learning devoted to a high but nonutilitarian purpose, Plato's Academy was never in troubled straits, and so it was never put upon to become a mendicant for financial favors.

ITS CURRICULAR AND EXTRACURRICULAR AFFAIRS

It was in the Academy itself—the main building one might call it—that Plato and his associates directed their search for wisdom. To snare this elusive prey, the scholars tuned up their mental muscles with philosophy and mathematics, subjects in which they were expected to possess some rudimentary competence before they were permitted to sit in class. It was Plato's view that true knowledge must be subject to clear and precise demonstration, as, in illustration, the ineluctable flow of a geometric proposition—hence the caveat written in stone over the entranceway: "Let no one enter here without geometry." For its time, the Academy's mathematical offering was substantial, including the art and science of numerical theory (advanced arithmetic), higher geometry, and astronomy. In addition, the seekers of wisdom applied themselves to music and letters, with a bit of history and law. Needless to say, in the quest for intellectual light philosophy, with all its tributaries, played a capital part. Not only were its powers expected to help the postulants—those who had enough talent and diligence—to enter the select circle of those who have penetrated the mystery of the absolute, eternal, and crystaline truth—the "real truth," some might say—they were also calculated to speed the student's way to becoming an upright and virtuous person. Like Isocrates, Plato undertook to prepare his protégés to become leaders of a new and better state. His heart, hence—as in the case of the eminent rhetorician—lay in politics. "When I was a young man," the Athenian mused, looking back from the midstream of his seventies, "I wanted . . . to devote myself to politics as soon as I was my own master." Alas for him, but luckily for us, the Fates spiked his lofty hopes, and so he had to settle instead for immortality as a metaphysician, a writer, a teacher, a moralist, and a utopian.

Save for hearsay, we know almost nothing of Plato's merits as a teacher—if he was ever seriously appraised, the records on the matter are silent. But we know that he, as well as his aides, sought refuge in didactic diversity. Sometimes they lectured; sometimes they resorted to dialogue; and sometimes they sought to rouse the minds of their auditors by confronting them with a problem. How, for example, they asked them, can one explain the apparently ordered travelings of the heavenly bodies? How, indeed! The lectures, even when they emanated from the headmaster himself, who generally gave them without recourse to notes, were abstruse and technical, and except for a few rare listeners, as, say, an Aristotle or a Demosthenes, were extremely hard to follow. Much livelier and in high favor at the Academy were its occasional drinking conferences. Attended by both masters and students, and under the amiable stewardship of the vine-wreathed Dionysus, ubiquitous though invisible, such gladsome gatherings where the wassail flowed freely, never failed to incite a spirited colloquy.

Plato placed a high trust in the powers and capacities of women. In his *Republic*, for example, they stood on equal footing with men, enjoying the same rights and opportunities, the same duties and obligations. It should come as no surprise, therefore, that the Academy opened its doors to the fair ones, provided, of course, they were able to meet the school's mathematical requirement for admission which, since it necessitated a sufficiency of funds for special tutoring, was not always easy. Just how many women attended the Academy's sessions we do not know, nor do we know how they fared at its bibulous seminars, if they bothered to attend them at all.

HIS WRITINGS

Though Socrates wrote nothing, the heir to his sandals was a diligent literatus. Plato wrote with a gifted and imaginative hand. Unhappily, however, it cannot be said that his art is flawless. The nightingale's silvery note is often missing—some of his exercises in erudition are wrought out of heavy clay. Plato is at his best in his *Dialogues,* of which three dozen still linger to grace the world, and which he inaugurated, it is said, as a mere literary plaything for diversion. Written during indeterminate intervals over the years, they were never welded into a single piece. Consequently, they show a marked untidiness in unity and coherence, a violation of the rhetorical canon which aggrieves conscientious schoolma'ms, male or female, to this day. On the other hand, when taken separately, some of them, as witness the *Symposium,* soar into the empyrean blue. There Plato reaches his literary apogee, with his candid shots of an Alcibiades, petulant and somewhat etherized; an Aristophanes, more hilarious than the most comic figure he ever fashioned in any of his plays as he struggles to separate himself from the festive slab, heavily beladen and belching violently; and finally, that indomitable challenger of convention and bogus values, the ungainly and unforgettable Socrates.

CONCERNING THE *REPUBLIC*

The fullest explanation of the Platonic thought and its bearing on the state and education dwells within the covers of the *Republic.* A later writing, the *Laws,* records some alterations, besides amplifying and fortifying some of the more general points laid down in the earlier work. In addition, Plato had things to say about education in *Meno* and *Theatetus.* Let us proceed with our exploration of his pedagogy by examining what he set down in the *Republic,* and then glancing at the *Laws.*

Philosophically, Plato begins with the Socratic supposition that knowledge is virtue. But hardly has he said yes to his master's dictum than he takes pause, as every right-thinking philosopher must, to ask himself just what knowledge is. It is not, to begin on a negative note, what the Sophists were contending, something that we see and sniff and hear and taste and touch in the world of sense, nor is it, as the same brethren ventured to maintain, what an individual makes it out to be, for no one man can ever be, as the Sophists insisted, the measure of all things. Instead, knowledge can be gained only through Ideas, which is to say the generalized conception which assembles and arranges the aggregation of our sensations into a concept. The vast variety of details, for example, that we perceive among a million tables, their various materials and colors, their shapes and textures, and the like, we organize, if we care to pursue the matter, according to their common essence into a class. The result is not, to be sure, an actual table, but a concept residing in the nonsensory world of thought, or if you will, the mind. As a concept, or in Platonic parlance, an Idea, it is forever the same, absolute and inextinguishable, and it exists, whether we do or not. The tables we sense are made to serve us, but the work of the vandal years condemns them to decay and disappear; yet our generalized image of a table, namely a plane surface with legs or supports to hold it up, will endure forever. What holds for tables holds for all things, from cats and the lepidoptera to circles, parallelepipedons, virtue, love, and justice. Of all Ideas in the hierarchy of values the highest, according to the father of the Academy, is goodness, which Plato somewhat mystically identified with God.

To lift one's self from the world of sense perception into the seventh heaven of ethereal Ideas demands a capacity for intellection not given to the ordinary man. What is required, it seems, is some prodigious acumen which will enable its possessor to differentiate the real from the illusory, the true bullion, so to say, from the gilded brick, a wisdom vouchsafed, according to Plato, only to philosophers. This is not to say, however, as Plato was at pains to state, that the holders of this rare enfranchisement had a monopoly on living a clean and upright life. It simply means that they alone could fully apprehend and appreciate the meanings and implications of absolute and unadulterated goodness and lead their lives accordingly.

LIFE IN THE *REPUBLIC*—AND AFTER

Such is the philosophic underpinning of Plato's *Republic*. Although it took its key from an older Greece, schooling in the Platonic utopia projects a number of striking novelties. For one thing, as he says in all his discourses on the subject, education should fall under the iron hand of state control, an innovation to the Athenians, if not to the totalitarian Spartans. It was a view which, needless to say, reaped the disdain of every free-lance vendor of knowledge who happened to run into it. Further, until the age of twenty, education was mandatory, and its burdens weighed upon the female no less than upon the male. Though, speaking strictly, education did not start officially until the child attained the age of seven, it was preceded, as soon as the youngster could safely waddle, by a program which might be described as somewhat akin to our present nursery school and kindergarten, where boys and girls shared their exercises and fun, gladdening their ears with rhymes and stories—all meticulously decontaminated of the slighest unseemliness, moral and otherwise. When they broke the rules, they were punished, although not roughly. Unlike their current successors, however youngsters in the Republic carried on their activities clad in nothing but their bare skin.

Once over the line of six, the children were put under the complete authority of the state. The sexes were separated, each sequestered under the roof of its own quarters and under the never-absent supervisory eye of state-appointed teachers. Here, until their thirteenth birthdays, they were to be made literate, moral, and religious, in addition to getting acquainted with simple numbers and an even simpler geometry, not, however, merely theoretic, but with the practice of untangling problems involving actual situations.

Here too the young were to become intimate with physical training and music, the one to build and beautify the body, the other to enhance and exalt the "soul." Rather curiously, and altogether at odds with the Greek's natural propensity, was the philosopher's stand against inciting the competitive spirit. If Plato granted his countenance to gymnastics, then it was not only because he himself had once been a lusty practitioner thereof, but because, like earlier Greeks, he perceived in them, as did the fascist and communist master minds of a later millennium, the preboot training of tomorrow's soldier. There was the usual leaping and hurling, dashing and distance running, but there was also the more warlike enterprise of archery, swordplay, spear-throwing, wrestling, hunting, and rather oddly—for the Greeks were not noteworthy as a horsy people—the art of horsemanship. Finally came the physical *crème de la crème,* the engagement, namely, in sham battles of light and heavy infantry. Sometimes, when the occasion was right, boys were escorted into the vicinage of actual carnage to bulge their eyes at the gory spectacle.

On his sixteenth birthday a boy was considered ready for more strenuous martial endeavor, and from then until he was twenty his teachers concentrated on making him an effective soldier. In most of this industry, excepting the most taxing sort, girls were allowed no immunity, for as equals of males they too were to bear arms to fight for the Republic. But in the Platonic promised land gymnastics embraced not only physical and premilitary exercises. As in a Greece which used to be, participation in sports was expected not only to build the body, to make it hardy and handsome; it was also to mold the youthful character and personality. One still hears such ethereal voices in our current era—notably from the playing fields of Britain, and also, of course, from moralistic athletic directors at some of our great seats of academe.

Although Plato's views on gymnastics and their place in his best-of-all-possible states often enough bear the stamp of tradition, yet in at least one respect the author of the *Republic* entertained a fresh and wider outlook. Living in Hellas at a time when some of its advanced and forward-looking medicos were beginning to emancipate themselves from their quackish preconceptions, it was only natural for a man of Plato's cast of mind to pay their emerging arcana a little heed. As a consequence, he invested physical training with something his forebears had never heard of. Thus, he allowed it not only the role it had played in bygone days, namely, to make the body strong and comely, but in addition he gilded it with a hygienic purpose. Were he at large on the American scene today, he could say that he had conjured up our department of physical training and hygiene. In short, the end of gymnastics was not just the cultivation of a powerful and attractive body; it was also to teach its possessor how to maintain it in good health.

In his later work, the *Laws,* its author brings dancing into active membership of the gymnastic fraternity. The fact that a grip on this skill was a prerequisite to a youth's participation in choral singing, since the two went hand in glove, thus bestowed upon it a double affiliation, one with gymnastics, the other with the tonal art. An older man when he put forth the *Laws,* somewhat disenchanted and disillusioned by what seemed to him a downhill slide of the Athenian youth, and maybe even with one foot on the edge of senescence, Plato found it much easier to descend into pedantry. Thus, he went to great length to tell his readers precisely how the art of Terpsichore must be taught, and exactly how to infuse it into the festivals and the grand athletic spectacles as well as the incessant parades and processions wherein young Greeks were wont to play a part. Dancing, the philosopher insisted, was at bottom a form of discipline, an activity which not only served the public interest but which, by helping to let loose youth's piled-up steam, helped to calm its harried psyche.

But even as Plato was seeking to promote physical culture, all about him the Greeks were abandoning their gymnasiums and their steam cabinets to absorb themselves in other things, especially the delights of the literary and rhetorical arts. Plato strove valiantly to stem the onrush of this villainous tide. Not only were the young to learn how to sing and how to stroke the lyre; at the same time there were to be no artistic innovations. Like the current rock music in the ears of the classical addict, Plato found only pain in attempts at musical novelty. Though in him flowed the artist's noble sap, and his prose often sighed with the soft winds of poesy, Plato, for all that, was somewhat prissy—in sum, in the arts he suffered all the pud-eurs of a puritan. His own youthful lyrical twitters would not have found favor with the Republic's censor, and Zeus only knew what would have happened to the equivalents of such anarchists as Prokofiev, Stravinsky, and even Wagner. By the same token, the broad-shouldered one would have purged the heroic past of its Homeric legacy, not merely for its want of historical exactitude, but for its deficiency in moral rectitude. Homer's tuneful canzones Plato would have expurgated, or even replaced, as did the early Bolsheviki when they administered Santa Claus and similar capitalis-tic folklore figures their collective hoof, and supplanted them with fanciful heroes of their own that were more in keeping with their Marxian idealism. "We are poets too," Plato volunteered when, very likely with a muted chuckle he counseled the adoption of his *Laws* as an altogether suitable schoolbook for the young.

So boys and girls were to pursue their appointed tasks in the state-run schools, whether they savored them or not, until at the age of twenty their years of academic conscription reached their possible end—providing their sufferers had run through a series of physical, mental, and moral tests—and had failed. For the overwhelming majority, to whom learning was a bore, this was easy enough—and for them schooldays ceased. Mustered out of the academic ranks, they became the Republic's artisans, its jug-makers and flute fabricants, its husbandmen and tradesmen, though, somewhat curi-ously, Plato, for all his sagacity, had offered them not the slightest vocation-al training, or as the phrase glitters nowadays, career training. Nevertheless, the Republic was not ungenerous to its "failures." Granted a plot of ground, the erstwhile students were free—within totalitarian limits—to exe-cute their industry. Yet, though they were neither serfs nor slaves, like convicts beading sweat in their clammy cells for the rest of their days, they were condemned to remain where the state, in its infinite philosophic in-sight, had deemed fit to place them.

THE CREAM OF THE CROP

The far lesser number who had surmounted the examiners' grim exigencies were now assigned to another ten years of learning with a greater belabor-ing of their cortex, especially by means of mathematics, solid geometry, and astronomy, the latter in those days being a great deal more speculative than experimental. To brush the cobwebs from their brains, and to prepare them for the subsequent difficult and demanding rumination in metaphysics and dialectics, Plato held that the study of mathematics had no equal. It was, he intimated, the best "head-developer" known to civilization. Ten years later the students confronted another inquisition. Again most of them were destined to stumble and fall. Thus weeded out, they were put upon to spend the rest of their lives in safeguarding the interests of the state. The handful who came through all their tests were honored with five more years of forced study, concentrating on "divine philosophy" in all its multifarious phases, with special attention to logic and ethics, besides politics, law, mathematics, astronomy, and music. At thirty-five, heavily weighted with knowledge and understanding, they were committed to the Republic's corps of office-holders to render service to the state, howsoever it ordained.

If the gods granted them a further fifteen years on earth, then at the age of two score years and ten they were designated Guardian, and their long and wearisome years of trial and preparation were at rest. From then on, until sickness or death made an end of it, they were to engross themselves in deliberating upon the intangible reality of pure Ideas. The Guardians constituted the Republic's finest intellects, its treasure trove of wisdom. Philosophers, they were the Republic's highest social caste, not only for their vast sapience, but for the power and influence they exerted as well. For in the Platonic wonderland only the wisest were entrusted with the reins of government. They alone could frame its laws, and they alone could effect their execution. Philosophers—such was Plato's wishful thought—shall be kings, and kings philosophers.

Yet for all their exalted majesty, these learning-laden kings were hedged in by restrictions on every side. Personal wealth and property were denied them. Matrimony they could commit, but, strictly speaking, their helpmeets were never entirely their own for, under the demands of the Republic they had to share the conjugal couch "with the best as often as possible." By the same token, their philosophic spouses performed a similar patriotic duty with the help of some other Guardian's better half. Thus not even procreation was left to the heart's desire of the philosopher-king. When he and his wife—or some other civic-minded partner—were to multiply was set by the public need, and should they, betrayed by some booby trap of biology, deliver an offspring without state authorization, then the babe thus born was doomed to die. Their legitimate, authorized progeny they knew only while they were at nurse. Once free from the maternal bosom, the young were put under the custody of the state to start their long trek toward their place in Plato's Good Society.

The Republic, of course, was never more than fancy put on parchment. Even its maker entertained doubts about the possibility of putting it into actual being, and on various occasions, notably, as has been mentioned, in his *Laws,* he essayed to improve it, or even in some instances to settle for something less. Summoned, when he was sixty, to impart wisdom to Dionysius the Younger of Syracuse, the son and heir of the tyrant who had come into his ken so many, many years ago, Plato proceeded, as per the rubric over the gateway to his Academy, to introduce the youth to geometry. Unhappily, after an initial enthusiasm, the crown prince lost interest in Euclid and his theorems, and Plato's dream of incubating a philosopher-king turned out to be just another castle in the air. Years later, perhaps to ease his conscience, or, more likely, simply to gratify his vainglory, the younger Dionysius, now himself the empurpled tyrant over the Syracusans, and rolling in wealth and power, presented Plato with a gift of nearly a half-a-million dollars to accelerate the pursuit of wisdom at the Academy.

PLATO CONSIDERED

Although Plato's educational theory as he bared it in the pages of the *Republic* and the *Laws* never crossed the line into actuality, this does not mean that in the forwarding of thought the man played only a subordinate role. His identification, for example, of goodness, the highest-valued on his scale of Ideas, with God, however nebulously limned, offered some rather delectable intellectual provender to Christendom's pioneer theologians. His Academy, although it was preceded by Isocrates's extremely successful re-thorical school, was destined, nevertheless, to occupy a memorable place in intellectual annals. Despite the looseness of its methods, its want of system and definitude, the Academy gave the cultivation of reason a powerful boost. Aristocrat by blood, Plato declared for a political leadership of brains, as did Jefferson, an archliberal, and his antithesis, the imperious Hamilton.

As a metaphysician, Plato proposed to leave this vale of all-too-human sense perception and soar into the interstellar space of Ideas, absolute, pellucid, perfect, and imperishable, thereby siring the philosophy of Idealism, which in various avatars is still in active circulation. As a feminist, the broad-shouldered one—though he himself enjoyed the felicities of singleblessedness—went all the way for equal rights, duties, and responsibilities for women. It was a stand which at the time took some courage, and which marked him among the generality of the reigning superior sex as something of a renegade or, to say the least, an ass. As a eugenist, Plato stood for a wedlock entered into only by healthy partners under the eye and license of the state, their progeny to be produced under controllable biologic laws, and their breeding subject at all times to the requirements of the state.

Although, as has been said, his heart was full of poetry, Plato was also a puritan. Therefore, although he asserted a belief in exposing children to the presence of beauty because, he thought, their lives would be ennobled by it, yet that beauty was subject at all times to the interpretations placed upon it by the omnipotent philosopher-kings, an authoritarianism so complete as to make even the Nazis and the Communists offer it their deepest bows. As for his pedagogy, Plato had the good sense to understand that when the novice is to be introduced to philosophy, the one temptation his preceptor must by all odds avoid is to begin with an overpowering parade of the most important principles of the subject, an axiom in teaching nowadays, of course—or, more likely, a platitude—but in Plato's time not at all self-evident. There is no doubt that Plato caught a glimpse of the differences which characterize the human race. At the same time he was unaware that for a variety of reasons some of us need more time than others to attain our peak. This, combined with his disdain for the intellectuality of the multitude—the "rubbish," as Mr. Jefferson centuries later called them—predestined them to sweat on the nethermost social rung of the Republic until the gods reincarnated them as something better, a belief to which the philosopher gave a grave support.

Plato's influence on his own times bordered on nil. With the passage of antiquity into the Middle Ages, he was, if not unremembered, at least almost ignored. The laureate of ancient philosophers amongst medieval savants was not Plato, but Aristotle, his student. But after the Renaissance, Plato, like so many half-forgotten ancients, was rediscovered and acclaimed by the Humanists, and until the rise and growth of the natural sciences in the sixteenth and seventeenth centuries, with their stress on unending change and observable phenomena, Plato remained an intellectual powerhouse to be reckoned with.

Chapter 4

Aristotle

THE YOUNG ARISTOCRAT

Unlike Plato, his teacher, and Socrates, his teacher's teacher, Aristotle (384–322 B.C.) was denied the privilege of being a native Athenian. Hence, by the measuring stick of the standpat custodians of Old-Guard Athenian correctness, Aristotle must be set down as a "barbarian." He was born in 384 B.C. at Stageirus, a shoreland town on the Aegean's northwest and next door to the kingdom of Macedonia. There, his father was the king's physician. His son, it scarcely needs relating, obtained a first-rate education not only on the hard bench of formal learning but in the palace itself, the calling place of some of the great intellectual worthies of the era, of whom some must have made more than an ordinary dent on the lad's sharp mind. In fact, young Aristotle had not yet come to his beard when his father thought him ripe for instruction in anatomy, a task which, to make sure it was executed to his taste, he performed himself—so the story goes. Soon thereafter the doctor dispatched his son to Athens to study under the redoubtable Plato.

When Aristotle enlisted for study in the Platonic grove, he was a seventeen-year-old stripling. His teacher, although his salad days had long since gone to seed—he was almost sixty-two, had nonetheless sustained himself as a potent figure in the world of thought. Time, it is true, had laid its leaden hand on his adroit and wonderful utterance; but wizening though he was, and aware that his early dreams had not come true, yet flashes of the idealism which had once ignited them continued to flare. These were Plato's more sedate years of the *Laws* rather than those of the poet's imagination which had illuminated so many passages in the *Symposium.* In short, Plato the artist had metamorphosed into Plato the professor. But as a professor, the father of the *Republic* was still a man to be reckoned with—provided, of course, his students could keep up with him on the sinuous tours of his belabored abstractions.

AT PLATO'S ACADEMY

For a score of years, with a break now and then, Aristotle was an integral part of the Academy. His brilliance was not lost upon his mentor, and for the rest of Plato's twenty earthly years he worked assiduously with the gifted Stageirite. The upshot was that as the years took flight, Aristotle found himself warming to some of his master's favorite ideologies. He concurred with him, to illustrate, in the view that education is a necessary department of statecraft; and he agreed that by nature man is dowered with the capacity to acquire virtue. As an advanced thinker, Aristotle ventured into the cerulean heights which still attracted Plato even as the older man's future grew less and less. As an instructor in the Academy, the "barbarian" honed the Platonic theorems to their finest edge, making them understandable, if not always enjoyable to his listeners. As a man of action, Aristotle participated in the association of "friends," which comprised most of the student body, and under whose plaque he composed harangues and erudite essays, orchestrated in the Platonic key. Time saw him become the Academy's salient figure, a Platonist in the overwhelming main.

WANDERINGS AND ALEXANDER

After Plato's passing at the age of eighty, the Academy descended to one of his nephews, Speusippus by name, but in cultural annals scarcely more than a footnote. The new director displayed no great cerebral zeal, nor even a capacity to whip it into being, and so the Academy begin to slip downhill. Its better students deserted it for intellectually more attractive pastures; some, including Aristotle, made for Assus to join the ranks of a philosophic junto founded many years before by a couple of Plato's students. For three years or so Aristotle devoted himself chiefly to teaching. Then he betook himself to Lesbos where he made a connection with a small band of Platonists and applied himself to the study of natural history and the plant and animal goings-on in the ocean sea. Meanwhile, he ruminated upon the art and science of human governance, and presently when the tidings of his doings reached the ears of Philip of Macedon, that sovereign issued a call to the philosopher to undertake the tutoring of his heir, Alexander, at the time still only a youth, but destined to stride down the infinite aisle of history as "the Great." His majesty wanted the prince to ponder philosophy, so that, he purportedly told him, "you may not do a great many of the things of the sort I am sorry to have done." Philip's summons proved too seductive to resist, and so in 343 B.C. Aristotle found himself in the splendor of the royal ménage as teacher to the bright but headstrong prince.

For the next seven years Aristotle instructed and squired young Alexander day and night, save when his royal pupil went off on an extracurricular call. The philosopher had hoped to condition the youth for a maturity of wisdom and goodness so that when his time came to warm his father's throne he would put the peace and happiness of his subjects ahead of everything else. Unhappily, things did not turn out as planned. Although Alexander's ardor for forwarding knowledge never waned, yet at bottom his avarice for martial glory and territorial aggrandizement and his love for powerful vinous juices far outran his desire for knowledge and wisdom. Death felled him in Babylon at the age of thirty-three following a series of heavy tippling sessions abetted by complications from a fever.

THE LYCEUM

Soon after Alexander had slipped into his regal silks to discharge the kingly business, Aristotle left for Athens. There, with the aid of friends and well-wishers, including Alexander, he founded the Lyceum. With one of the city's finest gymnasiums as its main building, it was under the patronage of Apollo of Lyceus, the god of shepherds. Like Aristotle's alma mater, the Academy, the new school lay amidst dappled arboreal shadows, chromatic gardens, a placid pond here, a piece of statuary there, and sheltered walks all about. The school's head and director worked himself unstintingly. His mornings he devoted to teaching. Sometimes he gave a lecture, and sometimes he engaged his students in dialogue as he came upon them during his rambles about the grounds. Later in the day he mounted his rostrum to lecture to the general populace, simplifying any complexity to suit their wit and interest. The practice of the free public lecture rendered by a ranking scholar still obtains in most of the larger citadels of advanced learning both here and abroad.

As the years slipped by, Aristotle's early ardor for the Platonic idealism underwent some alteration. His master's absorption in the "heavenly things that are the object of higher philosophy," which a younger Aristotle had once regarded with the utmost respect, yielded more and more to an engrossment in things and events, in particular, the phenomena of science and history. The shift, as might be expected, was caught in the Lyceum's looking glass, which although it had begun as a promoter of rhetoric and philosophy, now directed its chief attention toward the natural sciences. To advance his newborn interest, the philosopher enriched the Lyceum not only with a large library, but with a museum of natural history, and even an entourage of living birds and beasts.

But if, for the sake of increasing our knowledge of the natural world, he evinced such an amiable disposition toward both the male and female fauna, he showed no such benignity toward the human female. Unlike the sagacious Plato, Aristotle held the human female in low esteem. She was, he maintained, a second-class human, at best an imperfect and underdeveloped male.

As Aristotle's interest veered more and more toward the study of natural phenomena his dependence on observation grew apace. Like the Sophists, he came to regard our senses as the wellspring of our knowledge; at the same time he missed no chance to rap their knuckles for hopping to conclusions about the essence of the universe without having troubled themselves to take a close and painstaking look at its discernible manifestations. Like Plato, he laid great weight on the importance of reason, but unlike the Idealist, he repudiated mere ratiocination as inadequate for grappling successfully with the conundrums of existence. The universals of Plato, and those who thought like him, Aristotle regarded simply as generalized ideas. Not inborn, they issue from numerous conceptions rather than real things. What the advancement of knowledge called for besides flight into the exalted metaphysical ether was a thoroughgoing examination of all observable phenomena. To such an end the Stageirite went to great lengths to get his charges to pry open their eyes and ears and, with all the precision at their command, to examine every field of knowledge from the social and political conventions of barbarians to the constitutions of Greek city-states, the organs of animals, their habits and social arrangements, the nature and distribution of flora, and so on. Whatever data their inspections availed them, they were to assemble in a systematic way to make them intelligible and useful to scholars scattered in other geographic parts. As still happens now and then in the academic community, the philosopher was not averse to helping himself to the fruits of his students' labors to place them in some of his own scholarly compositions, only to make the maddening discovery later on that some contained puerilities and gaucheries of the first magnitude.

WRITINGS AND GENERAL VIEWS

Aristotle was an extremely copious writer—it takes a large two-columned page for the *Encyclopaedia Britannica* to embalm the titles of his works of which we have any knowledge. Unlike Plato, Aristotle frequently wrote with a heavy pen—he lacked his teacher's light and lyrical touch. Even so, he toiled assiduously, confecting for the layman no less than twenty-seven dialogues, some of which, if we accept the verdict of Cicero, were on a par with those of Plato. Unhappily, too many of these writings have vanished, victims, very likely, of the rampaging Roman legions. What is left is for the most part abstract and technical, and at times not a little arid. From logic and rhetoric his writings swept into the natural sciences, and thence into metaphysics, esthetics, ethics, and politics. Nothing, apparently, escaped this man's intellect.

It is in his dealings with ethics and politics that we catch a glimpse of Aristotle as a pedagogue. His *Nicomachean Ethics,* which he named for his young son Nicomachus who fell in battle, is the first complete and systematic treatise on right and wrong of which we have any knowledge, and his *Politics,* although it has come to us only as the residuum of a fuller study, remains, for all its lacks, the first formal dissertation on what currently passes for the science of comparative government. In accord with Plato, Aristotle viewed education as a branch of politics. It is—it has to be—he insisted, a state monopoly, and to attain the ends of the state its education must reflect the nature of the society it undertakes to preserve. In Sparta, for example, a totalitarian military state where the individual is subject at all times to the fiats of its board of elders, the young must be brought up accordingly. But Spartan education would never do for the Athenians, who put a high value on a citizen's individual rights, whether private or public. Though the Aristotelian proposition that education must tailor the young to fit the nature of the state, whatever it may be, is currently under the frown of various clans of pedagogic sages, yet after more than two millennia it still carries the cachet of common sense.

Although Aristotle declared for an education which would fortify the existence of the prevailing social order, this does not mean that he was ready to grant it a free hand to crush any individual qualities that lurk, perhaps undisclosed and unavowed, within a normal man. Such a course, the philosopher believed, would be self-defeating, for it would fail to achieve its overriding purpose—the making of an active man of virtue. But for Aristotle such a fellow's goodness is not bottomed solely in wisdom. This, true enough, may be the most scintillating in the dramatis personae of human values, but beside it stand numerous others, some of a lesser sheen, and maybe even a bit homely, but virtues, nevertheless. Nor is virtue to be bagged primarily, as Plato would have it, by means of philosophic contemplation; for the goodness of a man, Aristotle contended, emanates not from his knowledge alone, but rather from its transmission into action. A man's knowledge of the good, in short, may rate 100 percent, but unless his deeds can be squared with what he knows, his progress to virtue is badly crippled. Finally, there are no such things as absolute, unalterable goods—in fact, overstressed, even a virtue may become a curse, as witness temperance transmogrified into prohibition. What is needed is moderation, the midpath between the opposites—a common sense which enables a man to row his boat between the extremes on either side which threaten to ruin him. The unvirtuous man, thus—to put it negatively—is the one who fails to fulfill his natural potential for good, the one who, by the same stroke, functions excessively or insufficiently.

BABES, MOTHERS, AND WOMEN

Like his teacher, Aristotle supported the view that by nature Homo sapiens is in part a rational being, but in a larger measure he is an irrational one. It thus becomes the task of education to wed these incongruous elements into a smoothly working partnership. In a way, the process is launched even before a man issues from his mother's womb, even, indeed, before he is conceived. For again, like the founder and headmaster of the Academy, Aristotle, endeavoring to effect the birth of a healthy and well-formed babe, announced for a state-supervised and antiseptical wedlock, with instruction and dietary guidance for the pregnant mother. Should the caprice of fate, nevertheless, condemn her freshborn offspring to sickliness or malformity, then, bowing to the ancient custom of heathenry, Aristotle would have it destroyed—a routine which, had it still been in vogue in later times would have robbed civilization of a Newton and a Voltaire, to mention only two.

On *les belles filles,* as one might figure, Aristotle wasted but little learning. Though he loved Pythias, his first wife, very dearly, and requested that upon his death his remains be placed beside hers, his general opinion of the female was scarcely flattering. Lacking in cerebral power, she is damned to suffer the consequence of her infirmity. Her natural and proper place, the sage let it be known, siding with a deeply tap-rooted Athenian tradition, was at the hearth, the bedroom—or, if you will, the breeding chamber—and the nursery. To give her help and counsel to enable her to play an effective role therein she was to be made privy to the common knacks and know-hows of the domestic arts and sciences. To the growing girl was assigned the duty of keeping herself healthy and physically efficient so that at eighteen she would be able to satisfy and comfort a mate to whom in the connubial enclave she was, of course, at all times subordinate. To obey him, to toady to his whims and wishes, to bear him a host of hale and hearty progeny—preferably male—was her unarguable function.

It was a view which men found very reasonable—in fact, some still do—and which subsequently sneaked its way into Christendom. Its early specialists in moral theology gave it an emphatic approbation, and presently some even enriched it with a corollary, to wit: not only is the female a second-class human; at heart she is also a rake and the root of all evil. Saint Augustine, for one, announced his astonishment that the All-knower should have created Eve at all, even though, it is true, He created her as an afterthought. As late as 1595, not quite twelve hundred years after the saint's elevation to a perdurable celestial bliss, deep thinkers at the University of Wittenberg were scorching their brains in formal disputation over whether women by any stretch of the imagination might rightfully qualify as human beings. Unfortunately, the question proved too staggering for even their high-powered genius. However, had the learned brethren hearked back to the researches of England's Bishop Aylmer, they would have had no problem. Women, His Lordship expostulated in a sermon he rendered in the presence of Queen Elizabeth I, were "foolish, wanton flibbergibs . . .evil-tongued, worse-minded, and in every way doltified with the dregs of the Devil's dunghill."

EDUCATION—MALE

Under Aristotle, males, needless to say, obtained a better deal. As a matter of fact, for even the lowliest among them—not counting those in slavery—he reserved no less than twenty-one years of schooling, which, as human life then spanned, was a sizable slice. The business was set in motion in the home, whose influence, for all the brow-wrinkling and throat-clearing of Plato, Aristotle continued to cherish. There, under parental vigilance, the boy was to take his first steps toward the development of a vigorous and virtuous maturity, which is to say a life of happiness. To scale the crags of this exalted ripeness, he was put to learning how to operate as a human being in accordance with whatever capacities nature had favored him, for only by successfully balancing the delicate equation between his natural assets and liabilities could he hope to pluck a fair share of life's gratifications. But inasmuch as a boy, by nature, is only dimly aware of life's harsh intricacies, and hence is obliged willy-nilly to wander for the most part in the mazes of irrationality, he must be safeguarded constantly against the pitfalls of his inexperience, whether in work or play, until he is safely over the line of seven. At that time, the state will communicate its greetings, ordering him to attend its schools in order to enable it to instruct and improve him in health, strength, and morality.

At school, where the curriculum was to be "one and the same for all," his duties were neither too exigent nor too indulgent, but as per the Aristotelian principle, they lay somewhere in between. Nor was the boy to be just a hearer; he was to be a doer as well. The words which entered his mind through his ears were to be translated into the reality of everyday practice, for what was all-important in the making of an upright and honorable man was not his holdings in accumulated knowledge, but his stock of good habits. At bottom, Aristotle asserted, virtue is a habit—or, in modern terms, it is an acquired response which by frequent repetition, like walking and talking, has become automatic.

From his first year at school until he was eighteen, Aristotle's nascent man of virtue applied himself to the study of reading and writing which, plainly, were imperative if he was to perform effectively as a good citizen. In addition, he directed some of his attention to music and drawing, because they would be a tonic to his psyche and thereby help to enrich and enlarge his living. His learning was to proceed at an agreeable pace, and its end was to be the liberal one of helping to make his adult life useful and happy. In no case was his education to be tarnished by practical and utilitarian motives. The learning which undertook to put butter on one's bread was for the mean man, not for the more well-bred one. Organized gymnastics, which among Greeks, whether Spartan or Athenian, had always rated high, Aristotle held in abeyance until the pupil was eighteen. The reason for their presence was not so much to lay the groundwork for the youth's eventual stint at soldiering, but rather to habituate him to keeping himself in good health and good physical condition, to afford him pleasure and well-being, and to develop self-control and a degree of athletic skill—not, however, to train him to win gauds at athletic shows.

STRIKE UP THE BAND

One of the philosopher's pet themes concerned the immeasurable value of the tonal art in the making of an upstanding citizen. Let the boy hear good music, and lots of it, while he is still in his childhood, for this, Aristotle held, would inevitably develop his later musical taste and understanding. Like so many Hellenes, the Stageirite subscribed to the curious delusion that music bore powerfully on the formation of good character. Hence, since it is a trait of music to display itself, like the common house cat, in almost infinite variety, it becomes a pedagogic urgency for the state to hold a relentless vigil over a pupil's harmonic intake, for it will work for his good or ill. Does he, for example, delight in langorous airs, in the sweet cooings of love and bucolic enchantment? Then let the state suppress such bon-bon stuff in its schools, for it is hemlock to the spirit, and in the long run it will surely rout the learner's ability to act with manly resolution. Let him—to transpose his ancient musical effusions into the more familiar equivalent of our own—be made to plug his ears to "Drink to Me Only with Thine Eyes," and listen instead to the "Marche Militaire," the "Marseillaise," or even "Strike Up the Band." Such robust strains are bound to fortify his will and spunk, and he will, as a consequence, grow into a loyal and up-and-doing citizen.

Teaching tomorrow's citizen to finger his lyre and chant his arias of heroic feats, like instructing the young in physical culture, was to be kept at all times on a strictly nonvocational level. Its purpose was not to bring forth a Kreisler or a Caruso, or even a Benny Goodman, for that to Aristotle carried a miasmic whiff of professionalism and was offensive to his nares. Never, in any case, was the budding citizen to divert himself by the seductions of the flute. Not only was its sound a pestilence to the ear, but the grimaces of the player were a pain to the eye. Lucky, indeed, was the Stageirite to have lived so long before the era of the lascivious waltz, not to say that of jazz and rock.

EDUCATION, CONTINUED

So much for Aristotle's program for the lower learning. Above that plane his educational recommendations are buried in the potter's field of history's numerous and unsung departed. Either he never bothered to compose them systematically in writing, or if he did they fell victim to the malice of the marauding years. Even so, from his own practice in the Lyceum and from remarks he let fall in some of his other writings, it is possible to piece together a fairly coordinate pattern. His main weight would lie on the natural and political sciences, with a persistent undertone in straight thinking. To this purpose Aristotle put before his students a course of study which in all likelihood comprised grammar, rhetoric, letters, including prose and poesy, besides music, geography, and, of course, the inescapable mathematics. Beyond that, for those who wanted still more, the philosopher favored the study of ethics, psychology, and politics, with its adjunct of education. Finally, for those hungering for the very richest intellectual provender, the *Philosophiae Doctor* of today, so to speak, the Lyceum's chief steward put the stamp of approval on such intellectual tidbits as biology, physics, and philosophy. All this, as has been hinted, is sheer inference, but in the main the estimate is based upon reason.

Rather noteworthy is that, in setting the school's educational policies, one of the controversies harassing the higher learning all over the contemporaneous world was resolved in practice in the Lyceum. There the advanced students, the juniors, seniors, and the graduates, as we think of them nowadays, not only chose their surrogates to plead in their behalf in discussions with the school's faculty over the school's policies; they also had a voice in the formulation of the course of study.

Although, as has already been mentioned, Aristotle stood in accord with his teacher on several matters, the Platonic gerontocracy, as laid out in the Republic, left him cold. In truth, he put no store whatever in the idea of the wisdom of old age. Consequently, any state in which the elderly make the laws and the young and the middle-aged stand by and obey, he regarded critically. Aristotle's view of old age, which rested on the unanswerable determinism of biology and the life span of the time, caused him to elbow out the elderly from positions of power, for the advancing years were bound to take their toll, and at fifty a man was caught in the outgoing ebb of time. Hence, rather than elevate aging philosophers to the throne of political command, as did Plato, Aristotle would remove them. Furthermore, instead of placing cerebrals, real or supposed, at the head of a state, the Stageirite preferred to rely on its police, the idea being for all citizens—not merely the senior intellectuals—to be upright and decent people, each to rule and to be ruled.

ARISTOTLE'S INFLUENCE

The impact of Aristotle's work and thought upon his own time, like that of Plato, was slight. The doddering city-state was too spent to respond even to the wonder drugs of the wise, and with its dissolution, the Hellenic ideal of the citizen-man glided into the irretrievable past. For Athenians life became a matter of every man for himself, a situation which so enfeebled what remained of even the best of Greece that her people fell easy prey to the arms of powerful might.

Yet, as so often happens in the study of our receding yesterdays, time saw scholars give Aristotle a second look. But the obtainable knowledge they had about him was scant. Indeed, in the Western world it had all but disappeared, and it was not until after several centuries that a fuller portrait of this remarkable Greek came to life through the searchings of the Arabs whose men of learning had long been his devotees. To them Aristotle was beyond any doubt the philosopher par excellence, "the master of those who know," and "the wisest of all Greeks." The man's secular knowledge made Christian scholars gape—verily, so stupendous was his knowledge it seemed almost to defy human credulity. The fact that this colossus was a heathen and that in many points his teachings were at sharp odds with those of Mother Church was not lost, of course, on the ecclesiastical powers. In fact, at least twice Rome had put down her official foot on the reading of Aristotle's works. By the thirteenth century, however, the interest in the publications of this pagan had become so overmastering that the church, yielding to pragmatic prudence, ordered a Latin edition of Aristotle's writings, exercising the necessary precaution, however, to warn the translators that the philosopher's works "be purged of all suspicion of error." Thus made safe for Christian decency, Aristotle climbed to a higher and higher eminence. So well was he regarded that in the esteem accorded him he presently not only joined the fraternity of the saintly fathers, but in the medieval world of scholarship his universal knowledge lay beyond dispute. By the middle of the thirteenth century, his revelations commanded so high a respect that, stitched into the church's official philosophy, they were being propounded in every European university.

What appealed especially to the medieval schoolmen—"the Scholastics," as they have been dubbed—was Aristotle's deductive logic, that issued therefrom even as they ignored all the while his stress on observation and inductive reasoning. The Stageirite was the first of whom we have any inkling who organized logic into a technical system of thought. Thereafter, any articulate man of normal rational capacity could teach logic as a formal mental discipline. Aristotle's book on the subject, the *Organon,* which was thus named after his death, sat in power in the textbook world for some 2,000 years, a best seller in any sense even though neither the composer nor his heirs, assigns, and successors ever collected a solitary drachma for his effort. The *Organon,* some pundits hold, though not without some contravening from others, was his most enduring legacy to intellectual history— some, indeed, have volunteered the opinion that, since Aristotle, nonmathematical logic has made slight progress.

If medieval savants fell hungrily upon the Aristotelian logic of deduction, they paid scarcely any heed to his reasoning in his *Nicomachean Ethics.* Therein, setting down the hypothesis that the primary end of a man's life is happiness, he proceeded to toss out all a priori presuppositions, insisting, to the contrary, on a step-by-step empirical procedure—which is to say he worked inductively. The best life, he concluded from the generalization of numerous particular examples, issues from a blend of all the manifold aspects of personality—the well-rounded man—a Goethe, for example, guided by reason, virtue, and self-restraint.

If in his *Ethics* Aristotle put his magnifying glass on the nature of individual happiness, then in his *Politics* he grappled with the nature of collective happiness. Based on an exhaustive dissection of more than 150 Greek constitutions, the *Politics* is the repository of Aristotle's political and sociological thought. The state, he let it be known, is a natural body, for "man is by nature a political animal." There is no best of all possible governments, he went on. When a state, be it a monarchy or a democracy or a timocracy, is governed efficiently for the general welfare, then plainly it has its points. Furthermore, he declared—treading his way along his favorite middle path—"though one form of government may be better than others, yet there is no reason to prevent another from being preferable to it under particular conditions,"—something evangelists of American democracy might well ponder.

SCIENTIFIC WRITINGS

Aristotle's most important scientific work is his *Historia Animalium,* which is for its greater part a piece of descriptive biology, and wherein, as has been hinted, he incorporated some of the findings of his students. In physics he was not so safely grounded. True, he rejected the influence of inscrutable ghostly powers and depended instead on explanations derived from observable natural cause and its effect. In this vein he applied himself to the study of the land, the sea, and the air. He came to grips with the clouds, the fog, the dew, and the winds. He turned a ferretlike eye to the mystery of lightning and thunder, the rainbow, and even the meteor. Man, it occurred to him, is an animal. The ape, he added as a corollary, is the link between Homo sapiens and the rest of the mammalian zoo, and the earth, their dwelling place, is a sphere, stationary, he was sure, and situated in the very center of the cosmos.

For all the power of his gigantic mind, Aristotle, being human, enjoyed no immunity from error. Some of his bungling, in fact, was prodigious, and in afterlight even somewhat droll. Without a snippet of evidence, for instance, he declared for the spontaneous generation of the eel. Though he had studied anatomy, yet he insisted that the human female possessed fewer ribs than the male. Plants, he gravely announced, are sexless. The organ of intellect, he was certain, was the heart, and when it cogitates too long and too intensely it becomes the function of the brain to pump phlegm into it to keep it from bursting into flame. Finally, hobnobbing with the theological doctrine of design, the Master of Those Who Know convinced himself that man was equipped with a behind, round, firm, and softly pillowed, because since he had but one pair of legs he needed such an appendage to set himself down in comfort.

The impulse to snicker at such profound balderdash is great, but let it not be forgotten that in the advancement of knowledge Aristotle was a pioneer; hence he was hobbled, as trail-blazers must always be, by inescapable obstacles. He had to devise his own methodology and he labored without the benefit of the simplest instruments, without a tube or crucible, without even a strip of litmus. For all his blundering, he was in a manner of speaking the remote father of the scientific method, furnishing it, as well as philosophy, with a nomenclature we still often find useful. Whenever Aristotle undertook a study, he attacked his problem not only with his senses, but laid down a barrage for his assault by combing all the writings which had dealt with his subject before his time—in short, he was on familiar footing with all available sources, whether genuine or spurious. Whatever data this wisest of all Greeks managed to snare, he carefully organized from alpha to omega. He was in this respect the first encyclopedist of whom we have any record—one of the most relentless pigeonholers ever heard of. Finally, he took infinite pains to embody his enormous knowledge in written form, allotting at least one dissertation to each of his specialties—thereby unwittingly making himself the forebear of what we currently designate as book learning. Although Aristotle was trapped on occasion by his fancy, yet sometimes that very fancy opened vistas which were unbeheld by others until the nineteenth century. To illustrate, he entered the vestibule of the temple of the evolutionary theory, and like contemporary scientists, he entertained an idea of a universe forever in flux.

A MOST REMARKABLE MAN

It is not given to many to rise to Aristotle's Olympian heights. In versatility, only Leonardo da Vinci surpassed him, and in the power of his intellect only Leibnitz, Newton, Einstein, and, give or take a bit, possibly Helmholtz, could rival him. But aside from these the Stageirite remains in a class by himself. His impact on medieval scholars, as has been said, knew no bounds, and for centuries his teachings, cleansed, of course, of their heathenry, stood without challenge. Then, as usually happens with anything that has enjoyed a long vogue, the philosopher fell into discredit. With the flowering of the Renaissance in the fourteenth century, Aristotle was not only pulled down from his pedestal; he was also accused of having been in error from start to finish—a thesis which a student in Paris publicly and successfully defended. No less contemptuous of the ancient philosopher was Martin Luther, who despised "the damned pagan Aristotle" as much, if possible, as he hated the Roman harlot. He had, Luther insisted, "debauched the Church with intellectual pride." Since then calmer minds have redressed the critical balance.

In pedagogy, the Aristotelian influence exhibited no great tremors. True, the philosopher's view that there is an inescapable affinity between the schooling of the young and the state whose interests it seeks to serve and safeguard has become a commonplace. So has his proposition that in order to benefit and prosper the commonweal, education must be a state enterprise. On the other hand, his disparagement of women as so many nobodies, educationally speaking, bedazzled and enticed a long line of his male successors, and it was not until the nineteenth century that his dubious thinking began to be seriously suspect. It was not, however, through philosophical meditation, but rather through the inexorable realities of the industrial and scientific revolutions that women's unfettering from the relics of a deep-seated prejudice got under way, and along with it, their inalienable right to an education on a par with their so-called "superior brothers."

The sunset of Aristotle's years, like that of Socrates, ended under a beclouded sky. His Lyceum, despite its worldwide fame, was excoriated by rival groups on every side. Jingoists, bemoaning the fact that its founder and director was an outlander, denounced him as a radical, an enemy of the people and of the legacy of their beloved decencies. Presently even his writings were under fire. They were, the town's experts in applied virtue accused, brimful of subversion, critical of right-thinking, and an affront to the gods. While his foes thus steadily added to what the French call the youngest of his sorrows, the dismoded Aristotle, loath to grant the Athenian planners of deviltries a second chance to sin against philosophy, made off for other latitudes. It was in the nick of time. Soon after, the state sentenced him to be executed. But luck played them false, and for a while at least the wisest of all Greeks kept out of reach. Then, at the age of sixty-two, he died, a casualty, it is chronicled, of a condemned stomach.

Chapter 5

Quintilian

ROME'S FOREMOST PEDAGOGIC THINKER

A people given to grappling with the realities of practice rather than to speculation, the Romans bred few writers on educational theory. Cicero, to be sure, dreamed about the subject, and so did Suetonius and Tacitus, but the light they shed was dim at best, and when set close to such blinding arc lights as Plato and Aristotle they all but fade away. Rome's foremost pedagogic thinker was Marcus Fabius Quintilian (ca. A.D. 35–95). He was born in the middle thirties of the first century in Calagurris, now known as Calahorra, a town on the banks of the Ebro in northern Spain. His father was a professional rhetorician, who also did a bit of moonlighting as a tutor of his specialty. Young Marcus fell not far from the paternal tree—in fact, he was still a youth when he undertook to make himself ready for a career in law by working as an apprentice to Domitius Afer, a successful jurisconsult at the time. Returned to his home town with his motor running, as it were, Quintilian presently found himself making his living as an advocate, dabbling betweenwhiles in politics, but after ten years or so of pleading the cases of his clients he exchanged his juridic robes for those of an academic. About A.D. 68 he settled in the city on the Tiber to keep school, where he also gave instruction in rhetoric, and, not unlike his father, he drifted into occasional moonlighting—in his own case, however, as a lawyer.

The Romans regarded him approvingly, and some of those who sat in his classes were destined to leave an imperishable mark on the pages of history. He was the mentor of Pliny the Younger, and of Juvenal and Tacitus, all highly intellectual, who not only read books but, when they became men, also wrote them. Even the imperial Vespasian succumbed to the fascination of this gentle and ingratiating man. The master of all the Romans not only entrusted his two adopted sons to the émigré from Calagurris for instruction, but in the year 78 he appointed him to the empire's first professorship in rhetoric—or for that matter in anything—with a lifetime chair and a generous emolument to make it worthwhile.

For some twenty years Quintilian lived a full and busy life, performing great prodigies as teacher, lawyer, writer, and speechmaker, not only under his exalted patron, the emperor, but under his successors Titus and Domitian as well. He became famed as Rome's supreme preceptor of the rhetorician's art, and in the process he was celebrated with an ever-rising stack of honors and rewards, culminating in the rank of senator with all its special usufructs, dignities, and immunities. Yet despite his glittering triumphs, in the year 88, while he was still on the good side of his fifties, he suddenly disengaged himself from all professional endeavor to devote the rest of his life to writing and reflection. He had chosen to free himself from the pressures and harassments of his work to "retire honorably," as he explained, "from teaching and speaking in the Forum while my services were still in demand."

Quintilian's life had its sunsets as well as its sunrises. Some of his days were bleak, and all too often his nights were wakeful. Death robbed him of his wife while she was still in her teens. One of his two boys died at the age of five. The other, to whose upbringing and education he had dedicated his main literary work, died soon after Quintilian had started writing. He had aspired to make it the most precious legacy a father could bequeath to his son in whom he had, as he said, placed all the hopes that should solace him in his old age. It should be no surprise that the dread of death should ride him, not in the sense that he was afraid to die, but rather that he might suddenly be cut down with his work unfinished. Thus roweled by the panic in his heart, Quintilian pursued his purpose without surcease, working day and night—sometimes all too hastily—until after two grim years his composition was ready for its publisher.

INSTITUTES OF ORATORY

The work which was produced by its author with so much sweat and tears is a treatise on the making of an orator, the *Institutio Oratoria,* or the *Institutes of Oratory.* It is an ambitious undertaking, cast in twelve parts, each embracing some seventy-five pages. Despite the narrow confines indicated by the book's title, its maker managed to peek over the wall to review a larger and often quite pleasurable landscape, as witness the Roman educational system, the prospective orator's boyhood years in the family circle, his toil and suffering at school, the rhetorician's refined and subtle mystery, the efforts to pin this down in the rhetorical school, the training in oratorical theory and practice in all their diverse and complex aspects, and, in the twelfth book, a grand finale on literary taste and criticism.

Though, like the typical Roman, Quintilian kept his feet on the solid ground of practicality, and in his labor of forging accomplished public speakers he was ever mindful of the actual world in which his students would some day have to function, yet at the same time he confessed an unblinking affection for the cultural. He was on friendly terms with Greek and recommended it wholeheartedly as a vastly nutritious ingredient in the curriculum of Rome's higher professional learning. Indeed, of such consequence did this master rhetorician regard the Greek tongue in the education of the Roman boy that he made it the learner's primary vehicle of instruction. "I prefer," he wrote, "that a boy should begin with the Greek language, because he will acquire Latin, which is in general use, even though we tried to prevent him." Besides, he went on, Greek should enjoy the right of precedence because Greek learning was, so to speak, the mother of Roman learning. Furthermore, he contended, in criticism of the established Roman practice, there is no reason why a boy's introduction to literacy should await his seventh birthday. Let him, suggested Quintilian, confront the ABC's as soon as he is able, which is to say, the professor hastened to explain with a somewhat wary Aristotelian caveat, whenever learning will not unduly hamper the youngster's budding powers.

Although Quintilian had himself done service as a tutor to the imperial young, he nevertheless entertained doubts about the value of such sequestered tutelage. There is no gainsaying, he conceded, that even the finest school has its shortcomings. Yet on the other hand there is nothing to take the place of a lad's flocking with others—a natural proclivity. Hence, to confine him day in day out in the singular company of his mentor, however laudable and companionable he may be, is at best a poor substitute for the social interplay to be enjoyed at school. To be held in quarantine in the parental home, even though it be a palace, is not only oppressive to a normal boy, but it can be the breeder of gross malaises, such as conceit, self-indulgence, shyness, insecurity, and similar pox upon human happiness. Finally, though the eminent Aristotle had discountenanced them, the competition and rivalry which only a school can generate can be an excellent tonic to make a pupil hustle; for his master, moreover, it is so much adrenalin, and the greater the assemblage of his students, the greater ought to be his incentive to surpass himself.

VIEWS AND DISSENSIONS

Roman schoolmasters, as is well known, brooked no nonsense from their wards, and they birched them frequently and even fiercely, not only for their trespasses but for their ignorance as well. Though flogging was the long-established rule, Quintilian, who was deeply sensitive to personal relationships, declared himself flatly against it. "That a boy should suffer physical punishment, though it be a custom," he avowed, "I by no means approve." It is a curious fact, at least when set in the context of his time and place, that Quintilian made a point of stressing that play and pleasure are no enemies of learning, but that to the contrary they can go a long way to make what seems unbearable, bearable, and even fascinating, when camouflaged with discreet fun and drollery. It should be no cause for wonder, therefore, to observe Quintilian urging pedagogues to festoon their drab offerings with soft enchantment so that not only will a boy be enticed to attend to his studies but in the long run "he will not reserve a dislike for what once had given him a pain."

Quintilian needed no master of the psyche to tell him about human diversity. His long span of service in the grove had brought him into the presence of every variety of student temperament. Taking one with another, most boys, he inclined to believe—somewhat optimistically one might say—were not only intelligent, but also eager to learn. Even so, he also had noticed that some were indolent; that others disliked to take orders; and that yet others were bogged in insecurity and were all too readily dispirited. Predictably, some would be pearls; but just as predictably, even more would be paste. Whatever the case, in spite of his predisposition to large classes, Quintilian went to great lengths to stress—as did Jean-Jacques Rousseau some seventeen hundred years following—that a teacher ought "to know the child," for only when thus forearmed can he expect to teach and guide understandingly. The model pupil, Quintilian believed, was the boy "who rouses when he is praised, who profits when he is encouraged, and cries when he is defeated." Such a fellow may be expected to apply himself and, given a little luck, he is headed for success and perhaps even fame. But let no one forget that his education is not intended to bring him wealth. "I trust," Quintilian wrote, "that none of my readers would think of calculating its monetary value."

THE MAKING OF AN ORATOR—PART 1

When Quintilian set down his views on the making of an orator—a man he described as "possessed of every moral virtue"—he was seeking to achieve two things: *one,* to delineate for parents and teachers a plan on how to go about making such a man; *two,* to return the art of public utterance to the high and respected eminence it had enjoyed in the preimperial times of Cicero, in whom the *Institutio's* genitor detected all the essential qualities of the superspeaker. To realize his heart's desire, the professor put his trust in the assistance of the home and the existing schools, but, as has been mentioned, mitigating the latters' strictness, as well as altering their offerings. To the home he assigned the task of laying a solid foundation. It was not only the matrix wherein the good man was to be molded; it was also the incubator of good speech. Needless to say, to bring these things about, parents were expected to play an active part. But, warned the professor, let us not overlook the influence, for good or ill, of the child's attendants. "Before all things," he insisted, "let the talk of the child's nurses be grammatical. It is they the child will hear first. It is their words he will try to form by imitation."

To teach the boy his letters, beginning with Greek and continuing with Latin, became the responsibility of the primary school, or, as the Romans knew it, the *ludus.* When reading ceased to be a closed art, which is to say when the boy had learned to fathom the meaning of simple written Greek and Latin sentences, he was considered fit to attend the sessions of the grammar school. To its teacher, the so-called *grammaticus,* fell the task of filling the pupil's head with the rules and regulations of grammar, doctoring his compositions when they were grammatically sick, and exercising their delinquent author relentlessly day after day in hopes of getting him to speak and write fluently and correctly. Meanwhile, his teacher also opened the door to the writings of the great luminaries of verse. Further, to equip the student for the sandals of Cicero, with the knowledge deemed necessary to his eventual practice of the oratorical art, his master set him on the path of philosophy, geometry, music, and astronomy.

But the organized love of wisdom that Quintilian contended with was scarcely the profound and formidable subject—with its intertwinings of ontology, epistemology, axiology, and such arcane concerns—that delighted the philosophical Plato and Aristotle and their endless successors. In fact, like the rhetorical Isocrates, his silent but eloquent Athenian predecessor, Quintilian held a rather sniffish opinion of the run of professing philosophers; and if he gave them any attention at all it was mainly for the light they so often cast on the effusions of the poets, which not uncommonly were obscured in the powdery mists of philosophic allusion. One may also wonder why a prospective orator, beset as he already was with an inordinately heavy load at school, should be called upon to study music. The answer, rather curiously, is to be found not in the domain of the beautiful, but in that of the practical. If tomorrow's rhetorician is bidden to surrender some of his precious time to the pursuit of the tonal art, it is not to transmute him into an accomplished tune-master, but rather to make him privy to his vocal resources, to help him develop and refine his voice, to cultivate in him a sense of tone and cadence, and finally to lift up his sagging spirit when his humors and megrims pester him unduly.

Does tomorrow's speaker in the forum grapple with geometry? Then once more the reason is predominantly utilitarian. Coming to grips with the Euclidian theorems, with their stout reliance on systematic deductive reasoning, would, Quintilian was certain, help to strengthen the student's ability to frame clear and ineluctable arguments. Like grammar, moreover, geometry was then regarded as the indispensable iron tonic for building up the powers of the mind. As for the study of the celestial bodies, even this can serve an orator usefully. Not only can his knowledge of the firmament and its ineffable lanterns be made to dumfound his hearers and fill them with awe, but reinforced with geometric computation it enables him to garb the cosmic mystery with meaning, however frail and esoteric.

THE MAKING OF AN ORATOR—PART 2

As is to be expected, the *Institutes of Oratory* burns the greater part of its candle to illuminate the last stage of the orator's development, namely, his more recherché studies in the rhetorical school. For all its specialized professional purpose, it permits no cessation of the student's general education. He must continue to press his pursuit of belles lettres, inhaling the exotic perfume of their prose and poetry, and give himself to meditate over their moral exaltations. He must bediamond his rhetoric and composition, sharpen his logic, and file the axioms of professional ethics in the cabinet of his memory. Though he lives in the present, he is not to disdain what came before; hence he is put upon to unlock the historical past. To sense its horrors no less than its delights will not only give him food for thought, it will also enlarge his professional stock for him to draw upon if the occasion presents itself, for cogent examples to inspirit his harangues.

There is no lack, of course, during this period, of professional training, including every jot and tittle of the speaking art. Thus, the rhetorical aspirant finds himself undergoing training in breathing in and breathing out. His gestures are under critical watch, and so are his facial expressions, his histrionism, his style, and his delivery. He practices his art before a living audience, rendering a simple speech, sometimes sad, sometimes glad; he argues the case of a suppositional client; and for festive occasions he is prepared to launch his oratorical rockets to shake the heavens, thereby lifting the audience out of its seats to buzz his ears with salvoes of applause. Finally, he is made familiar with every artifice in the lawyer's pouch of deception, for, in concert with Roman juridic ethics then in currency, Quintilian believed that to win a case a pleader might use any stratagem, howsoever ignoble.

THE HEIGHTS—SCALED

It is not often granted to teachers—even the best of them—to scale Quintilian's alpine heights. When he died, around the age of sixty, he was a celebrity, not only as a teacher but as a man. He was, said Martial, himself of Spanish provenance, "the best of guides for unstable youth." Juvenal, the ironist, who inclined more to damn than to hymn, pronounced Quintilian "wise, noble, and highminded." The one stain on his otherwise impeccable comportment, his base truckling, that is, before the Emperor Domitian, who among Romans is surpassed only by Nero as a practitioner of horror, was tactfully swept under the rug. Although an unkind fate robbed Quintilian of the joy of passing the *Institutio* as a legacy to his son, the bereaved father must have been somewhat solaced by the tremendous acceptance accorded his work. In fact, long after its author had taken residence among the eternal shades, though his work was imitated and even plagiarized, it continued to command the field. Then, like a spent meteor, it suddenly vanished into the silent void.

So things stood till 1416, when Poggio Bracciolini, while rummaging for fugitive manuscripts, came upon a complete copy of it resting inconspicuously in dust and dinginess in the cloister of Sankt Gallen in Switzerland. Copied in what must have been a breakneck speed by the ecstatic Poggio, the resurrected *Institutio* was restored to a lusty circulation in academia, bethumbed and reflected over by students for another several hundred years. To the generality of schoolmasters, whose pedagogical outlook scarcely diverged from that of their faraway Roman antecedents, the bulk of Quintilian's didactic views were so much balderdash, and if they deigned to give them any notice at all, it was simply to lash out at him with their catcalls. But liberal-minded scholars in Britain as well as on the European mainland beat the drum for them with wonder and admiration. Some, like Erasmus, even adopted some of the Roman's precepts, and some, like Vittorino da Feltre, actually ventured to employ them in the diurnal practice of his school at Mantua.

QUINTILIAN TODAY—AND THE DEATH OF ROME

Thus the professor's ideas found their way down the interminable route of time, and though nowadays, to the common classroom teacher, their fomenter and promoter is all too frequently only a name, vaguely remembered, if even that, yet the fact remains that not a few of Quintilian's theories, for all their hoary vintage, have imbedded themselves as self-evident postulates in contemporary education, as, in illustration, the importance of the home in the child's early education; the necessity of understanding the peculiar nature of the individual child, and, by corollary, the recognition of his rights and dignity as a human being, even though he is not yet fully formed; the value of play and joy as spurs to learning; the desirability of learning not from books alone, but from experience as well; and so on. The memory of the planter of these and other seeds of progressivism may have faded, but his pedagogy in the main has been kept alive.

Although time has spared the greater part of Quintilian's educational theory from dissolution, this is not to say that its invulnerability has been total. There is, for one, the man's view of the nature and functioning of the human mind, the so-called "faculty psychology," whereby the mind is plotted into assorted faculties, each an autonomous principality, performing its own task in complete independence of the others. This notion, firm on its pedestal to the middle of the nineteenth century, grew gradually suspect, and with the advent of scientific psychology it was toppled once and for all. So too was the case of the correlative theory of formal discipline—the doctrine, that is, that the mental faculties, whatever their particular function, could by the use of appropriate subjects be improved in their efficiency. In short, as the saying was, "the mind could be trained."

Rome's foremost schoolman, as has been duly remarked, was not a philosopher, at all events in the familiar sense that he ruminated with any system or depth over transcendent matters involving man and the cosmos. Quintilian restricted his ratiocination to the problems of the world wherein he lived and labored. Practical above all else, he viewed education, as did Plato and Aristotle before him, as one of the many fascicules of society which it served to uphold and protect—and, if reasonably possible—to improve. In this society the orator, as Quintilian conceived him, played a stellar role. He was a liberally educated person, but not in the Hellenic sense that the culture he had accumulated through the long and toilsome years was to give his life enrichment and thereby make it more enjoyable and tolerable. If in his passage from childhood through the halls of rhetorical learning the Roman youth was immersed in a general culture, the purpose behind it was preeminently utilitarian. It was in a word the prerequisite to the rhetorician's professional success. But for all his feet-on-the-ground practicality, Quintilian was not immune from inventing imaginary worlds. "I only hope," he mused, "that at some future day, the perfect orator who is to come will appropriate to himself the study of philosophy." The ideal orator, he went on, "will raise it once more to a place of honor. Like one who recovers stolen property, he will assign it again to its proper position in the world of eloquence." The pity of it is that Quintilian's hope bore no fruit. Rome died before his new world could come into being.

Chapter 6

Saint Augustine

THE WORLD OF AUGUSTINE

Aurelius Augustinius (354–430), known to us more familiarly as Saint Augustine, was born in the North African town of Tagaste in the Roman province of Numidia, now Algeria, and he died seventy-six years later in Hippo, some 30 miles from his birthplace. His sojourn on this planet thus traverses the years which saw the translation of one great civilization into another.

When Augustine entered upon this scene, Rome was under the scepter of one of Constantine's Christian successors. During the years of his youth he had seen the empire succumb to a successful pagan restoration under Julian the Apostate, only to be done in before long by the emperors Gratian and the second Theodosius, each of whom graced his throne as a Christian. As Augustine increased in years, paganism was fast going out of mode, and although, like the vestigial vermiform appendix, it still posed a threat to disturb a Christian's peace of mind, its days of unchallenged supremacy were done. Augustine's seventy-six years in this tormented vale were packed with momentous historical events. He witnessed not only the triumphant progress of the cross in the ancient world, but he also lived through some of its most hair-raising military and political spectacles, as, for example, the devasting rout of the Romans at Adrianople in 378, the disruptions and division of the empire in its bloodsoaked trail, the incursion of the Vandal hordes and others of no less ferocity, the decay and deterioration of Rome's once fearful military fist, and finally, in 410, the ravaging of the Roman capital by Alaric and his Germanic Visigoths. Twenty years later, as Augustine lay dying in Hippo, the Vandals were battering at the city's gate.

YOUTH AND THE GOOD TIMES

Augustine sprang from a pagan father and a Christian mother, a woman named Monica, exemplary in her piety and like her son, venerated nowadays as a saint. For all his mother's devoutness, her son followed in the track of his father's heathenry. Then, on some long-forgotten day, he became a devotee of Mani, a Persian mystic, who, under divine instructions, nominated himself a messiah to purge the world of its wickedness. But the Manichaean revelation, though tranquilizing enough to the flushed spirit of the future saint, offered an insufficient fare to his mind, and so, after a decade in Mani's fold, Augustine began to partake of the richer intellectual alimentation of the Neoplatonists.

The crucial point in Augustine's spiritual development came during his early thirties while he was living in Milan. There he "studiously hearkened" to the preaching of Ambrose, the bishop, more in the mood, however, as Augustine confides in his *Confessions,* of a "careless and contemptuous spectator," than of one seeking the benison of truth. But the bishop's gift of tongue proved irresistible. Before long, indeed, Augustine found himself constrained to grant not only "how well he spoke," but even "how truly he spoke." The upshot was that he dropped the mask of his prejudices and became a catechumen, and after a year or so of indoctrination, at the age of thirty-three he submitted to the baptismal sprinkling. As happens often enough in the ascendancy of a consecrated man—note, for example, the cases of the saints Benedict and Ignatius Loyola—Augustine had luxuriated in a wild and lubricious youth. He lied, he stole, he wenched. In truth, he was not yet twenty when he acquired a mistress who loved him in all respects and bore him an offspring—the Gift of God its father spoke of it. It is scarcely necessary to add that his submission to Christ made an end of such a lurid life once and for all.

EDUCATION

Although Augustine's father was a man of moderate means, he made it a point to give his son a good education. Accordingly, when the time came, the boy was enlisted for instruction either in his home town or in a small municipality nearby. He followed the course trodden by thousands of schoolboys before him, attending the *ludus,* or primary school, where among other things he was expected to learn a rudimentary Greek and Latin. His tutelage, it appears, was up to par, which is to say, it was unspeakably dull. Bored stiff, Augustine reacted in accord with the universal articles of boys' law—he took an acrid delight in making his master's life as miserable as possible, for which, needless to say, he got his lumps. At the same time he remained resolutely anesthetic to Greek. Life in the secondary school proved to be somewhat less forbidding. There, under the direction of the *grammaticus,* he was put through his paces in grammar and literature, with a special emphasis on the works of the poets. For the latter, in particular their leading virtuoso, Virgil, he conceived an unencumbered affection. "The wooden horse full of armed men. . .," he told God in his memoirs, was "a most pleasant spectacle of vanity."

At the age of sixteen he went to Carthage, where he studied rhetoric and public speaking and the usual satellite subjects of grammar, formal logic, music, geometry, and higher arithmetic. He emerged from the rhetorical school at the head of his class—unfortunately, the number of his graduating coevals has escaped the keepers of statistical records. In any case, his head bulged with knowledge. "Whatever was written on rhetoric or logic, music or arithmetic," he confessed—happily unhampered by modesty—"I understood without any great difficulty, and without the aid of any man." It was in this self-appreciating mood that he elected to become a teacher. He launched himself presently as a *grammaticus* in his native Tagaste, whence he proceeded to shine his light as an instructor of rhetoric, first at Carthage, then at Rome, and finally at Milan. Himself a master of a rich eloquence, he reached the peak of his professional eminence when, in the year 384, he was commissioned to supply the proper rhetoric for the Emperor and the Consul Designate for the year ahead.

It was during his Carthaginian school years—Augustine was then of the sophisticated age of eighteen—that he "came upon a book by a certain Cicero." The work, now extinct, was *Hortensius,* an exhortation to philosophy. Evidently, the author's message must have gone straight to its mark—or, to resort to the Augustinian locution, it "changed his affections." Looking back from his riper forties, he confided that it was his reading of *Hortensius* that "turned my prayers to you, Lord, and caused me to have different purposes and devices." It shattered all his previous aspirations which now seemed vain and hollow. Indeed, "with incredible ardor of heart," he now craved nothing less than "undying wisdom." The fire which Cicero had kindled in Augustine was inextinguishable. Time, in truth, was to see it flame into an educational philosophy, borrowing whatever served its end from the Graeco-Roman heritage, and adding the essential Christian elements to give form and substance to a God-centered education which he laid bare in the *Doctrina Christiana* of the *City of God.*

PROPAGATING THE FAITH

Three years after he had been diverted from his downslide to certain damnation, Augustine took holy orders. He performed with a messianic passion to promote the glory of God not only as one of heaven's ordained ambassadors, but as a traveling evangelist as well. He carried the Word to faroff places, haranguing audiences, which often enough were less given to hospitality than to hostility. All the same, the reverend father refused to be daunted, and in the procession of the years he became one of the most successful faith dispensers the church has ever had. Between his missionary work and the demands put upon him by his priestly duties, he continued to teach, not to be sure, as in his former beclouded years at Carthage, Rome, and Milan, but in the loftier role of instructing catechumens for baptism, and even—to climb several rungs higher—of preparing young men for service in the holy frock. At Hippo, where he performed the sacerdotal function, he founded a friary which presently stretched the trammels of its otherwordliness with a seminary for the training and edification of the city's nascent clerics.

One would imagine that a man so heavily weighted with things to do would find his working hours completely bespoken. But this was not the case. Busy though he was, Augustine was not too busy to compose a vast mass of tracts and philippics in defense of the new religion, to say nothing of several books, of which two at least, the *City of God* and the *Confessions,* still make the rounds as literary classics.

Like Luther some eleven hundred years later, the saint-to-be had a flair for argument and altercation. A master logician no less than a skillful rhetorician, he made it his task to deliver the world from its numerous beguilers. Some of his most exalted rage he directed at his former cronies, the Manichaeans, who beheld mankind caught in the crossfire of two warring worlds, the one under the sovereignty of a perfect deity, the other under the sway of some satanic führer in a dominion where evil was a principle ruling in its own right. In the same manner Augustine undertook to dispose of the heretical Donatists who ventured the opinion that unless a priest led a worthy and seemly life, the sacraments he administered were of no account.

Finally, he let loose a broadside of poisoned darts at the Pelagians, who were so indiscreet as to air the view that for a man to get into Heaven what he did on earth carried a greater weight than did divine grace. Mother Church was not unmindful of her son's lavish diligence; in fact, so alive was she to this man's extraordinary accomplishments that after he had served three years in the priesthood she raised him to episcopal splendor as Bishop of Hippo, an office he invested with honor and distinction until his death some three and a half decades following.

CHRISTIANITY AND PLATONISM

Augustine's quest for "undying wisdom" brought him willy-nilly into the sphere of philosophic reflection. Even before his conversion, as has been stated, he sought to slake his intellectual thirst with draughts from the Platonic spiggot. It was in the writings of the Neoplatonists that he caught his first glimpse of God and the Word, the creation, the divine light illuminating the darkness, and other glittering wonders. Although during his graying years the Bishop of Hippo perceived a broader cleft between Christianity and Platonism, yet the fact remains that he continued to regard the Platonic writings as his preparation for his acceptance of Holy Writ—the "solid ground of piety," as he makes reference in his confessional chronicle. In sum, his odyssey for everlasting wisdom, embarked upon in the port of Neoplatonism, bore him to the "haven of philosophy," that is, of Christianity. What differentiates one from the other, Augustine explained, is that the supporters of the former, no matter how appalling the extent of their knowledge and learning, put their main cofidence in reason, and in consequence they seldom are able to attain the whole truth—indeed, more often than not their cerebrations lead them to stray into the dead-end alley of error and falsehood. In contrast, the Christians' quest for truth is not grounded on guesswork, but on the holy Gospel wherein the Almighty holds the truth for all to see. In short, the Scriptures rather than the fallible human mind are the one and only authoritative rock spring of the "true Christian philosophy."

THE *CONFESSIONS* AND THE *CITY OF GOD*

Of Augustine's vast literary output, his *Confessions* and the *City of God* have been the most durable, and though their substance is somewhat remote from the nerve of the profane times we currently live in, the books nonetheless still attract an appreciable audience. Of the two, the former stands somewhat lower than the latter, though historically it is the first recorded attempt of a writer venturing to undertake such a thoroughgoing public self-unveiling. More important still is Augustine's unsparing candor—more than thirteen hundred years were to come and go before another such self-critical work was to be undertaken, a work which, rather curiously, was similarly titled, and whose author was Jean-Jacques Rousseau.

In the *City of God* Augustine set down what was to become known as the Christian epic, a boundless panorama of the unfolding of the divine scheme from Adam to the final tick of the mundane clock. Begun soon after Alaric's burning and pillaging of the ancient city on the hills, and especially in refutation of the popular lament that Rome's calamity was due to her neglect of her venerable gods and goddesses, the *City of God* came into being in 426 after a prolonged gestation. There are, the bishop tells us, two kinds of states, the one terrestrial and made by man, the other celestial and created by God. The first secular state, the City of the Devil, was the handiwork of Cain, remembered everywhere as the inventor of murder, while Rome was founded by Romulus, who, following in the track of the world's pioneer assassin, butchered his twin brother. Inaugurated in villainy, Satan's City is the habitat of all those of pagan heritage, whether enlightened or benighted, including all the ancient resorts of heathenry and all the current states and peoples who have flouted the beckonings of the Savior. Chin-deep in sin, the denizens of the earthly state are doomed to writhe in an agony of tortures and torments too terrible even for display on television.

By way of reassuring contrast, the City of God, pitched in its beginning in Eden, but elevated after Adam's disgraceful conduct to the dizzy heights of the ethereal blue, is a perfect state, peopled by angels, the saints, and God's Chosen, all basking in ecstasy in the presence of the Heavenly Father. The two worlds, it needs no saying, are oppugnant, and as in the case of the Manichaean blueprint, they are forever and implacably in conflict— at least until the awesome day of judgment.

On subsequent times Augustine's representation of history left its mark not only on faith and morals, and the attendant education, which, of course, was to be expected; but it also set the sights for the writing of history. In its image, for example, Orosius compounded the first account of ancient history. Later, Otto von Freising, a connoisseur in his day of medieval history, followed suit with a book in his specialty. In fact, so late as the seventeenth century, when Jacques-Benigne Bossuet—Bishop of Meaux and preceptor of the dauphin, but renowned in cultural annals especially for his sonorous valedictories to the recently departed—assembled the world's first universal history, he took the precaution to shelter it under the umbrella of the Augustinian assumptions.

Not a few of Augustine's axioms on good and evil reach far into the depths of his personal experience. Did Hippo's bishop, for example, preach that the good God "judges it better to bring good out of evil than to allow

no evil to exist?" The reason is that as a youth, having embraced the Manichaean fallacy that evil is an active principle operating independently of
Omnipotence, his conversion had happily snatched him from the thrall of
that delirium. And did Augustine pin the teaching of Christian youth to
antiquity's liberal arts even though a short while back these had served as
the indispensable mortar to compound tomorrow's pagandom? Then it is
because he himself had drunk freely from the ancient jug and found it
useful and, in some respects, even enjoyable. Finally, did the bishop entertain an abhorrence of sex? Then the clue lurks in his dissolute nonage.
Approaching his conversion, he was loath to forswear his venery, and
though he prayed the Lord to make him chaste, he was careful to add "not
quite yet." But once he had kissed the holy cross, his demeanor toward sex
suffered a violent turnabout. He not only excoriated it as offensive to God;
he even discerned it at the roots of all our woes and ills. Adam's fall, he was
certain, was the consequence of coition, an untoward act for which the
saintly man was quick to put the blame on Eve. As mentioned in the chapter on Aristotle, Augustine eyed the female with grim suspicion. Indeed, he
once confessed his public perplexity that God, in all his infinite wisdom,
had troubled to compose women at all.

Needless to say, Augustine's views in this department carried tremendous weight, and for at least a thousand years they were the rule. Indeed, it
was only the day before yesterday, speaking metaphorically, that Adam's
and Eve's descendants succeeded in attaining their present free-and-easy
state of permissiveness. The noblest character on earth, Augustine allowed,
is the one who abstains from the joys and gratifications of the world—a
monk, let us say, who, turning his back on temporal pleasures, lives in
austerity and keeps his natural appetites in commendable check.

It was the prelate's immovable belief that by nature human beings, the
youngest no less than the eldest, are utterly and totally depraved, and without the mercy of divine grace they are damned forever to be confectioners
of evil. For a tiny handful, the so-called "elect," God had reserved room in
eternity to disport themselves happily in the company of the angels and the
saints; the vast shoal of others, even before their conception, he had predestined to a burning hell, a pit crawling with hell worms, toads, and frogs,
besides a host of devils and tailed drakes, all doing their utmost to harass
them for eternity.

The doctrine, with its glum and sullen outlook, proved too grisly for
most of the later specialists in medieval moral theology, who mellowed it or
rejected it outright. But to Martin Luther, who esteemed Saint Augustine
highly, the theory of human depravity made sense, and he incorporated it in
his system of divine science as a cardinal article. So also did his fellow
reformer, John Calvin, the deviser and designer of Puritanism, who gave his

affirmation and approval not only to the doctrine of total depravity but to that of predestination as well. So strong in its sinister allure was the Augustinian teaching that as late as the seventeenth century it was given a renewal in the teachings of the Dutch Bishop Jansen, whose morbid effusions attracted droves of followers, even amongst Catholics. But Holy Church put them under her taboo, condemning Jansen as a heretic, and to protect the faithful from Jansenist toxins, she had their episcopal author clamped into a common hoosegow.

Thus the man and the essence of his outlook. To put him into a neatly labeled bottle is no easy task, for like the enigmatic Rousseau he was a person riven by baffling contrarieties. A man of titanic imagination, he was also the possessor of a vigorous and incisive mind. Though he was a devotee of the gentle and forbearing Jesus, he himself was sparse of warmth and tenderness. A zealot of the first water, he put faith above reason, and the authority of the one holy, apostolic, Catholic church above the freedom of individual thinking. He was at once a romantic and a scholastic, a mystic and a logician, a poet and a grammarian—a man, in sum, who eludes us in a haze of psychological vapors.

EDUCATIONAL THEORY

Augustine posed his educational theory on the same Platonic foundation he had laid for the *City of God,* a dualism comprised on the one hand of the world wherein we live and obtain our knowledge, and on the other of the transcendent world which lies in the unbeholdable beyond. The one wallows in error, deception, false thinking, and delusive and precarious persuasion; while the other is the seat of absolute and undefiled ideas, everlasting and unchanging truth, virtue, wisdom, and justice.

To enter this wonderland of intellectual grandeur is demanding—indeed, for the multitudes incapable of thought it is impossible. Still, this does not mean that they are doomed to the black abysm of ignorance. Let the quest for the ultimate truth be confined to the select few who have a head for ratiocination. As for the others, let them put their trust in Mother Church. Locked in the vaults of her authority, she has a store of knowledge—all, indeed, a plain sinner needs to have. Not only will she inspirit him with the sacred truth, but as the Lord's appointed surrogate on earth she is also vested with the right and duty to persuade him to accept it. If doubts gnaw a motley few, then let them abandon reason and abide by faith. If their doubts nevertheless persist, then let them believe or be damned.

One would imagine that a man who had populated the City of the Devil with pagans of every shade and shape would have been at pains to dispatch their cultural belongings with them. But, surprisingly, this was not so; the education the bishop endorsed was not unlike the academic fare he himself had put up with as a hapless inmate of the Roman educational establishment. Thus the young Christian savored the familiar canapés of the elementary R's, whereupon he followed with several years of ingesting grammar, rhetoric, and what then passed for nature study—all of which, however, were to be scrupulouly disinfected against the presence of any pagan streptococci.

The future saint's reliance on the ancient classical legacy evoked some hearty dissent among other Christian masterminds, but in the ensuing discourse Augustine, having bolstered himself with Holy Writ, cleared the field of his critics. "The Egyptians," he contended, "not only had idols and crushing burdens which the people of Israel detested . . ., but they also had vessels of gold and silver . . . which the Israelites, leaving Egypt, secretly claimed for themselves as if for a better use." By the same token, he analogized, all infidels have "counterfeit and superstitious notions" which every decent and upright person "ought to abominate and shun." But the heathen also entertain some liberal ideas "adapted to the service of truth"—aye, even "of God himself." Therefore, if Jahveh had ordained that it was all right for the Israelites to take from the Egyptians whatever could be put to a better purpose, it follows that it is also meet and proper for Christians to remove from pagans any items which they themselves could turn to a superior Christian purpose. In short, the ancient learning was too valuable for Christians to relegate to the dump without first having made a searching examination of its contents. As a result, throughout antiquity, setting aside a few special cases—notably in Syria—Christians founded no schools of their own; they simply reorchestrated the existing course of studies in a religious and moral key devised and required by the church.

The years, to be sure, were to see some modification of this simple procedure, and in his discourse *On Christian Education* Augustine laid the groundwork for a revised curriculum. No student, he mandated, was to study any secular subject in hopes of attaining personal happiness thereby, but rather he was to make use of his knowledge to serve God. To this purpose he was to give the profane learning a close and sober inspection, excising whatever bore the taint of superstition, indecency, and free-living, and retaining only what was essential for the business of a good life. To this end he was to apply his diligence to subjects concerned with material objects, as, say, the mechanical arts, the art and science of formal debate, and the science of numbers. Aside from the aforementioned, Augustine continued to look upon the ancient liberal arts with a certain deference.

Though the bishop spoke out against superstition and dubious thinking, to say that he was clothed in immunity against their influence would be

foolish. Like all his Christian confrères, the learned no less than the ignorant, Augustine insisted that numbers are endowed with mystical properties. "There are," he said with Pythagorean gravity, "three classes of
numbers—the more than perfect, the perfect, and the less perfect, according
as the sum of them is greater than, equal to, or less than the original number." Of all their representatives, six is the first perfect number, because the
Lord Creator allowed Himself six days to make the world, when, as a
matter of fact, He could have done the job with a simple clap of the hands.

Although there was a time in his younger years when Augustine held
the study of science to be futile, since, as had been foretold, the end of the
world was drawing closer and closer, in later years, when the Second Coming had apparently suffered some delay, the prelate underwent a change of
mind. A knowledge of nature, he had come to appreciate, was the unfailing
open sesame to the walled-in meaning of certain enigmatic passages in Holy
Writ. Not only was the student to know nature, he was also to observe it. In
this respect the saint went to some length to practice what he preached.
Indeed, by applying his own expert scrutiny, as he related in the *City of
God*, he had had his moment of awareness when he saw a headless man
with eyes in his breast. By keeping open his eyes and ears, moreover, the
bishop had observed that sundry innkeepers were wont to slip a drug into
the cheeses they served their guests, thereby metamorphosing these hapless
travelers into dogs, cats, and other domesticated fauna. Finally, Augustine
gave his support to the proposition that the peacock was a favorite of the
Heavenly Father, and that when it died its flesh would not decay. This
phenomenon, whether natural or divine, Augustine asserted, he has tested
and he knew it to be a fact.

WORDS TO THE TEACHER

From his long association with the schoolroom, both as a learner and as a
pedagogue, Augustine had some things to say to the practicing teacher.
Since it was his duty to divert his academic fledglings from wrong and evil,
and by his light and leading to put them on the straight and narrow path to
God, let him commence, like a good speaker, by gaining the confidence of
his hearers. Once they were under his spell, he should proceed to a clear and
concise exposition of the revelation at hand, avoiding the pleasure of wandering afield, however beguiling this promised to be. At all times it be-
hooved him to cast light on any difficult points, and never in any case
should he expect to increase his wordly store by his didactic enterprise. The
proficient master should never lose sight of the fact that his purpose is to
instruct and uplift his students, now by dulcet cajolery, now by solid persuasion, and always by the sterling example of his own impeccable life. To

attain his pedagogical ends Augustine counseled the teaching brethren to make use of summaries, a practice which they eagerly adopted, and which held sway even in the higher learning until the Middle Ages came to their end. Since then, whether they are believers or not, students have taken the saint's advice to heart, and a campus bookstore which did not sag its shelves with outlines on this subject or that would be an anomaly.

For all his sweet thoughts on academic law and decorum, Hippo's bishop stood foursquare with the masters under whom he had suffered as a schoolboy. Though he never ceased to tremble at the recollection of the beatings he had taken at the hands of these dauntless stickmen, yet the thought never crawled in his mind to reject their necessity. For children, like their elders, and even, he insisted, the inhabitants of the vegetable kingdom, bore the curse of the fallen Adam. Thus inescapably the youngest of them was trapped in the thick murk of natural depravity, and in no case was he to be granted any easement of his sentence. To checkmate his natural bent for wickedness, and to coax forth any goodness which might chance to repose inconspicuously within him, the switch and the fist were the sole therapy then known to enlightened man.

As has been said, up to his early thirties Augustine had partaken heavily of pagan letters, and even after his baptism he continued to regard them well. Because of his insistent pleading in their behalf, the ancient liberal arts were able to hold their place in the early Christian course of study. But as more and more years weighed upon him, qualms began to assail him. For all their unarguable literary merit, the fact remained that at bottom the ancient classics were the work of infidels, and for the innocent reader their thoughts could be as catching as cholera morbus. For awhile the bishop inclined to compromise. He would tolerate the reading of those heathen books which did the Christian teachings no harm, such as the works of their grammarians and rhetoricians. To strengthen his stand, Augustine searched his Bible where, as he had hoped, he found a providential concordance. But despite the prelate's radiant rhetoric and the authority that ran with it, the onslaught against the writings of the ancients refused to still. Contrarily, as the years passed on, it increased in force until, in 401, under the direction of no less a figure than the Bishop of Hippo—who in the meantime must have taken another look at Holy Writ—the Council of Carthage snapped its padlock on the pagan writings, thereby reducing their menace to Christendom to approximate zero.

Under its mandate no Christian, not even the church's sacred hierarchy, was to have any dealings with the ancient humanistic literature. Doubtless there would be an occasional disloyalist who, with the shutters drawn and the doors locked tight, would steal a candle-lighted glance at the forbidden works, but by and large for almost a thousand years, when the

Renaissance ran down the Middle Ages, Holy Church's edict proved to be a very potent anaphrodisiac to a man's passion for Graeco-Roman letters. Rather interestingly, the glacier which held medieval scholarship in its ice-bound grip with its hobbling of the human mind and will, which character-ized so many centuries of this period, was the consequence in no small proportion of the surpassing power and influence of the "father of Christian philosophy."

FINAL THOUGHTS

Yet when everything is brought into the final reckoning, Augustine stands out as one of the greatest figures that the church past or present has ever known. In spite of his antagonism toward the free exercise of the powers of the mind, and his eagerness to tether it securely to the iron clog of ecclesias-tical authority, the saint himself towers as one of Mother Church's most puissant intellects. As Aristotle epitomized Hellenic learning and Cicero personified its impact on Roman culture, so Augustine takes on the aspect of the salient narrator of the main currents of thought in Christendom during those difficult years when Christianity, after having suffered one distemper after another, finally triumphed over paganism. A systematizer second perhaps only to Aristotle, this foremost of the church fathers em-broidered the theme of the so-called "Christian epic," the first full Christian philosophy of history. The originator of early Christian theology, he elevat-ed his creation to a majestic standing, the recognized queen of all the sci-ences, a sovereignty that endured for most of the Middle Ages. Augustine's unyielding insistence of man's total depravity and his well-nigh certain pre-destined consignment to the gruesome horrors of an everlasting hell was applauded and accepted in part by Luther and in full by Calvin. Though Hippo's spiritual father was never on easy terms with Greek (he blamed his schoolmasters for his disability), yet as a Latinist he was supreme, and he wrote with ease and grace. Among Romans he alone comes close to the stature of Plato.

Augustine's wide and multifarious traffic with men of every sort af-forded him a shrewd and salty understanding of their wily ways, whether for right or wrong. His insight into human nature has caused some of his partisans to hail him as the "father of psychology," a title which has been thrust on several others of the faraway past, notably Aristotle. In education he offered the succeeding generations a clear and specific program for the instruction of their youth at a time when the light of learning everywhere was going out. His achievement was to give strength and reassurance to the newborn Christian culture through the ensuing centuries of wreck and ruin. True to the biblical teaching, Augustine also gave credence, utterly and undeviatingly, to the existence of witches and their wicked craft, and though he did not cause them to be done to death as the Sacred Scriptures (Exodus 22:18) command us, he nevertheless hated them violently. Like the great manswarm which currently enjoys the enlightenment Divine Providence has vouchsafed us, Hippo's bishop believed in the power of the heavenly bodies, not so much for their capability to serve us for good or ill, but rather for their illuminating portents of the Omnipotent's desires and designs.

Like all the early consecrated fathers, Augustine threw his full episcopal weight behind the doctrine that work must ever be the human lot not only as man's penitence for Adam's sin, but as a prophylactic against the seductions of the ever-lurking Old Deluder. Although Augustine stood up for the necessity of having to sweat for one's daily bread, he also gave his blessing to slavery, defending it as God's just and inescapable vengeance upon the sinful. In those days as in these, there was apparently no lack of such sinners—in fact, as late as the sixth century Pope Gregory the Great was doing his utmost to cooperate with God by collecting as many as he could in the largest horde of slaves owned by any prince in Christendom, whether sacred or profane. This is not to suggest, however, that either Augustine or Gregory thought slaves beyond redemption. In 597, after meeting some English slaves in Rome, the Holy Father dispatched Augustine of Canterbury to Kent to convert the Anglo-Saxons to the cross.

Chapter 7

Desiderius Erasmus

THE RENAISSANCE AND HUMANISM

What Western civilization designates as its "middle age"—that long procession of years which bridges the final crumbling of imperial Rome and the first quiverings of the modern era one thousand years or so later—reached its apogee in the thirteenth century. The activities of its men of learning, the so-called "Scholastics," ran at full tilt, and the cathedral schools and universities—at all events their superior representatives—were beginning to give tone to their mental muscle. But through it all Mother Church's insistence on the primacy of the faith persisted, and whenever her upholdings collided with the findings of reason, the latter was granted the charity to knuckle under. Scholarship, whatever its shape or substance, busied itself not with giving challenge to the accepted beliefs in hopes of replacing them with new and maybe sounder ones, but rather with seeking to nail them firmly down with the hammer of deductive logic. In consequence, though still hailed by some of its swains as the "greatest of the centuries," the thirteenth remained, as had all the Christian centuries before it, a period of bowing to authority—an age, in other words, of intellectual conformance.

Nevertheless, there were portents even then of a new spirit on the rise, restrained, to be sure, by the strangling embrace of Holy Church, but destined, as the years passed, to increase in juice and momentum, and in time even to burst the barriers. One may sense its presence in the stirrings of Islamic learning; in the reactivation of Roman law; in the rejuvenation of town life; and in the brisk trade and traffic of prosperous merchants—the Roebucks and Woolworths of long ago.

The fourteenth century saw the Middle Ages pick up their wraps and bid the world goodbye. Say fourteenth century to an experienced and cultivated Old Worlder, and his mind's eye will picture not just another marker of a hundred years, but the advent of an epoch—the Renaissance. This did not, like the Reformation, which was in a manner of speaking its child, involve countless thousands; rather it confined its joys and benefits to a small patronage, mostly male and usually with a substantial bankroll. Sprung up in Italy, and nurtured in such hustling hives of commerce as Venice and Florence, the Renaissance witnessed a return to some of the sumptuous paganism of Greece and Rome. Once again men leaned over the ancient classics, not, however, to dissect and explore them for their grammar and syntax, as was to become their sickly fate in afteryears. Read and reveled in by men fed up with the theological rumble bumble stored in so much of medieval writing, the classics fetched their readers not only for the ideas which glistened therein, all of a predominantly mundane tone without even a hint of Christian moralism but with recountings often enough of an unabashed and even bawdy indecorum, but also because not a few of them were swathed in a soft and soothing beauty.

Although the Renaissance came to being as a rediscovery of the forgotten grandeurs of classical antiquity, before long it was burgeoning with a vitality all its own. It invaded nearly every sector of life. It brought a new glint to letters and learning and the beaux arts. The prodigality of its spirit overflowed into the affairs of trade and commerce, of state and finance— even into the domain of social criticism. As the movement grew, its magic spread from Italy toward the north and west across the continent, and thence across the channel into Britain. High and mighty men were its intimates, but its essence at bottom was profane, and its chief support issued from the rich townsmen and the leisured aristocracy.

As might be expected, the cultural values cried up so fervently by the partisans of the Renaissance were presently siphoned into education. Like its medieval predecessor, the new learning, which came to be known as Humanism, leaned on the traditional curriculum, the old and vaunted Seven Liberal Arts, but logic no longer sat at the head of the table, having been dispossessed by grammar and rhetoric. On them fell the task of laying the foundation for a smooth and flawless utterance in written and spoken Latin. Once a learner had come to terms with this mystery, he was introduced to the great writings of the ancients, their master builders of prose and poetry, their sages and historians, tackling them first in Latin and after awhile in Greek. Now and then he made acquaintance with the rest of the liberal arts, namely, arithmetic, geometry, music, and astronomy. But such engagement was the exception rather than the rule. Predominantly the stress fell on the languages and letters of classical antiquity, or as the idiom of the learned put it then, the "humane learning and good literature."

Did the elders shortchange the young in science and mathematics? If so, they made amends for it in other ways. Down the drain went the bookishness of medieval schooling, its logic hashing, its piling up of facts and definitions, and down too went its dank and cheerless air, its kneeing to "authority," its hollow pedagogues and their ever-handy birch. What the new learning wanted at its best was to make a well-balanced man, his body, mind, and feelings pulsing in amicable coordination, a gracious and well-mannered person, confident and self-controlled, on good terms with himself and the world—in sum, the ideal of ancient Hellas.

Such an education was naturally beyond the average purse. Restricted, hence, to those in pocket, its amenities were dispensed by hired tutors, thoroughly marinated in the classical seasoning. Eventually the new learning was dispensed by schools. We glimpse them first in Italy, where the Renaissance grew its roots. There, among several, two stand above the others, the one under the banner of Guarino, a teacher in practice at Ferrara, the other at Mantua, under that of Vittorino. Presently similar groves appeared beyond the Alps in various European latitudes and longitudes, from Geneva to the northern Lowlands to London and beyond. Their promoters and principals were usually Humanists, which is to say, they smiled upon the classical humanities and curled their lips at the medieval learning. Into this cultural climate two boys were born, each destined to cut a historic figure, the one as a man of letters and great learning, the other as a founder of a new religion. The one was Desiderius Erasmus (ca. 1466–1536), the other Martin Luther. Both entertained educational ideas, and as to their examination, let us begin with the former.

ERASMUS—THE YOUNG YEARS

Among Humanists on the far side of the Italian Alps the one that reaches higher than all others was Erasmus. He was born in 1466 at Gouda, lauded even in those days for the fragrance of its cheeses; or as some contend, he may have come from Rotterdam, a more raffish town, renowned, if not for its dairy delicacies, then at least for the throb of its trade and commerce. A child born of indiscretion rather than deliberation, Erasmus sprang from the union of Margaret, the widowed daughter of a medico, and Gerard, a holy clerk in the Catholic cloth. The newborn had been preceded three years earlier, and before the ordination of his father, by a brother whose name was Peter. The passing years saw Erasmus give himself the name of Desiderius, the "desired one," which, whether ironical or merely an excitement to his fancy, was scarcely in keeping with the sinful pleasures of his begetters. Soon after the "desired one's" arrival, his father left his bedmate. "Farewell," he told her, "I shall never see you again"—a pledge, however, which chance thwarted him from keeping.

Though the cards were heavily stacked against young Erasmus, fortune, nevertheless, was not unkind. Thus, unlike the usual lot of boy bastards of that epoch—unless they happened to be the progeny of the high and mighty—Erasmus was granted an education. He was put upon learning his letters in his fifth year under the rattan of the ever-watchful Peter Winckel of Gouda, who, but for the later attainments of his pupil, would long since have fallen into obscurity. In 1745, after some four years in the Winckel seminary, Erasmus and his brother were sent to Deventer to attend the sessions of a school run by the Brethren of the Common Life. Organized almost a century before by Gerard Groot, a man with a heart as big as a clothes hamper, but given also to mystical vaporizing, the Brothers devoted themselves to living a simple life of piety, reading their prayer books and counting their beads, disdainful of the fatuities of metaphysics no less than the pretensions of formal theology, but seeking by their example and their teaching to educate boys for a useful Christian life, both here and in the celestial beyond.

Not all Deventer's masters lived up to the founder's idealism; Erasmus designated one of them as somewhat truculent—a "driveling ram." Another, he tells us, took pleasure in accusing his fledglings falsely—including Erasmus—whereupon, pronouncing a unanimous verdict of guilt upon his victim, he black-and-blued his hindquarters without mercy. Among the Brethren, however, such churlish fellows were the exception, and in their chambers there was probably less recourse to the prophylactic switch than in the run of schools. Instead, the devotees of the common life relied on cordiality, and when that failed, they resorted to fines. Boys were levied upon, for example, whenever they were caught speaking their maternal Dutch rather than the required Latin. To make sure that all rules and regulations were obeyed, and that lawbreakers would not easily elude detection, the Brothers encouraged a system of snooping, putting upon their pupils to spy and tattle not only on one another but also on their younger tutors. It was an underhanded trick, to say the least, and one which was at utter odds with boys' universal law, but for long years it continued to enjoy the support of adult acceptance, profane as well as pedagogic.

Even so, despite their all-too-human failings, with the aid of the Brethren Erasmus took his first steps in Latin. He was not as highly dowered as was the incandescent Voltaire, with a dazzling brightness, but if he was somewhat less scintillating, he was enormously studious, so that, as the years wore on, he made himself an accomplished Latinist, the finest the world has known, it has been said, since Saint Augustine. Like Voltaire, Erasmus broke into verse, not professionally but for fun. Hence his cantos were not so polished, but they were good enough. Indeed, like the Frenchman, when as a boy he sat in a Jesuit college in Paris, at Deventer Erasmus became the school's poet laureate, its star showpiece, called upon to invoke the muse to lubricate the ego of some visiting grandissimo or altruistic benefactor, whether actual or potential.

Deventer was one of the larger intellectual dispensaries of its time, meting out instruction, when it was operating under full load, to slightly more than 2,000 boys. Nevertheless, because the Brethren promoted poverty to the status of a virtue, life in the school was stark. Of amenities there were scarcely any; in fact, even necessities were in short supply. Roused from their dreams by the chapel bell at four o'clock in the morning, and after mumbling their Aves and Pater Nosters, the boys passed the ensuing hours in study, with a brief furlough now and then for food, exercise, and romping, until eight or nine in the evening, depending on the season of the year, when bell peals summoned them once more to their prayers and cots. As purveyors of the secondary learning, the Brethren stressed mainly the teaching of Latin—a Latin which, looking back from his riper years, Erasmus pronounced "barbarous." In the schoolroom there were no purposeless luxuries, no adornments, no exhibits or globes or charts to tell one where or how or why. In fact, save for the repose and comfort of the master, no space was wasted on stools or benches. For sitting down, the floor was roomy enough. There the boys huddled around the teacher who read aloud from some Latin text, translating and commenting thereon while his listeners scrawled his words into their copybooks, knowing that on the morrow he would harry and oppress them not only with queries on content and meaning, but on the syntax as well. Nine years of their lives the boys gave to such tedious rehearsal, advancing, of course, as time chased on, from what was rudimentary to pieces from the ageless classics, and since the moral brethren put so much weight on Christian piety, also to Holy Writ.

TAKING THE VOWS

When they were through with their schoolbooks, the two brothers made tracks for home, only to increase their knowledge when they got there with the harsh tidings that they were penniless. Their parents had fallen prey to the deadly plague, and though their father had provided the boys with a slight inheritance, their guardians had licked their fingers with it generously. One of them, meanwhile, had died, but the surviving one, a shrewd and far-reaching knave, worked upon the youths to ease their condition by taking monastic vows. It was a counsel they did not relish, but in the end Peter caved in, only to be followed resignedly by Desiderius. For six years he was out of the world, immured in the cloister of the Augustinians at Steyn, hard by Gouda, the prisoner of a pattern of life that brought him more grief than joy. Asceticism distempered his urbane cast of mind; the monk's coarse habit pricked and pocked his tender skin, and fish, the friar's frequent fare, almost killed him. "I hate a snake less than a fish," he remarked in later years, though, doubtless, he never addressed himself to a serpent gastronomically. He made a handful of friends, whom he loved dearly, and whose memory years later still warmed his heart. But the main surcease from his distress he found in the quietude of the abbey's library, where somehow the ecstasy of the wonderland of books made him oblivious, if only for a transient moment, to the depressing reality which bore so heavily all about him.

INFLUENCE OF LORENZO VALLA

Although Erasmus roved happily in the classics of an old and far-off time, this is not to say that he had no taste for the moderns—provided, of course, they were couched in a smooth and flawless Latin—the writings of such illuminati, for example, as the German Agricola (born Bauer), Pope Pius II (born Piccolomini), and especially the brash and impudent, yet supremely scholarly Lorenzo Valla. So well, in fact, did Erasmus regard this Italian, not only as a stylist, but as a critic, that often enough the spell he laid upon the Dutchman is plain.

On earth for only fifty years, from 1406 to 1456, Valla lived in an age when the tide of Humanistic learning was beginning to flood, and everywhere in the Italian states men of tone and substance were bowling one another over in their scramble to bedizen their household with the presence of a bearer of its flame. Valla's virtuosity as a Graeco-Latin scholar and critic, as well as an embroiderer of an exquisite prose, fetched him to Alfonso's Neapolitan palazzo and ultimately into the service and pay of Pope Nicholas V. Although, like so many other Italian Humanists, Valla measured himself as a man of unqualified excellence—he was a popinjay, grantedly, and not a little sassy—even so, the Holy Father, overjoyed to have such a rare and attention-getting treasure in his gem box, plied him with favors and set him to work. There followed an almost interminable procession of translations from Herodotus and Thucydides to Demosthenes and numerous others.

For all the pope's esteem and consideration, Valla, though he wore the sacerdotal frock, was scarcely Mother Church's loyal and compliant son. Given to a gamey commentary, he reviled not only the common clergy, but even the papacy. A crasher of idols, bold, derisive, and pungently cynical, he directed the full force of his intellectual and literary insolence to make a mockery of the Church, the imposition of her creed and ritual, and the ignorance of her clerks, not to mention their debaucheries and corruptions. What he called for was a return to the elemental teachings of Christ, a faith stripped of such meretricious accretions as Scholasticism and asceticism, to say nothing of relics, miracles, and suchlike inventions of the higher inscrutable powers. The old theologians to whom he was inclined he likened to bees making honey; their successors, on the other hand, were so many wasps looting the reserve of their betters.

To advance his iconoclastic views, he wrote with unflagging industry and not a little sting. The monastic life, he declared, was not worth the pain, and the asceticism whereon it beds itself was unnatural. "We have an imperious instinct to mate," he said, "and certainly no instinct for lifelong chastity." A harlot, even if she be a loose fish, he stated to a world of lofty flickering ideals, was more useful than a nun, for the former at least performs a gratifying public service. As for the Catholic Bible, the Vulgate, as it was known, it abounded in mistakes and mistranslations, and the sainted Jerome, its maker, had made a botch of it. Finally, as if to make sure he would have no friends in the holy cloth whatever, after long and strenuous study and meditation Valla announced that the *Donation of Constantine*, a document by which the Church had in large part justified her claim to temporal power—a final and absolute power, that is, over kings and emperors as well as over the laity—was bogus and full of lies. So relentless was his dissection of this ancient writ that Valla is recalled in the record of our rotting past as the faraway sire of the present-day more-or-less scientific historians. Despite the fury of his onslaught on Mother Church, time saw him lament his sinful ways and ask for her forgiveness. He ended his earthly days as a canon of St. John Lateran, and when he died his remains were put to rest in consecrated ground.

THE MOVE TO HIGHER STUDY

While Erasmus warmed his spirit in his book-environed world, he also worked a busy quill, practicing without letup to perfect his Latin, and fathering in the process an ever-enlarging correspondence, one which in the course of his three-score years and ten was to expand into one of the most colossal epistolary productions the world has ever witnessed. He applied his talents to making verses, declamations, and essays, none of which are especially worth remembering save, perhaps, for the Humanist's recurrent homage to the precious legacy of ancient letters, and his assault, contrarily, on the barbarians who would defile them. Like a well-constructed tale, however, they are a beginning, the portent of grander things to come in the middle and toward the end.

Erasmus's literary diligence bore him an altogether unexpected dividend, for it brought him to the notice of the Bishop of Cambrai, Henry of Bergen, who, as hazard would have it, was, like Erasmus, the product of illicit love. The episcopal Henry was laying plans to go to Rome in hopes of snaring a cardinal's hat, and to give him the essential literary help he needed, he engaged Erasmus as his official secretary. Unluckily, the bishop's expectations miscarried and the journey never got under way. But if Henry's aspirations were dashed, for the friar from Steyn the course of events took a happier turn: from his patron he obtained a slight viaticum and, better still, the episcopal sanction to betake himself to Paris to gorge on the higher studies. From that time forth, Erasmus's monastic travail was over. Not only was he free to absorb himself in study and writing, but by papal dispensation he might dine and wine as his palate recommended, even on fast days. Later, around 1516, when the despairing abbot of Steyn threatened to blackmail the slippery Dutchman in order to force him back into the fold—back, in other words, to an intolerable mausoleum—discreet and high-placed friends of the Rotterdammer, along with a respectable sum of money, succeeded in persuading the astute Pope Julius that his erring son merited not only absolution, but a dispensation which enabled him, so to speak, to join the world as a regular member.

Erasmus was the most traveled of all the Humanists. "I wish," he permitted himself to proclaim, "to be called a citizen of the world, the common friend of all states, or rather, a sojourner in all." And this is precisely what came to pass. His studies led him to Paris and his teaching to London and Cambridge. He called on the Holy City, spent years in study and writing at Louvain, several more in Freiburg, the vestibule of the Black Forest, and yet more years across the Rhine in Switzerland. Even now the dust that he has become reposes not in his native Lowlands, but somewhere in the earth of Basel, in Switzerland, where he died in 1536, at the age of seventy.

WRITINGS IN OPPOSITION—THE NEW TESTAMENT AND *THE PRAISE OF FOLLY*

In the kingdom of scholarship Erasmus's most praiseworthy achievement was, no doubt, his Graeco-Latin version of the New Testament, whose genitor may well have lurked in some of the mordant animadversions of Lorenzo Valla. In fact Valla's critical assault was scholarly enough to win the praise of Erasmus, who not only summarized its main points but put them to use in his own translation. Once the Dutchman embarked upon his research, it became an inseparable part of his existence. He toiled at it full blast for long and wearisome years, scrutinizing the older texts, making note of their deviations, their insertion of deceptive and even fraudulent material, as well as their abundant errors and contradictions, until at length, in 1516 (he was then just over fifty), he knew the pleasant glow of beholding his brainchild in print. For its digression from Mother Church's official version, and also doubtless for the effrontery of this monkish upstart to cast suspicion upon the certitude of her judgment, his translation brought him no loud huzzahs. Even so, in time the scholarship of its author, making all due allowances, has become plain. Since those very far-away days vastly superior editions have been composed—indeed, like the vernal equinoxes, they come upon us year upon year to give us hope and edification—but in one particular the Erasmian edition is the sire of them all: as the first critical version of this holy book, his New Testament, marks the beginning of the dawn of modern higher biblical scholarship.

Erasmus was not a writer of great literary fecundity—at least not on the uninhibited scale of a Voltaire or a Balzac, or, to step downward several rungs on the ladder, of the late genitor of Perry Mason, but the scenario which flowed from the Dutchman's stylus bore in the main the mark of quality. The words he put on paper sang; even when they were designed to teach, they were filagreed with a rich and impish wit. Clearly, this man paid no heed to the common notion, still current, that if a book of learning is inspirited with grace and pleasantry, its scholarship is thereby suspect. Yet because of his light touch, his writings entertained a stupendous audience, the largest of his era by any count.

His most engaging work, a mere midget as books by the learned generally go, was *The Praise of Folly,* which he dedicated to his friend and fellow Humanist, Thomas More. Begun on returning from Italy as a piece of self-amusement, this pastiche, which its maker completed in a little more than a week, was put into circulation in Paris in 1511. Next to Voltaire's *Candide* it is probably the most durable satirical compound ever put together, and like that other it strikes at its target not with indignation, but with an easy humor—one might even say a tolerant understanding. Cast into the mold of a speech which Folly flings off in self-adulation, the address pays tribute to a man's sempiternal silliness, from that of its highest magnificoes on earth to that of its slightly lesser fauna and so on down the line to its nethermost peasant.

The Praise of Folly was an instant hit. Edition after edition rolled from the hand-worked presses, not only in the original Latin, but in English, French, Italian, Dutch, German, Swedish, Danish, Russian, Spanish,

Greek, Czech, and Polish. Without a doubt Erasmus's sly view of Homo sapiens made its author a figure of international reputation, and were he at large today, a card-carrier in the Authors League and protected by the laws of copyright, he would surely make a mint. He had begotten, as he blithely observed, "a daughter like myself," one who "turns, twists, and bites like an awl," but he "as a fool had written of true folly." But as readers in the literate world rollicked in its mirth, underneath some of them sensed a more ominous tone.

Luther acclaimed it as "so jocund, so learned, and so ingenious" that he found it hard to resist. But when the sun of his years sank into the twilight, and a schizoid senility began to loom, he denounced the work with a magnificent ferocity—a distinction he was to bestow without exception on everything Erasmus ever wrote. To the wary eyes of Holy Church, meanwhile, there were many reasons for suspicion. Did the badinage of Erasmus make Leo X shake with laughter? If so, at the same time, to less risible critics, behind its clown show the work was a deft challenge to the high puissance of the church. "If you examine it," commented Etienne Dolet, a Humanist pundit, and slated, alas, for execution on some fateful tomorrow on the ground that he was an atheist, "the impudence of Erasmus will strike you rather than the language. He laughs, jokes, makes fun, irritates, inveighs, and raises a smile at even Christ himself."

WHAT GOES UP MUST COME DOWN—THE *COLLOQUIES*

If *The Praise of Folly* sold like hot cakes, then the *Colloquies* sold even better. A guide to Latin style, they were hatched in Paris in 1497, not for publication, but simply to extend a helping hand to a few of the Dutchman's private pupils. Himself an expert in the confection of a diamond-studded prose, Erasmus was not stumped by the subtle mystery of getting his learners to grant him attention when he inscribed his words in a schoolbook. Long ago, when he was still at school, his masters had commissioned him to draft a digest of Valla's *The Elegancies of Latin,* a manual on the finer nuances of Latin style, which at the time was enjoying a brisk academic favor. Curiously enough, when Erasmus assembled his first *Colloquies,* he held them in rather low regard. They were, he explained, mere "formulas for everyday intercourse, and again some conversations"—"trifles" he labeled them as he laid them to rest once his learners had tucked them in the garrets of their memories. But luckily for future apprentices in Latin letters, the unpredictable Fates intruded. A score of years or so after Erasmus had put the work out of his thoughts, they prevailed upon some rogue in Basel to get his hands on it and put it into print. To turn the tables on this bounder, the Hollander, reluctantly acknowledging his paternity of the *Colloquies,* contrived in his quietly aggressive way to enlarge and ameliorate them, whereupon in 1522 he offered the reading public a brand new version entitled *Formulas of Familiar Conversations,* which, he hoped, "would be useful not only for polishing a boy's (Latin) speech, but for building his character."

Sprung in large part from its author's personal observations, the new manual broke into a boy's everyday world, drawing a sharp bead on such concerns as his manner of eating and drinking, and—every bit as essential to his well-being and social standing—a variety of games then heartily esteemed in the better juvenile circles. To improve a lad's address Erasmus put together a lengthy list of salutations, fit for any occasion. To make youngsters privy to what, among their sophisticated elders, counted for a rudimentary decorum, Erasmus reminded them that whenever a person sneezed, he should at all times be granted the consolation of a "God bless thee!" or at least a "Gesundheit!"—in impeccable Latin, needless to say. But never in any case, should the situation occur, was he to unclasp his lips when, say, his companion's stomach growled, or when he belched.

For its saltiness and good humor, no less than for its common sense, Erasmus's schoolbook was something of a novelty. In contrast, those weathered standbys of Lily and Melanchthon, the one a Briton, the other a German, for all their improvements on the grammars of their Scholastic predecessors, were sadly lacking in vital sap. The upshot was that the *Colloquies* presently bade fair to knock them off their perch, to the delight not only of the effervescent young, but here and there even to that of a teacher. Even Luther, despite his bilious humor for the Lowlander, gave the volume his nod and went so far as to endorse some of its passages for use in Protestant schools. But as time dulled his judgment and his rancors began to fester, the Reformation's führer put the writings of Erasmus on his personal blacklist. "On my deathbed," he let it be known, with the paternal absolutism so typical of his time and people, "I shall forbid my sons to read Erasmus's *Colloquies.*" "He is much worse than Lucian," he went on, "mocking all things under the guise of holiness."

But the *Colloquies* had caught the public favor, and as the years edged on Erasmus applied himself assiduously to their improvement. In consequence, time saw one edition succeed another, the last one appearing in 1533, three years before its author's demise. As often happens when a book is cast in a new incarnation, it tends to take on a greater heft. Where the first *Colloquies* were simple and even spindly, their successor of 1522 was freighted with considerable religious talk. The year following saw the author apply his sagacity to the topics of love and holy wedlock, including their laughter no less than their hurt. His impartiality, on the surface at any rate, is that of an honest judge. Thus, though the *Colloquies* is a book for the instruction and edification of Junior, Erasmus does not shrink from laying down his warning to girls attuned to occult voices bidding them to enter a nunnery; nor, in the same vein, does he balk at setting down a conversation between a gawky stripling and a lady of scarlet in his endeavor to convert her to an upright Christian life. Nor, for that matter, does he refrain from flicking his satirical spitballs at some of his era's common foibles, the folly of its reliance on war to settle its disputes, the hollowness of many of its bigwigs, the vanities of its holy men, the futility of sacred pilgrimages, the idolization of Mary, mother of Jesus, and so on, all with a soft, but nonetheless insistent pedal.

For all its vast triumph, the *Colloquies* ran into heavy squalls. Although the book enchanted the young, from whom, despite its didactic purpose, it often elicited chuckles, yet all too often its author's potshots dismayed their elders. Experts in moral pathology bemoaned the contempt the book held for Christian decency and the havoc this would surely wreak upon the young and impressionable mind, in particular such a scandalous dialogue as that engaged in by an unpolluted Christian youth and a foul prostitute. Monks, who still smarted from the prick of Erasmus's satirical syringe, never forgave him. He had, declared Voltaire, "saturated the monks in a ridicule from which they never recovered." Apers of Cicero, who craved nothing more than to make their utterances a carbon copy of the great Roman orator, for which the Dutchman mocked them unsparingly, not only called for the intercession of Jupiter Optimus Maximus; they also proposed to put the unspeakable bastard out of business by working up a book of colloquies of their own. The most lavish hostility toward Erasmus, as one might expect, came from the clergy, both Catholic and Protestant.

With only a few exceptions, the Reformation leaders had never forgiven Erasmus for refusing to use the power of his pen to advance their cause. Even though he saw eye to eye with them on many things, he had nevertheless elected to walk alone. This insistence on intellectual autonomy, the right to be his own man, reaped him an outburst of calumny. The upshot was that in various Catholic lands his writings were eventually suppressed. In 1535, the year before Erasmus died, Franche-Comté, a shred of France, clamped the lid on the *Colloquies.* Belgium banned all his writings in 1540, and some three years following Milan burned them. The divine scientists, sitting in council at Trent in 1545, and for eighteen successive years thereafter, condemned Erasmus as a dangerous heretic and a Pelagian. It remained for Pope Paul IV to administer the final *coup de pied.* In 1559 the Holy Father put the Dutchman's entire literary output in the first class of forbidden books "even if they contain absolutely nothing against religion or about religion."

EDUCATION FOR THE VERY YOUNG

Although Erasmus's ideas on pedagogy are apparent in his various text-books, notably, of course, in the many-editioned *Colloquies,* yet he also gave his earnest attention to the subject in a number of special and specific treatments. There is, to begin, his *Order of Study,* a book on how to teach well and effectively, which appeared in 1511. "There are two kinds of knowledge," Erasmus states, "the knowledge of truths and the knowledge of words"—a solemn statement of the familiar even then. True knowledge, he continues, "includes the best in both kinds of knowledge, taught . . . under the best guidance." Of all the subjects the learner is expected to master, the most important are Greek and Latin, for "their literature contains all the knowledge we recognize of vital importance to mankind." Fifteen years later, in 1526, Erasmus followed with *Civility for Boys,* a primordial Emily Post for young males, revealing to them the punctilios of deportment, such as how a well-behaved lad should disport himself, what clothes he should wear, how he should behave at the dining table and properly handle his meat, noodles, and shifty peas, how he should act in church, in company, at play, and even in his sleeping chamber.

The first of its sort ever to be published, the *Civility for Boys* found a ready market, especially among the rising burgherdom. As might be expected, the book was widely parroted—in fact, through the nineteenth century such informative and uplifting manuals on juvenile etiquette were commonplace. They still make the rounds, of course.

Erasmus's views on pedagogy are interred in his *Liberal Education of Children,* which came out in 1529. There is little in it that had not been said before—indeed, when taken in the mass, it is little more than Quintilian and Plutarch redivivus—mostly the former—with a Platonic stencil here and an Aristotelian one there, and a light refrain by Mapheus Vagius. It is no more than just, however, to mention that grizzly as these theorems were, on the day-by-day schoolroom practice they had made barely a dent.

What is the essence of the Erasmian educational credo? For one thing, it was the Hollander's conviction that the cornerstone of a sane and sound education must be set during the child's earliest years. A child, he contended, is never too young to learn. Hence, his learning should be launched "while his age is tender and tractable and his mind ready and flexible to follow everything." His teacher during these budding years is for the most part his mother. At her finest she is a one-woman infant school, or as Comenius's euphemism was, several generations later, the School of the Mother's Knee. For a half-dozen years or so she stands sentinel over her child's health, manners, morals, and piety. She commends him when he is good and reprimands him when he is bad. In short, she prepares him for what the world will exact from him later. In all this the child's father, though absorbed in the essential enterprise of making a living for his family, must, nevertheless, play a part. Too many fathers, Erasmus laments, "take no care, or else they care too late."

None of this is to imply that Junior's life was all work and no play. On the contrary, Erasmus put substantial stock in the influence of play. Whenever he engaged professionally in schoolroom activities, and despite his fragile frame, he made it a point to cut a merry caper with his flock, as if he himself were a growing boy again. He could talk in the hushed tones of an embalmer if the occasion so ordained, but he could also holler or banter when the time was right. Work, he remarked, which in this case means study, "should begin by way of play."

Although Erasmus patterned much of his pedagogical thinking on the recommendations of Quintilian, yet he did not always follow in the ancient Roman's trail. Thus where the Roman put little confidence in a tutorial education, Erasmus, on the other hand, endorsed it highly. Hence, when Junior attained the age of five or six, he was to be kept under the family roof in the care of a private mentor, the reason being that in his educational aspiration, at bottom, Erasmus, like Plato, was an aristocrat. The schooling of the simple-minded commoners as urged and promoted by Luther left the Dutchman cold. If, for one cause or another, a cruel fate, nevertheless, insisted that a boy be packed off to a school, then Erasmus—his inner consciousness still writhing with intrusive memories of the worst moments at Deventer—felt that it should be a lay school rather than a religious one.

LATER EDUCATION

The main task of education, as Erasmus saw it, was to make a man who not only knows, but who thinks and feels as well—in sum, a cultivated familiar of the classical humanities. Like Quintilian—indeed, like any teacher worthy of his chalk and pointer—Erasmus had observed that "we learn the things most easily for which nature fits us," and that what X gobbles up with ease and interest, Y will consume with difficulty and distaste. Such differences in individuality, however, Erasmus went optimistically on, need be no barricade to successful learning. "There is . . . scarcely any discipline which the mind of man is not apt to learn, if we continue teaching and practicing"—a view which is subject to dispute, since not even the most furious pedagogy can create the essential capacity where it does not exist. To get on easy terms with ancient letters, the learner was to give himself to the study of the literary masterpieces of antiquity, Greek as well as Latin. After having mastered the necessary fundamentals, he proceeded *allegro con spirito* to a reading of the Gospels, followed by an assault on a Latin translation of Plutarch's *Apothegms.* The first Greek he ran into was Aesop, the fabricator of those unforgettable fables, so savory to the young that they have been rendered into nearly every language used by man. The study of the fabulous, and especially its ever-attendant moral, was a common enough practice in those days, yet centuries later it was to rile Rousseau on the ground that a youngster has insufficient wit to understand what a fable is all about. In any case, as the years advanced, so also, of course, did the pupil's reading. His literary diet was substantially what Quintilian had cooked up a millennium and a half or so before, namely, Cicero, Virgil, Caesar, in addition to Plautus, Terrence, and Sallust among the Romans, and Homer, Lucian, Demosthenes, Euripides, and Aristophanes among the Hellenes.

Curiously, although the primary stress fell on reading, when a student tackled an author, he read the work first for its grammar, then for its style, and finally for its moral message. To read a book at school for its own narrational sake, simply for the pleasure, was unthinkable, and a schoolbook which failed to inspire and ennoble the learner's character was not worth bothering about. Both the *Colloquies* and *The Praise of Folly,* for all their buffoonery, were at bottom full of moral purpose, as high-minded in this respect as the readers assembled by the illustrious Rev. William Holmes McGuffey in nineteenth-century America.

Next in importance to reading stood writing, the mastery, that is, of elegance in literary expression. Whatever the form and substance of the work under scrutiny, Erasmus exhorted the student to "write, write, and write again." To illuminate and assist the nascent literatus, he was made to study the style of the salient men of letters, inspecting their content minutely, like a customs official fishing through a traveler's luggage. He made note of the phrases they turned, the manner in which they plaited their words together, their idiomatic idiosyncracies, their orchestrations of humor and wit, of sobs and sadness, their recourse to similes, metaphors, and other pet devices. The idea was not to copy the art of these worthies, but rather to capture from them a feeling for literary expression and thereby develop an exemplary style of their own. It is a practice to which many serious aspirants in the literary art still subscribe.

The Erasmian course of study, it scarcely needs saying, is almost totally linguistic. To language verily all other subjects played second fiddle. Whatever history the student takes aboard he culls from reading Livy and Thucydides. The natural sciences, so prized by Aristotle, take no part in the making of an educated man, save insofar as they are encountered in the anteroom of the writings of Pliny. As for mathematics, so highly touted by Plato, Erasmus had little fancy for it, and consequently in his pedagogical garden he gave it no place. Nor was there even a tiny spot for the art of tone. He lauded the Englanders, it is true, "as [being] the most musical of all people"—forgetting the Italians and never having heard the Irish. Luther's stirring "A Mighty Fortress is our God" failed to raise his heartbeat, while the general run of hymnody in the reformed churches was sufficient, he confided, to make him writhe.

Yet, if Erasmus's course of study is barren of nonlinguistic proteins, in one respect he reaches far beyond the generality of his fellow Humanists. Though he conceived a distaste for the Platonic glow for mathematics, in the matter of women's education, the Dutchman walked arm in arm with the Athenian. Like the latter, he cherished the notion that the feminine head is by no means cerebrally destitute, and hence, he insisted, girls, like their brothers, should have a chance to exercise their minds in learning.

Chapter 8

Martin Luther

THE REFORMATION

The bold skepticism set ablaze by the Renaissance would not be snuffed. The more its votaries exalted their spirit in the warm glow of antiquity, the more some of them creased their brows over the gloom and dowdiness of the age into which an unkind fate had deposited them. They reviled its restraints and disabilities, the tyranny of its fixed ideas, the stillbirths of its scholarship, the stupidities of its folk. Time saw them sass even the old and hallowed church, thereby paving the way for the Reformation, or as certain historiographic sanitarians insist, the Protestant revolt.

Insurrection was no novelty to Holy Church. Heresies and schisms had oppressed her many times. But always she had been able to strike down false thinking or, failing that, to cremate its more stubborn adherents at the stake. But now the dissidence was manifold and of a more than ordinary strength. Not just theological, it revealed itself in a variety of forms, and its blasts howled from all directions—from heads of state, emerging from feudalism, whose national ambitions clashed with the fiats of Rome; from traders in the marketplace and their money lenders, eager to liberate their enterprise from ecclesiastic restrictions; from land-poor peasants, anxious for a slice of Mother Church's spacious earth; and from folk all about, high and low, fed up with the endless gougings of Peter's tithe grabber.

Roweled by mundane motives, often solely self-interested, these forces, coalescing with others, now closed in on the hitherto impregnable church to challenge her authority. Yet for all the ominous rumblings underneath the surface, the Reformation had started without much ado, even in a state of academic propriety, when Martin Luther (1483–1546), a monk draped in the Augustinian's baggy frock and also a professor of theology at Wittenberg, conscious of a bad odor in some of the church's money-raising tactics, gave vent to his displeasure in the *Ninety-five Theses,* which he nailed to the castle's chapel door. Composed in the scholar's Latin, the theses were committed, as per medieval university convention, to men of learning, in particular to its specialists in sacred science, inviting any or all to discuss and debate them with their propounder.

But the interchange of thought Luther had hoped for overran the expected bounds. Put into the vernacular by some forgotten busybody, the *Ninety-five* presently swirled over all of Europe like so many wind-blown leaves, involving its people in a virulent ruction, which in turn, as the years ticked on, swept Luther into an out-and-out rebellion and, in the end, into secession and excommunication.

THE YOUNG LUTHER

Who, one might ask, was this recreant brother, this defier of the mighty church and disturber of the Christian peace? Born in 1483 at Eisleben, Germany, the son of a peasant, Luther had graced this vale some six months when his parents moved to Mansfeld, a mining town, where the father was soon pouring his muscle and sweat into its pits. Much has been made by Lutherophiles over the family's hard-strained circumstances, and the horrible burdens these laid on the boy during his growing years. But this has proved to be a stretching of the facts. The truth is that the Luthers were plain people, pious, and industrious, even a bit penurious, who, though laboring for meager rewards, by hard effort and frugality, managed to get ahead—so well, indeed, that presently the elder Luther was able to put aside his pick and shovel and invest in a few smelteries. He even rose to the rank and dignity of elected membership in the town council—an almost miraculous feat for one born to peasant blood in those days.

Meanwhile, Martin's parents saw to it that their offspring learned his letters. They put him in the town school where he was suckled on the

Roman language and its literature, the rules and postulates of the Catholic rite, and its hymnody. At the age of fourteen the youth was articled for study under the Brethren of the Common Life, the same specialists in piety and good works who had launched Erasmus as a Latinist, but in Luther's case they practiced their magic in one of their other chapters. The Brothers drilled him assiduously in Latin grammar, rhetoric, and poesy, and when they were done, in 1501, the University of Erfurt, then the most renowned intellectual plant in Germany, was ready to accept him.

There he listened to lectures on grammar, rhetoric, logic, philosophy, metaphysics, and ethics, besides physics and mathematics. He was a man of diligent enterprise, an attribute for which his professors gave him his due when they converted him first into a bachelor and then into a master of arts cum laude. Thus stamped with approval and stuffed with knowledge, young Luther headed for the sittings of the faculty of law in hopes of making himself proficient in the juridic science. But his interest in torts and testaments and such legal sorcery paled, and he retired to the cloister at Erfurt where he applied his reflections to the study of theology.

In time he took the friar's vows, and in 1507 he received ordination into the priesthood. But for a while his main work was in teaching. Dispatched by his abbot to Wittenberg, he gave instruction in Aristotelian ethics, though subsequently, after he had invested himself in the reformer's mantle, he became a ceaseless damner of the ancient sage. Aristotle's works, he now knew, were so much "Satanic filth." He also resumed his pursuit of theology, hoping to master its more recondite arcana. After a year or so he returned to his monastic haunt at Erfurt, where he kept on lecturing and snared another degree. Finally, he was transferred permanently to the monastery at Wittenberg, where he continued to carry on academically at the university, bearing the torch in divine science and eventually making his ascension to the airy heights of doctorship. In 1512, after the doctor's hat had safely settled over his ears, the university elevated him to the chair of biblical literature.

THE MAKING OF A REFORMER

For all his monkish conditioning, Luther possessed an exuberant energy. A man of action, he could drive himself without mercy; but he could also become still and pensive for weeks and months on end, well-nigh drowning at such times in a sea of despair. For release he sought to soothe his aching soul with the wisdom of Holy Writ, the words of the church's saintly fathers, Saint Augustine in particular, and even the serenity of her great, but often suspect, and even misprised, mystics. Sometime in 1512 God vouchsafed him a sudden ray of light. Is not the Bible the Lord's inspired and

incontrovertible word? Then it follows that it is also God's edict and command—it alone, and not the pope, is the authority for Christian teaching
and comportment. Are the children of God naturally and incurably evil,
incapable ever since Adam of a solitary, unsullied act? Then the theological
doctors helped them not a whit. Let men, instead, bend their knee before
the Heavenly Father to implore His mercies, for only by their faith in Him
can they hope some day to fly with the angelic flock.

It was Luther's conviction that the baptized, abetted and upheld by
their faith and irradiated by the Holy Ghost, could, by a constant and
scrupulous pondering of Scripture, arrive at God's eternal verity. It was his
view—at least during his larval years as a religious reformer—that "a Christian is the most free lord of all, and subject to no one," and that, by corollary, "everyone ought to be allowed to believe what he will," for, he went
on, "if his belief be wrong, he will suffer punishment enough in the eternal
fires of Hell." Later, to be sure, when every Bible reader became, as it were,
his own supreme court in the interpretation of questions bearing on the
Good Book's inspired meaning, and in the process not infrequently reached
verdicts which were at variance with those of Brother Martin, Luther faced
about. Thus, where in the first skirmishes of his rebellion against the Harlot
on the Seven Hills he had insisted on Bible-reading as an obligation for
every Christian, whether in childhood or in dotage, he now found himself
devoured by doubts and misgivings. Had he, for example, during the infancy of his revolt, declared for every man's free and easy access to Holy Writ?
Then, with the passing human show, after numerous sessions in his praying
cell, and not a little self-examination and internal communication, he recognized with a pang that the simple-minded millions found thinking a pain,
and hence it would be futile to expect them to unravel the holy truth by
themselves. What the common man needed was a dose of sound religious
instruction, dispensed and controlled by the evangelical Lutheran church.
Otherwise, despite the kindly light of the Holy Spirit, his thinking was
doomed to failure. Such was the pitiful case, for example, of the Anabap-
tists, those deplorable souls who, by their misinterpretation of the Holy
Word, rejected infant baptism as a cardinal article of faith. For such damaged minds Luther reserved his most pungent dung-pile abuse, and when
these bullheaded people persisted in their heresy, it proved more than Luther could calmly take. "Let them," he lathered, "be put to the sword."

Although the Protestant revolt was engendered in part by the iconoclasm of the Renaissance's bolder Humanists—the dreadless Valla, for instance, and Erasmus, to single out only two—as the contest between the
church and her antagonists increased, the intellectual promise of the Renaissance succumbed to the blackout imposed by creed and dogma. In this
respect even Luther was no exception. During his salad days he too had

savored the Humanistic nectar, and had even hymned it highly, yet as his years increased, so also did his theological intolerance. The religious freedom he had formerly exalted, he now denounced and damned—save only when its benisons devolved upon himself and his fellow believers. "Reason," the years had taught him, "is a poisonous beast." "It was," he wrote as the buffets of time edged him toward his grave, "the Devil's harlot," a word to which he resorted freely, and which he also pinned on Mother Church. His mood reflected the temper of the epoch, a distressed and fanatical age, besot by bigotry and hostile to the free functioning of the human mind.

THE REFORMER AS COMPOSER AND WRITER

The first great mass movement in human annals to be carried on not only *viva voce,* but with the printed word as well, the Protestant revolt steeped Christendom in the flood waters of propaganda tracts and pamphlets, satires and caricatures, and, occasionally, a book. Written for the most part in a frenzied polemical vein, the bulk of this output was balderdash which has long since drifted into oblivion. But there were some works of worth. From Luther's genius, for example, flowed "A Mighty Fortress is our God," a lusty and stirring psalm, and the battle hymn, so to say, of the Reformation, but sung nowadays in the temples of the former enemy. Luther, who unlike Erasmus had a delicate ear for tone, wrote music as much to give voice to his inmost feelings as to fit it for an occasion. It was in this agonized mood that he composed his deeply personal "From Heartfelt Need I Cry to Thee."

Not all Luther's creations gurgled from the primal spring. His "To Thee Oh Lord We Sing Our Praise," he derived from the Latin *Te Deum Laudamus,* and his "From Heaven on High I Come to Thee" he adapted from a medieval text. It has become one of Germany's most beloved Christmas Carols. Among the hymnists of his day he takes on the guise, if not the stature, of a Schubert. In consequence, he not only left his mark as a master of tune; presently he was also being flattered by imitators among Protestants, and even, rather sardonically, in the camp of the accursed papists.

In the realm of scholarship, Luther's preeminent achievement, by staggering odds, was his translation of the Bible—*Die Bibel oder die Heilige Schrift.* The work, it is true, had been preceded by more than a dozen others, most in High German, the rest in Low German, but Luther's version, pundits allow, was the first generally satisfactory German rendition. Although the labor of its composition was Luther's, he had the wit to seek the help and counsel of a herd of established scholars, philological as well as theological, especially Melanchthon (born Schwarzerd [Blacksoil]), a learned and enthusiastic Hellenist, and Aurogallus (born Goldhahn [Gold-cock]), a mastermind in Hebrew. The work was begun in 1521, but Luther had aged thirteen years before it actually appeared in print. Written in a robust peasant German, the book was rewritten and rewritten as Luther refined his labor, transmuting it into the first literary utterance of commanding merit in modern German and setting by it a high and enviable standard.

On a somewhat lower plane in Germany's cultural history are the reformer's numerous epistles, sermons, and broadsides, where in one way or another he addressed himself to the problems besetting the advance of the new religion, among which the rehabilitation of German schooling was by no means the least. To this end, he put forth a pamphlet in 1520, *To the Christian Noblemen of the German Nation; On the Improvement of Christian Practices.* Four years later he came out with a long and profusely worded *Letter to the Mayors and Aldermen of All the Cities of Germany in Behalf of Christian Schools.* In 1530 he supplemented and fortified his earlier pronouncements with his *Sermon on the Duty of Sending Children to School.* There were other writings, but the three aforesaid contain the essence of Luther's educational views. Let us now wheel him into the observation room and put his ideas into laboratory jars.

REFORM AND LOWER EDUCATION—THE *CATECHISM*

When, in that fateful year of 1517, Luther unwittingly unleashed the Reformation, education in the German states had become debilitated. The province of Holy Church for almost a thousand years, it not only had supplied her with her holy clerks, but through her countless benefices and other stipendiums she had been able to extend schooling to many a talented but needy lad. But now the monopoly she had enjoyed so long had fallen under challenge not only of the skeptical Humanists who were derisive of her marble-niched Aristotle and her moldering Seven Liberal Arts, but also of a variety of secular potentates who put their educational stress on practical ends, and from heads of states and municipalities, who threw down their gloves to an education which the church had directed predominantly to her own self-interest. Hence, as the Protestant revolt picked up force, it was no wonder that its leaders should cast flirtatious glances at such malcontents— not only to woo them to the Reformation's cause, but, if possible, to persuade them to lend a political hand in laying the groundwork of a sound and substantial society.

Toward such a goal Luther launched upon a piece of rhetoric directed at Germany's ruling princes. It lay within their hands, he told them, to make their states fair and peaceful havens for a Christian, which is to say, a Protestant, to settle down. To bring this about, they should not only purge the church of her debaucheries and pollutions; they should also reform education. Let them end the decay in the higher learning, the "dens of murderers" and "temples of Moloch," as Luther on one occasion anathematized the universities, by revising their worm-eaten curricula. But let them give thought, too, to the learning below. Every reigning prince, Luther insisted, has the obligation to provide primary schools for girls no less than for boys, where they shall all be made privy to the immutable axioms laid down in Holy Writ. To make it easier for them, Luther had put the ancient holy book into a German which was at once instructive and upbuilding as well as readable. Later, in 1528, after he had turned his back on the idea of allowing every individual free access to the Bible, he nominated himself to concoct a *Catechism*—in fact, he concocted two, a short one and a long one, wherein he put down the tenets of his Protestantism in plain and understandable language for the German people.

The *Catechism,* its author confided, "is the right Bible for the laity." It contained the essence of doctrine necessary for every Christian aspiring some day to sprout wings. This little volume, which was much less costly than the Bible, became the Lutheran schoolchild's basic book for religious instruction, which, needless to say, Luther made mandatory. Not only was his *Catechism* the layman's "right Bible"; it also bore the cachet of official sanction, and hence had no competition. Pupils learned its contents from cover to cover, line by line, page by page, until finally they had etched them forever upon their memories. Like Noah Webster's famous blue-backed *American Spelling Book,* which entered these scenes several centuries following, the *Catechism* was often a child's only book—as indispensable to his welfare as his Blutwurst and his dog. The *Catechism* was in the vernacular German. Religion and the attendant morals were the only subjects—not counting gymnastics—dispensed in the maternal tongue. To supplement the Bible's postulates of Christian virtue, Luther translated the fables of the pagan Aesop, whose contributions to moral science Brother Martin pronounced second only to those of Holy Writ.

Although in his early crusading days Luther put considerable store in teaching the mother tongue, as his attitude toward reason and religious tolerance hardened, so did his attitude toward German as a language for instruction in the lower learning. Save in the business of religious—shall we say, indoctrination?—the reformer put its use under proscription. Teaching young Germany how to speak, read, and write its language, though by no means dismissed as needless or even unimportant, was nevertheless consigned primarily to the home. The fact that in most homes the families were illiterate, and there was therefore a question of just who was going to teach young Germany to read and write its language, was a point on which Luther, unhappily, did not elect to elucidate.

If Luther cried down the teaching of German in the lower learning, he cried up the teaching of Latin, which was to be the language of instruction in all subjects apart from religion and physical culture. Indeed, before the melancholy reactionary retrogression had entered into his being the reformer had panted to teach the young not only German and Latin but Greek and Hebrew as well, a passion which doubtless issued from his exposure as a student to the Humanistic bacilli. Needless to say, his aspiration was never more than a wish, and in his later years he renounced it.

RELIGION AND LANGUAGE—THE OLD OR THE NEW?

In the groves of higher knowledge the tongues of antiquity had always been essential for specialists in divinity, a practice which Luther approved and would not alter. But as the row between the new and the old religions grew, there was a precipitous drop in the number of students seeking preparation for the professions, and especially for the holy calling. The sacred vestment no longer offered its former security. University enrollments plummeted. In 1520, to summon examples, the University of Erfurt, at the time Germany's principal center of Humanistic culture, boasted some 300 students. Seven years later it could round up only fourteen—and it never recovered. In 1519 the University of Vienna had a student corps of 600; thirteen years later it could scrape up only a dozen. So academia's sorry plight went down the line from Cologne to Heidelberg, and across the Rhine to Basel and beyond. Very briefly, the University of Wittenberg, from whose ramparts the Reformation's first rockets had burst in the air, fared somewhat better. There for a number of years, with Luther and other Reformation leaders warming the professorial seats, enrollments soared—only suddenly to cease their climb, fade and disintegrate, as rockets do.

Doubtless the woe visited upon Teutonia's academic shrines was a reflection of the evils of the time, an angry, agonized time, not a little uncertain and even dangerous. Some, like the erudite Erasmus, placed the blame for Germany's academic downslide on Luther—on his objurgations against reason, and his slanderous name-calling, not to mention the stirring of his afflatus as a God-appointed missionary. "Wherever Lutheranism prevails," asserted the Dutch scholar, "there culture and learning perish"—a statement which, all in all, was doubtless more malicious than judicious.

The undressed truth is that Luther bore no antagonism to the teaching of the ancient languages in the strongholds of higher learning. Again and again he spoke up in their behalf, in his early years of hope and in the falling night of his disenchantment. When, for instance, after having given out the Holy Word in German, only to have the herd of common Germans then balk at putting their children to sacrificing so many years to studying any more Latin, Luther turned loose the full artillery of his invective. They had been gulled, he cannonaded, by the trickery of Lucifer. "Is it not enough, you ask," he told them, "to teach the Scriptures which are necessary for salvation in the mother tongue?" "To this," he went on, "I answer: I know, alas, that we Germans must always remain irrational brutes, as we are deservedly called by the surrounding nations." To turn one's back to the study of the original biblical tongues, he lamented on another occasion, is "a disgrace and a sin," for without them "we cannot preserve the Gospel."

The chasm between Erasmus and Luther in their attitude toward the classical learning issued from their oppugnant views of education. For Erasmus, a Humanist from head to toe, the ancient languages constituted the liver and lights of a liberal education, and without them no man could aspire to lead a truly civilized life. For Luther, on the other hand, the Erasmian Humanism, unmellowed by the dulcet touch of religion, was an artificiality. What the evangelist prized was not the "humane learning and good literature," but a God-serving Christian. For him, hence, the ancient languages were the handmaidens of theology—or, if you will, of the higher biblical study.

MUSIC, HISTORY—AND RELIGION

Closely connected with religious instruction in the lower school was the study and practice of hymnody, not only as an academic exercise but for the Sabbath's congregational devotions. Himself a first-class tune maker, Luther confessed that from his earliest recollection he had always been a wooer of melody. "I always loved music," he wrote, and he "who has skill in this art," he went on, somewhat carried away by his own good feeling "is of good temperament, fitted for all things." "Music," he avowed, "is a fair, noble gift of God, next to theology. . . . Youths should be trained in this art, for it makes fine, clever people." As a result, singing rooted itself as an established practice in the Lutheran school. Soon, indeed, its seeds scattered throughout the Germanic land, so that to this very day German schoolchildren still sing every day throughout the year, whether in a secular or a pious expression.

Luther's proposed elementary schooling was intended primarily to inculcate the faith. All other considerations were minor. Not only was instruction in religion its paramount function, but in some way all other instruction—except gymnastics—was related to it, from music to the fabulous apologues of Brother Aesop. Even the study of Latin, though it was exacted from all boys for so-called "cultural reasons," bore often enough on matters of faith and morals. Even history, which in those days was not commonly included in the lower-learning curriculum, had religious overtones. Not only did it shine its light on man, his inherent propensity for evil, for example, his acts of right and wrong, as well as the rise and growth of institutions, sacred and profane, but, as Lorenzo Valla had so convincingly demonstrated by his demolition of the *Donation of Constantine,* a thoroughgoing grip on history could serve the reformers as a powerful arm in their assault on the frayed pretensions and fabrications of the ancient church. "Historians," asseverated Luther with characteristic hyperbole, "are the most useful of men and the best of teachers." Ah, that it were so simple!

THE WAR FOR EDUCATION

The gist of Luther's educational doctrine is set down in his *Letter to the Mayors and Aldermen of all the Cities of Germany in Behalf of Christian Schools.* A harangue rather than an epistle, it was compounded in 1524 when its author was still on friendly terms with reason. Be that as it may, in spite of his later renunciations, the letter is fairly representative of the reformer's general educational outlook. Although he stood under the church's ban, and hence was officially muzzled, he told the mayors and aldermen that even though Rome had commanded him to hold his tongue, this, nevertheless, he could not do, since God had bidden him to speak. "I wish to declare," he announced, "that if you hear me, you hear not me but Christ." Thus authorized by the Lord on High, he went on to tell his readers that he knew the truth, and that anybody in his right mind could easily realize it.

For a start, let the mayors and aldermen open their eyes to the sad condition of Germany's schools. Her shrines of higher learning have become "unchristian and sensual" and her monasteries have debased themselves into nurseries of sloth and corruption. And "because selfish parents see they can no longer put their children upon the bounty of the monasteries and cathedrals, they refuse to educate them." All this makes the Devil chuckle into his beard. Indeed, "who can blame him . . . ? How could he consent to a proper training of the young?" For in order to maintain himself in power Auld Horny well knows that he must possess the young.

Let it not be forgotten, however, Brother Martin reminded the politicos, that the "right instruction is a matter wherein Christ and the whole world are concerned." Moreover, since "the highest welfare, safety, and power of a city consists in able, learned, wise, upright, and cultivated citizens . . . ," it behooves the secular authority not only to wipe out these seminaries of satanism once and forever, but, more important, to create and support Christian schools in their place, open freely to every boy and girl. To accomplish this bold maneuver, every loyal citizen should give a friendly boost, a consideration which, Luther took pains to explain, was no longer a fragile dream, since divine grace has "released them from the exaction and robbery" and other extortion by the pontifical banditi. A child's claim to an education is not only inalienable; it is the command of Omnipotence. "Why," the former friar asked, "do old people live except to take care of, teach, and bring up the young . . .? Because, he went on, answering his own question, "God has commended them [the children] to us who are older and know what is good for them." But parents being the posterity of the sinful Adam, and hence inescapably depraved, are inclined much too often to shirk their responsibility, and thereby suffer their offspring "to grow up ill-bred, and to infect other children till at last the whole city be destroyed like Sodom and Gomorrah. . . ." Such being, in Luther's opinion, the incontrovertible truth, it befell the civil government not only to provide schools, but even to make attendance obligatory.

There are those, in and out of public office, as Luther well knew, who would howl down his proposal as too extravagant, a drain on the general pocket, and beyond the bounds of practicality. Let such argufiers make note, the reformer reminded them, that year after year Germans "spend large sums on muskets, roads, bridges, dams, and the like. . ." Why then, he demanded, "should we not apply as much to our neglected youth in order that they may have a skillful schoolmaster or two?"

Then there are those, not so numerous perhaps, who laid down the dogma that schooling the youth had always been the care and responsibility of the church, and that the civil government thus had no business sticking its nose into such a pious endeavor. Such a view Luther rejected out of hand. "If there is a village which can do it," he reassured Johann, Elector of Saxony, in 1526, "your Grace has the power to compel it to support schools, preaching places, and parishes." Did the village still refuse to comply? If so, then Johann's correspondent reminded the elector that by virtue of his office he was "the supreme guardian of the youth," and if necessary he should resort to force. Compelling a town to support schools, Luther explained, is no different from requiring it "to contribute and to do work for the building of bridges and roads. . . ."

Four years later, in 1530, the father of Protestantism was still of the same mind. "I maintain," he sermonized ex cathedra, "that the civil authorities are in duty bound to compel people to send their children to school . . . . If the government can compel such citizens as are fit for . . . martial duties in time of war, how much more has it a right to compel the people to send their children to school, because in this case we are warring with the Devil."

PLANS FOR EDUCATION

Besides exhorting Germany's secular dignitaries to establish and support schools in their various domains, and to compel parents to commit their small fry, male and female, to their tutelage, the reformer felt impelled to keep the rulers abreast of just what such schools should teach. But this we have already dwelt upon: the schools should teach Lutheran orthodoxy. However, such seminaries were not to occupy their recruits for six hours a day, five days a week, during ten months or so a year, as they are apt to nowadays. "My idea," Luther volunteered, "is that boys should spend an hour or two a day at school, and the rest of their time at home, learn some trade, and do whatever is desired" (by their parents, one may safely bet). The sauce for the gander was also sauce for the goose. Girls, however, were to help their mothers with the household chores. "For," as the holy man expanded, "she sleeps, dances, and plays away more than that." During the seedtime of the year and the harvesting later on, when every able man and woman worked in the fields, the young, as might be expected, were conscripted to help their elders, and at such time, naturally, they were excused from becoming educated. Finally, let it be underlined that, except in religious instruction, Luther's primary school was not a vernacular school, at least not in the sense that we know today.

Even though mothers and fathers fulfilled their obligations to Christ, whether of their own free will or not, by sending their children to school "an hour or so a day," this by no means relieved them of the duty of safeguarding their young against the designs of Satan and his evil helpers, who, as Luther had often plainly warned, baited their traps in all places and at all times. Consequently, it was in the home that the child was to be disciplined in such imperative Christian virtues as modesty, honesty, work, frugality, and above all, honoring and obeying his seniors, so that in time he would ripen into an acceptable citizen, which is to say, he would mind his betters, sacred and secular, unquestioningly—like a puppet on a string.

Although the father was at all times the commander-in-chief of the household, and was expected to tolerate no nonsense from his underlings, yet Luther issued a declaration that the paternal mandates, such as they were, should always be brushed with tenderness. The home, like the school which Luther envisioned, should not be a hell or a purgatory with a reign of endless fear and flogging. In his own younger days when children, like animals, had no rights, Luther enjoyed no such domestic felicity. Consequently, as year followed year, the boy amassed abrasions, welts, and bruises which damaged not only his body but his psyche as well—though in fairness it must be said that his parents were probably no harsher than was then the rule. Nevertheless, to his dying day, Luther, true to the fourth

Mosaic injunction, continued to honor his father and his mother. In their home Luther's children fared better than their father had in his, and thus the recourse to arnica was much less frequent. It is reported that Luther loved his children devotedly, and that the family relationship was one of happiness and contentment. Even so, loyal to the Holy Word, to his last breath Luther believed that as father of his offspring, he was also their governor and director.

As if Luther's demand upon the heads of German states and municipalities to invest some of their treasured coin to assure their young ones a decent Christian schooling were not enough, Luther proceeded in addition to press upon them "to procure good libraries in suitable buildings, especially in large cities which were able to afford it." Such edifices, it goes without saying, were to crowd their stacks with Holy Writ in every language in which it existed, old as well as new. Next, they should stock books helpful in the mastery of tongues "the poets and orators, without considering whether they are heathen or Christian," because "from such works grammar must be learned." Then, there should be books "treating of all the arts and sciences"—decorous and respectable, and in full accord with the "scientific" revelations of Holy Writ. Finally, there should be volumes dealing with law and medicine, though here again Luther warned that "discrimination is necessary." Beelzebub was no idler. At all times this archdeceiver "designs that we should torture ourselves with Catholicons, Floristas, Modernists, and other trash of the accursed monks and sophists, always learning, yet never acquiring knowledge."

THE MAN AND HIS CREDO

Thus the man and his educational credo. Let us review its salient articles to see what they amount to. There is, to begin, Luther's pronouncement that an elementary schooling, however paltry it may look to us in retrospect, is the just due of every child, rather than the monopoly of a few. Next there is the related doctrine that a proper schooling is the right of girls as well as boys, at all events in learning's nether valley, and certainly in religion and virtue. This is not to suggest, however, that, like Plato, Luther was ready to grant the female equal rights even if her wit and ability matched that of the male. The inventor of Protestantism reprehended such sexual egalitarianism on the ground that it was against the divine will. The father, said Luther, proving his points by the Bible, was God's appointed master of the hearth, and his spouse, like their biological reproductions, owed him respect and obedience at all times and in all matters.

Lest parents should seek to deny their young their Heaven-sent right to an honest Christian schooling, Luther called for the inauguration of compulsory education—nothing new, of course, for the long since ghostly Spartans but in Luther's Germany a dazzling innovation. To attain his end, the reformer went on to advocate the establishment of schools which would be controlled and supported by the state, an old idea again, as old, indeed, as Plato's imaginary republic, but one which, when proposed in all earnestness as a reality for Germans living in Lutherland, stood out like a neon sign a hundred feet tall.

If Luther offered the checkrein of education to the state, at the same time he insisted that the school's primary function was not secular, or even intellectual, but religious and moral, a task wherein the fireside was to assume a full and responsible partnership. It was in the home where the child was to learn to walk the straight and narrow path. Finally, following in the track of some of the Renaissance's most progressive schoolmen—as witness, especially, such a glittering star as Vittorino da Feltre—the recreant Luther, hamfisted though he could be, was at odds with the schoolmasters' harshness with the attendant "flogging, trembling, anguish, and wretchedness." "Children," Luther wrote, "delight in acquiring knowledge . . . ," and "it is not well to check them in everything."

Chapter 9

Saint Ignatius of Loyola

THE CATHOLIC REFORMATION

Even before Luther flung out his challenge in Wittenberg, numerous Catholic prominenti of the lay and ecclesiastical noblesse—including even the Holy Roman Emperor—had been imploring Mother Church to put a stop to the widespread abuse and corruption in the hierarchy. But from such pleas the Holy Father kept himself aloof. In fact, Luther's eventful act at Wittenberg had been in history for almost thirty years before the church awoke from her torpor, seized her mops and buckets, and set herself to work to put her house in order. For this purpose Pope Paul III, after several aborted attempts, summoned a council "to extirpate heresy and to reform morals," to convene in 1545 in the Italian city of Trent. Fevered by disunity, a good deal of hotheaded talk, and on at least one occasion a case of physical combat between two of its episcopal participants, the council faced a staggering assignment. Indeed, before its sessions were over, eighteen years were to pass, and so were Paul and his three successors to the chair of Peter.

From its massed assault of prayer, outcry, and disputation emerged a program—even a campaign—which has since been celebrated by cultural memoirists as the Catholic Reformation. Not only did it venture to make an end of ecclesiastical unseemliness, but for the instruction and welfare of the faithful it also undertook to redefine and bolster the church's fundamental axioms. To set the old religion on a strong foundation the council, following the example of the errant and heretical Protestants, put much of its trust in the potency of education. Every diocese, its dignitaries ordained, was to garrison itself with a seminary to educate young men for the holy calling. Such schools were to be staffed with qualified professors, and to make certain of their competence, the council drew up a code of standards. Finally, it instructed its clergy, from parish priest to the mitred higher-ups, to spare no pains to give schooling to the common child.

It did not take very long before a number of religious organizations answered the council's educational call, and among them the Society of Jesus, commonly spoken of as the Jesuit Order, was far and away the most important. It was germinated in 1534 when Iñigo de Oñez y Loyola—or, as he is more generally known, Saint Ignatius Loyola (1491–1556)—and a handful of disciples, discontented with the sordid facts of existence, dropped to their knees in the chapel of St. Mary on Montmartre not only to vow that for the rest of their lives would they keep themselves chaste and poor, but that presently they would undertake a pilgrimage to the Holy Land where, armed with the papal blessing and the power of soft persuasion, they would melt the iron hearts of the infidel Turks and win them for the cross. Unluckily, Loyola's crusade ran aground in Venice—but not his dreams. Although he did not know it, it had gone into hiding in the subbasement of his consciousness, to emerge again several decades later. But by that later time its possessor, more attuned to life's grim realities, removed its original mellowness and now bellowed for money, men, arms, and hundreds of vessels lodging cannon to put his crusade into effect. But sad to say, his plans went awry.

BIRTH OF THE SOCIETY OF JESUS (THE JESUIT ORDER)

Who was this Loyola, this mixture of romanticist and realist, this dreamer of preposterous dreams, and organizer of one of the most powerful religious associations the world has ever witnessed? He was the son of Don Beltram Oñez y Loyola, a Spanish peer, whose wordly estate was slight, far slighter than his propensity to increase the number of his progeny of which, with the aid of his spouse, he begot thirteen. Iñigo was at the age of seven when he became a page in the royal summer palace, where one of his better-heeled kinsmen chanced to be the governor. Thus brought face to face with courtly life, the lad toiled his way up to knighthood, consuming as he moved along its prized punctilios of virility, of strength and valor, of discipline and service, besides its vices and artificialities, its bowing and kneeling, its simulated politesse, its love play, its intrigues and politicking. Intellectually, chivalry—or what remained of it, now that gunpowder was literally blasting it to bits—was as sterile as it had been in its golden medieval heyday. In consequence, as the youth grew to manhood, apart from his reading of a few chivalric romances he had remained a stranger to the world of books.

Meanwhile, though, he relished the pleasures of his world and sowed his wild oats, like the high-stepping Augustine during his early pagan days, with lavish abandon. But again like Augustine, on some unforeseeable tomorrow Ignatius would renounce his false and fatuous ways and devote his remaining years to the furtherance of God's glory. The way toward this extraordinary transformation was prepared when, in combat, Loyola's right leg collided with a hostile cannonball.

There is no need to rehearse the details: the result was that during his long and gruesome convalescence, Loyola gradually turned into a man of fanatic piety. Henceforth, he let it be known, he would fight as a soldier in the army of God. Someday, he even permitted himself to fancy, he would have his name enshrined in the catalog of the saints. There followed a long period when, oppressed by a feeling of guilt and shame, he imposed upon himself a bizarre and desperate penance. He gave away his material goods, donned the pilgrim's coarse costume, and sustained himself by begging for his food, but in no case would he accept meat. He fasted, sometimes for days; he flogged himself regularly thrice a day until his bare skin was flecked with blood; he prayed incessantly. Finally he undertook a pilgrimage to Jerusalem.

Whatever Loyola did, he did without stint. It is said, for example, that when he wrote a letter, even a casual communiqué, say to his uncle, he would make it a major production, reading and redacting it again and again before sending it on its way. The same ordered and painstaking procedure he applied to his *Exercises* and *Constitutions,* wherein he set down the basic principles and rules governing the order, and over which he sweated with scarcely any surcease for several decades.

His thirties were upon Loyola when the realization came to him that his ignorance of books would put a heavy burden on the progress of his missionary labors. With that realization, grown man though he was, he took his place on the schoolboy's bench to cross swords with Latin grammar. Presently we encounter him in Paris attending sessions in the secondary school and, true to his vows, living chastely in the poor house and appeasing his stomach by begging for bread. It was in the ancient city on the Seine that he gained his first adherents, a trio of comrade ascetics, sworn to a pure and penniless existence, and who with Loyola nominated themselves to serve and obey "the Roman pontiff as God's vicar on earth"; and "to execute immediately and without hesitation or excuse all that the reigning pope or his successors may enjoin upon them . . .," no matter where. It was a dedication which was too attractive to be ignored, and in 1540 Pope Paul gave official recognition to the Society of Jesus. The year following, Ignatius was elected general. Inaugurated as an effort to save and redeem the Moslems, after Trent the order enlarged its enterprise to teach and preach at all times in any place ever heard of, or even unheard of, "for the benefit of souls or for the propagation of the faith."

THE RATIO STUDIORUM

The society executed its industry under the regulatory hand of a constitution, the work of Ignatius, and of which the fourth part delineates his views on education. As the years went on, these were assiduously curried and glossed in actual schoolroom practice, after which they were amended and renovated to become the Ratio Studiorum, the all-embracing statutes for Jesuit education the world around. Framed with infinite pains, the Ratio was assembled only after a long and searching study of Europe's outstanding pedagogical practice as manifested, for example, in the schools of the Brethren of the Common Life, Johann Sturm's famed Gymnasium at Strassburg, and some of the better colleges in France. Yet, however exemplary these practices may have seemed when they were first observed on their home ground, they were refused official admittance to the Ratio until they had proved their mettle in the Jesuit classrooms. The Ratio's first draft was ready in 1586 when the head of the order transmitted it to the provinces for study and comment, but thirteen years went by before the writ was given its final form and content and was allowed to go into print. From that time forth it suffered no alteration for almost two and a half centuries until 1832, when, yielding to the realization that certain newer disciplines were apparently here to stay, the society made delicate concessions to the study of mathematics and the natural sciences as well as to history and geography. Thereafter it closed the door to any further tinkering with the Ratio until 1906, when it slackened the taut checkrein of its general compulsion and granted the right to every Jesuit province to bring its teaching into greater concordance with local needs.

THE JESUIT CURRICULUM

Although the Jesuit fathers recognized that the conditioning of the young was all-important to its broad objective of delivering Christendom from its moral and religious dinginess, yet, save in rare and extraordinary instances, they did not concern themselves in particular with the elementary learning. If parents pressed upon them nevertheless to make an exception and teach their child the fundamentals, then they were under instruction to say "that we are not permitted." Hence, to speak of a Jesuit elementary school is, at least 99½ times out of 100, a contradiction in terms. The run of Jesuit academies fell into two classes: either they were "inferior," which is to say they were on a plane with Europe's secondary schools, or they were "superior," which means they were on a level with its colleges. The lower school welcomed its freshmen when they were at the age of twelve, and the upper school greeted them some four years later. At the age of twelve, as everybody knows, the boy who understands precisely what he aims to do in his adult years is a rarity. To the Jesuit fathers it made not a shade of difference, for the course of studies they laid before their students was the same for all. Nor did it matter whether a pupil's blood ran blue as well as red, or whether he was rich or poor. What counted was his capacity to learn and his moral character, not the family's standing, whether social, political, pecuniary, or whatnot. In no instance, moreover, did his schooling cost him one cent, a custom which had enjoyed the favor of the old-line Greeks and Romans, but which in sixteenth-century Europe had been pretty much forgotten. When temptation sometimes tapped at Jesuit doors and recommended the imposition of fees, as was the wont among their academic competitors, then their founder's reminder was always there to inform them, "Freely you have received, freely give."

To be accepted for instruction in a Jesuit school, a boy was expected to be able to parse a simple Latin sentence, and to know how to read and write a rudimentary prose. Once he was admitted to its sessions, he was under the obligation to speak Latin on all occasions, whether in the chambers of learning or on the playground, save on holidays, when he might speak in any tongue that suited him. Needless to say, an unremitting emphasis was laid on religion and morality, and every device known to moral jurisprudence was resorted to in order to make the boy a true and abiding Catholic. To get his instruction rolling, appropriately enough, every master began by asking divine assistance for the proceedings. There were, of course, student prayers as well, which, fortified by daily confession, communion, and Mass, were calculated to keep the student safe from Satan's deadly traps not only during his years at school, but henceforth and forever. From beginning to end his course of study was prescribed—as was still the situation at Harvard a century or so later. To make sure that an instructor, however keen his acumen, would nevertheless not fall prey to the pitfalls that lurk between the covers of some subversive book, as, let us say, the lethally attractive *Colloquies* of Erasmus, the Jesuit high command mandated not only what a boy should study in the classroom, but also what he should read.

The Jesuit lower learning was divided into three parts, of which one was allotted to three years of grammar, one to the humanities, and one to rhetoric. During the first year of his grammatical conscription the learner, besides striking up a casual acquaintance with Greek, devoted the major part of his attention to Latin grammar. He eased himself into Latin letters by beginning as did the Romans in their time, with such verbal custards as the *Lives* of Nepos and the fables of Phaedrus. The next two years saw him strengthen his intimacy with Roman grammar, rehearsing himself in its mystery again and again until he was privy to its every quirk. As he increased in years and proficiency, his reading matter naturally was adjusted to his augmented capacity, and he now matched wits with the highest Latin literati from Caesar, Cicero, and Virgil to Ovid, Catullus, Tibullus, and yet more. In Greek he grappled with Aesop, Saint Chrysostom, and a few others.

A master—or at all events a near master—of the grammatical lore, the boy was now turned to eloquence. He was directed toward amplifying his erudition and studying the simpler principles of rhetoric. He pondered the writings of the historians, the poets, and the orators in Greek no less than in Latin, noting not only their substance but also their style. But Cicero was still the grandmaster of them all, and no day was allowed to pass without savoring at least a sliver of his prose. The senior year bore upon making the boy an accomplished practitioner of the speaker's craft, in all its varied branches. He was drilled relentlessly in every form of public utterance, with Cicero as his lodestar, but with supplementary guidance from Aristotle and Tertullian.

THE PROBATIONER

For most, completion of the study of rhetoric brought their schooldays to an end. The few whom the Heavenly Father had inspirited with a desire to continue, which is to say to become Jesuits, now entered upon a two-year novitiate—provided, of course, they were accepted as likely candidates for the holy calling. Being a probationer in the Society of Jesus was not easy; like the boot training of a United States Marine, its requirements could be immensely taxing. Immured from the world, the novice abandoned its agreeable delights, seeking instead to exalt his soul in a kind of noble purity through spiritual and religious meditation. Discipline was stiff, but it was never brutal. What was demanded above all was an absolute obedience to authority and, by corollary, a complete abnegation of the individual will. "We ought always be ready to believe," declared the society's general, "that what seems to be white is black if the hierarchical Church so defines it."

The probationer was given to believe that his was a "holy obedience," and that in submitting to the orders of his superiors he was actually obeying the mandates of God. As might be expected, the novice was under constant surveillance, not only by his superiors, but even by his comrades. In fact, he himself was pledged to report to his masters any miscarriage of deportment on the part of his mates—a practice of espionage which was common enough in academic circles in those days.

Once the novitiate had run its course, the candidate's qualities were minutely weighed and measured. He was to be, as Loyola had set forth in his *Constitutions,* "of sound doctrine, or apt to learn it." He should possess "discretion in the management of business." He should have an elephant's capacity to remember, and "he should be burning with zeal for the salvation of souls." To put these qualities to effective use, he needed to be able to speak fluently and convincingly. He needed to be strong and healthy to enable him "to undergo the labors of our society." Finally, the unsightliness of Socrates notwithstanding, he would benefit by "a comely presence for the edification of those with whom we have to deal." Did the candidate's attributes show a favorable balance? Then he took the oaths of obedience, chastity, and poverty, though if he happened to have piled up any material estate he was allowed to retain it so long as any income from it went to the bursar of the order, and when he died the organization was his sole and rightful legatee.

He now undertook a three-year exploration of philosophy. Cicero still hovered at his side—in fact, so total had been his immersion in the old Roman's humanism that its influence would never entirely rub off. Still, what was cardinal now to the rising Jesuit's mode of thinking was a stiff dosing from the Aristotelian bottle. Restored by the fathers to the heights from which the classical Humanists had dislodged him, the ancient thinker now ruled the Jesuit intellectual enclave. "Never," commanded the Ratio, "deviate from Aristotle." Thus Jesuit pedagogy undertook to amalgamate the classical heritage, which had been revived and revitalized by the illuminati of the Renaissance, with the Aristotelian philosophical tradition, which for so many centuries had held the great theological doctors of the medieval church in its thrall.

THE MAKING OF A TEACHER

Once his philosophic studies were out of the way, the young man—he was now just over twenty—was assigned to teach grammar in one of the society's farflung lower schools, where he might have to suffer for the rest of his life. But if it had pleased a gracious Providence to reserve him for the performance of a higher service, his trials as a grammatical don obtained for only a couple of years, whereupon he was ordered to a Jesuit seat of the higher learning to prepare himself for the priesthood. When, four years following, he was ready, he stood for ordination, and in most cases he devoted his remaining working years to the sacerdotal practice. But if his professors had detected in him a glint of talent for teaching, he was granted a chance to prove his gift with another two-year period in the student's bench to make himself ready to offer instruction in one of the Jesuit colleges. When he was through, he was not only as educated as his professors could make him; he was also thoroughly versed in what then passed for the art of teaching. By modern lights this had its serious limitations, but in its own time it was without rival. Into the crucible of its making had gone not only the collective thought and ingenuity of the society's master pedagogues, but also their effort to fashion teachers of a surpassing merit. In consequence, the general run of Jesuit preceptors, whether in the lower schools or the higher, was of a superior order.

The superlative care the Jesuits took in bringing out the talents of their teachers did not cease once they began their classroom work. To ensure that their instruction would not deteriorate, they were subject to a monthly inspection by their superior, the rector of the college, who not only observed their classroom practice but was required to offer his critical commentary and counsel. The rector's legman, so to say, was the prefect of studies, to whom was assigned the chore of visiting every class once a fortnight to take account of its general progress, besides passing judgment upon the performance of the teacher. He was under instruction to keep an especially sharp eye on new teachers to guard against their deviation from the settled method and the expression of any proscribed ideas. Did the teacher satisfy the prefect? Then the supervisor was to grant him his commendation. On the other hand, if he had flunked in one way or another, he was to be told of his deficiency firmly but politely. In any case, he was to "obey the prefect of studies in all matters pertaining to studies and the discipline of the classes."

The fathers gave much time and thought to the forging of first-rate teachers, and obviously their training was not of a type that permitted innovation. Hence, unless novelty lay within the prescribed bounds of the official method, invention was taboo. "If there are any too prone to innovation," warned the ever-ready Ratio, "or too liberal in their views, they shall be removed from the responsibility of teaching."

THE ORGANIZATION OF A CLASS

The same meticulous care that went into the confection of their method of teaching went also into the organization of their classes. Taking a rather friendly view of competition, the Jesuits split every class into two opposing units, each constantly eager to outshine the other in its collective luster. Again, every class was arranged into crews of ten, each under the direction of a monitor, or in Jesuit lingo, a *decurion,* who not only heard his comrades rattle off their learned-by-heart assignments, but also reported on their assorted derelictions, mental, moral, spiritual, and the like. Ordinarily, such a fellow should have enjoyed all the popularity of a member of the Gestapo, yet somewhat surprisingly the monitorial office was well regarded and was even accorded a decent respect. Finally, every boy was pitted against a personal rival, who, like a terrier lurking at a rathole, was forever on the alert so that he might catch his rival in an error. Should such luck befall one, then he was under orders to disclose the faux pas forthwith before both master and classmates. Naturally, the victim, who was a rival to his rival, enjoyed similar rights and prerogatives.

Besides the general class recitation, with rivals leaping to their feet to challenge rivals, a teacher might resort to a quasi-lecture, wherein he undertook to explore and clarify the matter under study. Selected from Cicero's sumptuous spread of literary tidbits, this might range from an uncomplicated declaration of a couple of lines to a paragraph of some length and bafflement. The professor began with a recital of the entire piece. Next he unriddled its intent and meaning. Then he proceeded to dissect it, at first sentence by sentence, then word by word, reflecting upon its syntax and organization, its bearing upon history, geography, and letters, and anything else that caught the preceptorial eye. Rather curiously, an almost identical procedure had been given the world by Quintilian as long ago as the first century, and in France, in the guise of an *explication de texte,* it still has its defenders. While the professor performed his surgery, his students listened to his running commentary and took notes. Finally, to make sure that nothing had escaped, the professor recapitulated the whole passage.

It has been charged by some that in this performance the students were so many wooden Indians who listened passively and jotted down an occasional remark. But the facts ridicule the accusation. Not only were the hearers incited by the narrator to participate vocally, they were also expected to raise questions which their mentor was under obligation to answer with clarity and good conscience. Like all masterful explanations, those of the Jesuit teacher were richly stocked with pertinent comparisons, or as the cliché of the moment runs, they were given relevance. But in no case was he to allow his thoughts to wander. His assignment, he should ever remember, was to teach Ciceronian Latin. Nor should he entertain the delusion that he had a right to speak his own views. "Even on matters where there is no risk to faith or devotion," the Ratio cautioned him, "no one shall introduce . . . any opinion that does not have suitable authority without first consulting his superior." In sum, within the walls of his classroom, the teacher was never to let himself be carried away by the passion of his pedagogy; his first and only task was to hammer the orthodox viewpoint into youth's malleable mind.

Finally, the fathers invested heavily in the educational value of debates, or, as these had been designated since antiquity, disputations. These zesty give-and-takes were the students' special delight, the demitasse and cognac, as it were, that imparted a warm glow following the consumption of the more solid academic rations. There was a debate every day, and to give it an ear the entire student body assisted at the session. Some debates, however, were strictly private, and they took place behind closed doors. The more pretentious disputations, as might be expected, were scheduled on gala public occasions.

Since memory has a way of cheating, the fathers went to great lengths to persuade it to become a trained and trustworthy servant. For this purpose they put a hearty emphasis on drill and review. Thus, following the morning's prescribed spiritual overture, the boy's instruction began with a rehearsal of what he had learned on the preceding day, and before the present day was past he was made to recount point for point what new material he had stored in the filing cabinet of his memory. There was a review at the end of the week, another at the end of the month, still another at the end of the term, and an imperious, comprehensive one at the end of the academic year.

The idea currently aired in some groves of academe that examinations can be ruinous to the student's health and psyche would have amused the fathers. Examinations were as certain and inexorable as the flow of time. No one with eyes and ears was spared, neither the quick nor the slow nor those in between. The interrogation they confronted was always viva voce rather than in writing, and it was executed with the entire student body looking on. Those who had set their hopes on becoming teachers or theologians were required to pass cum laude; the rest were granted a greater latitude.

CONCERNS FOR THE STUDENT

Like their founder, Jesuit teachers were keenly aware of the subtle ways of Homo sapiens, whether he was a fledgling or fully plumed. At a time when the belief prevailed that to make learning effective it had to be administered in repugnant doses and in a dismal atmosphere, the fathers advocated moderation. Never should a teacher show partiality, and in no case was a pupil—or a master—to be treated unjustly. The travail of learning was to be tempered with play—outdoors when the weather was affable. That human beings vary in attributes and capacities was an obvious fact to Jesuit mentors long before psychologists made it a scientific truth. Hence, although in his *Constitutions* Ignatius had stressed the importance of uniformity, yet he also recommended that masters should give boys of some particular talent extra help and counsel. In addition, a boy could be promoted at any time, but he could also be put back.

In a day when disease and death scourged the land with forbidding frequency, Jesuit schoolmen, for all their intellectual bent, had the acumen to do everything then within the human ken to encourage and promote the health and well-being of their protégés. Their concern doubtless issued directly from the experience of their founder. His austere and excessive penitential exercises almost destroyed him, and as the years brought him wisdom he trod more or less in the Aristotelian path of moderation. In fact, as early as 1539, in its first statutes, which were substantially the work of Ignatius, the order put its prohibition on "fasts, scourgings . . . , hair shirts, or other mortifications under penalty of grievous sin." "We must look after the body and keep its health," Loyola wrote some years later to Francisco Borgia, Duke of Gandia, who was destined to become the society's third general, "inasmuch as it serves the soul and fits it for the service and glorification of God."

The Jesuits were strict, but they were not inhuman—indeed, for their time, when schoolmasters, taken as a lot, were so many Simon Legrees, the fathers by comparison were gentle men. Like Switzerland's renowned Pestalozzi of a later day, Ignatius held the opinion that "discipline is a thinking love." "Let there be no haste in punishment," bade the Ratio, "nor too much accusing." When Jesuit pupils performed meritoriously, the fathers plied them with praise. But being boys, and hence presumably human, their will was sometimes weaker than their good intentions, and they broke the rules. To deal with minor offenses, as, for example, making a tour of the classroom or even leaving it altogether without the teacher's approval, the master privileged one of the boys to act as "censor," and empowered him to impose small penalties. For major wrongs the Jesuits employed the services of a specialist. Known as a "corrector," he was not a member of their society; nevertheless, within the confines of his practice he enjoyed what amounted to plenary powers. Whenever he was summoned to employ his art, however, the Ratio invited his affable discretion. But when wickedness became a habit which not even the corrector's sorcery could repair, then in the last resort the malefactor might be condemned to exile, either temporary or permanent.

IN RETROSPECT

Contemplated in retrospect, Jesuit education falls considerably below that of today. But regard it against the dark shadows of its own time and you will see a radiant incandescence. No other system of schooling of those times had been so scrupulously planned and executed. The blueprint from which it emerged, the Ratio Studiorum, was thorough and comprehensive, so all-embracing, indeed, that it left nothing to chance, neither organization nor curriculum nor method, nor the qualification and preparation of Jesuit teachers, nor even the details of their supervision. So notable was the attainment of the Jesuit groves that they incited the envy of Sir Francis Bacon, a Briton and an Anglican. "Such as they are," he vouchsafed, "would they were ours."

With so much stress on a high educational quality, Jesuit pupils were hard pressed, and of those who presented themselves as freshmen, only a small proportion would reach the finish line. Those who succeeded were magnificently schooled. They could write and speak a suave Latin; they were on familiar terms with the cream of the ancient writings; and they were as erudite and disciplined as the most advanced pedagogy employed by expert teachers could make them. Against them, however, the indictment has been placed that they were ignorant of whole continents of human, intellectual, and cultural experience—in particular, in the budding natural sciences and the fine arts; that they were ill at ease in the practice of original and independent thinking; and that the ideas they favored and expressed were like so many Model T's, standardized and assembled in accordance with the official Catholic design. For the large horde of Jesuit graduates this was undoubtedly so, but it was not altogether so. Like the issue of any other school, the bulk of Jesuit alumni have long since been sucked into anonymity, but for this predominant multitude there remains the compensation of the scintillating exception, creative and free-thinking men like Corneille, Descartes, Lamartine, Molière, Calderon, and Tasso— even such incurable scoffers as Diderot and Voltaire. "What did I observe during the seven years I spent under the Jesuit roof?" asked that deadly foe of Mother Church. "A life," he replied, "of diligence, moderation, and order. They devoted every hour of the day to our instruction or to the fulfillment of their strict vows. As evidence of this," he went on, "I appeal to the testimony of the thousands who, like myself, were educated by them."

The reputable supremacy of Jesuit instruction, besides the fact that from its lowest through its highest learning it was dispensed gratis, even to non-Catholics, compelled the respect of its natural adversaries. "How many of us," a Protestant man of God permitted himself to ask, "are so learned and well educated as the Jesuits?" And how many, he continued, "are so zealous and skilled in teaching as these emissaries of the Roman Antichrist?" Nor was there ever a shortage of benevolent Catholics who stood ready to grace their wealth with good works by providing the capital needed to erect and furnish a schoolhouse, and the chapel and buildings which were their necessary accessories, and last but by no means least, a sufficient endowment for the perpetual maintenance of their staff, pedagogic and profane.

In 1550, a decade after the society had obtained the papal authorization, its first school, the Collegium Romanum, in Rome, was ready to shine its scholarly light. It was, in a manner of speaking, a pedagogic experimental station where, so Loyola hoped, the order would try out various curricula, methods, and textbooks, and then would recommend those that met its rigorous requirements for general adoption in the entire Jesuit academic chain. The year following saw the establishment of the Collegium Germanicum, also in the Eternal City. True to its name, the new school purveyed its instruction for the most part to German youths, handpicked by the Jesuit fathers for their brightness, and destined in the long run to play an effective part in persuading numerous German Prostestants to mend their ways and return to the bosom of a forgiving Mother Church. As year followed year the increase in the number of Jesuit schools and missions gathered force, and presently we observe them carrying on not only in various parts of Europe, but in such faraway lands as India, China, and Japan in the East, and in various latitudes and longitudes in the West. In 1556, when Loyola died, there existed some one hundred Jesuit centers of learning; a century or so later one could poll four times as many; and by 1706, the sesquicentennial of the saint's demise, with a string of some eight hundred schools enrolling around 200,000 students scattered over the globe, the figure reached its flood height. Thereafter the flow began to ebb, and in slightly more than half a century the number of schools receded to some 725.

THE JESUITS IN CHANGE

It was on the continent that the Society of Jesus exerted its most strenuous effort. There, as self-declared soldiers in the army of God, the members drove themselves unsparingly, preaching and teaching to arrest, and, if possible, to reverse the onward sweep of the Reformation. So devoted were they to their mission, and so indomitable in their determination to fulfill it, that when they were through they had the satisfaction of having regained a good part of Germany, nearly all of Bohemia and Hungary, and the whole of Christian Poland for worship in the Roman rite. Seldom, if ever, had so small a host won a victory of such far-reaching consequence; and just as rarely had an institution been so vividly etched by the work and thought of a single personality.

In their zeal to liquidate the Reformation, the fathers relied not only on the power of their teaching and preaching; presently some of them undertook to support their exegetics with the sidearm of politics. There is no gainsaying, politics being politics, that in their eagerness to advance the interests of the papacy at any cost—or as the refinement of their casuists expressed it, the greater glory of God—all too often they polluted the probity of their devotion, and that in consequence, their methods were frequently devious and even shameful. The years saw their operations fall under opprobrium not only among Protestants, but among Catholics as well. Nation after nation took steps against the society, proscribing its activities and ordering its members into exile. In 1772 Pope Clement XIV closed the Jesuit seminary in Rome, and shortly afterward he shut down the order's remaining seminaries in the Papal States. Finally, in 1773, recognizing that "the Society of Jesus was not in the position to produce the rich fruits and remarkable advantages for which it was instituted," the Holy Father pronounced its universal suppression.

Some two score years following, the Society of Jesus enjoyed a glorious rebirth. But during the long span of its dormancy the world had changed. The festerings which had fevered the proponents of the Counter-Reformation against the fallen-away Protestants, though by no means healed, had nevertheless ceased to be a paramount concern. True, the Jesuits—or, as their American students later nicknamed them, the Jebbies—still swore their solemn oaths, and they still unleashed their zeal to enhance God's glory, and to extend their utmost support to the incumbent heir of Peter. To this end they still ran their schools and missions the world around. In the springtide of their labor, the Jesuits had proferred Europe the most advanced and proficient scheme of education ever heard of, the product of a never-remitting, trial-and-error, and pragmatic success. Set down in its beginnings in Loyola's *Constitutions,* the scheme was the essence of his educational creed. Subsequently, in a more elaborate and methodical arrangement, it was translated into the Ratio Studiorum, which has gone into our chronicle of human achievement as the first recorded endeavor in modern times to give order and system to the entire educational enterprise. At the same time, the Ratio, lacking resilience, barricaded the passage to the values and requirements of a world in continuous flux. Consequently, as the years drove on, Jesuit education lost its youthful buoyancy, and with the fashioning of an improved and more up-to-date pedagogy in the hands of such adroit educational reformers as Comenius, Rousseau, and Pestalozzi, its once vaunted superiority suffered the rust of time. Not until the Ratio's moderate overhauling in the thirties of the nineteenth century and, more important, the general unbinding of its restraints in the twentieth, were the Jesuits in a position to catch up with the educational progress which in the passage of the many years had left them stranded.

Chapter 10

Jan Amos Comenius

THE TIMES OF COMENIUS

Jan Amos Comenius, born Komensky (1592–1670), a miller's son, originated in Nivnice, Moravia, now in the heartland of Czechoslovakia, and he died in Amsterdam seventy-eight years later. The period his life spanned is celebrated among other things for the accomplishments of a long line of notable men, such mental wizards, for example, as Isaac Newton, René Descartes, and John Locke, to speak of only three. But like our own age of resplendent wonders, the seventeenth century was cursed by the incubus of man's inhumanity to man, inflamed by bigotry and fanaticism, and afflicted by the tragedy of the seemingly endless Thirty Years War, in which Catholics and Protestants undertook to exterminate one another. Though Comenius was a man of peace, the war snared him in its web. His home was twice destroyed; his family dispersed; and his treasured library and manuscripts put to the torch. Uprooted for much of his life, he was, as it were, a man without a country, living and working now in Poland, now in Sweden, now somewhere else, and when his time was up, dying an expatriate in the low and clammy flats of Holland.

Although destiny had labeled the miller's son for a scholarly life, his early schooling was of the sparest sort, embracing little more than a feeble jousting with the three R's, learning the catechism by heart, and exercising his larynx in hymnody. But what his schooling lacked in substance, it more than made amends for by the ferocity of its discipline. It left its mark on young Komensky, both physically and psychologically, and in later years when he himself adorned the magisterial stool, he still bemoaned the blisterings he had suffered as a schoolboy. Like too many others, his school, he said as he reminisced, had been "a slaughterhouse of the mind." When he was sixteen, which is to say, ten years or so beyond the then customary starting age, he betook himself to a Latin school to get a grip on the Roman tongue without which no one in those days—not even an Einstein—could hope to be a man of learning. A person of deep religious feelings, Comenius said his prayers as a member of the Moravian Brethren, a sect of small proportion which patterned its beliefs on the doctrines of Jan Huss, who met a heretic's death at the stake.

It was Comenius's hope that a day would come when he would be called to shepherd the Brethren as one of their ordained men of God, and to make himself fit and ready he frequented the lectures in divine and moral science at Heidelberg. When he was through, a year or so later—he was now twenty-two—the Brethren turned him down. They admired and commended his zeal and erudition, but as older men and, therefore, wiser, they regarded him as too youthful to make an effective pastor. Instead they cast him in the schoolman's role, and set him to perform in their village school at Prerov. A schoolmaster, hence, by accident rather than by choice, Comenius found teaching the young surprisingly agreeable, so much so that, when some years later he was elevated into the sacred cloth, he insisted on continuing his teaching in conjunction with his pastoring—a fairly common practice in those free and easy times, and one wherein he engaged in one way or another to his end.

Save for his casual observations as a schoolboy, Comenius was guiltless of any pedagogic knowledge until he was twenty, when the name of Wolfgang Ratke came to his notice. A German and a fanatical Lutheran, given to self-handshakings, Ratke—or, as he preferred to be addressed in the circle of the learned, Raticius—had fathered a new method of teaching, the finest ever heard of, he freely admitted, "for the service of Christendom," by which he meant especially its Lutheran sector. Although Ratke took great pains to keep his method safely padlocked in an impenetrable vault of secrecy in hopes of unloading it presently to some well-heeled patron, Comenius was privy to its essential theorems, most of which he found attractive, and some of which he even honored with a few fragrant words. In truth, when subsequently he himself incubated his own treatise on the pedagogical art, he incorporated a number of Ratke's doctrines.

Stronger than the suction of Ratke was the pull of Francis Bacon and his bullhorn blasts for the advancement of learning by way of objective and systematic experimentation. Although Comenius toiled as a professional surrogate of the Lord, he was not, like so many of his reverend colleagues, lacking in hospitality to the new revelations of the natural sciences. He regarded them not with fear, but with hope. At one time he even owned a copy of *The Revolution of the Heavenly Bodies,* that grisly Copernican concoction, though in frankness it must be added that the Moravian rejected its theory—not, however, on grounds of an insufficiency of empirical evidence, but rather for its gainsaying certain passages in Holy Writ.

THE GREAT DIDACTIC—A SYSTEM OF EDUCATION

Except when he was imparting knowledge in the classroom, or sermonizing the Brethren to lead a devout and upright life, or when he was traveling under his own steam or being driven by militant Catholics baying at his heels, during his working hours Comenius applied his industry to writing. His pen was seldom idle, and the ink it consumed and the paper it filled must have run to a large wagonload. The range of his composition was not only of an almost incredible heft; it was also of an infinite variety. He was just a year over twenty when, as a student at Heidelberg, he began to put together a Latin-Czech lexicon, but it was more than forty-odd years later, at a time in life when most of us are lolling in a state of mandatory retirement, that he put down the work's final period. Not content with having just one pot simmering on the stove, in 1616—he was then twenty-two—he began preparing another, this time a Czech encyclopedia. He called it *A Theater of All Things,* and it required sixteen volumes. He had scarcely installed himself in the Brethren's Prerov school when the idea seized him that what the world sorely needed, especially its youth, was a new Latin grammar. Completed in a comparative romp, the book was ready in 1616. It was the first of several grammars, each an alteration and improvement of its predecessor until, with the appearance in 1658 of the *Orbis Sensalium Pictus,* or in English *The World in Pictures,* Comenius reached the top of the schoolbook writer's pole of glory.

Comenius's pedagogical canon lies conserved between the covers of *The Great Didactic,* which he wrote while he was a fugitive in Poland. It showed itself at first in a Czech incarnation—the year of its appearance was probably 1632. Its publication incited no shattering acclamation, probably because to most people the language of the Czechs made no sense. A quarter of a century passed before the book was put into the scholar's Latin, but even then, though Comenius's views became more widely known, the mass of pedagogic practitioners were anesthetic to its merits. Not unaware of such a likelihood, Comenius, like Luther before him, had the foresight to address a letter to all men of good conscience, especially those to whom God had given something to say in the everyday affairs of government, the church, or the home, to remind them of their sacred responsibility toward the little ones and to urge upon them the providing of the young with a decent education. Only thus, he concluded, could the wickedness of mankind be curbed and, possibly, even extirpated. The first comprehensive treatise on education to issue from the pen of a Christian man of learning, *The Great Didactic* essayed to lay bare "the whole art of teaching all things to all men," and how to do it "quickly, pleasantly, and thoroughly," by giving instruction and counsel "in all things necessary for the present and for the future life," including "true knowledge, gentle morality, and the deepest piety." Lest some potential reader might be crushed under the impression of the prodigious magnitude of such a proposal, Comenius hastened to reassure him that what he had in mind was in reality "an easy and sure method."

If Comenius's premise—that the purpose of education is to prepare the sons of man for happiness on earth as in heaven—is not without logic or sense, then it follows that the boon of learning should be within reach of every child, rich or poor, in skirts or pantaloons. This was especially true, as Comenius was sure, since, all men having been created in the image of the Heavenly Father, they needs must have a common destiny. Nor should the business be postponed until the child has celebrated his sixth or seventh anniversary. Let him start instead in the so-called "Mother School," which in actuality is not a school at all but the home, where among the many other duties her role of housewife has imposed upon the mother, she will steer her offspring along the precarious path to knowledge, virtue, and piety. Let her begin to teach him what is right and what is wrong as soon as he is able to understand, and let her continue along this line until he is ready for his books at school. To give mothers a helping hand in their pursuit of the pedagogical enterprise, Comenius accommodated them with a special handbook, *The School of Infancy,* wherein he recorded the cardinal facts they needed to know. Comenius's appointment of the mother as the child's first teacher during the years that count, an age when he is still very young and formative, is the first of its sort to be put forth in Christendom. In some of its purpose it resembles the kindergarten, in which certain family-tree specialists have detected a lineal descendant.

At the age of six the youngster, having suffered his early conditioning for happiness in the present as well as in the endless time ahead, is ready to take a look at his first schoolmaster. The meeting is achieved in what Comenius called the Vernacular School, so denominated because its instruction was to be in the mother tongue, a practice which is taken for granted nowadays, of course, but which in Comenius's time was still rare. Just as rare was Comenius's insistence that education must be for both girls and boys, a dictum which had been laid down by Plato and seconded by Erasmus, but which was still far removed from universal acceptance. Just as striking, albeit altogether in accord with the ideology of Prostestantism's foremost deep thinkers, was Comenius's contention that since education is a Christian duty, attendance at the sessions of the lower school must be made compulsory for every child until the twelfth birthday.

Pursuant to its elementary nature, the Vernacular School grounded its pupils in the three R's, besides offering them some fleeting glimpses of history, including the creation, fall, and redemption of man, geography, the stars and planets, and the trades and occupations then in currency—all in all a rather amplitudinous offering when set against the ordinary curriculum of the time. To promote the "gentle morality and the deepest piety" so dear to the Comenian heart, the Vernacular School put as much stress on ennobling and elevating the character of its clients as it did on enlarging their stock of "true knowledge." To this end it imparted to them the biblical truth, reinforced with the contents of their catechism, tales about ne'er-do-ills and their unfailing rewards, and about ne'er-do-goods and their inevitable agonizing retribution, besides the usual regular recourse to prayer and hymnody.

Once set free from forced attendance in the lower school, the mass of its graduates celebrated their deliverance by making an end of their contact with formal learning and going their appointed ways. Awaiting those who, in the Comenian phrase, desired something "higher than the workshop," was the Latin School, which got its name because Latin was its specialty. That girls should have any dealings with that outland tongue ran against the prevailing grain of opinion; not only did they have no need for it professionally as did their brothers, but they also lacked the mental and physical capacity to cope with it successfully. Although the province of the Latin School was to convert its pupils into first-rate Latinists, it also treated of some other learning, such as the mother tongue, physics, mathematics, astronomy, logic, geography, history, and chronology, besides a bit of Greek and Hebrew. Needless to say, Comenius tolerated no cessation of his campaign to protect the young against moral contamination. Hence, he made his grammarians continue to ponder their worn and dog-eared catechisms and to make the rafters of their schoolroom quiver with the performance of their hymnal prodigies. In addition, God continued to be much bespoken.

After lending themselves to such endeavor for a half-dozen years, the

Latin scholars—they were now in their elderly teens—were rewarded with the right to sweat through a rather searching examination. If they passed, they were granted admission to the higher learning. But if they failed, then their academic hopes were dashed, and in lieu of having a chance to snare the prized doctoral bonnet, they had to settle for something less, a scrivener's clerkship, say, in the employ of some commanding man of God or some nabob of international trade, or even a job on the public payroll.

Those taken for grooming in the higher grove were put upon during the next six years to devote their "undivided energies to that subject for which [they are] evidently suited by nature," for example, law, medicine, divine and moral science, teaching, physics, public speaking, music making, and suchlike arts and sciences. To inoculate the student against the toxicocity of a deadening bookishness, he was bidden to take an occasional respite from his studies and to fare forth into the living world, asea and ashore, to savor its complex phenomena at first hand. If he happened to be one of the few men on earth endowed with a conspicuously consuming mind, Comenius— doubtless holding the mirror up to himself—proposed that the young man "be urged to pursue all the branches of study that there will always be some men whose knowledge is encyclopedic."

With the end of their university years, for most students the prowl for knowledge ceased. They had engaged in it formally for eighteen years, and most of them no doubt discharged a prolonged sigh of relief when the business at last was done. But not all. A few remained whose cerebrums were forever bestirred by the lure of the intellectual chase, and for these addicts Comenius proposed a Universal College, an Everest, as it were, in the mountain range of scholarship, where the great savants of the world were to open their mental throttles, singly and in congress, to bring new light and truth into the world. Inspired, it may well be, by Sir Francis Bacon's visionary House of Solomon, the Comenian congregation of high-voltage intellects was to encourage research and the exchange of thought so as "to spread the light of wisdom throughout the human race . . . and benefit humanity by new and useful inventions."

What was peculiarly novel in Comenius's plan of school organization at the time he commended it to the world was that it created an articulated structure—an "educational ladder," as the *genus Americanus* calls it— whereby every school from the rudimentary to the graduate is brought together into a single entity. What the Europeans entertained instead was three separate schools—elementary, secondary, and higher—each conceived at a different time in history, and responding to new cultural forces, and each addressing itself to its own purposes and social groups. The Comenian arrangement was of course purely theoretical, and so, for all its inherent common sense, it was to remain for many generations to come.

Indeed, the twentieth century was on the calendar before various European nations, endeavoring to rid themselves of their crippling organizational relic, undertook to coordinate their schools into a more coherent system. But tradition, especially in the domain of education, is tenacious, and so, except for Communist Russia among the larger powers, an educational system à la Komensky, brought together like a string of beads into a single piece, from the infant school through the university, is still in the process of evolving rather than of actual being. Meanwhile, in the American republic, blessed by good fortune and impelled by the invocations of democracy, over the years an articulated school system, the educational ladder, actually materialized.

LUST FOR KNOWLEDGE—PANSOPHIA

Comenius's lust for knowledge, his passion to collect and exhibit it for all the world to behold, drove him, like an insatiable hunger, throughout his long and incredibly productive life. One first discerns it in his early twenties with the compilation of his Latin-Czech dictionary and his many-volumed Czech encyclopedia. One glimpses it in his schoolmastering as he tells his pupils to learn not only as they read about things in their books, but by constant scrutiny of actual things in nature and in the man-made world about them. And one sees it in his copious writings, particularly in his textbooks. Finally, one notes it plainly stated in his plan to assemble a posse of the world's foremost scholars for the purpose of putting together every shred of knowledge from A to Z in a work which was to be known as *Pansophia.* The idea was scarcely a striking morsel of news, such confections having been attempted as long ago as the Middle Ages, not only in Christendom but in Islam as well. In fact, during Comenius's own lifetime, his friend and erstwhile teacher, the Rev. John Henry Alstead, had braved such a wonder in his *Encyclopedia of all the Sciences,* a 120-volume project. What was new about Comenius's pansophic proposal, however, was his suspicion that the body of knowledge had grown so large that no one person, however gigantic his erudition, could possibly hope to track it down.

Plagued by difficulties from the start, Comenius's brainchild was doomed to die in embryo. For one thing, the intellectual luminaries needed to produce such a work were in short supply. Still more damaging was the lack of money. Nevertheless, so agog for knowledge was this man that he simply refused to harbor the thought of possible failure, and in 1641, at the urging of his friend and fellow thinker, Samuel Hartlib, he made for England in hopes of drumming up support for his project. With Hartlib and several of his big-brained associates—including John Milton—to cheer him on, Comenius presented his pansophic blueprint to Parliament, but the lawmakers, enmeshed in their conflict with their mulish sovereign, the first Charles, were in no mood to ruminate over encyclopedias. At that moment, moreover, as if to make sure that Comenius's scheme would stand no chance whatever, the Fates prompted the rambunctious Irish to erupt in one of their perennial rebellions. When the rumor mill presently ground out the tidings that the insurgents had made cadavers of 200,000 Englanders in the course of a single night, Comenius wasted no time in deciding that he needed a change of scene more than money, and he straightway made for cover on the Continent.

One such experience is usually enough to daunt any man, but not this irrepressible Moravian. As the years chased on, his vision continued to enchant him. To nurture its materialization, he worked with an endless diligence, searching and studying, the while piling up a colossal pyramid of notes. But all his zeal and labor was doomed to nothingness. In 1656, enraged by the unseemly politicking of the Moravian Brethren, then enjoying asylum in the Polish town of Nissa, a mob burned Comenius's house to the ground. In its smoldering wreckage lay the ashes of his books and writings and the myriad notes he had so laboriously collected over the years for *Pansophia*.

WRITINGS

Not all of Comenius's dreams were idle. Indeed, for a specialist in pedagogical theory, he was remarkably practical, even utilitarian. To be sure, many of his exalted hopes did not come to fruit until long after he was in his grave. But during his stay on earth his educational practice was considerable. He taught school in his native land as well as in Poland and Hungary. It was in the latter at a place called Sarospatak that he came close to transforming his diaphanous world of pedagogical idealism into reality. There he aspired to convert his school into a vest-pocket Latin state, wherein the learners would be quarantined from the world outside. It would be a mini-Rome, so to speak, with everybody speaking in Latin, a state which was subject to its own jurisprudence, governance, and mores—Christian, needless to state, rather than pagan. Unhappily for Comenius, his plan fell into discredit even among his brothers on the faculty who rejected it as too radical, not to say somewhat tinged with insanity, and so it came to grief. In Sweden, where Comenius lived for ten of his many more than three score years, he devoted his time and energy to the practical job of overhauling and revitalizing the Scandinavian schools.

But it was in the composition of Latin textbooks that he set off his greatest glitter. True enough, the dour Latin grammars which for centuries had pressed so heavily on the natural jocosity of medieval boyhood had long since been done in by the newer grammars of Lily and Melanchthon, both classical Humanists, the one an Anglo-Saxon, the other a Teuton. But even these inclined to be tedious, and all too often their abstract wordiness put them beyond the comprehension of their readers. Erasmus, it may be recalled, had given them challenge with his pert and joysome *Colloquies,* but its drollery had given offense to serious upholders of Christian decorum. Comenius, as has been mentioned, had scarcely begun to pace the class-room floor when he made up his mind to enrich the world with a Latin reader which would be more in key with his own pedagogical principles. It appeared in type in 1631 as the *Janua Linguarum Reserata,* or the *Gate of Languages Unlocked.*

Designed to serve beginners as a simple introduction to the Latin idiom, the *Janua,* true to its author's obsession to teach everything to everybody, attempted a great deal more. It was, Comenius made known, "an easy way of understanding any language, as well as the beginning of the liberal arts." To gain his end he packed its pages with some 8,000 Latin words and their vernacular equivalents, many of them relating to things discernible in the everyday world, which he thereupon stitched into several hundred sentences. Bottomed on the Comenian theme that in learning one does best by proceeding from the simple to the complex, the *Janua*'s material was graded accordingly, beginning pianissimo with short pronouncements about the familiar, and maneuvering to more intricate observations on remote matters. The general idea of such a manual was no novelty, a very similar one having been written by an Irish Jesuit named William Bateus (born Batty), a teacher in Spain. Not only was the Irishman's composition in type some fifteen years before Comenius's, but even its title, *Janua Linguarum,* while no pearl, seems to have inspired Comenius sufficiently to have caused him to cabbage it.

However that may be, Comenius's handbook achieved what in the textbook world must be set down as a delirious success. Acclaimed around the globe as "the golden book," it was translated into one language after another, including Arabic and Mongolian. Yet for all the panegyrics heaped upon it, whether emotional or otherwise, the *Janua* had its blemishes. For one thing, to unroll the immense panorama which the author envisioned it brooked no repetition—a pedagogic instrument for more years than one can remember, and without which learning becomes difficult or even impossible. For another thing, the *Gate of Languages* essayed to unlock too much, with the result that it laid an inordinately heavy burden on even the brightest of its consumers—a situation which Comenius, sound teacher that he was, was not long in grasping. The upshot was that presently he resorted to his corrective clippers, and in 1633, two years after its introduction to the schoolroom, the *Janua,* judiciously sheared, gave way to a simple successor, the *Vestibulum,* or *Vestibule* (or as a more recent verbal decorator has put it, the *Entrance Hall),* which, like its antecedent, soon acquired a large and international audience.

Comenius wrote several other Latin books, including a grammar, the *Atrium,* and an anthology, the *Palatium.* But his greatest schoolbook coup was a picture book, the *Orbis Sensalium Pictus,* or *The World in Pictures.* Printed in 1658 at Nurnberg, it presented some 150 illustrated subjects, from birds and bees to a tailor's workshop, a cobbler's, and a ropemaker's to justice, temperance, the phases of the moon, vermin, disease, human disfigurements, a burial, and, fittingly enough, the Last Judgment. Like athletes in a sports arena, each illustrated object bears an identifying number to which reference is made below the picture in two columns, one in Latin and the other in the reader's native tongue. The volume, its maker was at pains to have us understand, was "a pleasant introduction to the Latin language" as well as "in the learning of the mother tongue." As the astute Moravian had the psychological horse sense to foresee, children were awed and entertained by his pictorial wonderland, not only the young per se, but the youngster that lurks in even the most oxydized gaffer among us. In consequence, many a father found himself putting down his pennies on the counter for a copy of the Comenian gallery.

Like its precursors, the *Janua* and the *Vestibulum,* the *Orbis Pictus* had the effect of the legendary mouse trap, and so presently it was attracting readers in droves. It visited its lessons upon them in school after school, and before it terminated its sensational run it saw itself translated into several dozen languages. To Europeans it offered its intellectual ministrations for not quite two centuries, while over here, where the study of Latin fell on dark days much earlier than in the Old World, it was still disarming and instructing the sons of the New York élite so late as 1810. To be sure, licentiates in the department of antiquarian affairs have on occasion issued outraged protestations to dispel the view that Comenius invented the illustrated textbook, and to insist that it had actually been anticipated by several others, notably in the *Ars Memorativa,* published in 1477 at Augsburg, but scarcely ever heard of nowadays, and, more notably still, in a work put out even before that by a Chinese metaphysician. But who cares? The plain fact is that Comenius's little offering, so strainlessly and modestly put together, was the first illustrated text to enjoy a prolonged engagement in the shrines of learning. Not only did it have a long life, but, reexamined from the current vantage point, for all its obsoleteness it still retains a bit of its original fizz.

For some reason that even scholars have been unable to make out, the common saw that success breeds the flattery of imitation did not apply in the case of the *Orbis Pictus.* Perhaps such a notion is a mere delusion. In any event, for all the high testimony to the book's surpassing excellence, it was not until 1774, or 116 years after the *Orbis Pictus*'s birth, before another schoolman, a Hamburger by the name of Johann Basedow, made an earnest effort to compose a pictured schoolbook.

THE MAN AND HIS APPROACH—A SUMMARY

The bulk of Comenius's educational theory, as has been said, lies imbedded in the passages of *The Great Didactic,* but it is in his work and life that he gave it form and substance. A man of deep reverence and devotion, he placed virtue and piety at the head of his educational want-list. Our schools, he wrote, should seek "to make us as like to Christ as is possible" for only thus may we indulge the hope of attaining "eternal happiness with God." Meanwhile, as we await that day of days, whatever we learn at school, be it knowledge, morality, or devoutness, should serve some useful purpose in our everyday life. "We learn," Comenius declared, "not for school, but for life"—an apothegm which has long since become a pedagogic stencil, but which, when he uttered it, was still fresh. To this end it behooves the pupils to approach their learning through things rather than words. They should "be taught to become wise by studying the heavens, the earth . . ., and they must learn to know how to investigate things themselves." The most direct way to study things, needless to say, is to observe them at first hand. Should this be impossible, then let the child look at pictures of the unavailable object. Let him contemplate "the living book of the world instead of dead papers."

If, as Comenius contended, education should enable us to achieve happiness not only as eventual residents in the golden beyond, but even on earth, then there is no reason that happiness should be excommunicated from the schoolroom. Let learning be made a gladsome process, Comenius implored, and let it be carried out in a congenial setting, in a school so trim and tidy that it lifts the heart, its chambers asmile with pictures, a garden of flowers to rejoice the eyes and the nose, and a large and grassy yard where the young can run and play—a place, in short, where children can be children. By the same yardstick, what a child is asked to learn should not be dull. Nor should it be too difficult. Instead, let it be adjusted to his powers and capacities. Let the master break with the precept then in common currency that one learns best when the going is galling, and instead let him infect his audience with the exuberance of his humor and enthusiasm. Then his classroom will become a place of intellectual excitement, and his listeners will learn readily. Indeed, since it is the child's nature to want to learn, given agreeable conditions he cannot be curbed.

It should scarcely be necessary to state that Comenius took a dim view of the brutish discipline which was then the established pedagogical vogue. Education, the Moravian remarked, should "be conducted without blows, rigor, or compulsion." Not only is the child entitled to respect, but since he is "God's most precious gift," let it ever be remembered that "rods and blows are quite unsuitable for free men, and should never be used in school." For all such ethereal wisdom, when he dealt with concrete cases in the classroom, Comenius showed no reluctance to adjust his sights. Since, as he believed, children are not born human, but have to be directed to this high estate by counsel and instruction, there will always be some acts of juvenile malfeasance. There will be those with wickedness in their hearts, the foulmouths, the scofflaws, the blasphemers, and suchlike miscreants. For these Comenius recommended strong measures—only, after having said his piece, to soar again into the clouds of optimism with the exhortation that they "should be exercised with such frankness and sincerity . . . the pupils may feel that the action is for their own good," which, as our everyday American vernacular puts it, will be the day!

Like Rousseau, though more naïve, Comenius cherished the belief that in education nature is our most reliable director—hence his stress on learning through the senses; hence too his insistence on play and his call for learning by practice, or, as the phrase is today, learning by doing. Do artisans, for example, "learn to forge by forging, to carve by carving, and to paint by painting?" Then, urged Comenius, "let children learn to write by writing, to sing by singing, and to reason by reasoning." To support his pleading that we should use nature as our pedagogical prompter, Comenius resorted freely to analogical comparisons—he was, indeed, something of an analogy maniac who allowed his reasoning to lead him often enough into irrelevant conclusions. Do birds, in illustration, hatch their eggs in spring? Then, Comenius argued, "the education of men should be commenced in the springtime of life." And does a chicken develop slowly without any abrupt change during the progress of its unfoldment? Then it follows that "all studies should be graded by minute steps." But let us not belabor the point. Despite his schooling in dialectic, Comenius was a shoddy logician. A mystic who on the one hand gave credence to the signs and the portents and the soothsayers, Comenius on the other hand was also an admirer of Francis Bacon's commanding stress on observation, induction, and experimentation in the forwarding of our knowledge. The two are scarcely handmaids, so that, as one might expect, the Moravian, like Rousseau, occasionally meandered from the path of consistency. It was his belief—to cite a few examples—that education should be tailored at all times to the capacity and temperament of the individual learner. Yet he also declared for a single teaching method—his own, needless to say—to be employed in all subjects and in large classes, preferably of some 200 pupils.

Comenius, as has been said, occupied himself year in and year out with writing schoolbooks that made their instruction vibrant and delightful the world around. Yet, for all his tremendous success, he pronounced the business of composing his little gems to be "nauseating." In his *Great Didactic* he strove to develop a science of education, with a body of specific universal principles to be undeviatingly adhered to in the master's act of teaching. Yet, rather curiously, in his writings he calls his didactic straitjacket the "art of teaching." There are yet other discrepancies. Throughout his life he cooed for peace, apart from the occasions when his own ox, the Moravian Brethren, was being gored. Then he became as bellicose as a munitions maker. Finally, he stood 100 percent for a unified Christendom. Yet from this ecumenical circle he would exclude all adherents of the Roman Church, which he despised.

The specter of tragedy haunted Comenius through much of his life. A man of boundless magnanimity, he was powerfully sensitive to the sorrows of the world. Still, he was chronically full of hope, and he never permitted his dream of universal peace to dim. Unfortunately, the world in which he lived was infected with hate, and if he ever celebrated the happiness he craved so heartily for all God's children, then it was not in the mournful here-below, but with the angel host on high. The largest part of his life he devoted to instructing his fellowmen, but in a world keyed to the rich and powerful, Comenius's beseeching on behalf of freedom and equality for all was too slight to stand up against the hurricane raised by his antagonists. Even before his passing, his critics were roasting him in the fire of their raillery. He was the eternal quester, but somehow the power of his vision, great though it was, failed him, and when he died, he was already more than half forgotten.

Even in education, where his mind went adventuring in almost every nook and cranny of the whole pedagogical domain, he carried scarcely any weight. His schoolbooks, of course, continued to be thumbed and esteemed for well over a century after he died. But his *Great Didactic,* in which he had placed his highest hopes, had long since been sealed within the walls of the forgotten past, and it was not until the nineteenth century that it began to receive some of the respect it deserved. Meanwhile, some of the doctrines for which the Moravian is noted today had been embodied in the theory and practice of several other educational reformers. There is Rousseau, a Genevan, who in the eighteenth century urged that in education we should take our cue from nature; Pestalozzi, a Swiss, who made a point of learning by observation; Froebel, a German, who, stressing play and learning by doing, gave the world the kindergarten; and even Herbart, another German, who, for all his forbidding intellectuality, stood in full accord with Comenius on the thesis that nothing can be learned without interest to ignite the child's will to learn.

Perhaps, in the long span of time, Comenius received the recognition he was denied while he was still on earth. Even so, one must wonder at Fate's cruel capping of this man's life work. Some have blamed the ferment and upheaval of his era, the arson and hemorrhage of its protracted wars, ever the bane of bold and articulate thinking. Others point the accusing finger at the Comenian prose. He could write exhilarating books for the young at school, but when he addressed their elders, particularly his peers among the learned, he strung his words together as if they were an army pacing its monotonous two-step without the tooting and booming of a band of brass to give it life. There remains the fact that Comenius worshipped as one of the Moravian Brethren, a despised and badgered sect, cast out of their land of origin, and cried down by many as subversive and dangerous. Jan Amos Comenius may have had numerous lacks; but it cannot be said that he suffered from a shortage of detractors, or even those who would have been overjoyed to assist at his funeral.

Chapter 11

John Locke

THE FIRST THIRTY-FOUR YEARS

While Comenius was giving birth to his pedagogic wonders on the Continent, beyond the channel's other shore an Englishman was bidding fair to become renowned for his intellectual virtuosity. His name was John Locke (1632–1704)—"the wisest of human beings," as Voltaire often spoke of him. Born not far from Bristol, at that time Britain's largest city next to London, Locke was the son of a lawyer, a Puritan who mixed his legal engagement with the management of his country acreage, and, when the time came, with soldiering as an officer in the parliamentary army in the civil war against the Stuarts. There was evidently enough money in the paternal stocking to permit young John a first-rate education, commencing, as was then wont among people of his order, with tutorial instruction under the family roof until the lad turned fourteen, and continuing then with his attendance at Westminster, called by the English a "public school," but which was actually a private institution ministering largely to the carriage trade. After all these many years the school, founded in 1384, is still in active—though considerably altered—practice.

Six of his seventy-two years Locke spent at Westminster, studying Greek and Latin besides being grounded in the settled principles of Christian piety and good and peaceable manners. When he lagged or lapsed either in scholarly zeal or deportment, he received the specialized service of the school's headmaster, the eminent Dr. Busby, whose intensity in its department of correction had brought him recognition as Britain's fiercest flogger. Indeed, long after old age had weakened his arm, he still gloated in recounting that during his lifetime he had rattanned a good half of the English bishops when they were boys.

From Westminster Locke's path wound to Oxford. There he obtained a stipend, small but sufficient to maintain himself in the comfort and respectability expected from the son of a rural jurist. He held his post over thirty years when, on a writ from Charles II, he was cashiered. Meanwhile, however, besides dispensing instruction in Greek, rhetoric, and ethics, Locke had festooned himself first in the bachelor's regalia and then in the master's. He had come to Oxford in hopes of preparing himself for holy orders, but the years saw him change his mind. Instead he read Descartes, at the time all the rage among France's more or less liberal intelligentsia. Though he found himself at odds with several of the French philosopher's doctrines and, as we shall see, was to give at least one of them a potent dressing-down, it was Descartes, nevertheless, who awakened in him a life-long attraction to philosophy.

But the Frenchman was not the only inspiration to Locke's inquisitive mind. There was also Thomas Hobbes, another robust thinker; Robert Boyle and his experimental pryings into chemistry; and Thomas Sydenham, a successful medico, who, like Boyle, did not sympathize with the vaporous a priori presuppositions of the workers in his specialty, and who put his trust instead in the findings brought about by careful and systematic observation. The healing mystery was apparently to young Locke's taste and he worked at it, diligently seeking to master its arcana and frequently accompanying Sydenham on his expeditions to the ailing. In time Locke metamorphosed into a practitioner in his own right, although he never heightened his professional standing with an M.D. In truth, his forties weighed upon him, his student days long since past, when his alma mater, upon a peer's advocacy and the sovereign's approval, gave recognition to his demonstrated competence by translating him into a bachelor of medicine, *honoris causa,* a high distinction, to be sure, but for its recipient by this time more cosmetic than substantial.

ENTER LORD ASHLEY

Locke doubtless would be the first to allow that the year 1666 was one when his lucky star was shining its brightest, for it marked his introduction to

Lord Ashley, who later became Britain's first Earl of Shaftesbury. Despite the inequality of their stations in life, the two men soon shed a pleasant glow upon each other, and after a year or so Locke waved good-bye to his Oxonian quarters to install himself at Exeter House, the lord's London home. There for fifteen years he acted as his lordship's secretary and doctor, and as the guiding light and mentor of his offspring. Although Lord Ashley's personal healer was in the main a practical man, yet he also thrilled to a session of lively intellectual palaver. It was at one of these sessions with some friends at the house when they found themselves stymied in their deliberation upon certain "principles of morality and religion," that Locke set himself the task of determining what he called the "limits of human understanding." Little did he dream that the business would occupy him off and on for almost twenty years, and that when he was through it would hatch a book, *An Essay Concerning Human Understanding*. Meanwhile, his patron engaged in politics, climbing high as he progressed, only presently to fall far lower than he had risen. The upshot was that discretion commanded him to take an indeterminate leave of absence in Holland, where his secretary and doctor, alias Dr. Van der Linden, gave him the encouragement he so badly needed, and where, as a friendly counselor to political refugees, the artful doctor came to the attention of Prince William of Orange.

In 1689, when James II was forced to take to his heels and the joint sovereigns William and Mary replaced him, the fugitive Shaftesbury and his aide deemed the motherland safe enough for them to hazard a return. In his luggage Locke toted the completed manuscript of his *Essay Concerning Human Understanding,* which some connoisseurs have lauded as the "most important philosophical treatise" to flow from the pen of an Englishman. Presently Locke also put the final period on *Two Treatises on Government,* in which he not only let loose his most powerful ratiocination in defense of the revolution against the headstrong James II, but also inflicted the coup de grace on the moribund doctrine of divine right, which held that a monarch is divinely appointed, and that his relationship to his people is akin to that of a father and child. Locke's argument, which, like all his prose, he set down with a sort of surgical precision, was accorded an agreeable approbation, if not by the disordered James, then at any rate by that sovereign's undoers. Accordingly, what Locke had sown presently reaped him a bountiful harvest not only of fame and money, but even a royal appointment as commissioner of trade. The burden of his office was light, as such acknowledgments of a man of literary stature were expected to be, and so he had time aplenty in addition to a small but continuous revenue from his commissionership to enable him to continue his busy relationship with his inkstand.

HIS WRITINGS—INTRODUCTION

The passing years saw him turn out one work after another. His *Letters on Toleration* appeared in 1672. Christianity's first and fundamental principle, he asserted therein, agreeing with Spinoza, is love; hence, those Christians who are bent on the persecution or injury of others because of their faith stand in contempt of their basic canon. The state, Locke went on, holding with the Quakers, should tend to its temporal business, and abstain from imposing a single official religion on the people, even though all other faiths may seem ridiculous and even dangerous to holders of the one and only truth. Indeed, it was Locke's opinion that all beliefs, save Catholicism and atheism, should be granted toleration. Romanists could not be vouchsafed religious freedom because their primary allegiance belonged to the Pope, who was clearly an alien potentate. Atheists, being nonbelievers, had no right to expect religious toleration.

Some *Thoughts Concerning Education* appeared soon after the *Letters*. It saw five editions during its composer's lifetime, and an unending train of them ever since. Locke's last production, the *Conduct of the Understanding,* appeared in 1706, two years after its author's death.

PEDAGOGICAL VIEWS, SUMMARIZED

The bulk of Locke's pedagogical views may be found in *Some Thoughts Concerning Education,* which came out in 1693; *An Essay Concerning Human Understanding,* which had come out four years earlier; and the *Conduct of the Understanding,* which, as was remarked, was put into print after its author's death. The *Thoughts* began life as a series of letters which Locke composed in response to a request from his friend Edward Clarke to aid him in the upbringing of his eight-year-old son. Not intended for the vulgar eye, the *Thoughts* were cast in what in those days passed for a genteel epistolary discourse, rambling at times, and repetitive, but happily free from the schoolmaster's cocksure prattle. The *Thoughts,* one might say, are not so much a generalized pedagogic credo as a custom-built body of theory designed to suit the particular educational requirements of a gentleman's son. Locke's more extensive pedagogical thinking, his philosophical and psychological trumps, he laid down in his other works, his "Deeper Thoughts on Education," one might call them.

In his approach to philosophy, Locke began by cleaning out what he regarded as so much moldy rubbish. Because the human mind is what it is—that is, handicapped by all sorts of limitations and disabilities—philosophers, Locke insisted, should restrict their cerebrations to problems that such minds can reasonably hope to cope with. The real world, and the only one Homo sapiens can deal with on terms of parity, is not some transcendental world of spirit, but the solid terrestrial one he actually inhabits—a world, in short, of discernible things. Like the Sophists of old, Locke beheld man as a sentient and reflective being; accordingly, he argued that philosophers should perform their thinking empirically, which is to say, they should base their reflections on knowledge they had obtained through experience. Thus, with a flick of the hand, as it were, Locke tossed into the discard a vast congeries of problems over which theologians and metaphysicians and such artisans of the higher thought had sweated ever since God had said, "Let there be light!"

Not content with putting the philosopher's searchings on an empirical footing, Locke employed a similar tactic in what in those days passed for psychology. Thus, with Thomas Hobbes, a fellow notable, Locke loaded his musket again and again to make war on some of psychology's prized but baggy-eyed preconceptions. It was a combat which over the years gathered power and acceleration until at length in the latter nineteenth century it was brought to an end when the study of the human psyche was made an object of laboratory investigation.

Locke directed his heaviest fusillades against the doctrine of innate ideas, a doctrine which had been given prominence by Plato and Saint Augustine, only to become a casualty to the neo-Aristotelianism of the medieval Scholastics. The doctrine, however, had not actually succumbed. Time saw its resuscitation and, thanks to the persuasive reasoning of the redoubtable Descartes, it was once more on sturdy legs. Reduced to its basic elements, the doctrine contends that a human being is born with a complete set of ideas, ranging from such a simple one as, for example, that the same thing cannot be absent and present in one place at the same time, to such a baffling one as the idea of God.

After long years of diligent probing, Locke could unearth no evidence to uphold the ancient doctrine; contrarily, in the course of his study he gathered a whole bagful of arguments against it. In consequence, he concluded that at birth a babe's mind is barren; it is akin to a sheet of "white paper void of all ideas." "How comes it then to be furnished?" he asked, anticipating the inescapable interrogatory barrage of the learned. How does the mind obtain "that vast store the busy and boundless fancy of man has painted on it with an almost endless variety?" The answer, in one word, is *experience.* On this piece of blank paper—the mind—our senses impress their perceptions; they thus constitute the wellspring of all our ideas. In addition, however, there is also the experience which the mind derives from its own operations. Simple at first, our ideas increase in intricacy and sagacity by means of reflection. For his stress on experience as the fountainhead of psychological data, Locke has been garlanded by some of his admirers as the father of modern psychology, a paternity, which, as has already been alluded to, rival cheerleaders have ascribed to others, notably Aristotle and Saint Augustine.

SOME THOUGHTS CONCERNING EDUCATION

"A sound mind in a sound body is a short but full description of a happy state in the world." So runs the exordium of *Some Thoughts Concerning Education,* which, as has been said, Locke wrote as a series of letters to help his friend Edward Clarke in the rearing of his son. Its sole reason for being is thus preeminently practical, namely, the preparation of a boy for "the Gentleman's calling."

Locke wastes no time on pedagogic twittering, but plunges into his task head-on. What, he pondered, slipping into his medical role and giving thought, perhaps, to his own fragile physique, is essential to maintain an English boy of quality bursting with health, strength, and high spirits? The first thing is to allow nature her just and rightful chance. "It seems suitable both to my reason and experience," counseled the philosophical medico, "that the tender constitution of children should have as little done to them as is possible, and as the absolute necessity of the case requires." What children need are such elemental things as fresh air, exercise, recreation, and plenty of sleep. Let their food be light and plain with more bread and gruel than meat, flushed down not with spiritous fluids, not even a mild and amiable wine—as was then a common practice among gentlefolk—but with milk or plain water. Their cots should be hard and firm, and their coverlets spare. They should bathe frequently in cold water, and their toilet habits should be kept regular "with little or no physic."

Besides being subject to this simple regimen, which was generally looked at askance as the radical effusion of some eccentric, the rising gentlemen, like the Spartans of yore, must needs be physically toughened. To such a purpose let them stand against the elements, both summer's heat and winter's chill, sparsely and loosely clothed, their shoes ruptured with slits and holes "so as to hold water." Thus conditioned, they would be inured against nature's threats—save only, as Herbert Spencer was to remark some centuries following, in cases where the treatment had not previously killed them.

Like the body stalwart, the mind needs to be given a thorough and constant workout, and thereby brought under discipline. The business should be attended to early, the earlier the better, for it is bound to leave its mark on the boy for the rest of his life. Where many parents go off the track is in their failure to make the mind of their progeny "obedient to discipline and pliable to reason when it is most tender."

CONTINUED . . .

What at bottom does a young man of quality need to know? The answer, stated baldly, is simple: the tools of his trade, which, besides the knowledge of how to run his estate with an able hand, include such attributes as virtue, wisdom, good breeding, and learning. Of these Locke puts virtue at the top of his list. Not only will it "make him valued and beloved by others"; it will also allow him to look into the glass of a morning and recognize the wise and prudent man his reflection proclaims him to be. That Locke should make learning the low man on the pedagogic totem pole is no accident, since his standard was utilitarian. The gentleman's proper calling, he reminds us, is "in the service of his country." Accordingly, most of his hours he will spend not in the scholar's carrel, but on his land, or in some government bureau, or even in some administrative branch of trade or commerce. The generality of scholars left Locke cold. Indeed, on them he once delivered himself as follows: "I imagine," he said, "you would think him a very foolish fellow who should not value a virtuous and wise man infinitely before a great scholar," which is perhaps another way of stating that on the scale of human worth a Saint Augustine outranks a Newton.

But if the "wisest of human beings" placed virtue above learning in the molding of a man of quality and at the same time took a dank view of the professional men of learning, this is by no means saying that he excused his gentleman-to-be from getting a grip on the essential tools of learning. Like Comenius, whose work and thought had apparently passed him by, Locke believed in starting the process while the child was still a toddler. As soon as he could peep his first understandable words he should be introduced to reading. Let the business begin gently and pleasurably with a few letters at a time, proceeding as if it were a game, until he knew the entire twenty-six. Next, let the blossoming alphabeterian fashion his acquisition into syllables and then into words. Once he knew some simple words, let the tie be made more intimate by putting him on a book, beginning by teaching him how to make sense of the lines of, say, the cherishable *Fables* of Aesop, and proceeding to simple Bible tales. Once he is on easy terms with reading, let him be handed a pencil and paper and learn to transcribe his thoughts and feelings into the written word. He will glory in it as true artists always do.

Although, as Locke had observed, in education "Latin and learning make all the noise," yet he contended that a gentleman's needs are better served by grounding him thoroughly in his native tongue. After he has gained a sufficient fluency and competence therein, then he may apply his talents to some other language, preferably French, at that time the recognized medium of polite expression among the continental *haut monde*. French may be followed, should circumstances so suggest, by a study of Latin. All those tongues, whether foreign or domestic, are to be acquired conversationally, and if grammar is to be allowed any consideration at all, then it is to be reserved for those bent on embarking on some sort of advanced linguistic enterprise. If a learner shows signs of being thus inclined, then he at least carries the advantage of being old enough to know what he is doing.

To be worth his gentlemanly salt, a man of quality must know arithmetic. Not only, declared Locke, is it "the easiest and consequently the first form of abstract reasoning which the mind commonly bears or accustoms itself to," but scarcely anything in life or business can be done without it. Hence, "a man cannot have too much of it or have it too perfectly." Although Locke seems to be at pains to occlude from his readers any specific information on how to teach arithmetic, he launches his pupil in the primordial manner by having him learn the numbers' looks and names, and how to count. Once the boy has cemented this acquaintance, he is taught how to subtract and to add. Later he is to follow the first six books of Euclidian geometry from axioms to theorems to corollaries; geography with its meridians, latitudes, and longitudes; and astronomy, the mother of the calendar.

A gentleman who is not privy to the theory and practice of politics and government, and at least the rudiments of civil law, may find himself heavily handicapped, and so Locke endorsed their study. Logic, however, he minimized—not for any skepticism on his part toward the logical processes, but rather on account of the logician's common addiction to splitting hairs and his frequent resort to a crafty sophistry to win his argument. Locke's disdain for the dialectician's art and science was more than redressed with a hearty admiration for history. "History," he discanted, "is the great mistress of prudence and civil knowledge, and ought to be the proper study of a gentleman or man of business in the world." History, he continued, not only teaches; it also delights. As a teacher, it recommends itself "to the study of grown men"; as a delighter, "it [is] the fittest for a young lad."

Like the generality of their medieval antecedents, the knights, the English gentry were generously provided with servants; their slightest needs were attended to by hired hands. A man of quality thus frequently suffered from the pain of excessive leisure. Some of this he was able to alleviate by setting aside some hours for reading and, maybe, even reflection; and some he filled with social enlivenment. To make life more tolerable for a person afflicted with too much time on his hands, Locke proposed, as we do nowadays on a much grander and gaudier scale, a program of instruction in what Franklin later called the "ornamental arts." To such an end Locke put in a favorable word for learning how to dance. But toward music he entertained a rather sniffish attitude. Not only was the learning of the tonal art not worth the time it took, but, more important, "men of parts and business do not commend it." As for poetry, Locke dispraised it utterly. " 'Tis a pleasant air," he pontificated, "but a barren soil," a view which was generally in concert with that held by the Babbitts of his era.

Although he was somewhat chary about the value of fencing in the production of a model Englishman of class and affairs, he was amicably disposed toward the fine art of wrestling in which, it may be recalled, Plato took delight before he succumbed to philosophy. Of the playing field, which was an integral part of any self-respecting English public school, and which nineteenth-century legend-doters esteemed with awe and wonder as one of academia's surpassing gifts to Anglo-Saxon supremacy, Locke was no votary—indeed, he regarded its high jinks mainly as a squandering of time which he was sure could be turned to better account. Instead of shedding cataracts of sweat in sports, for example, let a youth seek gratification in gardening and woodwork, two "fit and healthy recreations" for gentlefolk. Not only will they keep intact the sterling virtues of the soul, but they are useful as well.

Like most men of wisdom, the tutor of Shaftesbury's offspring cherished a number of pet ideas about certain aspects of the schoolman's art. They are best forwarded, he concluded, in the home rather than at school, though neither one is without its shortcomings. Yet "the faults of a private education [are] infinitely to be preferred." In any case, for implanting virtue in the young, there is no place like home.

It used to be the accepted practice among chroniclers of the educational past to catalog John Locke as a disciplinarian—a supporter, that is, of the formal training of the mind and the herald of what in a later age psychologists were to set down as the doctrine of transfer of training. Up to a point the historians put up a good case. For did not the estimable John put a tremendous store in the physical toughening of the young, the so-called "hardening process"? And was it not the same frail-bodied sage who laid such a heavy weight on the importance of disciplining the will? "He that has not a mastery over his inclinations," Locke let it be known, "he that knows not how to resist the importunity of present pleasure to what reason tells him . . . is in danger never to be good for anything." A well-bred man, he concluded, should know how "to deny his own desires, cross his inclinations, and purely follow what reason directs as best."

It was Locke's contention that to learn how to reason with sharpness and address, the mental powers must be given frequent rehearsing. "As it is in the body," he remarked, "so it is in the mind; practice makes it what it is." But to put an edge on the mind, Locke repudiated the schoolman's traditional grindstone of grammar, rhetoric, and logic. To teach a person how to reason well and to observe "the connection of ideas," nothing serves as well as mathematics which, per consequence, Locke was convinced, should be studied by "all those who have the time and opportunity"—in short, the lucky ones whose parents have the necessary wherewithal. The purpose of mathematics, however, Locke took pains to state, was not so much to make gentlemen mathematicians "as to make them reasonable creatures."

In Locke's time, and for a long time to come, it was commonplace to put a schoolboy to stuffing his memory not only with all the questions and prefabricated answers in his catechism, but also with an endless herd of Latin passages. Once he had these securely stanchioned in his memory, it was thought that not only would they delight him as he aged, but that also his schoolboy memorizing would be bound to fortify his capacity to remember things in general, and so he would have no difficulty in recalling anything he put his mind to, from the birthday of his rich and sickly spinster aunt to the family tree of each of his pack of hounds.

It was a view, however, which met Locke's turned-down thumbs. "Strength of memory," he was convinced, "is owing to a happy situation, and not by any habitual improvement got by exercise." The belief that training a boy to memorize something specific, such as page after page of Latin, would eventually generate a capacity in him to recall anything and everything, became known, as the years rolled on, as the theory of transfer of training. Because of its beguiling plausibility the doctrine enjoyed a vast support, and time saw it grow to a bewhiskered old age—in fact, the twentieth century was inside the gates before the searchings of modern experimental psychologists gravely damaged it.

Although Locke had declared for the training of our mental prowess through exercising it, he did not, as was stated, at all accept the transfer doctrine. "Learning pages of Latin by heart," he asseverated, "no more fits the memory for retention of anything else than the graving of one sentence in lead makes it more capable of retaining firmly any other characters." For another thing, he added, "we see men frequently dexterous and sharp in making a bargain, who, if you reason with them about matters of religion, appear perfectly stupid."

AN EVALUATION

In the large concerns which related to teaching and learning Locke's views were, in the main, advanced. Not only did he adorn his own day as a progressive, but a number of his doctrines offered inspiration to later pedagogical seers, including some of the great immortals. Some of his views, in fact, are still generally accepted. At a time, for example, when the knowledge of child behavior was still, so to say, in diapers, Locke held the then somewhat suspect opinion that children, like grownups, are people, different to be sure, but still people. As miniscule representatives of Homo sapiens, moreover, they are rational beings. In consequence, it behooves their elders not only to give them the respect which is their due, but, by the same score, they should help them to bring their latent powers to full flower.

Long before William James, the father, some say, of laboratory psychology in America, Locke caught a glimpse of the notion that nothing can be truly learned unless one is ready to learn it. "The fittest time for children to learn anything," he explained, "is when their minds are in tune and well disposed to it." (So powerfully did this idea implant itself in after years in the thinking of Rousseau, that the Genevan put the lid on all formal learning, including reading—that abomination—until his fictional Emile was of an age of no less than twelve, and by that time presumably ready to cope with it.) In addition, Locke's recognition of the importance of agreeable surroundings as an effective inducement in the training of the young, although all too often dishonored in our day-to-day practice, would certainly be generally upheld as a sound and sensible theory.

But readiness and surroundings alone are not sufficient to engender learning: the pupil's experience must be made felicitous as well. Like the ancient Quintilian, Locke entertained doubts about the value of forcing the young to learn. Nothing they are to study, he insisted, "should ever be made a burden to them or imposed upon them." Not only will forced learning become irksome; it may also breed a deep aversion—and flogging reluctant scholars, the birchman's usual sure cure in such cases, will only make a bad matter worse. "Whereas," Locke concluded, "were matters ordered right, learning might be made as much a recreation to their play, as play is to their learning." In short, with the progressive pedagogues of his time, the philosopher held for the doctrine that learning should be made as exhilarating as pedagogic ingenuity can make it. "Masters and teachers," he declared, "should raise no difficulties to their scholars, but on the contrary should smooth the way."

AND THE POOR?

Although the author of *Two Treatises on Government* has been hymned as the defender of a people's right to unhorse a distempered sovereign—and, in so doing, minting much of the basic rhetoric of democracy—it would, nevertheless, be a mistake to conclude that the revelation Locke preached so bewitchingly on paper applied to all God's children on equal terms. The truth is that despite the glitter of his liberalism, Locke's thinking failed to pierce the trammels imposed upon him by his time and class, of which he was a favored somebody. Accordingly, when he turned his thoughts to the education of the lower orders, Locke put a curb on his progressivism. "The knowledge of the Bible," he said, "and the business of his calling is enough for the ordinary man."

Locke's views of what should be done for the masses whom fortune had palpably passed by, the disregarded and voiceless poor, was expressed in a proposal he issued in 1697 while he was active as a commissioner of the board of trade. In it, he called for the compulsory impressment of pauper children at the age of three in public workhouses, of which there was to be one in every parish. There the young were to be housed and trained to be "sober and industrious," their health and morals under constant watch, and their daily appetite attended to with "a bellyful of . . . bread," and during winter's chill, "if it be thought needful, a little watergruel." Every day, except on the Sabbath, the children were to be instructed in spinning, weaving, and suchlike useful crafts. The products of their labor were to be sold, and whatever money accrued therefrom was to go toward their board and looking-after. God's day, needless to say, was set aside to do Him reverence and to reinforce instruction in His religious and moral ordinances. To this end, all children were to be "obliged to come constantly to church with their schoolmasters and dames." In this vein of debit-and-credit charity the progeny of Britain's poor people would come into their own. Not only would they show their betters a due and decorous deference, but "from infancy they would be inured to work," while at the same time their mothers would be freed to go to work. Thus the child labored at his required tasks until his fourteenth birthday, whereupon, "inured to work," he was pronounced ready for apprenticeship.

TO SUM UP

Locke's concern in education was personal rather than professional. Even so, in Britain and in some of her far-flung colonies his opinions won him an agreeable reading trade, especially among men of means. Regarding his intellectual pick-and-shovel work in philosophy and psychology, there is no gainsaying its impact upon the world of thought. Nor is his liberalism invisible in his pedagogy. In his *Thoughts,* it displays itself over and over again. But Locke's educational ideas were scarcely virginal—in fact, when his *Thoughts* were given to the world, his progressive theories were already stale. Their essence had been set forth long before by Quintilian. We see them again in the writings of Erasmus and several other luminaries of Humanism for whose classical niceties Locke professed a frank abhorrence. In Montaigne, too, a member of France's landed noblesse, we find progressivism aplenty, and better still, voluptuously and waggishly expressed. Finally, in Comenius the theories show themselves in all the simple nobility of the real thing.

Locke, it has been said, is of consequence for the questions he ignited. What education is of most worth? Is its purpose to breed scholars? Or is it to fit a person for everyday living? Should it put book learning above experience? Or should it lay its primary emphasis on the development of good character? Should it train youth to bow to the dictates of law and order? Or should it train them to live as men who are disciplined to freedom? Grappling with such conundrums doubtless serves a useful purpose—in fact, they are still being grappled with. More revealing, however, than Locke's questions are his answers, and these, even when they are given their due allowance in the light of a kindly hindsight, must sometimes be given a low mark.

The ineradicable fact is that Locke was born and bred within the confines of the seventeenth-century Anglo-Saxon culture, and for all the puissance of his mind, his undoubted charm and affability, his thinking was beset at all times by a hard-grained class prejudice. He could not, like Montaigne, for example, engage in easy colloquy with the lower and meaner folk. Like Comenius, he was a believing Christian, but the warmth and tenderness of the gentle Czech eluded the Englishman completely. He observed the world in which he found himself with a penetrating eye, but all too often with the false vision of a man of privilege. Thus, where Comenius preached the brotherhood of all men, and took steps to bring this about, Locke was at pains to pen them in separate enclosures as castes, classes, sects, and even factions. The chasm between the two men reveals itself plainly in their pedagogy. Where Comenius spoke up for a single school system for all, Locke, dividing his world fastidiously into one of masters and servants, vouchsafed the best education that money could buy to the former, with only an anemic sort of leftover, as it were, to the latter—which is to say, the overwhelming horde.

Comenius, an exemplar and executor of democracy and not merely its mouthpiece, opened his elementary school to every child, whether girl or boy, rich or poor—in fact, he even had the temerity to recommend that attendance be compulsory. Locke, though a supporter of democracy, tolerated no such hobnobbing. To those he knew he was of a kindly heart, and for his friends his affection was warm and unquenchable. But the vast swarm of mankind left him flat, and when he granted their education some thought, it was not, as with Comenius, in the spirit of compassion, but with a sense of impersonal utility.

Reference has at times been made to Locke as being typically English, an opinion for which there is much to say. As a philosopher, for example, he entertained neither the logical acuteness of the French nor the verbose weightiness of the Germans. His proposal to educate the poor was stillborn, but what did it in was not its callous and shameful insufficiency, but what was then regarded as a threat to the ordered world which Omniscience had ordained. Nonetheless, as year chased year, the education which took form in England carried the recognizable seal of Mr. Locke, namely, a set of schools of unqualified excellence for those of high estate, but only a paltry provision for the lowly multitude. Not until the nineteenth century, when social reform picked up momentum, did the English undertake to come to grips with the nation's educational inadequacies.

Chapter 12

The Changing Intellectual Climate

THE ENLIGHTENMENT

While Puritans, living and dead, awaited that inescapable day of doom when Jahveh would store all but a chosen few of them in a deep and blistering hell, in the Old World a new spirit was on the wing. Embodied in the Enlightenment, it showed itself first in the motherland, then on the Continent, and finally in colonial America. Precisely when the Enlightenment got under way is uncertain. Some savants have detected traces of it in the writings of Francis Bacon, who died in 1626, especially in his *Novum Organum,* but also in a somewhat lesser measure in the *New Atlantis* and the *Advancement of Learning.* Others discern surer signs in the deliberations of John Locke, the inspirer in a later day of Jefferson and the intellectual godfather, so to speak, of the Declaration of Independence. Finally, there are those who mark the advent of the Enlightenment with the publication in 1686 of Sir Isaac Newton's stupendous *Principia Mathematica,* or, in English, *Mathematical Principles of Natural Philosophy.*

Regardless of exactly what year it was that the Enlightenment came to being, its groundwork in good part had been set during the Renaissance assault on medieval values, fortified as this was by the individualism and worldiness of many of its worthies. But the Renaissance lacked a method which would yield a rational explanation of the cosmos, so that when time finally plowed it into history it had raised many more questions than it had answered.

A start toward tracking down such answers was made in the sixteenth century as the Renaissance ran into the surge of the Reformation. Unhappily, the latter age was in no mood to encourage the free journeying of the mind. The delicate forbearance Holy Church had permitted herself in this respect during the high day of the Renaissance was abruptly terminated as she buckled on her armor to put down the heresy-breathing Protestants. But let it be noted that here the banner-wavers of Protestantism stood side by side with their Romish adversaries. The theological gulf which separated the contending factions may have been wide, but when it came to granting dispensations to the freedom of thought, both sides balked. Both sides howled down the nascent natural sciences, and for those who would steal the Promethean fire they reserved their most sizzling maledictions.

Nevertheless, there were some who would not be daunted. Their ranks, to be sure, were spare, but their feats were on a vast and protean scale, ranging from astronomy, botany, and chemistry to geology, mathematics, zoology, and yet more. Scan their puny roster, and again and again you see some memorable name, such as Andreas Vesalius, the first in modern annals to explore a human cadaver and to report intelligently on his findings; Gerhard Kramer—or, as the world more often speaks of him, Mercator—the father of the science of cartography; Valerius Cordus, the reputed genitor in the West of experimental chemistry; William Gilbert, the coiner of the word "electricity" and the author of the world's first dissertation on its powers and properties; and finally, the most glittering of them all, Nicholas Copernicus, whose work, *The Revolution of the Heavenly Bodies,* which was published soon after his death in 1543, disposed of the papier-maché medieval cosmos by making the sun and not the Earth the center of our solar system.

Despite the prohibitions and repressions put upon scientists, their venturesomeness did not stop. On the contrary, their explorations gained in strength and significance to such a degree that later recorders of intellectual history referred to their work as the Scientific Movement of the Seventeenth Century. There is not much to be gained by summoning its prominenti one after another to take a curtain call from an applauding posterity. Let it be noted simply that in the penetration of their arcana not a few were giants, and some, indeed, were mastodons—such as Galileo, Leibnitz, Harvey,

Boyle, and that crusty old bachelor Newton, whose feats in physics made his name synonymous with the era.

The knowledge of the observable universe which the seventeenth century unveiled, the eighteenth augmented and expanded. Thus the hunt for the precise facts about nature has been carried on for century upon century until in the present day it bids fair to strain even our most extravagant fancy.

DEISM—OLD WORLD TO NEW

As more and more of nature's mysterious workings yielded their secrets to the searchings of the men of science, the authority which metaphysicians and theologians had long wielded in this department was not only challenged, but, as the years drove on, fell into a state of minor consequence. The authority of revealed religion, once of an all-embracing sweep and of an almost irresistible power, gradually descended from its high dominion to confine its operations largely to the task of the advancement and maintenance of virtue and piety.

As so many of Christendom's cherished theorems fell under the impact of science, thinking men, drawing deeply from the jug of skepticism, took a fresh look at God and His creation. Intellectually, the dominant concept of the Heavenly Father and the sidereal universe had remained pretty much what it had been in the flush days of the medieval church. Like the leading Catholic thinkers, those of the Reformation put their store in a universal order wherein God was the beginning and the end of all. A personal deity, omniscient and omnipotent, He took a frequent hand in human affairs, speaking from burning bushes, dispatching angels to deliver his communiqués, giving an ear to man's prayers and exhortations, granting or denying him aid, and in the end meting out rewards and penalties as His illimitable mind and taste saw fit.

But where the medieval exemplars of divine science and their Reformation analogs sought to fathom the cosmic riddle by presuming a universe centered in Almighty God, the cerebrals of the Enlightenment flashed their searchlight on a universe wherein man was at the core. And where the former relied heavily on revelation and other ghostly data to uphold and sustain their argument, the latter, loosened from the bonds of ecclesiastics, leaned not on faith but on reason. They turned their backs on supernatural evidence, resorting instead to the objective and impartial findings of the natural sciences and their indispensable handmaiden, mathematics. The upshot was a new explication of the cosmic mystery, namely deism.

Deism is a word bred in the seventeenth century by the Swiss Pierre Viret to describe the viewpoint of men who put their credence in God but not in the divinity of Jesus. Neither atheistic nor agnostic, it repudiates orthodox Christianity, with its trappings of prophecies and miracles, its portents and providences. Its roots lie in the Newtonian astrophysics, in the rationalism of John Locke and his followers, and in the findings of students of comparative religion which seemed to suggest that Homo sapiens, no matter where he lived or what his color, entertained a number of common religious beliefs.

The first to give a systematic expression to the new outlook was an Englishman, Lord Herbert Cherbury (1583–1648), the author of the *Ancient Religions of the Gentiles,* so erudite a work that it is now rarely read. A universal natural religion, his Lordship contended, holds that there is a God, solitary and supreme; that He ought to be worshipped; that the chief end of worship is the promotion of virtue and piety, which is to say, better living; that the prerequisite to this is the repentance of our sins; and that God dispenses rewards and punishments and justice both here and now and in the extraterrestrial life to come. Centuries later, Franklin emitted similar reflections, and so did Jefferson, the last American writer of any eminence to declare himself on the subject while it was still of moment.

The deistic current which flowed out of the Newtonian revolution laid down its challenge to the timeworn Christian cosmology, holding instead that the universe was a mere mechanism, infinite in its reach and orderly in its functioning, the breathtaking handiwork of the Almighty, regulated and run by natural laws. Self-operating, it performs eternally, like a gigantic perpetual-motion machine, requiring no further attention from its all-fore-seeing author. "God's arm," remarked Thomas Paine, an avowed deist, "wound up the vast machine," whereupon its owner walked off to let the machine run by itself. "God," volunteered another deist, "created the universe in six days, and he has been resting ever since," a flippancy at first blush, but on sober reflection a great point, for so perfectly had the Eternal presumably fashioned His universe that it needs no further direction.

DEISM IN THE NEW WORLD

From the Old World, the deistic postulates betook themselves to the New. Franklin and Jefferson were among their adherents. The latter, as a matter of fact, went to great lengths to let his convictions be known, declaring himself on the side of reason and urging its use at all times even if, as a consequence, one is led thereby to reject the existence of God. Both Washington and Madison fancied a deistic view, but they preferred to speak their views privily. John Adams confessed to Unitarianism, a somewhat tonier and, at the time, a slightly more respectable deistic avatar.

The most voluble partisan of deism in America was Thomas Paine, a bankrupt corset maker, grocer, teacher, preacher, but a fellow of considerable sauce. He had come across deism in England and in France, and thereafter it never ceased to fever him. A tireless propagandist for enlightenment, like Franklin and Jefferson, Paine summed up his deistic dialectic in the *Age of Reason,* in our present world a classic, but for a time embarrassingly suspect, and in England even under the censor's heel. The work, for all the uproar it caused, is of modest size, flowing and clear, and of a sledgehammer directness. "The true Deist," it tells us, "has but one Deity." He is the first cause and "of a nature totally different to any material existence we know of. . . .The God in whom we believe," it goes on, "is a God of moral truths. . . ." And "it is a duty incumbent on every true Deist that he vindicate the moral justice of God against the calumnies of the Bible." To this constructive idealism Paine addressed his talents with an unabated passion, attacking Holy Writ with force and wit if not with scholarly discernment. He himself, he reflected, could compose a book without forgetting on one page what he had said on another. God Almighty, he allowed, should "do as well."

On the generality of people, whether of the Old World or the New, the deistic teachings had no great bearing. Man in the aggregate is not readily amenable, or even hospitable, to strange ideas. On the other hand, it is easy enough to alarm him. Somehow the belief would not dissolve that deists were Antichrist and the raveners, hence, of all that was good and beautiful and true. For his resolute deism and his verbal aggressions on the reverend fathers, and especially their Calvinistic representatives, Jefferson was barbecued as an atheist. Paine fared no worse. So late, indeed, as the present century the first Roosevelt, a man who took pride in that he never swore or drank—unless he had to—set Paine down as a "filthy little atheist." Yet today, the filthy little atheist is lodged in his niche in the nation's Hall of Fame, to be gaped at so long as the republic stands.

Despite its slender harvest of converts, deism was not altogether void of consequences. Rocklike skeptics, it is true, remained unmoved, for its rationalism, they found, was vitiated all too often by its a priori assumption. Nevertheless, the deists' onslaught on the shortcomings, contradictions, and even puerilities of Sacred Writ, for all the antagonism and hubbub it incited, launched an intellectual revolution of the first magnitude. Without it, advanced thinkers of a later day, the skeptic, the agnostic, and the atheist, would have found their progress infinitely more beset. The deistic movement began to peter out along with the eighteenth century, but its essence remained, and in the nineteenth century more and more it found its place in one guise or another in the intellectual's wardrobe.

Although deists were despised and denounced in the Old World no less than the New, it is only fair to remind one's self that the run of them were folk of goodwill. Their great concern was to develop virtuous people, impervious to selfishness and self-seeking, and thereby, they hoped, able to promote the common good. But the virtues the deists stressed were not, as Jefferson took care to make known, out of "sectarian dogmas" but the "genuine precepts of Jesus himself." From his Philadelphia diocese Franklin issued similar pronunciamentos. And to attain their end, both men, as will be noted later, invested heavily in education.

PROGRESS, CHANGE, AND THE AMERICAN ENLIGHTENMENT

The great expectations a handful of scientists put in the power of observation and experiment to pry the secrets from nature, along with their slowly increasing stock of information, presently gave rise to the thought that, put to useful application, the knowledge of scientific theory could be made to serve man's material needs. The idea itself was far from being a novelty. As far back, indeed, as the early seventeenth century, Francis Bacon had given it a grandiose invocation when, in his *New Atlantis,* he limned a great society wherein scientists rather than metaphysicians and theologians, or even priests, would lead the rest of us to a glorious fulfillment. The passing years heard other thinkers intone variations on the Bacon theme—Blaise Pascal, for one, who, until he succumbed to the Jansenist theological frenzy, pinned his intellectual hopes on the powers of his own generation to lead, rather than on the wisdom of a faraway antiquity. From the perspicacious René Descartes, a superb mathematician and philosopher, came the manifesto that to compound a logical and dependable body of knowledge, philosophers, like their comrade pursuers of truth, the scientists, must divest themselves not only of their preconceptions, cherished though they may have been, but also of the venerated authority of the ancients.

It remained for another Frenchman, a Cartesian familiar, Bernard de Fontenelle, to compose our first fairly systematic and substantial treatise on the theory of progress, *A Digression on the Ancients and Moderns* (ca. 1689). Though he was content to let the old-time Greeks and Latins rest on their laurels, Fontenelle was averse to the all-too-prevalent notion that the attainments of the moderns were inferior. Progress, he observed, was cumulative. It was a forward-moving process wherein every advancing step depended on a preceding one. Hence the moderns, building on their heritage, were inevitably ahead of their antecedents.

The first to lay down the theory that man might conceive a better world, and by planning and assiduous effort might even succeed in bringing it about, was yet another Gallic worthy, the celebrated Abbé Castel de St. Pierre. Not concerned, like some of his forerunners, with proving the obvious, namely, that since antiquity a great many things have improved, in his *Observations on the Continual Progress of Univeral Reason* (1737) the Abbé affirmed that not only is progress possible, but that the making of a better future rests in man's own hands. St. Pierre's theory stands much closer to our own views than does that of any of his predecessors, and for this conception the Abbé has even been nominated as the father of the theory of progress.

It is a curious fact that neither the Greeks nor the Romans nor the medieval Europeans had even the faintest glimmer of what has since come to pass for the doctrine of progress. Far back, when civilization was still in puberty, the world's great sages were in thrall to the concept of changelessness. Change was unsettling and suspect. Whatever underwent change, weighty minds agreed, was somehow inferior to what did not. Change brought decay and deterioration. "All things change," meditated Marcus Aurelius, "and you yourself are constantly wasting away, and so is the universe." "Times change," brooded another Roman, "and men deteriorate." Witness, in contrast, the high respect reserved for what was immune to change. "I am the Lord. I change not." So it was writ in the Old Testament, in Malachi 3:6, some time about 300 B.C.

The classical ancients held with Homer, Hesiod, and Seneca that their forefathers had lived in a golden age, and that for reasons known only to the high inscrutable powers they had fallen from this height and were doomed, generation after generation, to keep on skidding downhill until extinction. Christians too had lost their paradise, and with it the ecstasies our primal parents had once savored. True enough, Christian thinkers were willing to grant that under the cross things were better than under heathenry. But Eden was irretrievably gone, and life on earth, in comparison, was onerous, sorrowful, hopeless. And man being what he is, which is to say depraved and wicked, human progress in this tear-drenched valley was unthinkable.

Yet, as the eighteenth century edged toward its close, in one way or another the idea of progress fired the thinking of the era's foremost intellects in Britain, Germany, and especially in France, where some of the so-called "philosophes" gave it an eager courtship. Its most striking wooer was Jean-Marie Antoine Nicholas de Condorcet. A mathematician, he was also a brewer of metaphysical vapors, and a blooded marquis to boot—a distinction, however, which in the deadly heavings of the French Revolution, aroused the displeasure of the lovers of liberty, equality, and fraternity. While hiding from the Terror, whose headsman he cheated by dying of pneumonia, Condorcet devoted his moments to writing his *Sketch of an Historical Picture of the Progress of the Human Mind* (1795), wherein, for all the menace of his pursuers, his belief in human reason and man's rise to a higher and higher perfection remained unshaken. "Nature," he proclaimed, "has assigned no limit to the perfecting of the human faculties." "The progress of this perfectibility," he continued, "has no other limit than the duration of the globe on which nature has placed us." Such is the theory of progress without end, or, as the phrase goes in the parlance of the learned, the doctrine of man's infinite perfectibility.

Unlike some of his fellow philosophes, such as Voltaire, Condorcet insisted that all of us, the meanest no less than the loftiest, are naturally dowered with a capacity for reason, but that to bring it to its full maturity, education is necessary. Hence, to assure every child a chance to attain his natural fulfillment, it behooves the state to guarantee at least a minimum education to all its young. Thus conceived, concluded the philosophical marquis, "education is for the government an obligation of justice." And only by paying it heed may the state expect its people to better themselves and the world in which they live, and thereby to move ahead, if only a microscopic stride, in the sempiternal march of progress.

The guiding star of countless thousands fretting to deliver themselves from the burdens and oppressions of the Old World, America very early came to be regarded as the one place where the possibility of improving the human condition could become something more substantial than the promise of a philosophic theory. Not only was the new land tremendous—a *Lebensraum* so vast it staggered even the wildest imagination—but for a man to acquire a modest part of it as his very own was not, as in the Old World, beyond the ordinary reach. Add to this the fact that nature had blessed this land with a manifold climate, with numerous large and navigable waterways, and with a happy abundance of untapped resources, and you have a lure which enterprising folk, struggling to advance their fortune, found well-nigh irresistible.

Nor was the lust for progress merely personal. From the very start, the American people have again and again manifested a propensity to dream up a better world, and by the manipulation of their institutions to seek to bring it into being. One discerns its subtle wine and seductive music at work so long ago as the eighteenth century when the fathers of the republic applied themselves to the writing of the Constitution. One perceives it in the happy aspirations of the nineteenth century, and in the progressive movements brought forth to give them form and substance. It is inherent in the Wilsonian New Freedom—even, indeed, in the ill-starred Eighteenth Amendment. And it is shot through the New Deal, the Fair Deal, and, only yesterday, the Great Society. Although the masterminds of the American Enlightenment showed little inclination to share Condorcet's romantic optimism on the future progress of human reason, and although none of them echoed his supporting rhetoric, nevertheless several of them had things to say on the importance of education. Two of them, Franklin and Jefferson, rose above the others not only in what they said, but also in what they did, and these two we are now ready to examine.

Chapter 13

Benjamin Franklin

OVERVIEW OF A SELF-MADE MAN

The first American of any consequence to give some earnest thought to an education not suffused with religion, and who sought to turn his ideas to account in actual practice, was Benjamin Franklin (1706–1790). An inheritor of the Old World's humanistic tradition, he was also a participant in its Enlightenment, especially in its scientific revelation, which, as was mentioned before, came to blossom in the seventeenth century and has been enjoying a lush florescence ever since. Franklin not only prized Europe's humanistic ideals, but some of them he also aspired to realize, even going so far as to tutor himself in Latin long after his father's stunted purse had obliged him to become a reluctant dropout from Boston's celebrated Latin School. He also sought to repair his literary deficiency with a copious reading of the masters, both ancient and contemporary, including Plutarch, Xenophon, and Cicero, besides Shakespeare, Bunyan, Defoe, Locke, Hume, Shaftesbury, and similar magnificoes.

From the Enlightenment, Franklin plucked an interest in the search for experimental truth, its striving to bare nature's hidden workings and its rejection of the authority which philosophers and men of God had preempted in this domain since civilization first began. Finally, from the Enlightenment Franklin derived his confidence in man's capacity for self-improvement to the end of making himself an understanding, useful citizen. But it was a confidence which was at times unsteady and on occasion even wobbled badly, as witness his observation in a letter to Charles Carroll in 1789. "We have been guarding against an evil," he wrote, "that old States are most liable to, excess of powers in the rulers; but our present danger seems to be a defect of obedience in the subjects."

Of the founding fathers, Franklin was the eldest by a whole generation, yet in the audacity and freshness of his outlook he might well have been the youngest, and so he steps closer into our ken today than do any of the others. A youth sowing his wild oats when Cotton Mather was steaming the dank New England air with his harangues on damnation, Franklin was still active long years later when Clay, Webster, and Calhoun were stooping over their schoolbooks, making ready without knowing it for the day when the national limelight, political rather than divine, would beat down upon them.

No other American except Jefferson has borne upon our country's life from so many directions, and none has left a deeper and more impressive trail. In Franklin worked the mysterious alchemy of genius, the versatility and many-sidedness which mark the giants of the Renaissance, and the rare talent for executing whatever he projected with a superb and seemingly effortless ease. Printer, publisher, writer, politician, statesman, diplomat, thinker, scientist, inventor, educator, organizer, and administrator, he could conjure up a scheme for a colonial union or a new commonwealth as readily as he could one for a subscription library in Philadelphia. He paved the way for advertising and salesmanship, now known to some of their professors as sciences, and, as one might expect of so prudent a man, he believed in the safeguards and protections of insurance, then just in infancy. He contrived a new-style stove, so excellent it is still being made, and that bears his name to warm and comfort us today. He perfected a lightning rod, a new harmonica, a rocking chair, and the first pair of bifocals the world had ever heard of. He tracked the winds, the ocean's ebb and flow, and the Gulf Stream's currents. And he flabbergasted sober-minded mathematicians with a set of magical squares.

An émigré from the classroom after only a couple of years of formal education, he schooled himself in the elements besides geometry and navigation, in addition to Latin and its progeny of French, Italian, and Spanish. The passing years saw him elevated to honorary brotherhood in more than a score of learned societies around the world, and celebrated as a master of arts, *honoris causa,* by the grace of Harvard and Yale, and not long after by William and Mary. Not to be outdone, St. Andrews of Scotland festooned him in its doctoral robes, and so, soon after, did Oxford. Respected in Britain, adored in France, he was beloved and esteemed no less in America. "There was scarcely a citizen . . . ," observed John Adams, not without a touch of amazement, "who . . . did not consider him a friend of human kind. When they spoke of him, they seemed to think he was to restore the Golden Age."

MORAL EXCELLENCE?

For most of his eighty-four years Franklin was enmeshed, as he testifies in his *Autobiography,* "in the bold and arduous project of arriving at moral perfection." Striking out in his still unleavened nonage, he undertook a diligent analysis of what constitutes moral excellence. His quest presently brought him a considerable quarry of human virtues, of which he set aside a baker's dozen for his personal cultivation and, he hoped, ultimate possession. To effect his purpose he drew up what has come down to us as "A Plan for Moral Self-improvement," a sort of do-it-yourself directive in which he laid down a number of principles for the making of a virtuous man, a scheme which at bottom bears some resemblance to Cotton Mather's *An Essay on the Good,* which in turn is a blend of Aristotelian and early Christian ethical doctrine. Did Franklin round up such old and homely goods as humility, temperance, justice, chastity, and the like? Then he also added a small gallery of his own, such as industry, frugality, order, sincerity, and cleanliness—all of a mundane materiality and greatly admired by the traders and worshipers in the temple of debit and credit where Franklin stood forth as an apostle of the first carat.

Unlike Mather's treatise on how to advance the good, Franklin's discourse is not orchestrated in some far-off spectral key, but in an ever-impinging earthly one. Set down to help him make his way past the soft blandishments of a hard world, he used it, however, not just to develop his own character, but also to put his moralities to work for the betterment of his fellowmen. Nowhere in Franklin's reflections on right and wrong is there any reference to godliness. Indeed, like the ancient Aristotle in his *Nichomachean Ethics,* the Philadelphia sage put little store in supernal sanctions, whether from the Throne of Grace on high, or from its ordained commissioners here below. But thereafter the resemblance fades.

Lacking the Greek's amplitudinous mind and spirit, Franklin could not break through the trammels of his middle-class virtues, and though his postulates were fashioned in the mode of a well-barbered respectability, at bottom they remain little more than the sublimated gospel of how to make a success in the world. They are summed up neatly, in the vein somewhat of Shakespeare's doddering Polonius, in a letter Franklin wrote to John Alleyne: "Be studious in your profession," he exhorted, "and you will be learned. Be industrious and frugal, and you will be rich. Be sober and temperate, and you will be healthy. Be in general virtuous and you will be happy."

... AND RELIGION

Born and raised in the manners and persuasion of a decaying Calvinism, Franklin had not yet crossed the frontier of fifteen when he fell prey to doubts and became, as he confided in later years, a "thorough deist." But as he took on years, he shed his adolescent theology, holding—outwardly at least—to his father's not-quite-conformist Presbyterianism, but adulterating even this to suit his taste, sometimes even with tartly skeptical savorings. In the greenery of his youth, for example, he arched an eyebrow over the inconsistency of a deity, ubiquitous and all-powerful, who nonetheless failed to make an end of sin. But shortly before his death he viewed the scene with different eyes. "I believe," he wrote in answer to a question put to him by Dr. Ezra Stiles, president of Yale, and hence, in those days, a man greatly concerned with the ghostly science, "in one God, creator of the universe. That he governs the world by his providence. That he ought to be worshipped. That the most acceptable service we can render him is doing good to his other children. That the soul of man is immortal, and will be treated with justice in another life, respecting its conduct in this."

Rather curiously, almost the same words had been offered the world as far back as the seventeenth century by Edward Lord Herbert of Cherbury, sometimes anointed by his admirers as the founder of deism. Less reassuring for the president of Yale must have been Franklin's view about Jesus of Nazareth of whom, he confessed, he held "some doubts as to his divinity." But Franklin was then too far gone in years to care to explore the problem. "I expect soon enough," he wrote, "an opportunity of knowing the truth with less trouble."

THE MAN HIMSELF

A practical man laying a capital stress on the attainment of useful ends, Franklin invested no large confidence in the pursuit of pure and ethereal ideas, the delight ever since Genesis of metaphysicians and divine scientists everywhere. He took pleasure in acclaiming himself a reasonable man. "So convenient a thing it is," he wrote in his *Autobiography,* "to be a reasonable creature, since it enables one to find or to make a reason for everything one has a mind to do." The rightness of opinions, he contended somewhat in the tone of John Locke, should be appraised not by the force of passion with which they are given utterance, but by their effects alone. Franklin was in this respect a vanguard shadow of latter-day pragmatists who declared that ideas, when untested in action, are little more than illusion, entertaining, perhaps, but in themselves of no ponderable significance. Again like the pragmatic brethren, though scarcely so sophisticated, Franklin viewed education as the constant and never-ending process of increasing, overhauling, and reassembling our stock of experience, be it solitary or collective.

If in his day-by-day doings Franklin betrayed an aversion to theory, in his scientific endeavor he faced about. He was a staunch supporter of experimental research even when it promised to be barren of any practical results. In Paris, while observing man's first balloon ascension, when some within his earshot impugned the whole business as useless, it was the utilitarian Franklin who riposted, "What good is a newborn baby?" At work during his experimental searchings, seeking, as he said, "to let light into nature," he was an amateur, perhaps, but certainly no dallier, a meticulous searcher with no other purpose than to unearth scientific truth for its own stark sake. This is not to suggest, of course, that the harvest Franklin culled from his numerous investigations was solely theoretical, as witness his perfection of the lightning rod, the natural offspring, so to say, of his experimentation in electricity. Nor does it mean that Franklin cherished no dreams of a better world—not in the sense of a massive moral improvement, it is true, but rather of a world infinitely ameliorated by the application of the theoretic findings of the laboratory. The day may break, he mused a decade or so before he died—in a letter to Joseph Priestley, a fellow scientist—when a man will be able to fly through the air without wings "for the sake of easy transport"; when farmers will sweat and suffer less, yet produce more; when disease will no longer rack and raven us; when our years on earth will surpass even the overflowing measure apportioned to our Old Testament forebears; and when even senility will have its charms.

But such ventures into reverie were few, and save in science and invention, Franklin rarely rose to the shimmering peaks of great fancy. Not given to dreaming, Franklin was insensitive to sheer beauty. The poet's poignant flights, exultant violins and murmuring harps, the awesome mysteries of philosophy or of religion, were all beyond him. Doing good, preserving man from moral dereliction, making money, and sunning himself in the respect and approbation of his audience—such, in epitome, were the interests that consumed him when he offered his words to the multitude.

Thus the man, his dominant views and values, which, as usual, serve as the vessel from which flowed his educational doctrines. A moralist, he made virtue the head god in his pantheon. "Virtue," he concluded after long years of reflection, "is sufficient to make a man good, glorious, and happy." A connoisseur of business and practical affairs and an exemplary success in their manipulation, Franklin spared no pains to urge an education which put its grip on the useful as well as the ornamental, but a deal more on the former than on the latter. A humanist and a scientist, he inveighed against a flyblown classicism with its concern for pigeonholing facts and learning by rote. Instead, he stood up for an educational program which would render due respect to the needs of a burgeoning commerce and the rising natural sciences.

POOR RICHARD'S ALMANAC

Franklin never wove his educational thoughts through the woof of a single educational piece. His writings on the subject are for the most part brief, put forth on scattered occasions, and directed to some special purpose. Here, for example, you will find him animadverting upon the formal schooling of the young; there on the self-education of their elders; and somewhere else on the importance of giving education to the free Negro. Today he may put his talents to work on the promotion of scientific research; tomorrow on plans for the establishment of the American Philosophical Society; and the day after on a batch of aphorisms to instruct and elevate the common mind.

Let us fix our eyes first on the latter. Not only did Franklin express a boundless trust in the powers which purportedly dwell in most of us, as well as in the capacity to pipe them into an endless flow of self-improvement, but to bring this about he also gave freely of his advice. We see it in several of his effusions, as witness "Advice to a Young Tradesman," "The Way to Wealth," "Father Abraham's Speech," and time and again in *Poor Richard's Almanac*, which made its debut in December, 1732, and which continued thereafter to show itself under Franklin's editorial hand for a quarter of a century. It was a blunt imitation of the English *Poor Robin's Almanac*, and like all such literary delicacies it dispensed its views on almost every subject ever heard about, from astrology and animal care to matrimony and madness. Directed, as the American phrase currently has it, at the "mass market," the almanac concentrated on the art and mystery of money-making and personal success, enlivened its discourse often enough with pleasantries, and garnished itself now and then with an apothegm.

Leaf through its pages and you will learn not only that foretelling the weather is "as easy as pissing abed," and that "he who lives upon hope, dies farting," but also, as doubtless you already know, that "early to bed and early to rise makes a man healthy, wealthy, and wise"; that "a penny saved is a penny earned"; that "time is money"; and should doubts about such axioms assail you, then remember Franklin's caveat that "a word to the wise is sufficient." Stale and fatuous in today's cynical world, such ditties for good works and human uplift were fatigued even then. In fact, most of them had been purloined from the world's available store, then dusted and glossed to suit his audience, the vast mass of plain Americans.

Franklin evidently knew his customers well, for *Poor Richard's Almanac* was an immediate and immense success. Within a month it ran through three editions. During the twenty-five years it emblazoned Franklin's name on its masthead its average annual sale embraced some 10,000 copies. It was translated into almost every European tongue, and parts of its 1757 issue, its last and most celebrated one, were worked into a schoolbook, *La Science du Bonhomme Richard,* to give instruction and high-mindedness to young France. All this, of course, gratified its maker not a little, and although it failed to make him healthy—his gout continued to oppress him—at least it deluged him with fame and yielded a very handsome revenue. Clearly, of the countless thousands of Poor Richard's emulators, eager for self-development and all that was said to follow unfailingly in its wake, Franklin was the shrewdest striver of all.

THE JUNTO AND THE AMERICAN PHILOSOPHICAL SOCIETY

A gregarious man, Franklin had scarcely begun his twenties when he persuaded a few friends to join him in the Junto, a society for the self-improvement of its members who, hand on heart and eyes toward Heaven, stood up to tell the world that they loved "truth for truth's sake" and "mankind in general." To show this devotion each member agreed to enlighten his brothers four times every twelvemonth with an address on some praiseworthy theme, such cerebral aphrodisiacs, for example, as, "Is it justifiable to put private men to death for the sake of safety and tranquility who have committed no crime?" "Which is the least criminal, a bad action joined with a good intention, or a good action with a bad intention?" and, "Why are tumultuous, uneasy sensations united with our desires?"

Meanwhile, to augment their knowledge and understanding, and thereby, they hoped, to put down error and wrong, they met every Friday evening in some friendly tavern where, as they assaulted their victuals and their tonics of fermented grape, they discharged their thoughts on the nature of sound and vapor, the way to win friends, fame, and fortune, the dangers of bad laws, and, giving pertinent notice to the presence of Bacchus at their board, the unhappy effects of intemperance.

The Junto's success presently led Franklin to lay plans for another fellowship, grander than the Junto, and one which, though not averse to occasional epicurean delights, was dedicated first and foremost to the advancement of knowledge. The child of Franklin's contriving was the American Philosophical Society, the first guild of learned men in the New World, still alive and in meritorious service, and as we visualize it across the infinite path of time, still one of the nation's historic intellectual wonders.

With Franklin warming its first presidential chair, and with a register of selected "ingenious men residing in the several colonies," the society made its advent in 1743. The passing years, however, saw its membership conferred upon non-Americans, especially the French, as witness Condorcet, Lafayette, Lavoisier, Du Pont de Nemours, and several others. The society's statutes, its minutes announced, "were adopted from the rule of that illustrious body, the Royal Society of London, whose example the American Philosophical Society think it their honor to follow in their endeavors of enlarging the sphere of knowledge and the useful arts." It undertook to give assistance to the "useful subjects . . . in physics, medicine, astronomy, mathematics, etc." At the same time its founders entertained a lively interest in the development of its natural resources. Time saw its virtuosi—so its members officially called themselves—apply their intellects to an almost inexhaustible array of subjects. They cogitated over electrical devices, over plows and mowing machines, and over smoke-free chimneys. They pondered ways to improve the trades and manufactures and the practical arts. They sought to better the colonial agronomy, to battle its hordes of natural enemies in the air and in the soil, and, not the least by any civilized score, to gladden the American palate with better provender and liquors. Now and then Franklin's society would lay up funds to underwrite a cash award for the best paper on such diverse subjects as street lighting, vegetable dyes, foolproof stoves and fireplaces, and the "most expeditious method of computing the longitude from lunar observation." Following the Revolution, the society offered a cash premium for the best essay on "a system of liberal and literary instruction adapted to the genius of the government, and best calculated to promote the general welfare of the United States; comprehending also a plan for instituting and conducting public schools in this country, on principles of the most extensive utility."

ON EDUCATION

So much for Franklin's endeavor to promote and extend the Enlightenment, whether on the lowbrow level of Poor Richard or on the higher intellectual crags of the American Philosophical Society. Like the major portion of Franklin's own education, it directed its attention to an audience of adults, outside the academic cloister, and bereft, therefore, of both its advantages and its hindrances. This is not to imply, however, that Franklin took a dim view of formal education. What he talked down was not its form, but its substance. Like William Penn, he held a low opinion of the higher learning then on tap, especially at Harvard, whence, as a teenager, his identity camouflaged with a pen name, he wrote in his brother's *New England Courant*, "every beetle skull" issued, "well satisfied with his own portion of learning, though perhaps he was as ignorant as ever." These words were evidently put together during a moment when Franklin's resolve to imitate Jesus and Socrates in humility was on leave of absence. Harvard, it is pleasant to recount, bore their composer no long grudge—subsequently, in fact, it canonized Franklin as one of its honorary masters of arts. By this time Franklin too had mellowed sufficiently to let bygones be bygones.

What avails it, Franklin presently wanted to know, to prepare a youth for a station in life which, in all likelihood, he will never occupy, to crowd his head with Latin and Greek—"the quackery of literature"—when all the while he was inadequately broken to the knowledge he needed to make him efficient when he came to man's estate and was expected to provide for himself? What was necessary was a thoroughgoing transvaluation of educational values, a new kind of school which, unlike the senescent Latin grammar school, would undertake to prepare its debutants not only for admission to college, if such was the desire, but for the trades and professions as well.

Even in those days such a boosting of an education addressed to realistic and practical goals was no longer singular—nor did Franklin ever make such a claim. He had drunk from the same Pierian waters as Locke and Milton, and he had ingested some of Defoe's shorter pastries, besides a few confections from Samuel Hartlib, William Petty, and several half-forgotten worthies suffering to reform education in Cromwell's Puritan utopia. All these writers impressed Franklin, but it was Locke and Milton, the former especially, who left the deepest mark. When Franklin, for example, submitted an exhortation for the establishment of a school calculated to keep its pupils "in health and to strengthen and render active their bodies," it was Locke who, antecedently, in his *Some Thoughts Concerning Education*, had urged that "a sound mind in a sound body is a short but full description of a happy state in the world." And when Franklin held for teaching "those things that are likely to be most useful and ornamental" to prepare the young for any office, whether in a trade or profession, it was Milton who had earlier expressed more or less the same idea in his *Tractate on Education*.

PROPOSALS RELATING TO THE EDUCATION OF YOUTH
IN PENNSYLVANIA

The year was 1749 when Franklin, then forty-three, well heeled, well regarded, and a figure of no small say in communal affairs, published his
Proposals Relating to the Education of Youth in Pennsylvania. The embodi-
ment of his educational views, they addressed a summons to Philadelphians, bidding them give a helping hand to the founding of a school to be
known as an academy (the name is out of Milton with a bow to the archpa-
ternal Plato), which would put English and certain modern subjects on an
equal footing with Latin and Greek. To bring this about, the academy
would offer its learning under two headings, the one to be featured in the
English School, and the other in the Classical School.

In its English sector the academy bore heavily on the teaching of English, and unlike its elderly relation, the grammar school, it conducted its
instruction not in Latin but in the vernacular; yet the groundwork for mastering the English idiom, namely, its grammar, rhetoric, and logic, though
laid in the native tongue, was, nevertheless, in the classical—one might even
say medieval—tradition. Once this historic trinity had been brought under
reasonable rein, the learner was ushered into the heritage of English letters,
reading and examining them, as had Franklin himself, in his youth, discovering the manner of their expression and thus developing a literary mode of
his own. He studied both prose and poetry, but the latter, somewhat oddly,
he dealt with not to elevate his spirit but to exercise him in grammar and
syntax and to improve his written style.

Besides expressing its predilection for the maternal tongue, the academy proposed several other departures from tradition, such as courses in
mathematics and natural science, both theoretic and applied, besides commerce, navigation, the mechanical arts, and the modern languages. Nor
were geography and history passed by. To the latter, in fact, the academy
granted a fat and juicy part. Though Franklin formulated no philosophy of
history, as did his illustrious contemporary, Voltaire, yet in the
Frenchman's very mood he looked upon it as something more than a mausoleum for the bones of dead events. As a tale of man's doings seen through
the many-windowed past, history disclosed the record of his experience, his
hopes, his triumphs, and his disasters. It was Franklin's contention that
most subjects—even, in a measure, the matter-of-fact cold sciences—could
profit from an understanding of their significance in man's long and gory
struggle to become civilized. From the life stories, for example, of the
world's immortal standouts, the wicked no less than the virtuous, enlighten-
ing lessons on good and evil could be drawn. The everyday value of public
speaking in its power to sway the general mind could easily be demonstrat-

ed by a scrutiny of the world's salient speechmakers through the ages. The rudimentary postulates of good government, Franklin declared, were plainly visible in the telltale light of the lamp of history. Even the advantages of a public religion and the "excellency of the Christian religion above all others, ancient or modern" could be supported by a comparative examination of historical peoples.

The first physical-fitness addict in this land of whom we have any inkling, Franklin, serving himself freely from the thoughts of Locke and Milton, agreed with them that a proper education of youth must concern itself not only with the inculcation of knowledge, but also with the cultivation of a healthy body, such as he himself had enjoyed in his youth. To such an end pupils taking their fare in the academy commons were to be put under gastronomic regulation. They were, said Franklin, "to diet together plainly, temperately, and frugally." It was a simple enough prescription, and one which, in his almanac, Franklin offered his customers over and over again, but also one which his own gargantuan love of food and drink forbade him personally from observing.

To keep the academy boys in health and to fortify their bodies no less than their wits, Franklin, taking his lines once more from the Messrs. Locke and Milton, called for a program of regular and frequent exercise. Thus they were made to run and leap, to wrestle and swim, the latter an activity which was not only salubrious but which might turn out to be supremely useful. Franklin himself was an expert swimmer; in fact, for a spell he had toyed with the notion of making himself a professional teacher of the watery art. Swimming, the tubby Franklin argued, is not only "a reducer of fatty tissues," it is also a comfort to the psyche. " 'Tis some advantage . . . to be free from the slavish terrors many of those feel who cannot swim when they are obliged to be on the water even in crossing a ferry." Interestingly, when America's Swimming Hall of Fame was founded, Franklin, along with fourteen Olympic champions, was granted an honorable niche.

Of the pursuit of knowledge for its own sake the doctor was intensely wary. "Some men," he cautioned, in the false face of Poor Richard, "grow mad by studying too much to know, but who grows mad by studying good to know?" Nor should it come as a surprise that Franklin, the espouser of practical action, should lay great weight on reinforcing book learning, whenever possible, with actual practice. Let the theories picked up, say, in natural history, be put to work in a little plain dirt gardening, with planting, grafting, and all the other essential knacks and know-hows. And by the same token, let excursions be taken to inspect the lands of master farmers, "their methods observed and reasoned upon for the information of youth."

Finally, let it not be overlooked that for all of Franklin's concern to bring the schooling of young America into concert with the country's mounting secular interests, at bottom he was still directing his effort, as he had in the Junto and in his almanac, toward moral uplift, both individual and collective. "I think with you," he wrote his New York friend Dr. Samuel Johnson in 1750, "that nothing is of more importance for the public weal, than to form and train up youth in wisdom and virtue. Wise and good men are, in my opinion, the strength of a state; much more so than riches or arms, which under the management of ignorance and wickedness, often draw on destruction, instead of providing for the safety of the people." The idea, again, was neither new nor startling. It had fed the meditation of the ancient sages in the East and West, and though cynics have flogged it persistently, even now, in our own convention-shattering era, it remains in high popular regard.

THE PHILADELPHIA ACADEMY—UNIVERSITY OF PENNSYLVANIA

In 1751, two laborious years after Franklin had put forth his proposals, the Philadelphia Academy was ready to attend its first clients—who were restricted to males ranging in age from eight to sixteen. Although nearly all its trustees addressed their confidences to God as congregants of the English Church, the academy drew no religious line, nor did it drill its neophytes in catechism and prayerbook, as was then more or less the rule. Had Franklin had the last word, it is not improbable that he would have put a hard brake on the classics and a sharp spur to the practical and modern subjects. But the school's governors were more discomposed by such an apostasy than the iconoclastic Benjamin. As a result, when their school opened its doors, Latin and Greek were on the scene as they had always been in the grammar school. But Franklin's grove also stood prepared to traffic in such challenging newcomers as English, French, and German. In addition, as it had taken pains to announce in Franklin's *Pennsylvania Gazette,* it offered courses in "History, Geography, Chronology, Logic, and Rhetoric; also Arithmetic, Merchants Accounts [nowadays known as bookkeeping], Geometry, Algebra, Surveying, Gauging, Navigation, Astronomy, Drawing in Perspective, and other mathematical sciences, with natural and mechanical Philosophy [physics], etc." If requested, moreover, the school was ready to take a fling at teacher training.

Aside from undertaking to beam its light on the birchman's art and science, the Philadelphia Academy, despite its amply stocked curricular larder, actually displayed no new material. Both above and below the Potomac private drummers of knowledge were dealing in pretty much the same staples, besides a number of others not listed by Philadelphia's newest purveyor of learning. The demand for tutoring in the bread-and-butter subjects arose as Americans responded more and more to the idea of advancing themselves in the world about them. Needless to say, the demand obtained almost wholly in the flusher towns where the chances for such advancement were more numerous than elsewhere in the land—and in this respect Philadelphia was far from being an exception. The upshot was that Franklin's academy enjoyed a fine prospering. In truth, the school was still in early childhood when it became clear that it had already outgrown its britches. Rechartered and rededicated in 1755, its name enriched to match the enhancement of its mission, it now faced the world as the College, Academy, and Charitable School of Philadelphia. Henceforward, the classical and philosophical lore was reserved for the college and the English and mathematical subjects became the concern of the academy. The charitable school continued, as originally, as a sort of side attraction to grant free instruction to a small flock of orphans.

The sixth shrine of higher learning to rise in colonial America, the College of Philadelphia, like the five others which had preceded it, has survived the remorseless crush of time. In 1779 it was christened anew to become the University of Pennsylvania, the name it currently carries, and which, as everyone knows, is lauded the world around.

In spite of the promise of its fine beginning, the English School presently fell upon dreary days. Its first trustees, though academically of a somewhat more timorous cast of mind than Franklin, were nonetheless in accord with his general outlook. But as the years gradually retired the original governors, their replacements inclined more and more toward the classics and less and less toward the modern learning. In consequence, the English School suffered a sad debility which eventually reduced it to playing the role of Cinderella to its classical step-relation. There is, observed Franklin, as he unbosomed himself in later years when he reviewed his disappointment over what had happened, a baffling prejudice in human nature "to favor ancient customs and habitudes, which incline to a continuance of them after the circumstances which had made them useful, have ceased to exist." And so, one may gather, Franklin was willing to let it be with the school's trustees.

WOMEN AND BLACKS

Although the greater part of Franklin's work and thought in education was pointed at forwarding man's self-improvement, by adult learning and by the reformation of the secondary school curriculum, as he gave it shape and content in the English School, a number of other matters attracted his attention too, and to them also he applied some of his virtuosity.

There is, for one, the subject of girls. At a time when men ran the roost and commonly held themselves to be superior to women in all but child-bearing and, maybe, keeping house, it was only natural that less weight should have been laid on the education of girls than on that of their masculine betters. Even Franklin had little to say on the general improvement of female education. It may well be that the overwhelming run of women needed to know very little beyond the kitchen, the parlor, the bedroom, and the nursery, and for this the prevalent instruction was patently sufficient. In sum, Franklin, applying his utilitarian yardstick, gave his approval to the prevailing notion that what a girl needed was instruction in the three R's to fill her head with knowledge, in virtue and religion to keep her sweet and straight, and in such useful and pleasant accessories as needlework, maybe a little music, and, as in the case of his own daughter and others as fortunately circumstanced, the ability to carry on a passable causerie in French.

But this is not to say that Franklin shared his era's conventional view of the limitations of womankind. He had, it is no secret, a fond eye for the ladies, an amiability which, both here and in far places, they were not loath to reciprocate. They attracted Franklin not only for their natural feminine attributes, but often enough for their competence in practical matters. When the relict of one of his deceased partners proceeded to handle her departed spouse's business affairs with unexpected ease and alacrity, Franklin was not only jubilantly astonished, he even convinced himself that a knowledge of accounting was essential for the thrifty housewife, and as a preparation, moreover, should those days of heartbreak ever befall her, for the bereft and lonesome state of widowhood.

All things considered, Franklin put a rather high confidence in the intelligence of the female, and though he did not foresee the advent of a flock of lady Bacons, Boyles, and Bernoullis, yet some of his best epistolary efforts on science were addressed to women, especially to Polly Stevenson. Some of his young women correspondents of a metaphysical inclination he encouraged, egging them on to indulge their interest, but he called upon them at the same time in the name of common sense to do it *sotto voce*. And if some of the young women were interested in science and philosophy, then there was no reason on earth why they ought to abstain from the affairs of trade and commerce. The sun would rise on some tomorrow, Franklin was sure, when women would take their place beside men in business as well as at the fireside. But not in politics. Here even the enlightened Dr. Franklin put down his gouty foot.

A bitter foe of slavery, Franklin was alert to what in his day constituted the Negro question. He not only worked and politicked to make an end of black enslavement, but he also made a stir to render aid and counsel to such Negroes who were so lucky as to be free. For their benefit he concocted his *Plan for Improving the Condition of the Free Blacks*. He submitted it for the guidance of the Pennsylvania Society for the Abolition of Slavery. What it proposed was simple enough, though for its time it was not only a little suspect but even violently denounced. True to Franklin's inexhaustible trust in organized action, the plan declared for the formation of a commission of twenty-four members to be distributed into four committees, one to give its leadership to non-slave Negroes in matters of moral rectitude and civil comportment; another to supervise the placement of the Negro young as apprentices; a third to find suitable jobs for Negro adults; and a fourth to take steps toward providing schooling for their offspring. Rather interestingly, slavery was the last public question to concern Franklin when, in a defense of Quaker "meddling" in the slave trade, he went to some length to air his disapproval of that dismal industry and to recommend its prompt extinction. As makers of drama, the Fates outdid themselves. Within less than a month Franklin was dead, and his words against human bondage became his final civic pronouncement, a fitting valedictory, if ever, to the career of one of the most extraordinary men to come to growth in America.

A REVIEW

Let us now turn back the past few pages to review some of their points. Like Jefferson and Washington, Franklin ran afoul of his commentators. For years venerators gurgled over him in ecstasy, while debunkers, following in their trail with snickers, picture for us in either case a man who never existed. He was actually a rare man, but like any other he had his faults and even, though less richly, his vices. He was, above all, a respected gentleman of the middle class, well tubbed, ease-loving, cautious of his utterance (save among his intimates when his facile curbstone humor could make a sailor blush), prosperous, given to good works and public service, a moralist expounding the bourgeois virtues of work, efficiency, honesty, thrift, order, and common sense.

So enrapt was Franklin in his middle-class presumptions that, in the end, they held him in thrall. That education is an instrument for social progress he perceived with clarity. Again and again he stood up for causes that challenged the existing class blockades and the religious rationalizing which so often sought to give them sanction. But never was he able to commit himself, as was Jefferson—a much younger man, to be sure—to the advocating of a school system which would help to narrow the gulf that stretched between the classes. A predominantly self-educated man, Franklin had made an artful use of the passing opportunities. Yet aside from the instruction of a small number of orphans, dispensed without charge by the Philadelphia Charity School, Franklin breathed no life into any proposal that might enlarge and improve upon the scant educational chances of the vast aggregation of depressed folk. To provide such people with free education, Franklin feared, would vitiate, or even dissolve, their incentive for self-instruction, a notion which rode the self-made Franklin like a witch on a broomstick. Historically, of course, one has no right to censure a man for accommodating himself to the currents of his time, but glancing over one's shoulder from the vantage point of the present day one may at least wonder at the infirmity of his reasoning.

To bring into being an education aimed at practical and useful ends, Franklin worked with a will, and in 1751, with the consecration of the Academy, his labor fructified. But Franklin, a man of action rather than rumination, successfully avoided coming to serious grips with the formulation of a fundamental educational theory. For his pedagogical canon, such as it was, he leaned largely on others. It was, in short, something of a grab bag, reasoned, no doubt, but certainly no more original than most of Franklin's philosophical cargo. Like Herbert Spencer, some hundred years following, Franklin was sensitive to the chasm which yawned between the wearied offerings of the Latin grammar school and the demands of the new world rising beyond its ramparts. To bring the secondary learning into concordance with the culture of his time, Franklin made appeal, on the one hand, for a substantial relaxing of its classical bias, and, on the other, for a vastly augmented stress on what he deemed essential to success in the new America whose lineaments were just emerging. All this makes sense. But there are other things that count in life besides the practical. Even captains of industry—even, indeed, its corporals and privates—have been known to seek relaxation with brush and palette or through the exhilarating tonic of music.

Unhappily, Franklin's passion for the utilitarian played hob with his usual acumen, and so too in a measure did his own lack of sensibility to the joys to be had from esthetic fulfillment. In consequence, what Franklin proposed was at bottom no more than a replacement of a narrow classical schooling by a heavily weighted utilitarian one. Time, however, saw this fault repaired, and as academies gained in popular acceptance there was nothing they disdained to teach—provided their clientele made a sufficient jingle with its cash—from double-entry bookkeeping and business jurisprudence to wax modeling, needlepoint, the piccolo, the zither and the archlute—even, indeed, Latin and Greek, which though sorely beset by the moderns, were far from being routed.

Chapter 14

Thomas Jefferson

FRANKLIN AND JEFFERSON

Like Franklin, Jefferson (1743–1826) was an active devotee of the Enlightenment, and even more than the Philadelphian, he bore the mark of Europe's humanistic experience. Unlike the staunchly middle-class Franklin, however, Jefferson descended from parents of high estate, the richly landed gentry on his father's side, and the Virginia quality on his mother's. In consequence, their son's schooling was easily managed. It was the best then obtainable in the South, beginning with private teaching in the elementals, followed with a grooming in Latin and Greek, and ascending to a baccalaureate from William and Mary, with an apprenticeship in law for a chaser, speaking freely, under the guidance of the celebrated jurist and patriot, the charming and erudite George Wythe.

In their intellectual and cultural endeavor, Franklin and Jefferson were, often enough, grubbers in the same soil. Both applied themselves to the advancement of knowledge. Both performed feats as scientists and inventors. Both drank heavily from books and gathered and stacked them in their homes, although Jefferson, with a hoard at one time of almost 10,000 volumes, was clearly far more gone in his bibliomania than Franklin. Although they fueled their minds with the learned lucubrations of John Locke, and even translated some of his theorems into their own thoughts and actions, neither of the two was at ease in pure philosophy or, more especially, in the gauzy mists of metaphysics. Even when spun by the wizardly hand of Plato, such transcendental matters floored them, and they dismissed them without much ado as a waste of time. Both men, as every schoolboy knows, glistened in the public service, and both gave liberally out of their personal accounts to succor the less fortunate, but for all his munificence, when Franklin took off for the Heavenly shore he left behind him a respectable bankroll, while Jefferson, once a man of substantial wealth, made the spooky trip on the brink of insolvency.

In religion, the two men announced for deism, though they made it a point at frequent intervals to proclaim themselves Christians, a description which standpat sectarians have often and heatedly disputed. Both gentlemen frequented the Sabbath convocations, Jefferson rather regularly and Franklin whenever the mood bespoke him. But for his lapses Franklin earned absolution, one may hope, with recurrent contributions to Philadelphia's numerous churches, no matter what the nature of their particular credos. It was a practice for which Jefferson had no stomach.

As educated and cultivated men, despite Jefferson's head start, the two founding fathers ran about even. Franklin, as has been recounted, acquired much of his knowledge for his own practical use. Even Latin, whose belles lettres he sniffed at as so much charlatanry, he nevertheless went to great lengths to master, if only because to keep abreast of the world's scientific writing, an understanding of that ancient idiom was indispensable. Jefferson, though certainly not the man to hang crepe on the pursuit of practical knowledge, was a cherisher at the same time of the beautiful. The familiar of Greek as well as Latin, he made use of them not only in his working hours, but after the day's struggle was done he liked on occasion to consort with the ancient masters, hobnobbing and relaxing with them and their euphoric paganism as did the humanists of an earlier date. Jefferson's esthetic passion glowed insistently. It communicated in art and music and architecture—even, indeed, in education. One may still descry it in the colonnaded grandeur of Monticello and the rolling fields and wooded slopes which frame it so simply, yet so gracefully, in the enveloping country quiet. Even more, one glimpses it in the columned calm of the University of Virginia, against the climbing background of the Blue Ridge wall, a lovely testament to the vision of the man who gave it life.

JEFFERSON AND RELIGIOUS FREEDOM

Let us expand a bit on some of the aforementioned points to see how they work themselves into Jefferson's educational beliefs. There is, to begin, his deism, and its assumption that a man has a right to think freely for himself. Next, there is his interest in science. And finally, there is his confidence in the doctrine of natural rights.

The deistic revelation we have already put under the glass, and there is little to be gained from another inspection. Let it be enough to note that from it sprang Jefferson's belief in an ordered universe—"God's machine"—wherein, man, playing his bit in the divine design, was equipped to fathom the cosmic wonder and, as one millennium shuffled off after another, to fulfill his ultimate assignment therein. Human progress in the scheme of deistic things was at bottom no more than the unfolding of the divine plan, and the record of bygone events was simply testimony to the Eternal's infinite wisdom.

Does a man have a right to do his own thinking? Then he also has the right to worship God as he sees fit. Man, Jefferson was convinced, could pilot his soul to the heavenly harbor under his own direction, or, if he preferred, he was free to head his ship for the joys of an abiding hot beyond. "The care of a man's soul," Jefferson insisted, "belongs to himself . . .," and not even the Lord of Hosts, he ventured to add, would save a man who chose to be damned. With the Almighty Himself at such caution to abstain from interfering with a man's freedom to make his postmortem bed as he chose, then obviously that man was entitled to the same deference from his fellows while he was still on earth.

As a member of the Virginia House of Burgesses, Jefferson fathered the commonwealth's historic Statute for Religious Freedom. He had submitted it to his colleague Justinians as a bill as early as 1779, shortly before he became governor, but seven years of talk, delay, hostility, and compromise dragged by before they could steel themselves to enact it, somewhat altered, into law. Effecting the divorce of state and church in all public affairs, the statute required that all men be "free to profess and by argument to maintain their opinions in matters of religion, and that the same shall in no wise diminish, enlarge, or affect their civil capacities." Needless to state, the enactment of the law did not make short shrift of the antagonism it had bred. Right-thinking churchmen, especially among the disestablished Episcopalians, put little stock in Jefferson's dictum that "truth is great and will prevail if left to herself," and for years they continued to assail the measure and to pour sharp words upon its maker—in fact, some of Jefferson's best enemies were men of God. But time has a way of cooling the hottest of controversies. Not only did the Virginia Statute for Religious Freedom endure, but before long the principle for which it stood was to be translated into the Bill of Rights.

THE SCIENTIST—AND THE UNIVERSITY OF VIRGINIA

"Nature," Jefferson once disclosed, "intended me for the tranquil pursuit of science"—a self-estimate which was somewhat dreamy, not to say a bit wide of the mark. Even so, his ardor for science seldom flagged, and whenever the chance offered, he took up the pursuit. His Monticello home contained a veritable arsenal of scientific apparatus, from familiar springs, knobs, cranks, and pulleys to mysterious and sinister-looking polygraphs, chronometers, batteries, and dynamometers. A fellow in the American Philosophical Society, Jefferson became its third president. His scientific studies, like Franklin's, varied and they ranged through many fields. Thus at one time or another Jefferson cast his nets for knowledge in mathematics or physics or even astronomy and meteorology. He was versed in anatomy and physiology, and in an emergency he could stitch torn flesh together or set a broken tibia. In France he directed his attention to the science of ballooning, for the moment the *dernier cri* in the Gallic wonderland, and before he was done he had delivered himself of several dissertations on "The Aeronautic Art."

But it was in biology that his lamp glowed the warmest. "What a field we have at our doors to signalize ourselves in," he wrote in 1789 to the Reverend Joseph Willard, president of Harvard. "The botany of America is far from being exhausted, its mineralogy is untouched, and its natural history or zoology totally mistaken and misrepresented." His passion to explore the land and water, to discern their hidden resources, and to know at first hand their flora and fauna, eventually worked its findings into his *Notes on Virginia,* the only book he ever published. And doubtless his zeal for nature had some bearing in later years when, as President of the United States, he prevailed upon Congress to grant the wherewithal for the epoch-making expedition of Lewis and Clark. "I am for encouraging science in all its branches," he remarked in 1799 to Elbridge Gary. The ideal spurred him through his many years, to his very end, in fact, at eighty-three. A pulsing, breathing aspiration, it tantalized his dreams, sustaining him in his hunt for scientific truth, and culminating triumphantly in the opening shortly before his death of the University of Virginia. Mr. Jefferson's University—so it came to be known—was dedicated to the advancement of all the sciences, from anthropology to zoology, for the betterment and happiness of every man.

THE PEOPLE, THE GOVERNMENT, AND EDUCATION

Let us introduce ourselves to the ensuing lines with a text: "All men are created free and equal, and are endowed by their creator with certain unalienable rights, among which are life, liberty, and the pursuit of happiness." The words, of course, are from the Declaration of Independence, and they were put together by Thomas Jefferson, affirmed and undersigned by his colleagues in Congress, assembled at Philadelphia in 1776. No man was ever more steadfast in his commitment to human liberty than Jefferson, and none was a more implacable foe of its detractors. The natural human rights for which Jefferson spoke so fervently we still cherish—indeed, without them no people could be truly free. In a world, moreover, where everything, if given time, may alter, our natural rights, Jefferson asserted, must be counted as a singular exception. "Nothing," he declared, "is unchangeable but the inherent rights of man." Such rights, he insisted, are the equal possession of all, whether high- or lowborn, rich or poor, and regardless of race or religion.

One of man's inalienable rights is to establish governments and to participate freely therein. "Every man and every body of men on earth," Jefferson wrote, "possess the right of self-government. . . . Individuals exercise it by their single will; collections of men by that of their majority; for the law of the majority is the natural law of every society of men." But lest the majority become despotic, an individual was free to oppose—even, indeed, to rebel—and to do this he had the right to air his grievances in speech or in writ, without fear of jeopardy. It was Jefferson's view that man's capacity for self-government, for all its natural provenance, was not innate, and that to be effective, representative government must needs be grounded on popular enlightenment. "Every government," he observed, "degenerates when trusted to the rulers of the people alone." Therefore, he went on, "the people themselves are its only safe depositories." And to render them safe their minds must be improved. To make this possible, he continued, somewhat in the vein of France's Condorcet, it behooves Virginia to "come in aid of public education."

BILL FOR THE MORE GENERAL DIFFUSION OF KNOWLEDGE

In 1779, the year Jefferson began what was to become a seven years' struggle for religious freedom in Virginia, he also confronted the lawmakers with a Bill for the More General Diffusion of Knowledge. Seeking, as its sponsor explained, to make education available to every child in the commonwealth—not counting the blacks—and thereby to lay the "principal foundations of future order," Jefferson's plan called upon every county to divide itself into "wards," or "hundreds," each some five to six miles square. Every estate thus laid out was to maintain a school where, for at least three years, the young—both girls and boys—were to have a chance to introduce themselves at public cost to the three R's, and "much longer at private expense as parents, guardians, or friends shall think proper."

Besides coming to grips with the ancestral fundamentals, the learners were to give some of their thought to the lessons of the past, especially the historic tidal marks of Greece, Rome, England, and America. Thus fortified, Jefferson hoped, they would be better prepared when they attained maturity to judge the quality of their own government, and be alert to any abuses and corruptions of the public trust. As might be expected, they were also to be inoculated with the high points of morality, but not with the truths of Holy Writ, which, because of Jefferson's proclivity for the separation of church and state, he did not regard as suitable study in the state-supported houses of knowledge.

When the three years of free schooling had run their course, the district's smartest boy—provided his parents could convince the state that money was a stranger to their pockets—was to be appointed by the state's overseer, or superintendent, for further free illumination in one of a score of state-appointed Latin grammar schools. There the boy would nourish his genius with formidable doses of Latin and Greek, English grammar, a dash of geography and higher arithmetic, including common and decimal fractions, and the mystery of extracting square roots from, say, 4,469 or even 2,255,314.

After a couple of years of such intellectual tussling, the best twenty of the state-supported scholars were to be "raked from the rubbish" to continue their cerebral skirmishings for yet another four years. Of these wonder boys, finally, the ten brightest were to be picked every year for further expansion at the College of William and Mary, there to be "educated, boarded, and clothed," once more as guests of the state. Thus Jefferson, who believed in "a natural aristocracy among men," hoped to "avail the state of those talents which nature has sown as liberally among the poor as the rich. . . ." As for the ones not so blessed—the rubbishy ones—unless the Lord took pity and staked some of them to an unexpected windfall, their presence in the halls of learning came to an end.

Unhappily, girls never had occasion to find out whether they were members in good standing or not. True to the custom of that day, the grammar school offered its learning exclusively to the male, and so under the Jeffersonian dispensation the most the girls could count on was the three years of free instruction in the rudiments. Whatever schooling a young miss snared beyond that, whether she was the owner of a high intelligence or not, depended on the capacity of her parents to finance it.

Jefferson's bill came to naught. It succumbed not for its limitations, such as they were, but for what posterity has since extolled as its virtues. Reprehended by the beneficiaries of the established way, it collided, for one thing, with the lingering Southern tradition that education of the young, like feeding, clothing, and roofing them, was the concern not of the state, but of their parents, a doctrine which, when put to practice, invariably shed its favors on the privileged few to the detriment of the hard-pressed many. As might be expected, the bill also ran into the opposition of ecclesiastics who, over the centuries, had come to regard the schooling of the common child, if he were to be schooled at all, as their prerogative, and who, needless to say, did not countenance Mr. Jefferson's unbiblical curriculum.

What brought about the bill's demise, however, was something far more strangling than the bonds of custom: the universal reluctance to pay taxes. To enable the children of the commonwealth to make themselves literate was all very fine—maybe, in a sense, even noble—and only the most intransigent of Virginia's ruling gentry would openly gainsay it. In fact, as long as Jefferson argued his case on purely theoretical grounds, it even evoked a ripple of approval. But when he moved beyond the limits of the suppositional into the sphere of practical action he ran head-on into the planters' unwillingness to foot the bill. In consequence, Jefferson's project was decried as an extravagance, and the givers of law found it prudent to vote it down. Down with it too went Jefferson's proposal to found a public library at Richmond. More than a quarter of a century following, in 1817, the Great Libertarian formulated another bill to establish free tax-supported schools for all the white children in the Old Dominion, the "keystone of the arch of our government," as he called it, but like its martyred predecessor, it too was laid in the grave.

Controverted when it was still young, Jefferson's plan has generated contention ever since. There is no doubt that its main assumptions were not original—for that matter they were not even American, but French—but this is, of course, immaterial. More to the point is the indictment that the plan is committed to the doctrine of an intellectual aristocracy, that it fails to make attendance mandatory, and that it allows no place for the utilitarian and practical subjects that are so essential to forwarding the comfort of the vast run of common Americans.

All these objections hold water. But this is not to say that Jefferson was unaware of them. If, for example, he declared for an intellectual elect, then it was because he was convinced that only through the cultivation of the best minds can man achieve a better civilization. If he turned his back on coercing parents to put their offspring to school, then it was because he placed the freedom of an individual to lead his own life, within the bounds of decency and decorum, above all else. And if he—unlike Franklin, the Swiss Pestalozzi, and the latter's great disciple, Fellenberg—eschewed the utilitarian studies, it was because his motive was not to train the youth vocationally, but rather to inculcate in them the irreducible essentials for the exercise of intelligent citizenship. To this end a full command of reading and writing was indispensable, not only to make effective civic participation possible, but also to serve its owner fruitfully in the years ahead as an instrument for his continued self-enhancement.

Jefferson's proposed legislation to bring enlightenment to the people of Virginia at public expense was the first of its species in the republic. Dedicated to the advancement of a better self-government, it was secular through and through. And if the Monticello squire embraced the doctrine of a class system of the intellect, an idea which romantic democrats even now regard as something of a shame and scandal, then at least let it be remembered that Jefferson looked askance at the proposition, all too frequently bruited about in his time, that in the principality of the mind there is no room at the top for the poor. To give the poorer folk of high intelligence a chance to fulfill their natural powers, Jefferson made special provision—meager, perhaps, and insufficient as the science of social pathology looks upon such things today, but still a chance.

REFURBISHING WILLIAM AND MARY

In 1779, a banner year, as has been indicated, for Jefferson's legislative invention, the commonwealth made him its governor. Though his term of office ran for but a year, whereupon he was reelected, unluckily he was out of his depth, and as a result his administration reaped him more sorrow than joy. When time at length brought his tenure to an end, the hapless governor made his exit under a pall of gloom, a disenchanted man suffering the humiliation not only of alleged incompetence but of failure as well, and resolved henceforth to live in bucolic solitude.

But in all this cloudbank of blighted hopes there appeared now and then a rift. Besides discharging his gubernatorial duties, Jefferson also acted in the capacity of a visitor for the College of William and Mary. It was a position much to his intellectual inclination, one which not only offered him a temporary respite from his political travail but which enabled him also to exert his liberal influence in the effort to rejuvenate his aging alma mater.

The college had come into being in the shank of the seventeenth century, in 1693, the auxiliary of the Anglican church and a nursery for her nascent men of God. The years had seen it undergo some alteration, slow to be sure, but even so, as the Revolution drew closer, William and Mary was showing definite signs of worldliness with an ever-swelling interest in secular affairs and a shrinking concern in those of divinity. The new spirit and the skepticism it wooed occasioned a number of novel and at times disconcerting consequences. The yoke of piety and moral rectitude, for example, which in those days pressed so heavily upon life in the higher learning, was slightly eased, affording students a somewhat greater leeway in their comportment, academic as well as profane. Even some of their instructors inclined to unstarch, at all events once they were beyond the college precinct. A few of them, in truth, grew somewhat careless of decorum, to exult their egos in taproom shindies, racing their metabolism with alcohol and playing cards into the far watches of the night in order to strengthen their minds.

Such jinks, needless to say, grieved the college fathers, and in 1779, led by Jefferson, they seized their sanitary mops and brushes to cleanse the school of its indecencies, and while they were about it to bring its stock of learning into greater consonance with the emerging mundane mood. They refurbished it with new chairs in medicine, mathematics, physics, moral philosophy, law, and economics. Divine science, not so long ago the shining star in the academic firmament and the chief reason for the college's founding, now fell under critical eyes. The sacred chair, asseverated Jefferson, the foreman of its deriders, was "incompatible with freedom in a republic," and so, foreshadowing the commonwealth's eventual separation of church and state, the reformers made an end of it. To solace the mourners, and as a vent, perhaps, for its conscience, the college conjured up a professorship of civil and ecclesiastical history. At the same time it commissioned the appointment of a "missionary . . . to the several tribes of Indians" who, besides instructing the Red Men for their baptismal consecration, was "to investigate their customs, religions, and . . . their languages." In addition, the renovators, again flagged on by Jefferson, introduced the elective system and broke ground for a student honor system.

MR. JEFFERSON'S UNIVERSITY—CONTINUED

With so many of his pet ideas adopted by William and Mary, the governor, one would think, should have been thrilled. Under his counsel and direction his ailing alma mater had been rescued, her moral malignancies uprooted, and her curricular arteriosclerosis assuaged, if not routed. But Jefferson had set his mind on something more. What engaged his thinking was not just the resuscitating of an elderly college but the making, in the process, of an entirely new athenaeum—a state university promoting the highest learning in every branch of science. "Have you ever turned your thoughts to such a plan?" he queried in a letter to John Adams in 1814. "I mean," he went on, "to a specification of the particular sciences of real use in human affairs, how they might be grouped as to require so many professors only as might bring them within the views of a just and enlightened economy."

To such a scheme Jefferson had addressed his reflections even in his greener days, and when, as a young Virginian, he returned from the universities of France, his plan was pretty well thought out, almost ready, in fact, for submission, through the Honorable Joseph Carrington Cabell, to the Virginia legislature. But that fateful day, like many another of mark in the annals of human progress, took its own good time in coming, and it was not till 1817, when Jefferson was in his middle seventies, that the givers of Virginia law granted their assent for the establishment of a state university, and even had the good sense to implement their jurisprudence with a slight subvention.

From this gentle seeding sprouted the University of Virginia. From its conception to its materialization it was Jefferson's baby, the only one of his sundry educational aspirations to attain fulfillment. No other great grove of the mind was ever more the handiwork of a single author. Indeed, the maker's sign is omnipresent. It was Jefferson who picked the land whereon it rose; it was he who designed its edifices; he who hired and directed the hands that fashioned them; and he again who scoured civilization to round up its first professors, comprising several Englishmen, a German, and a Virginian.

Then as now such things ran into money. Again it was Jefferson, the weaver of dreams, who went out to raise it, cajoling funds from tight-fisted lawmakers, begging and borrowing from likely altruists, and digging into his own pocket to keep the venture going. Jefferson inspired the school's requirements for admission and for graduation—he even worked out the details of its administrative government. There was to be no hierarchy of professors; instead, all were to be put on equal footing, with the same rights, privileges, and immunities. The university was to put itself in the hands not of a president, the prevailing title in America, but of a rector, a designation of medieval vintage but still in use in much of contemporary Europe.

Further, although the man from Monticello held a bachelor's degree from William and Mary and honorary letters from a number of other institutions, Virginia's first students could look forward to no such gauds and gratifications. Upon graduation the college invested them with no patrician baccalaureate but with only a plain, plebian diploma. And if some of them should later rise to high renown, their alma mater, though certainly pleased, would not award them letters in *honoris causa.* In fact, to this day the University of Virginia has abstained from granting its degrees for any reason other than the successful completion of its prescribed courses.

When, in early March of 1825, the university swung open its doors to conduct its first services, it was the most up-to-date institution of its sort, the first frankly secular university the republic had ever seen, and the nearest in its purport and quality to our own conception of a state university. Eight schools made up the academic family, each staffed by a single professor—one apiece for ancient languages, modern languages, mathematics, natural philosophy, natural history, anatomy and medicine, moral philosophy, and law.

"This university," Jefferson had proclaimed some five years preceding, "will be based on the illimitable freedom of the human mind." To the attainment of this ideal, professors were assured the right "to follow the truth wherever it may lead," regardless of what sacred gods were manhandled in the process. By the same stroke, students were free to study according to their own lights in whatever schools they preferred. Not only were they free to elect their studies, they were also free to attend classes or not, as they chose. They were at liberty to expose themselves to the learned recitals of their professors, or thinking the better of it, to absent themselves to engage in larking or snoozing or some other form of constructive leisure. Such voluntary attendance at lecture sessions is a hoary practice in much of the European higher learning, and one which to a large degree still obtains, but it is one which with us is, even now, the exception rather than the rule. "Our institution," Jefferson went on record, "will proceed on the principle . . . of letting anyone come and listen to whatever he thinks may improve the condition of his mind." All that was asked of a student was an "elementary qualification . . . and sufficient age."

Although Jefferson cast an emphatic vote for stiff and frequent examinations, he had no liking for the familiar faculty policing of such engagements. A libertarian of the first order and, more important still, a man of unquenchable honor, he was contumacious to the notion esteemed by specialists in righteousness, that people could be made virtuous by law. Jefferson's first concern was the cultivation of honor, not morality, and to enable young men to develop a sound relish, if not for what is moral, then at least for what is decent, he laid his weight not on coercion but on self-discipline. As for the student's freedom of expression, and even his open dissent, the university's liberal rector delegated all disciplinary powers to a council of student "censors." The consequence was the genesis of self-government besides the unproctored examination—or the honor system. Sprung from the soil of man's unalienable rights, these boons, beset and berated though they were by conservatives and obscurantists on every side, grew for all that, slowly and toilsomely, until at length the passing years saw them ripen into a tradition, prized and powerful and solidly set, and, rather interestingly, one which still renders effective service at Mr. Jefferson's University today.

PRINCIPLES

The University of Virginia, as has been said, was the only one of Jefferson's educational dreams to come true. His other educational proposals, for all the logic and eloquence he could muster in their behalf, succumbed to the cultural prejudices and preconceptions of his day. But surely this cannot be said of the principles which gave them their vital sap. Not a few, though they were rejected or given a hard time during their sponsor's days on earth, have since implanted themselves in the national custom, as essential to the pursuit of happiness in our incomparable republic as pizza palazzos, football hippodromes, and bumper-to-bumper traffic.

There is, first, Jefferson's insistence on the separation of state and church. In these present days, for good or for ill, the law of the land has imposed a proscription on the teaching of religion in any public houses of learning.

Second, there is Jefferson's declaration for complete and unfettered religious freedom. This principle too has worked itself into the nation's juridic writ, and by virtue of its presence it assures parents and guardians the right to put their young into the school of their choice, whether sacred or profane, private, parochial, or public.

Third, there is Jefferson's gigantic trust in a man's right to do his own thinking. A right with no strings attached, it is nature's offering to Homo sapiens. Even professors—aye, even students—are its beneficiaries, and it must be allowed to function freely at all times. Does such thinking turn out to be naïve, specious, or even meretricious? It makes no matter—so long as reason and free inquiry, "the natural enemies of error," are not hobbled in their warfare on the false and fallacious. Truth, Jefferson was sure, "has nothing to fear . . . unless by human interposition disarmed of her natural weapons, free argument and debate; errors ceasing to exist when it is permitted freely to contradict them." Reason, in short, is not the corruption of freedom, but its salvation. Translated into pedagogic lingo, this doctrine has become known as academic freedom, the right, that is, of a teacher to teach and the right of a learner to learn without hindrance from any source.

Needless to say, this ideal was not fully realized—nor, for that matter, is it even now. In fact, its most glowing advocate, forgetting that he was a liberal, found himself constrained to exact an oath of loyalty from schoolmasters before letting them perform their mystery upon the young. The Jefferson who cried out for a man's right to disagree with the accepted articles of the current orthodoxy was the same libertarian who dreaded the subversive possibilities in the teaching of government, especially the diableries of the Federalists. A newcomer in the teaching frock, and hence an unknown, Jefferson warned, had better be thoroughly looked into. For all one knew, the fellow "might be one of that school of quondam federalism, now 'consolidation,' " a deadly danger. It is our duty, he went on, "to guard against such principles being disseminated among our youth, and the diffusion of that poison, by a previous prescription of the texts to be followed in their courses." Thus the logic of even the best intentioned when they stand in the shadow of fear and prejudice. Even so, let the full peal of bells ring out the man's praise. His lapses were rare, and after one has made the necessary allowances there is no doubt that in the struggle for academic freedom Jefferson stands at the front of the line.

Although several of the founding fathers trumpeted hosannas to the power of education to improve humankind, and hence the public weal, it was Jefferson who came closest to the ideal we cherish today, a system of universal schooling, publicly organized and operated, and supported by taxes. And of the fathers, only Jefferson—save possibly, Madison, a pianissimo exception—spoke out strongly for the idea, almost axiomatic in these later days, that the fortune of an effective democratic governance rests inescapably in the hands of an educated and enlightened citizenry. Jefferson's plan to furnish free public schooling to all young white Virginians, male and female, for three years, and more beyond that to selected boys, was a step to such an end. Interestingly, for its execution his scheme involved a single coherent school organization, ranging from the elementary grades through the secondary ones and the college—the so-called "educational ladder," a commonplace today, but extraordinary in Jefferson's time, so at odds, in fact, with the wonted practice that more than a hundred years came and went before the American people were able to achieve a ladder of free, tax-supported public education, complete rung upon rung from kindergarten through higher learning.

Chapter 15

Noah Webster

EDUCATING YOUNG AMERICA

While Jefferson was expounding his views on public education and trying
in vain to induce the Virginia planters to frame them into law, several
others undertook to discharge their own ideas on the subject of educating
young America. Like Jefferson, most of them had been brushed by the
breezes blowing out of intellectual France. Patriots all, and pillars of the
middle class, they followed various callings, from doctoring the sick to
preaching God's holy ordinances, and though none of them was a professional educator, yet at least two of them are known to have resorted at some
time to schoolmastering.

The educational ideas of these worthies were often at variance, but for
the most part they saw eye to eye on the presuppositions which grounded
their thinking. Education, they wholeheartedly agreed, is the seedbed of
individual and social progress. Neglect a youngster's schooling, and you do
it to the damage of the man, of whom, as the saying goes, the child is the

father. And if the adult citizen's well-being is impaired, so, in consequence, is that of the nation. Education not only is indispensable to the furtherance of the common weal, but it is the natural right of every child. To assure its attainment, the republic needs to provide for a new education, freely available to all, one which will not only advance the general enlightenment but will also cultivate intelligent leaders to cope with the problems of tomorrow. So vital is education to the national progress that its course may not be left to chance; it must be made a state responsibility.

So much for the general design. Let us now, in this chapter and the following two, turn to some of the details as put forth by three of its foremost advocates, namely, Noah Webster (1758–1843), a lexicographer, Benjamin Rush, a physician and surgeon, and Samuel Knox, an ordained man of God.

WEBSTER THE AMERICAN

Of these worthies the most publicized, both during his lifetime and after, was doubtless Noah Webster. The composer of the *American Dictionary of the English Language,* which is the father of all the Websters of today, he was also the architect of one of the most successful books ever published, the *American Spelling Book.* Appearing in the fall of 1783, priced over the counter at 14 pennies a copy, it multiplied with all the abandon of a cockroach, passing through edition after edition to reach, by the latest reckoning, at least a hundred million copies, read and pondered, it is estimated, by no less than a billion readers. The book was resorted to all over the land, and save for his lunch and bean shooter, often enough it was the only cargo a schoolboy toted to the academic bench. "Above all people," observed the Honorable Jefferson Davis, some years, to be sure, before Sumter, "we are united, and above all books which have united us, I place the spelling-book of Noah Webster." Famous last words, alas!

Though posterity recalls him mostly for his successful word-mongering, Webster was nevertheless a man of extensive interests. He studied and wrote about epidemic diseases, beginning with a slight allegro exercise thereon and ending up fortissimo with a two-volume history of the subject. He sought to fathom the nature of dew and delivered himself of an essay of some consequence on his findings. He edited John Winthrop's historic journal, and all by himself he undertook to pin a similar honor upon the Bible. Although he disparaged the teaching of such mildewed tongues as Latin and Greek, he himself was a veritable Berlitz, a *Sprachschule* on legs, as it were, the familiar not only of the languages of Homer and Virgil, but a score of others as well, including Sanskrit. Finally, to him we ascribe the paternity of the copyright law in America, and if he was not the actual genitor of the census, then at least he assisted as a midwife in ushering it into life.

For all his brontosaurian endeavor his excursions into the ways of the deliquescent dewdrop, his panting to correct and improve Holy Writ, besides his exploits in lexicography, spelling, geography, history, and suchlike, wet blankets on the natural joys of childhood, Webster must still be set at the second table. The vigor and freshness that glisten through the pages of Franklin and Jefferson eluded him. His mind bulged with knowledge, but at bottom it was merely a collection, hungrily but indiscriminately assembled, dedicated neither to lighten nor ennoble life nor to exhilarate the spirit, but to such earnest and practical ends as, say, bagging definitions for his dictionary. He gave music lessons, but music dwelt not in his heart. He was religious, but not in the sense that the love of God and man was woven into the fibers of his existence, but rather in that religion was the calisthenic which preserved him from moral annihilation. Poetry without moral or religious purpose he dismissed as futile.

Though Webster made his escape from the harsh labors of schoolmastering while he was still in tender years, the dust of chalk clung to him to the end. No wearer of the magisterial mantle ever fevered with greater heat to instruct and to correct error among the old no less than the young. And yet he actually entertained very little confidence in youth—the sad reality, indeed, is that all too often they depressed his psyche. A stickler for linguistic exactness, he fondly hoped to find the same attribute among his educated compatriots. Linguistic indecorum he could not tolerate even from his wife. It is reported that when she caught him being overfamiliar with the maid, she exclaimed that she was "surprized." "Nay, madam," Noah corrected her, "*You* are astonished; *we* are surprized."

Some of Webster's portrayers have called up pictures of him as a waxen, mirthless Yankee, self-serving, self-important, and devoid of passion. But if an overflowing love of country may be described as a passion, then surely such derogation needs to be redressed. Cold and cocksure the man was, without a doubt, and bilious too were his suspicions about the generality of the human race. But about his primary motives there is nothing discreditable. Whatever his limitations, they fade before the memory of his patriotism.

It was in the mood of the 100 percent American that Webster addressed himself to the composition of his major works, his histories and geographies, and even his grammar. It was no accident that he called his speller an *American Spelling Book,* nor was it mere hazard that he named his dictionary an *American Dictionary of the English Language.* In the one he attempted to offer his countrymen a spelling which reflected their pronunciation. In the other he defined words in the native idiom. And in both he braved the motherland's sneers by conferring linguistic legitimacy upon words which in origin and use were totally American, and never even whispered at Buckingham. Webster waged a relentless war for a simplified spelling of the American vernacular, and if today we write *honor* and *odor* in place of the British *honour* and *odour,* the reason behind it is preeminently Noah Webster. He snipped the *k* off *physick* and *tactick,* and he gave his countrymen a *plow* to replace the Englishman's *plough,* and when an American needed the law's correction, he stored him in a *jail* instead of a *gaol.* And so on and on.

THE SIAMESE TWINS

As might be expected, the nationalism which vibrated so powerfully in Webster's heart set off an echo in his pedagogy—the two are, so to speak, Siamese twins. The aim of education, he let it be known, is to make good Americans. "Americans," he bristled, "unshackle your minds and act like independent beings. You have been children long enough subject to the control . . . of a haughty parent!" To such an end the native schooling must be made to reflect the American culture. Cast out the Briton's hand-me-downs. Cry up America instead, her land and people, her freedom, her hopes and dreams, and instill them in the child while he is yet a babe. As soon, indeed, as he opens his lips to talk, "let the first word he lisps be Washington."

A man of action rather than ideas, Webster radiated no glory as an educational thinker. His pedagogy, such as it was, derived not so much from any deep reading and reflection on the subject as from his day-by-day experience as a schoolmaster sweating to lodge the rudiments of knowledge in the pates of his rustic and far-from-eager fledglings. He had ensconced himself in the teacher's pulpit when he was barely out of his teens and at the time was still burning the lamp at Yale. From this venture in didactics and a few others which followed he gathered a number of ideas which, true to the schoolmaster's immemorial wont, he carefully stored between the covers of his notebooks. He laid them aside for a decade or so when, the itch to be heard overmastered him, and he embroidered them into an essay "On the Education of Youth in America," which he proceeded to spread in a half-dozen installments in the pages of his own *American Magazine.* Although there was little in Webster's views that had not been expressed by others—often enough in a far more ingratiating rhetoric—yet he himself entertained a rather high opinion of them, high enough to sanction their being reprinted several times in various organs of opinion.

AMERICAN SCHOOLS!

What stands out in Webster is, of course, his patriotic passion. Again and again it inflamed him. It ran in his blood like the germs of love or the streptococcus. We perceive its fire in some of his essays and harangues and even in his schoolbooks—even, in fact, in the calmer reflective moments of his educational theory. When Webster undertook to persuade his countrymen to make their schools American, they were in large part still what they had been before the Revolution, which is to say, recognizably British. The knowledge they served the American young bore a lingering British redolence, the same aroma in the main as that which permeated the ancient halls of learning in the kingdom overseas. The books they used were ordinarily English, concocted by Englishmen for English youth, as witness Thomas Dilworth's *A New Guide to the English Tongue.* Endorsed and recommended by England's loftiest nabobs of both the laity and the clergy, this tiny volume stood high in the esteem of British pedagogues, if not in that of their pupils, and for years it sold expansively not only in the motherland but in her far-flung dependencies as well. In this respect America was no exception. In fact, years after the colonies had become the states, Dilworth's guide, for all its British fats and starches, continued to be common provender in scholastic America. Patriots, needless to say, found such a diet disgraceful, and it was to rectify this situation that the industrious Noah devoted a large portion of his long life.

What the man could do showed itself as early as 1785 when, in his *Grammatical Institute of the English Tongue*—Webster's challenge to the contaminating Dilworth—he not only confronted America's rising generation with familiar standbys from Swift and Shakespeare, but he regaled them as well with gems from Thomas Paine's *Crisis,* and even a couple of oratorical pearls dropped in the august chambers of Congress. Five years following, in 1790, the gauge of Webster's nationalistic pressure shot several notches higher. His *Little Reader's Assistant,* a revision and renewal of his earlier effort, but with the free-thinking Paine discreetly deleted, included "stories from the history of America . . .," besides "a Federal catechism, being a short and easy explanation of the Constitution of the United States [Ah, that it were so!] . . . and several principles of government and commerce . . .," all of which, happily, pupils could learn without even trying, for they "were adapted to the capacities of children."

Besides actively upholding the national honor on the textbook front Webster emitted patriotic pronunciamentos in several other sectors. Teaching, he insisted, is something of an art, and its practice must be entrusted to none but the ablest hands, and these must be American. When Webster heard that Washington was about to put his heir in the keeping of a Scottish tutor, he upbraided the father of our country with so much heat that the man abstained from his incipient treason and hired a New Englander instead.

Even worse than confiding a young American to the care of an outlander in his own home was the pernicious custom, especially among the Southern quality, of exporting their offspring for enlightenment in some foreign grove. Such doings, Webster felt, might have been seemly enough in the colonies' paleolithic period—perhaps they might even have been unavoidable—but now that Old Glory billowed o'er the land the practice was un-American, and it had better be stopped. Let young people master their lessons over here, and when their task is done, and if they still smart to savor the world, then let them commence with a tour of a year or more of these United States. Thus, Webster believed, they would not only become privy to the country's geography and the varied culture of its people, but thereby "all jealousies should be removed . . . and a harmony of views and interests be cultivated by friendly intercourse."

Like Jefferson, Webster believed that every child, whether in skirts or pantaloons, should be assured a chance to go to school, not because nature may or may not have ordained it as an inalienable right, but because without knowledge no people, however admired by God, can effectually govern itself. "The more generally knowledge is diffused among the substantial yeomanry," Webster asserted, "the more perfect will be the laws of the state." The first step toward achieving such a fair and happy land is simple enough: Let every hamlet bedizen itself "with a school, at least four months in a year, when boys are not otherwise employed. . . .Here children should be taught the usual branches of learning, submission to superiors and to laws, the moral or social duties, the history and transactions of their own country, the principles of liberty and government." And here too their natural animal spirits will be appropriately curbed by instruction in the "principles of virtue and good behavior." Rather curiously, Webster issued a ban against Bible-reading in the schoolroom, although it was then still a common practice in American learning.

PATRIOTISM AND UTILITARIANISM

Side by side with Webster's overriding patriotism marched his unflagging utilitarianism. Whatever is taught, whether it be how to spell "cat" or how to bound Pennsylvania, should be taught with an eye to its eventual usefulness. What avails it, he lamented, to belabor a boy's gray cells with Latin and Greek when all the while fortune has him marked for service in the cowshed, or, if he is lucky, for an accountant's perch in some bureau of higher commerce? "Every man," Webster declared, "should be able to speak and write his native tongue with correctness, and have some knowledge of mathematics. . . ." But besides the learning which is of common use, he should be directed to pursue those branches which are connected more intimately with the business in which some day he hopes to make a living.

Like the male, the female needs to be made literate in the vernacular, and like him she should make acquaintance with the arithmetic of everyday use. Like the male, she should be on easy terms with the republic's history and geography. The disposition of the fair ones being what it is, which is to say, full of "delicate sentiments" and the "finest feelings," these creatures of finer clay should be plied with lovely literature, especially the verbal apéritifs of the great poets. The ability of a young miss to hold converse in French, though carrying the justification of both Franklin and Jefferson, received no bows from the practical-minded Noah. Not only is the French language unnecessary for American girls—so much excess intellectual baggage—but the French themselves, and especially their literary artists, are, as everyone has heard, a notoriously loose people. Better it is by far for a girl to read Addison's *Spectator* than to fritter herself away on French, which is for "those whose attention is not employed by more useful concerns."

As for the pursuit of the nobler arts, these are for the city-bred, and even at their best such enterprises "hold a subordinate rank." Keeping company with a harpsichord, a canvas and a brush, or even cutting a sightly figure in a minuet, are right enough. But they bear no relation to the immovable fact that woman's real merit is nothing "when it is not supported by domestic worth." In fact, the very point of schooling these aureate beings is to enable them to rear and educate their own children, "to instill in the tender mind such sentiments of virtue, propriety, and dignity as are suited to the freedom of our country." Finally, it should not be forgotten that in shaping the national manners, and especially those of the male, there is no overestimating the distaff influence. Let woman, therefore, major in purity.

One more item in Webster's portfolio needs to be explored, namely, his conviction that no matter how meticulously we lay our plans for the education of our youth, their success, in the last analysis, hinges on the ability of the teacher to put them into effective execution in his daily rounds. The idea at least was as ancient as the first-century Quintilian's somewhat similar theorem. Nevertheless, for all the noble patina of its years, by and large the proposition had remained a stranger to the common practice, especially in the lower schools, whose principal defect, Webster complained, "is the want of good teachers." All too often, he ventured to add, parents commit their children to the ministration of trashy men, "low-bred clowns or morose tyrants," or other "worthless characters."

What the situation called for, obviously, was a thoroughgoing inquest into the qualifications of every candidate for the tutorial smock. He should be a man of impeccable rectitude, of dignity and understanding as well as knowledge, the complete master of his materials—in short, superior. Such magnificoes, Webster felt, were readily available—if not, then the republic could certainly produce them. Lest there be a hitch, however, education should be made the "first care of the legislature, not merely the institution of schools, but the furnishing of them with the best men for teachers."

Chapter 16

Benjamin Rush

THE MAN

No less devoted to his native land than the irrepressible Webster, though a calmer and more amiable crusader, was Benjamin Rush (ca. 1745–1813). He was born on the eve of Christmas in 1745, hard by Philadelphia, where he spent the bulk of his years until he died at the age of sixty-eight. Like Webster, he had recourse to the taps of higher learning, taking his first letters at Princeton, and then shipping for Edinburgh and London, and after a while for Paris, to study the natural and medical sciences. Time saw him become one of the foremost medicos in America, a performer so magnificently meritorious that he was heaped with honors and awards throughout the world, the Old as well as the New.

A man of ideas as well as acts, Rush declared for American independence even before that fateful fourth of July in '76. When the schismatic moment finally fell, he not only put his signature to the Declaration; he also backed his belief wth active service in the cause of the struggling country, first as its surgeon general and then as physician general. It was in many ways a singular experience, and one which did not easily rub off. To it the doctor attributed not only the surge of his republican idealism, but the disruption of his early medical views as well. "To the American Revolution," he commented long after he had returned his saws and scarifiers to his war bag, "I ascribe in great measure the disorganization of my old principles of medicine." So insidious were the ptomaines of patriotism that they impelled him to seek to create an American system of medicine, with prescriptions restricted to the "domestic remedies of the United States," in plain collision with his maturer and sounder judgment that "in science of every kind men should consider themselves as citizens of the world." Even so, to the last he remained convinced that the interests of science are better served under an elected executive than under a sovereign, however divinely appointed.

The utilitarian stripe, so visible in the thinking of Franklin and Webster, ran also in that of the doctor. To make an end, for example, of the country's appalling gunpowder shortage during the Revolution, he applied the full inventory of his knowledge of chemical theory in an effort to produce saltpeter. Again, in a series of lectures he read at the Young Ladies' Academy in Philadelphia, he undertook to show his amazed hearers the practical applications of chemistry to household cookery, subsequently enshrining his teaching in a syllabus entitled *Domestic and Culinary Purposes.* In 1793, when yellow fever was slaughtering Philadelphians in droves, although the doctor was utterly innocent of any knowledge of the reasons for the being of the jaundiced marauder, he worked with a startling pragmatic success to thwart death time and again, although in the process he also translated not a few of his patients straight into the hereafter. Finally, to make the best medical care available to the poor he worked indefatigably to bring into being the first free dispensary in the United States.

For all his utilitarian stresses, Rush was a man of tremendous vision, and—for a laboratory man—immoderately romantic. Like Franklin, his friend and fellow townsman, he was something of a moralist, less sacchariferous than the benign doctor, no doubt, but of an expansive optimism just the same. Science, he was sure, would in time sweep human suffering off the earth. No man, he contended, sloughing off his Calvinistic heritage, is ever completely depraved. If he is antagonistic to his fellowman, either alone or in a pack, it is simply because he is in the clutch of overpowering physical and environmental forces. If he is a convicted felon, an arsonist, or even an assassin, nevertheless at bottom he is still a human being, entitled like any other afflicted creature of God to the boons of a redeeming therapy. The primary reason for storing a wrongdoer in a cell, Rush contended, should be to salvage, not to penalize, him. Almost solitary among the men of his generation, the doctor diagnosed lunacy not as an act of a willful Jahveh, or even the work of Satan, but as a human illness, and like a nihilistic gall bladder or a kidney run amok, subject to medical treatment and study.

More sophisticated in philosophy than either Franklin or Jefferson, Rush seldom sidestepped a chance to raise a metaphysical wind, especially in the domain of moral science. Even so, he was convinced that the "moral faculty" was "visible in actions," and that on some tomorrow the hour would surely strike when its nature and workings could be ascertained scientifically, which is, of course, one of the things the world's current horde of testers and measurers of human behavior is still striving to achieve. Despite his materialistic outlook, the doctor was of a powerful religious conviction. To his very end his faith remained unclouded by doubts of any kind, and there was for him not even the frailest shadow of a conflict between science and religion. The truths of both, he was certain, dwell in the Creator's mind, and the laboratory as well as the altar is the work of divine benevolence. It behooves their respective votaries, therefore, to work together for the advancement of human happiness.

Thus Dr. Rush and his repertoire. He was a man of great and astounding breadth. A materialist and a utilitarian, he was also a man of faith and unbounded piety. A scientist and a realist, he was at the same time a man of sentiment, an impassioned patriot, and above all a humanitarian. His diverse talents, contradictory at times though they seem to be, he addressed to a single purpose, the making of a better people, a better America, and thereby, he hoped, a better humanity. As usual, his dreams found their way into his educational ideas. He gave them substance in the tangible consequence of his striving, in the conjuring up, for one, of Dickinson College and Franklin and Marshall College (born Franklin), and in his direction, for another, of the department of medicine at the College of Philadelphia, founded in 1765, the first of its sort to grace the American higher learning. He also wove them into the tapestry of innumerable essays and speeches. Of the former, three stand above the rest: "A Plan for the Establishment of Public Schools," "Thoughts upon Female Education," and "Thoughts upon the Mode of Education proper in a Republic." It is to these, the last-mentioned in particular, that we now turn.

SUGGESTIONS FOR A SYSTEM OF EDUCATION

It was in 1786, the year before the nation's chosen elders gathered in the summer's swelter in Philadelphia's Independence Hall to draw up the Constitution, that Rush offered his countrymen his suggestions for an American system of education. The two events were not unrelated. For both issued from the same overriding desire to weld some 4 million persons, divided in outlook, cast of mind, and regional loyalties, into a solid body of united Americans. Where the framers of the Constitution fashioned a plan of government to bring about this miracle, Rush, for his part, envisioned a system of national schooling to fortify the process. Under the circumstances, it would be flattery to call the man objective. His proposal is plainly that of a patriot seeking to render service to the republic, so young and spindly, and so delicately rooted. "The principle of patriotism," Rush said, "stands in need of the reinforcement of prejudice," and since everyone knows that we seldom get over the way we are brought up, it is of the utmost importance to inculcate this love of country while the child is young and pliable, and to do it right here in our own country. To ensure the development of this purest of all mundane loves, Rush called for the formation of a national system of public schools. Only thus would the mass of young Americans, the low no less than the high, be broken to the proposition that "there can be no durable liberty but in a republic." The behavior of young people, he had convinced himself, like the latter-day Pavlov and his history-making dog, can be conditioned. "Organized life," he noted, "as well as the life of an individual is largely a matter of habit. . . .I consider as possible," he went on, "to convert men into republican machines," which is to say, into automatic right-thinking and right-acting Americans.

What should such prodigies of 100 percent Americanism be taught? They, said Rush, echoing Webster, himself an aftertone of Franklin, should learn whatever is palpably useful. Why, demanded the doctor, should young people overload their brainpans with Greek particles, Latin periphrastics, and the conformation of the ruins of Palmyra, when all the while they should be wooing "those branches of knowledge which increase the convenience of life, lessen human misery, improve our country, promote population, exalt the human understanding, and establish the domestic happiness?" It was a stupendous order, of course, as staggering as the declared purpose of the American Philosophical Society, which it loosely resembled—though naturally it was tailored to a beginner's capacity.

"Let the first eight years of a boy's time be employed in learning to speak, spell, read, and write the English language," Dr. Rush proceeded, again to the appreciative nodding of the Messrs. Webster and Franklin. When the boy is old enough to endure the harassments of arithmetic, he should be put upon its study, along with the lighter elements of mathematics. In a predominantly rustic land such as the adolescent republic, with its flora and fauna all about, an understanding of natural history also becomes imperative. Not only is it a study "simple and truly delightful," the object often enough of a boy's inherent wonder; it is also "the foundation of all useful and practical knowledge in agriculture," besides "manufacturers and commerce, as well as philosophy, chemistry, and medicine. . . ."

Needless to state, every American should in addition know the lay of the land, and for this the study of geography is necessary. "It is a simple science and accommodated to the capacity of a boy under twelve years of age." Did the magnanimous doctor emancipate the youth of the republic from the study of the accursed classics? Then he felt no qualms over disturbing their peace with French and German, for these, he had noticed, could later be made to serve gainfully in the pursuit of "commerce, physic, or divinity. . . ." But to make them function effectively "they should be acquired by ear." For the chronic grammatofanatic, the former surgeon general had little use, and he put his ban on the study of their specialty until a boy was safely past the elementary learning. If, thereafter, he still elected to chase the Muses, then presumably he knew what to expect, and he was turned not only on the study of the grammar of the vernacular, but also on "oratory, criticism, the higher branches of mathematics, philosophy, chemistry, logic, metaphysics, chronology, history, government, the principles of agriculture and manufactures, and . . . everything else that is necessary to qualify him for public usefulness or private happiness."

Although Rush strove at all times to be a man of the highest moral punctilio, rather curiously he put no stock in the talismanic powers of the prevalent teaching of ethical science, whether its moral pathology or its related therapy. All too frequently, he contended, the ethical revelation has been pressed into the young by masters who are unfriendly to the Christian belief, or, worse, yet, whose thinking has fallen afoul of the subversions of heathenry. Rather than seek to make men good by means of the conventional vaporizings on right and wrong, the doctor proposed to lay the foundation of all education in religion. Without it, he syllogized, "there can be no virtue, and without virtue there can be no liberty," and liberty, after all, is the life stream of the republican purpose. In sum, he said, "a Christian cannot fail of being a republican," and presumably vice versa. Unlike that iconoclastic Bible-banner, Thomas Jefferson, Rush ordered a diligent classroom study of Holy Scripture, with daily readings and exercises and regular quizzes thereon. It is, he proclaimed, the one sure "means of acquiring happiness both here and hereafter."

HISTORY

Next to man's duties to the Heavenly Father stand his duties to his country. To understand and appreciate them, let him ponder the lessons of history, not only of the American fatherland, but also of the ancient republics. Better than anything else they will afford him insight into the rise and fall of freedom in lands once great and glorious, but now lying in dust and rubble. Convinced not only that perpetual human progress is possible, but that, like the shifting tides and seasons, the advancement of man and civilization rests on ponderable natural law, Rush announced for a study of the laws that govern human progress. To unlock the portals to such recondite matters, once more the master key is a knowledge of history, especially its light on those movements in human annals which have helped to promote the general progress. Every true red-white-and-blue-blooded American should be on easy terms with the workings of his government. He should be well heeled with knowledge of "all the prerogatives of government." He should know all about the "nature and variety of treaties . . ., the difference in the powers and duties of the several species of ambassadors . . ., the obligations of individuals and of states . . ., and all the laws and forms which unite the sovereigns of the earth or separate them from each other." He should apprise himself of such affairs not only by means of the books of the *eruditi;* he should also supplement what he has learned with frequent visits to the chambers of justice, where he can form a realistic understanding of matters pertaining "to the preservation of life, liberty, or property."

A NATIONAL UNIVERSITY

Very precious to the doctor's overflowing heart was the idea of founding a national university. He glimpsed it in his dreams as early as 1778, when he delineated its substance in an essay, "A Plan for a Federal University." The pinnacle of his proposed national system of public schooling, it was to spread its illumination upon graduate students seeking to perfect themselves for the public service, not only by filling them with the "republican knowledge" essential for the execution of their occult art but by inspiring them as well with the indispensable "federal principles." Such a national Sorbonne, its architect maintained, would confer a singular dignity upon the country's higher learning. Moreover, in a land honeycombed with diversity and dissension, it could be relied upon to forward a common national spirit. Finally, its presence would spare young Americans thirsting for the highest learning from hazarding the long, costly, and even dangerous voyage overseas.

Some of the country's foremost statesmen favored the doctor's prescription. Washington, in fact, not only gave it his stout approbation, but while he presided over the republic he even took the trouble of looking for a suitable site for the new school. Better still, in his will he set aside several thousand dollars in prime securities to start the projected shrine of democracy on its way. Unhappily, the men of Congress were of another mind. Some were concerned lest such an institution might incline toward a bureaucratic tyranny. Others regarded it as a menace to the existing private colleges, already in unhappy financial straits. Yet others felt that education, no matter what its purpose, was a local concern, and that the national government had no authority to meddle therein. Finally, not a few of the Congressional Pericleses were convinced that the cost of launching and maintaining a federal university would run into astronomical figures. Be all that as it may, the people's ambassadors looked upon the business with ill grace, so that Rush's idea, despite its transparent merit, never emerged from its dream-spun cocoon.

WOMEN . . .

Dispraised by the imperious Hamilton as a radical, Rush, as might be expected, was highly partial to the idea of extending knowledge to American womanhood. In this department the doctor strode several thousand steps beyond either Franklin or Webster, and the prescriptions he compounded to promote the education of the female were much more boldly conceived than any of theirs. Although, as he was well aware, fate had imposed many cruel handicaps on the daughters of Eve, nevertheless, like their brothers, they were citizens, and as such they owed their share of duties to the republic.

"To qualify women for this purpose," Rush declared, "they should not only be instructed in the usual branches of female education, but they should be taught the principles of liberty and government," and especially, he added, the "obligations of patriotism." For all their feminine peculiarities, their education, like that of their masculine counterparts, must at all times be useful. Even in those early times, it seems, there was a shortage of well-trained servants, and, thus confronted, every woman, whether she covered herself in silks or calico, should be prepared to tend the hearth and prepare a savory meal. Although in those days woman's right to own tangible property was heavily hobbled, even so, the freethinking Rush, contrary to the consensus of his era, held that women should be trained "to be the stewards and guardians of their husband's property." Most important of all, though, was woman's role of motherhood. Upon her devolved the principal responsibility of rearing the very young, and to fulfill this awesome obligation properly a woman needed to be given "a suitable education," by which Rush meant she should be heavily bottomed "in the principles of liberty and government and the obligations of patriotism. . . ."

. . . AND THEIR EDUCATION

What noble metals go into the minting of such female paladins of true Americanism? For one thing, like their brothers, they should be made intimate with the American language to enable them to read and write it fluently and well. Naturally, they should know how to make effective use of figures not merely the ones an all-merciful God had given them, but the more profane ones of the counting room. And a knowledge of geography and history, as everyone knows, is as essential to the proficient patriot as the pipe is to the snake charmer. Furthermore, every American woman should know how to sing, and to this purpose her "vocal education should never be neglected." Not only will her warbling help "to soothe the cares of domestic life," it will also prepare her "to join in that part of public worship which is known as psalmody." For extra measure, from the depth of his everyday practice, the doctor had observed that because of its "exercise of the organs of her breast," singing is highly salubrious to a woman's health.

For the instrumental tonal art, however, Rush conceived a grave dubiety. For one thing, guitars and trumpets and the like run into not a little money, and so do the tutorial services needed to learn how to strum and tootle them. Even more burdensome is the frightful sacrifice of a daughter's time. To become a middling fiddler, or even a fifer, requires much time and practice. How much more useful it would be to direct such time and trial to the gathering of "useful ideas," stored within easy reach in "history, philosophy, poetry, and the numerous moral essays with which our language abounds." In the long run, the ability to talk freely about such subjects, as, of course, modern Americans need not be reminded, will not only win friends and influence people, it will also "add to the consequence of a lady with her husband. . . ."

What goes for learning how to make good music goes also for learning French. To gain competence in this outland idiom takes a deal of time and effort. The chances are, as the doctor had become painfully aware, that before a girl has found out how to ask "What time is it?" in French, she finds herself instead with a husband and children, and no time, alas, to maintain her foreign relations. Is she, by way of stubborn exception, at home in the Gallic tongue? Nonetheless, her conquest is for naught. "Of those who have acquired it," he remarked, "how few have retained it?" And even if they have held on to it, what chance do they have to use it? How much better it would be, the doctor mused, in the interest of "female delicacy" and the "natural politeness" of the French nation, for François, Alphonse, and other gallant Gauls "to learn to speak our language in order to converse with our ladies than for our ladies to learn their language in order to converse with them." And so, like Webster, Rush found himself obliged to pronounce his anathema on the feminine pursuit of French, not only on utilitarian and patriotic grounds, but also on those of the economy and hygiene of learning.

For the dance, however, the doctor had only pleasant things to say. Despite his Calvinistic background—or maybe because of it—he had an eye for a shapely feminine ankle as well as its clinical condition. And so, both as a connoisseur of beauty as well as a guardian of the people's health, he stamped the dance with his personal and professional approval. "Dancing," he avowed, "is by no means an improper branch of education for the American lady."

All this female learning, from the three R's to patriotism, household husbandry and administration, singing and dancing, and the rest, is indispensable, Rush believed, to the sound training and upbringing of our daughters. Yet it constituted only the cultural superstructure, and unless it was firmly settled on the bedrock of religious instruction, the edifice would surely crumble. "The female breast," Rush had learned from long study, "is the natural soil of Christianity," and so long as this was carefully cultivated, right-minded Americans need have no fear of the lures of such artful scoffers as the Messrs. Voltaire and Bolingbroke.

DOUBTS AND BROODINGS

Although Dr. Rush was in a high mood when he discoursed on the necessity of universal education in a democracy, yet he was also wrenched by doubts and misgivings. "I am not enthusiastic upon the subject of education," he once confided to a bevy of startled lady academicians assembled in Philadelphia. Like Jefferson and Franklin, he had sampled the bewitching wines of the Enlightenment, and like them he had cultivated a rosy glow for the infinite possibilities of the powers of science to rid us some day of all our sorrows. But unlike the aforesaid sages, Rush lacked transcendent confidence in the earthly destiny of the human race. Perhaps his inherited Calvinism was not altogether extirpated and its ghosts were still repining in the dungeons of his subconscious. Or perhaps, as a doctor, he had been too close an observer of human folly to let himself suffer from any optimistic delusions. In any case, the promise of the immediate years ahead seemed to him anything but bright. By and by, he brooded, "we would follow the footsteps of Europe in manners and vices." And the beginning of our decay and deterioration, he ruefully submitted, will show itself first among our women. "Their idleness, ignorance, and profligacy," he predicted, "will be the harbinger of our ruin."

Chapter 17

Samuel Knox

THE NEWCOMER

The Reverend Samuel Knox (1756–1832) arrived on this planet in Ireland, and he departed it seventy-six years later in Maryland Free State. In the nation's educational archives his name has been memorialized for a prize-winning essay on American education which he submitted to the American Philosophical Society in 1797. An impressive and admirable performance in its own right, Knox's achievement was all the more remarkable in that he had set foot on these shores but a bare two years previously. Educated at the University of Glasgow, then one of the world's great refineries of the intellect, Knox made himself ready for an eventual career in the holy cloth, concentrating, as is still the rule, on divine science, with its imposing array of collateral learning, especially philosophy and the ancient languages.

But unlike the general run of specialists in consecrated knowledge, Knox evinced a lively interest in the natural sciences, even, indeed, in the scary mystery of the medico. As a Presbyterian of Irish provenance, and particularly one who had ingested his higher learning among the Scots, Knox took naturally to politics, both physically and metaphysically, and in Maryland, where he passed the bulk of his American years, he gave them an active play. As was then not uncommon among the learned clergy, for a while Knox kept school—time, in fact, saw him rise to the prestige of a headmastership of an academy in Frederickstown, Maryland. Of a liberal outlook, he developed a liking for some of the ideas of Thomas Jefferson. Indeed, in 1800, despite the Calvinism in his veins, the Marylander found it possible—even compulsive—to issue a manifesto in defense of the religious views of the man from Monticello.

Like some of the essays we have already inspected, that of the Reverend Mr. Knox concerned itself with the subject of a national system of education. His piece is more of a monograph than an essay, laboring its way through eleven chapters and a conclusion, each heralded by a flourish of trumpets from the works of some classical master, from Quintilian and Horace to Erasmus and Meander, a Hellenic concocter of jocose verse and drama. The essay's title alone is a singular spectacle, a brontosaurus, so to say, measuring from bow to stern more than a half-a-hundred words. Keyed to the specifications of the American Philosophical Society, and with an eye cocked on its prize of $100, Knox's essay directs its attention both to "a system of liberal and literary instruction adapted to the genius of the government" and to "a plan for instituting and conducting public schools in this country on principles of the most extensive utility." Knox searched every educational crack and corner then within the human ken—and sometimes even beyond—from its aims and ideals, the organization of its schools, their curriculum, their relationship to church and state, the advantages of public schooling over the private variety, the preparation of first-rate teachers, and so on, down to the one and only way to teach the alphabet.

FUNDAMENTAL POSTULATES

Let us pass to a scrutiny of Knox's fundamental postulates. What, to start, should be the paramount purpose of education in the American republic? It should seek, asserted the pastor—not unlike his fellow cogitators on the subject—to instruct and improve the mind and to perfect the youth "in those arts on which the welfare, prosperity, and happiness of society depend." To assure an equable distribution of the blessings of knowledge, Knox—again raising his voice in chorus with his comrade seers—called for the creation of a national system of schooling, one embracing every scholastic plane, from that of the freshman in the primary school to that of the unfolding Platos and Aristotles in academe's highest learning. "In proportion," proclaimed Knox, waving the grand old flag with Webster and Rush, "as our government is superior in its nature and constitution, in its principles and practice, to the systems of those which have been instituted for enslaving the minds, as well as the bodies, of their ignorant vassals, so should the most general means of promoting and diffusing knowledge be adopted, be patronised, and supported in this and every other portion of the union."

To cultivate and better the minds and bodies of young Americans for a useful and happy life in our great democracy, youth should have access to instruction "in every science and branch of knowledge." Some of the learning they are expected to achieve, as, say, the three R's, is indispensable, and hence it becomes the function of the public seats of knowledge to impart it to every child, be he headed for practice in commerce or a profession or for just plain everyday civil life. But, proceeded Knox, there is another aspect of education which, though not essential for the commonality, is, for all that, no less important. Specialized and diverse in its component elements, it is classical and scientific, albeit not entirely so. Its purpose, at bottom, is the advancement of the general welfare, or as the parson phrased it in a somewhat transcendent prose, it is the "exertion of that refined and sublime knowledge on which the improvement of genius, science, and taste, rather than worldly circumstances, chiefly depends." Thus conceived, American education obtains a double purpose. One of its sights is trained upon every child to prepare for life, while the other is directed at the youth whom God and his parents have appointed for collegiate edification.

Teaching the indispensables, as per common custom, Knox assigned to the custody of the primary schools. Unhappily, he found them inadequate to their task. Not only was their number grossly insufficient, but all too often they had fallen into a low and discredited state. What the republic needed was a prompt increase in the stock of its seminaries of rudimentary knowledge, along with a vigorous correction of their offerings and methods. It was Knox's belief that the long climb up the ladder of learning would be surer and swifter if, before the young were put upon it, they were fortified with a knowledge of reading, as was the practice then in several places in New England. Rather curiously, the Marylander betrayed a dislike for the method then prevailing of teaching Johnny how to read. A relic from the past, it confined his "attention to long, dry lists . . . of words and syllables" which, however skillfully put together, succeeded chiefly in being dull. In place of this, let the novice be launched with thoughts, however light and fluffy, expressed in simple declarations. Once he is able to make sense of these "with tolerable ease and readiness," then let him progress into the exemplary books of Noah Webster, beginning, for example, with the *Institute,* and proceeding to snippets of the loftier thoughts of the "best historians" and those shimmering in the pages of Addison's *Spectator* and other organs of taste and airy sentiment.

With instruction in reading, of course, went such correlative bracers as spelling and composition, and eventually grammar. No amnesty was accorded to the study of arithmetic. Not only was the subject resorted to as a whetstone of the mind, but, with an eye on its eventual utility, Knox insisted that it ought to be related more closely to everyday life—a stunning thought in those days.

Although Knox was almost forty when he set himself down in America, its freedom and opportunity warmed his heart, and it was not long before he was serenading the country's grandness, less lavishly, perhaps, than the ebullient Webster, but with gusto just the same. Finally, like Rush and Webster, Knox made a place in his curriculum for the natural sciences, in those days for the most part still an ugly duckling in the pond of the lower learning.

Like so many other men of learning primed and perfected in the Scottish grove, the Maryland divine bore a liking for pedagogical colloquy. He reveled in its every aspect, from volunteering his counsel on how to teach the ABC's and the most rewarding way to read a book to such quiddity as the type and paper most suitable in the making of schoolbooks, which, he affirmed, should be uniform throughout the land on every academic level from the primary school to the university. Rather interestingly, now and then he intoned notions of an almost modern air. In illustration, pupils should be given leeway "to habituate them to call forth their own exertions." Rather than to be made to ape their elders, they should be spurred to think and act for themselves. Finally, in an age when schoolmen frayed their rattans more often than the pages of their books, Knox put in a word for moderation. Let the master guard against dispiriting the learner, he urged, thereby echoing Aristotle and Quintilian. "To cherish and keep up his ardor," Knox reflected, "constitutes no small share of a good teacher."

NO RELIGION IN THE PUBLIC SCHOOLS!

Although Knox was a practicing clerk of the Lord, and hence, one might suppose, inspired by the Holy Ghost to declare for religious instruction in the chambers of learning, in this matter, somewhat surprisingly, he made camp not with the pious Dr. Rush, but with the secular-minded Jefferson. Like the Virginian, he was perfervidly partisan to the idea of separating church and state. "No circumstance . . . can be brought to view in the history of scientific improvement," he stated flatly, "that has more retarded its progress, or tended to enslave the human mind, than that of admitting any combination to exist between the interests of academical instruction and the, too often partial, interests of particular religious bodies." Under such circumstances, Knox put the teaching of religion in the public school under an absolute ban. No public institution of learning, he told Maryland's lawmakers, can be "suited to the constitution of this state that would tend either to dissolve or establish any religious principles which may have been inspired by their parents or religious instructors of that particular society or denomination to which they belong." And what held for public education in the free state on the Chesapeake, this vicar of God insisted, applied also in his proposed national system. If Knox opposed religious instruction in the public school, this does not mean to suggest that he nursed any doubts about the merits of religion in its purest state. To make sure that the young would not ripen into infidels, or even agnostics, he relied on sustaining them in the history of natural religion and morals.

PUBLIC ACADEMIES

In the springtime of the republic the number of children completing primary school was conspicuously sparse, and the number of those who volunteered for further toil on the secondary studies was even sparser. The bald fact is that despite the romantic visions of Jefferson and other speculators in egalitarian ideals, the era continued to look upon education not as the inarguable right of every child, but as a prerogative which by God's will went hand in hand with money if not with brains. In consequence, the free-and-easy access to the middle learning, such as Americans take for granted nowadays, was extremely scarce. To remedy this affront to democracy, Knox applied his corrective snickersee, cutting vastly deeper, while he was about it, than even the audacious Jefferson.

His first step was to recommend the establishment of national public academies, one in every county, and open without fee to boys who had successfully navigated the primary course and who, in testimony of their acquired competence, could pass a far from perfunctory test for admission. Such lads, who were usually of an age of no less than thirteen, the academy would undertake to refine and polish with "a classical and thorough mathematical education." Where Franklin and Webster lamented the stress on the ancient tongues in the schooling of the American youth, Knox felt no such pangs. On the contrary, he insisted on powerful dosings of Latin and Greek so that his graduates would have a firm enough grip on them to enable them "to translate with propriety and ease either prose or verse, to be able to write Latin, if not classically [which is to say like Cicero, Virgil, and similar performers], then at least grammatically."

If Knox's envisioned academy sought to restore Latin and Greek to their former grandeur, this is not to intimate that thereupon he called a halt.

Instead, Knox recommended "a like knowledge of the French language," especially for those destined some day to answer the call of trade or commerce. For a soothing analgesic the young academician was set upon "ancient and modern history, geography . . . , prosody, Greek and Roman antiquities, rhetoric, criticism, and composition. . . ."

What distinguished Knox's intellectual stronghold from the Latin grammar school of, say, Boston, in its days of unpolluted classicism, was not only the concessions it granted such intruders as French, modern history, and geography, but, even more, the tremendous weight it laid on mathematics. After refreshing his recollection of the arithmetic and practical mathematics he had soaked up while sitting on the primary bench, the academy student was shepherded into the geometry of Euclid, "at least the first six, and the eleventh and twelfth books," including all the axioms, theorems, and corollaries down to the last jot and tittle. Before he was through, he was also to stuff himself with conic sections besides "algebra with its applications to geometry." From there, he went on to plane and spherical trigonometry—then, like all mathematical study, believed to be vastly nutritious for the growing mind. The only exceptions were to those for whom the academy was to be the end of the learner's trail. For them Knox proposed a reduction of the learner's mathematical ration, to permit them more time for practical subjects, especially some of those which currently fall under the jurisdiction of the business scientists.

Nor is this the end. Besides the learning aforementioned, the academy was to throw its searchlight on the "principles of ethics, law, and government," in addition to astronomy and natural and experimental philosophy, now spoken of as physics. With so many trees at every turn, Knox realized that the students might run the risk of never seeing the forest. Accordingly, he suggested that it might be a good thing "occasionally, to give the students a view of what constituted the complete scholar and man of science."

Despite the pressing stress the preacher laid on the training of the intellect, he was not bereft of magnanimity. For example, he relaxed his pressures with courses in such accomplishments as drawing, painting, music, physical culture, and fencing. Then, catching a prophetic vision of things to come, he ventured to impress upon his audience the opinion that there are some nonintellectual things which every cultivated young man, college bound or not, should know. "It would be a great acquisition to a place of public instruction," he wrote, "could such tutors be procured, as would teach dancing, a polished address in conversation, and also the proper attitudes, gestures, and actions in elocution." Finally, since Mars—like Satan, his colleague—lurked around every corner, Knox, on grounds of health as well as national security, advocated training all his academicians in the specifications laid down in the *Manual of Military Exercise.*

PUBLIC COLLEGES

To enable young men of sufficient capacity but little money to continue their intellectual life beyond the county academy, Knox laid plans for the establishment of a national system of colleges, one in every county, each to be free, public, and tax-maintained. Designated as state colleges, they were nonetheless to be under the governance of a federal authority, the so-called "Literary Board," whose duty, among others, was to effect as much uniformity as was possible among buildings, equipment, curricula, scholastic standards, admission requirements, and the qualifications of employes, savants, and others.

To be allowed entry to a state college, the prospective collegian was required to have fulfilled the prescriptions of the primary school and the county academy, or some satisfactory substitute. But to make sure that the candidate had been more than a mere classroom presence, and that he actually remembered the essence of the things his masters had tried to teach him, he was made to suffer a searching public inspection of his "classical and mathematical proficiency." If he emerged successfully, and had celebrated at least fifteen birthdays but in no case his nineteenth, he was granted entry.

His studies, he soon found out, were substantially like those of the academy. Like his previous preceptors, his professors still beleaguered him with the Greeks and Romans, but now the doses were heavier and more potent. Half his freshman year, for example, he surrendered to "exercises of classical criticism," amplified by lectures on literary history, the "names and customs of the Greeks and Romans, and on . . . taste, criticism, and composition." Nor was there any less belaboring of his encephalon with mathematics, for this subject, Knox was convinced, was unfailingly essential for the development of a man's mental horsepower.

The next year witnessed no recession of the classical and mathematical floodwaters. But the student's preoccupation therewith was somewhat mitigated with "a concise view of rhetoric, logic, and moral philosophy," besides geography, "the laws of motion, the mechanical powers, and principles of astronomy." By this time it may well be that a conscientious student, suffering attacks of cerebral vertigo, might have begun to wonder what it was all about. To give him aid, his professors turned him upon Locke's *Essay on the Human Understanding* and Bacon's *Novum Organum*, both respected authorities on the nature and operation of the human mind. In his third and concluding year, the student's main grappling was with natural philosophy, or physics. Moreover, to safeguard the collegian from the danger of sealing himself too tightly within the academic cloister, Knox took steps to bring him out into the glitter of the sun to adventure among men beyond the academic wall. Students, he commented, "should have time to mix a little in society, see their friends, and know something of the world as well as books."

As a young man of learning, a state college alumnus, whether he continued to satisfy his ardor for knowledge in Knox's projected national university or settled into the pleasures of civilian life, would doubtless be called upon from time to time to declare himself on all sorts of questions, public and otherwise. To compose him for such occasions, his professors were to spare no pains to freight him with the teachings of "moral philosophy," larded with "natural theology, economics, and jurisprudence." Finally, before he was set loose upon the world, his mentors were to make sure that he knew how to "write and produce essays."

AND A UNIVERSITY

Like Rush and Washington, Knox fevered for the founding of a national university. To be sure, the lofty dismissal of such a proposal by the fathers of the nation's law had rendered the curate somewhat sour. Even so, in his essay he went to not a little length to sketch the main features of a national seat of learning. Connected "with every branch or seminary of the general scheme of education," it was to be the crowning fulfillment of the republic's school system. Above all else it was to stress excellence so as to make it the "fountainhead of science, the center to which all literary genius of the commonwealth would tend. . . ." Unlike its inferior cousins—the primary school, academy, and college—it was to enjoy the felicity of an almost unheard-of flexibility, both in its curriculum and organization, so as to allow it to make adjustment to new and changing conditions. Its purpose was to give light to youth "in every circumstance of life and also for any particular business or profession"—a prefiguring of an up-to-date, fully groomed American university, without, of course, any national organizational overtones.

Knox's university was to staff itself with the supreme scholars of the day, with fixed salaries and thus not dependent for their bread and butter "on the precarious attendance of many or few students in the respective sciences or arts." The faculty which took shape in Knox's mental eye was the largest ever heard of in Christendom, larger than those of either Oxford or Cambridge, or even, when it materialized in 1825, Mr. Jefferson's University of Virginia. There was to be, of course, a professor of the classical learning in all its intricate network, from grammar and syntax to literature and composition, flanked by a professor of Greek and Roman antiquities. Needless to say, there was also a professor of mathematics, besides one of astronomy, and another of rhetoric, logic, and moral philosophy. The department of natural philosophy, which Knox anticipated would do a land-office business, was graced not only by the presence of a full professor, but with an assistant professor as well. In addition, the insatiable cleric called for chairs in history, law, and government, elocution and oratory, and even Hebrew and Oriental languages. These and the aforementioned, reinforced by the medical department's own professorial ménage, and those of its savants striking sparks in "ornamental arts," Knox was certain, "would compose that respectable faculty to whom the important charge of this seminary should be entrusted under the direction of the Literary Board."

Chapter 18

Jean-Jacques Rousseau

THE UNLIKELY CHILDHOOD

In 1712—less than a decade after the passing of Voltaire's "wisest of human beings"—there was born in the Free City of Geneva one who in later years was to elicit from the Frenchman the opinion that he was "completely mad." His name was Jean-Jacques Rousseau (1712–1778). The son of Isaac, a watchmaker on such occasions as he chose to exercise his craft, and Suzanne, who stood a notch or so higher than her spouse in the Genevan bourgeoisie, Rousseau wrote of his birth as the first of his misfortunes. The impulse to deride the remark as so much claptrap is strong, but when it comes down to tacks, it happens to be more fact than fiction. For less than a week after Jean-Jacques had drawn his first breath, his mother drew her last.

Following her death, the task of raising the child rested on the shoulders of the father who, not unexpectedly, was baffled and dismayed by even the simplest ground rules. To give him counsel and reinforcement, the widower mustered the services of an aunt, but her competence left something to be desired. The result was that young Rousseau roved through childhood without ever being made to feel the sharp teeth of discipline. An amiable lad—by his own admission—he strove to please his elders; even so, a trial balance struck at the end of his first ten years on earth would have indicated his vices to be more numerous than his virtues.

With aid from his father, a baptized but scarcely an unremitting Protestant, he made his way through Calvin's gloomy catechism. It became the practice of the elder Rousseau, who suffered from an incurable addiction to book reading, to make his son stay up through the long hours of the night to listen to him read. His favorite literary hashish ran to sentimental romance, of which his departed wife had left him a slight supply. But there was solid and serious stuff as well: Le Sueur's *History of the Church and the Empire,* Bishop Bossuet's *Universal History,* La Bruyère's *Characters,* the works of Ovid and Tacitus, and the *Lives* of Plutarch. The experience, needless to say, was instructive, though hardly to be recommended for general adoption. Still, through these nocturnal recitals the father taught his son how to read—whereupon he presently introduced him to the second R. There is no gainsaying that the boy had a first-rate mind; nevertheless, when Papa Rousseau essayed to teach his son the Copernican heliocentric system, his pedagogic art collapsed completely.

Much more exhilarating than his father's discourses on matters of cosmic significance was the singing of his aunt. She had a sweet and simple voice, and its charm enchanted her nephew. It is to his aunt Suzanne that he subsequently credited his lifelong passion for music. Taking one day with another, life in the Rousseau household may have lacked some of the comforts and conventions of the ideal home life, and it may have been at times disordered, but it cannot be said that it ever suffered unduly from the sorrows of a heavy heart.

But nothing good lasts forever. Late in 1722, Isaac Rousseau made the mistake of drawing his sword against one of his patrician betters, and when the Genevan magistrates sought to bring the watchmaker to their hall of justice he reminded himself that discretion often is indeed the better part of valor and made for safety across the border, never to be seen again in his beloved city. Meanwhile, he had unloaded his son on one of his uncles who, in turn, settled him with a clerk of God and his helpmeet who put the finishing strokes to his learning—and sometimes, to motivate him, to his hinder parts.

Done with his schoolbooks some two years following, the boy was put out as an apprentice in the office of the town clerk in hopes that he would elevate himself into a notary, but his ineptitude was more than his master could calmly take, and after a few weeks he turned him loose. A year or so later Jean-Jacques was back in Geneva, an apprentice now under contract to an engraver. But the lad had no zeal for the graver's art, and, except for a sightly hand and some fierce batterings from his jug-devoted master, he gained very little. In fact, after three or so years, he ran off. His vices, meanwhile, had augmented far more prodigally than his virtues.

FINALLY, A MARRIAGE

The events of the next few years are not a matter of present concern, and there is no need to dwell upon them. Let it suffice to note that in their course he headed for the home of Madame Françoise-Louise de la Tour de Warens, a baroness known far and wide for her charm and comeliness if not for her moral impeccability. She established the youth in her villa as her protégé and later as her lover. But let it not be supposed that in the molding of his career the lady was a cipher. Through her insistence he increased his knowledge with tutoring in music, Latin, philosophy, and the natural sciences. A fevered convert to Catholicism, the baroness made it a point to have him effectively instructed in the Roman rite. Presently, indeed, he was willing to renounce the false teaching of Calvin, that prophet of infant damnation, for the truth of Holy Church, which in later years he discarded, like a pair of old pants, for the more attractive Deism. As the years streamed by, the relationship between the two began to cool, and when the madame gave lodgment to a rival buck, he became the object of Rousseau's dudgeon. In any event, in 1741 the couple bade each other a moist farewell.

Rousseau now made tracks for Paris, where he drudged for a spell as copyist for a publisher, busying himself also in the composition of an opera. Next we see him in Venice, a sinful city, where he rendered secretarial assistance to a French diplomatic officer. His stay, though brief, was not without moment, for in his courtly compound he found himself in a gilded world, full of sham and double-dealing, a Latin Gomorrah, as it were, whose follies and fripperies worked him into a lather, and the likes of which in his riper years as the Advocate of Nature he was to reprehend with a very telling rhetoric.

Returned to the French capital in 1744, at the age of thirty-two, Rousseau began to consort with the so-called "philosophes," who, with Voltaire as their chief sharpshooter, were waging a war of pen and ink against the deviltries of the Old Regime. It was during these years that he fell a casualty to Thérèse Levasseur, a creature of no special account, save perhaps that she was his woman and he was her man. They set up house together, living in what the clergy commonly decry as sin. From their experimental union issued five children, each of whom their father donated to a foundling home—an instance of paternal altruism that is perhaps unparalleled in

Christendom. There have appeared a number of doubting Thomases who contend that the whole business defies credulity; that because of his prostatic deficiency Rousseau must have been impotent; and, finally, that if Thérèse brought any issue into the world her partner in their production was certainly not Jean-Jacques, despite the tears of remorse he dripped into his *Confessions.*

After the Rousseau-Levasseur coalition had endured for over twenty years, its male associate resolved to make it legal; and so on August 30, 1768, at Bourgoin in a wayside tavern, in the presence of the mayor and his nephew, and with Jean-Jacques as master of ceremonies, he and Thérèse became Monsieur and Madame Rousseau.

WRITINGS

On several occasions Rousseau had broken into serious writing, but it was not until 1750 that he marched off with his first success. It was visited upon him by an essay he submitted to the Academy of Dijon, a high-toned intellectual association, for its prize in answer to its question of whether the progress of the arts and sciences had contributed to the improvement of morality. His response—prompted, it has been said, by Diderot—was an absolute and unapologetic "No!" "Almighty God!" he palpitated, "deliver us from the fatal arts and sciences of our forefathers; give us back ignorance, innocence, and poverty, which alone can make us happy and are precious in Thy sight." Although such thinking veered sharply from what Dijon's academicians had allowed themselves to expect, they nevertheless appraised it as of sufficient merit to honor its author with their prize of an enormous gold medal and a small sum of hard cash. More important, however, was the fact that at thirty-eight, after years of groping in a maze of indecision and frustration, Rousseau suddenly found himself bathed in a great glare of publicity not only at Dijon but in the entire civilized world.

Persuaded by the sudden illumination fortune had beamed upon him that he had been marked for a career as a writer, the Citizen of Geneva, as he now signed himself, turned on the literary tap. He let if flow at full draught and, save only when his spirit suffered a calamity or his four humors laid him low, he was at the business without intermission. From his vivacious pen flowed a cataract of verses, plays, songs, operas, a novel of appalling length, besides essays, treatises, and dissertations. Three years after Dijon's sages had engauded and enriched him, he nominated himself to repeat his earlier triumph, this time with a *Discourse on the Origin of Inequality.* It got the medalist some laudatory comments, but neither laurel nor lucre. In 1760 he published the *Nouvelle Heloïse.* A novel in epistolary form, full of sentimental sauce, it simmers for over a thousand pages wherein Rousseau brews exotic odes to nature and its greatest glory, the Noble Savage, and expostulates, while he is about it, against civilization, blaming it for all our woes. Attacked by bluenoses on the ground that its pages are littered with prurience, the novel, as usual with such assistance, enjoyed an agreeable trade. On the heels of the *Nouvelle Heloïse*—the year was 1762— appeared *The Social Contract* and *Emile,* two lucubrations in prose which, notwithstanding their occasional recourse to soapbox rhetoric, have assured their author a front seat in the congress of the world's most eminent literati. The one represents the Genevan's version of the best of all possible governments, and does not concern us here. The other offers Rousseau's matured deliberations on education, and it is to them that we now turn.

CRITICISMS OF TEACHING

Emile was not Rousseau's first brush with pedagogy. He had borne in on it some twenty years before as a tutor of the children of Monsieur de Malby, a shining light of applied statecraft at Lyons. The experience had been anything but a grand success. Indeed, so disquieting was its impact upon the tutor that before he was through he found himself filling the ears of his astonished employer with the lament that he regarded "the education given young children both senseless and absurd." They are pumped full of Latin and Greek, but are "left ignorant of the history of their own country." They speak Latin with correctness and ease, but they "speak the worst possible French." They are asked to make sense of a God "who is three persons in one, none of which is the other, yet each one of which is the same God." They are told about original sin, for which they were being made to suffer for trespasses they had never committed. They are taught about the efficacy of the sacraments "which make the soul virtuous by a purely physical application." Finally, since "they are told nothing about the fundamental truths of Christianity or the basic principles of moral science," when it comes to understanding "the universal obligations of humanity" they wallow in the muck of ignorance.

For all his trial as a tutor, his interest in educational reform did not slacken—indeed, if anything, the passing years saw it blaze into an active passion. As in the case of John Locke, Rousseau's friends—especially those in skirts—beleaguered him for help and advice in matters pertaining to their children's education. But unlike the eminent John, the Genevan usually kept his counsel general and often beautifully vague, and he never honored his admirers with a full and candid treatise. Nevertheless, the indubitable concern of these women over the education of their young served at least to rouse in him a glimmer of understanding of the vast importance of the problem. He had come to grief at Lyons, he gave himself to believe, because he had broken faith with himself. Shackled to the conventions of the age, he had followed the old and well-worn route instead of daring to blaze a trail of his own. What he needed to do was to conjure up an ideal situation wherein he tooled his ideas in gaunt honesty with no heed whatsoever for the immemorial mores of society, however hallowed they might be. Of course, he knew that such a work would not only abrade man's perennial pet ideas and pruderies; it would also risk the pundits' charge that it was not an educational treatise at all, but the delusions of some moonstruck romantic. Whatever fate awaited him, he would, nonetheless, write the book. The labor of composing it, even though he was already in the throes of sweating forth both the *Nouvelle Heloïse* and *The Social Contract*, would scarcely cause him to blow a blood vessel. In fact, all he had to do was to translate to paper the ideas that were swarming in his head, ideas, he wrote, of the kind "that determines the happiness and unhappiness of the human race."

EMILE

Arranged in four parts which trace Emile's education from infancy to the heady heights of early manhood, *Emile* was launched, as it were, with the roll of rhetorical drums. "Everything," its confector asserted, "is good as it comes from the hands of the Author of Nature; but everything degenerates in the hands of man." Although the doctors of the sacred faculty differed vehemently with such unprofessional ignorance, holding instead that man is born with the stain of Adam's sin, Rousseau stuck to his guns. Thus, for all the testimony assembled by the reverend fathers, original sin, he countered, is a palpable swindle, and so is its associate of total depravity. Rousseau's insistence that man is born good, and that our so-called "civilization" pollutes and ruins everything it touches, is the recurring and undeviating refrain not only in *Emile* but in all his writings of any consequence. Is the newborn child naturally good? Then it follows that his education must at all times be attuned to the strings of nature. Bearing on this task, Rousseau identified three distinct types of education, or "teachers." The first is simply the process of growing up, letting our bodies and all our capacities develop unhobbled and uncaged—in sum, letting nature take its course. Next there is the education we pluck from our surroundings—that fire burns, that water is wet, and that the rose, despite its friendly smell, bears painful thorns. Finally, there is the education imparted by man. Over the first we have no control; over the second, very little; but over the last, a great deal. Since the cooperation of all three "is necessary for their perfection," Rousseau explained, "it is to the one over which we have no control that we must direct the other two."

Before Rousseau's imaginary pupil was brought into the world, his inventor provided him with well-heeled parents; thereby, this friend of mankind confided, "we shall at least be sure of having made one man more, whereas a poor man can become a man of his own accord." Next, the Genevan endowed his brainchild with excellent health as well as strength and sturdiness, for, he argued, it would be nonsensical "to teach someone to live whose only thought is to keep from dying." Finally, Emile is to be entrusted to the care and guidance of the best of all teachers, who turns out to be no less a worthy than Jean-Jacques himself.

The first part of *Emile* takes its leading character from his birth to his fifth year. The primary task during this period, as has already been said, is to hearken to nature's cues. Does the infant yowl for food? Then let his mama put him to her breast. Does he labor to move his arms and legs? Then unswathe him from his hampering wraps. Let him instead wear not a stitch more than the weather demands, for only thus can he function freely and happily. Let him work his senses and muscles so that they may attain their natural strength and power. Play, which comes naturally to children, should be allowed copious leeway, but Emile's playthings should not be the gaudy contrivances whose chief pleasure is for the adult who buys them. Rather let them be some modest product of nature, such as "branches with their fruits and flowers, or a poppyhead wherein the seeds are heard to rattle." Above all else, let Emile be spared from the medicos and their pills, salves, elixirs, and embrocations, and their inevitable sweatings and bleedings. Call in the Galens only when Emile's life is in grave peril, for then "they can do nothing worse than kill him."

What holds for the professional healers also holds for the development of Emile's habits. They are at odds with impulse, declared his tutor, and so they are against what is natural. In consequence, the formation of habits is proscribed, the only exception being the habit "to contract no habit whatsoever." It was Rousseau's conviction that since "man's breath is fatal to his fellow-men," both literally and metaphorically, it behooves his pupil to be brought up not in town but in the country. There in the heart of nature's eternal mystery, his early education unfolds.

"We are always looking for the man in the child," observed Rousseau, without stopping "to think what he is before he becomes a man." Parents fall into the common human error of supposing their offspring "can reason as soon as they are born, and so they talk to them as if they were grown persons." The facts, Rousseau contended, ridicule the elders' gallant optimism. Indeed, Rousseau went so far as to hold it an axiom that up to the age of twelve Emile, poor fellow, lacks all power to reason. In consequence, in the book's second section the chief stress still falls on the cultivation of the muscles and the senses. "Develop the body and keep the mind fallow," is Rousseau's incessant drumbeat. "In order to think," he elucidates—somewhat muddily it would seem—"we must exercise our limbs, our senses, and our organs, which are the instruments of intelligence." To such a purpose Emile learns to swim. He takes long hikes over rough terrain. He climbs to the mountain's crag-crowned height. Thus he gives his muscles tone and toughness, and thus he whets his senses. For added measure he puts a hard bulge on his biceps by lifting weights, and to rehearse his perceptions he estimates distances, whether vertical or horizontal. To train his eyes and hands he is put upon sketching, using what he discerns in nature as his models. To exercise his ears and larynx he resorts to song.

During this period of the untilled mind, Emile is to have no truck with the elemental R's. Reading, in truth, caused Nature's Advocate to throw fits. "It is," he tells us, "the scourge of childhood." If instruction in the simple R's is taboo, then plainly there can be no room for any of the other branches. History, for one thing, puts an inordinate burden on the memory, and this nature had not yet brought to ripeness in Emile. For another thing, the scriveners of history lay too much emphasis on kings and their political and warlike enterprise. What goes for history goes also for geography, for it too demands a mental capital that Emile does not yet possess. Even benign old Aesop falls to Rousseau's ax. Although his fables carried the endorsements of such illuminates as Erasmus, Locke, Luther, and several others, and had been made available to the French in the bewitching rhymes of La Fontaine, Rousseau nevertheless found them beyond Emile's powers. Through the ages adults had used them in the belief that they incite the young to moral rectitude. But, countered Emile's tutor, his fledgling is not yet a moral being, and so Aesop's moralizing defies his boyish understanding.

To protect the child from such and other parental blunders, he must be taught only what he can understand. "Let us allow childhood to ripen within the child," he exhorted. Not only must he be safeguarded from the snares of book learning, but until he reaches young manhood, and awakes from reason's prolonged slumber, lecturing him on right and wrong goes for precisely nothing. Does he, nevertheless, disport himself like a nascent Nero? Then let him experience the "natural consequences" of his misconduct. Does he, to come to cases, smash a window? Then let him sit in the chill and perchance even come down with a case of first-class sniffles. Or does he pull up his neighbor's sprawling melon vines and plant himself a sack of beans in their stead? Then let the man next door dislodge this felon's infant bean sprouts and thereby impress upon him "the sanctity of private property."

THE TWELFTH BIRTHDAY

On his twelfth birthday Emile stands at the portal of what his mentor characterized as "the time for labor, instructions, and inquiry." Although he is still growing in length and breadth, the stock of his accumulated corporeal power is now in excess of his bodily needs. Consequently the brakes are put on Emile's physical and sensory training to afford him more time to come to grips with knowledge. Unhappily, the division between the two is immensely disproportionate. "Time was long during early childhood," Rousseau ruminated, "but now it is the other way."

To even the difference somewhat, Emile's tutor limits the goal to "useful knowledge," and once again the clue to what is of use—the "sacred formula" is the Genevan's phrase—is to be found in the boy's natural desires. Knowledge, in short, is to be the bond between nature and himself. As might be expected, a high place is granted to the natural sciences, but their manifestations are to be examined not in books but directly by experience. Emile, his tutor would have it understood, "is not to learn the sciences," but is to develop "a taste for them," and to reveal to him "the method for learning them." If on some tomorrow he craves to know them more familiarly, then the method is at his door. He makes acquaintance with geography not from globes and atlases and suchlike schoolmasterly devices, but by exploring his surroundings and proceeding thence in an ever-expanding orbit to places more and more remote. To translate his observations into some sort of tangible meaning, he makes his own maps.

The venerable phenomena of astronomy are brought to Emile's attention by having him feast his eyes on the celestial grandeur of the rising sun. Electricity is sneaked into the boy's innocent awareness by the bamboozlement of a juggler who, by the devious use of hidden magnets, appears with his bare hands to be snatching metal ducks out of the air from almost everywhere. In all this questing, whether simple or complex, Emile is expected to construct whatever apparatus he may need, say a funnel or a piece of pliable tubing, or, should he yearn for a closer look at the heavenly bodies, even a spyglass. Makeshift though such implements may be, Rousseau was certain his ward would cherish them more fondly than the finest ones obtainable for money. "I wish," the Citizen of Geneva let it be known, "we might make all our own apparatus; and I would not begin by making the instrument before the experiment." Instead, he would tarry long enough to catch a glimpse of an experiment in actual progress. Then, "as by hazard, I would invent little by little the instrument which would verify it."

Although Emile is now engaged in gathering knowledge, his mentor has not ceased firing his cannon against books. "I hate books," he stormed, for "they teach us merely to talk about what we do not know." At this time in Emile's life only one book is granted a dispensation, namely, *Robinson Crusoe.* Not only is it "the best teacher of an education according to nature," but for a long time it will form his entire library. Just how and when Emile learns to read—save for the drop of a vague hint that the mystery will somehow be mastered incidentally—the Geneva sage does not specify.

From Rousseau's horror of book learning issued the essence of his pedagogical method. "Never," he warned, "substitute the sign for the thing itself, except when it is impossible to show the thing." Again, "I shall never repeat enough that we give too much power to words. . . .We are making nothing but babblers." In place of talk, let there be action. "Let all the lessons of young people take the form of doing rather than talking." There is an emphatic echo here, of course, of Erasmus, Comenius, Locke, and several other advanced-thinking pedagogues before them. It was to resound again and again in the century following—in fact, it is still making itself heard in our current era of enlightenment.

Up to the age of twelve Emile had been left pretty much alone— indeed, except for his tutor, and now and then some scanty contacts with village boys, his eyes have had little chance to explore a fellow primate. To repair this lack, the youth's education now directs itself cautiously to the social. Starting by the simplest route, the business is got under way by having Emile observe the plain people performing their specialties in their shops and workrooms, and in the fields, streams, and woodlands. Thus the lad is to find out for himself that "in society a man either lives at the cost of others or he owes them in labor the cost of his keep." If this pronouncement is valid, then it follows that in one way or another everybody, whether in pocket or out, stalwart or spavined, is under the obligation to work. In this matter Rousseau permits no exemptions. An idler, in fact, "is a thief." To spare Emile from such an ignominious fate, his guide and mentor sets him upon learning a trade, "one in which his hands work harder than his head." After some circumspection Rousseau declared for the carpenter's ancient craft, not only on the ground that it is "nearest to nature," but also because "it is clean and useful," besides exacting a measure of skill from its practitioner, and, by the physical exercise it provides, setting his blood racing through his veins. Finally, "while fashioning articles for everyday use, there is scope for elegance and taste."

ADOLESCENSE TO MARRIAGE

In Emile's middle teens adolescence sneaks upon him, and for the next few years he will sense the presence of strange and potent inner urgings. "Here," Rousseau exulted, "is the second birth . . . when a man really begins to live." It is, he added, "the epoch where ordinary education ends," but "where ours properly ought to begin." If, for reasons primarily personal, Emile has been made aware of man's interdependence, his social education now gathers a greater vigor. "We have formed his body, his senses, and his intelligence," Rousseau wrote, "it remains to give him a heart"—which is to say Emile must master the art of living peaceably and compassionately with his fellows. Toward this end he strikes out over the road of personal experience. But his introduction to the human mammal is not to start at the peak with generals, bankers, bishops, and similar celebrities. Such encounters, the Genevan warned, are full of risks—indeed, in years not far removed, they might even infect Emile with a mass of uncomfortable longings. To become mellow and sympathetic to his fellowmen, he must meet their common representatives and share with them draughts from the ancient goblet of humility. Especially must he enlighten his understanding of the rejected wretches, the voiceless and forgotten people caught in the elemental agonies of life. And so, like a social salvager, he observes the inhabitants and their concerns at hospitals and orphan homes, even in jails and madhouses.

This is the time too when Emile must make acquaintance with the fine nuances of human values. He must become privy to the causes of inequality and the evil role played by prejudice in the shaping and shattering of human careers. It was a subject on which Rousseau, having dwelt upon it in bygone years in an essay of some length, spoke with unruffled assurance. Lest man's frauds and foibles throw Emile into a complete dither and thereby convert him to an irreparable cynicism, Rousseau now bestowed his tutorial approval upon the subject of history. Of all the historical brethren, Thucydides appeared to Emile's teacher to be the most suitable. Simple in style, he embroiders his tale with beauteous words, yet he never permits himself to descend into the puerilities of Herodotus. Nor does he disfigure his shapely record in the manner of such paler luminaries as Sallust and Polybius. But the study of history, Rousseau served notice, has its pitfalls, For one thing, it concerns itself all too much with the melodramatic. It plays up wars and kings and popes and forgets the men of every day. Though the past is many-windowed, the historian, peering through its panes, tends to discern mainly what is bad. In the common historical confection, the Genevan lamented, "only the wicked become famous, the good are forgotten or laughed to scorn, and so history, like philosophy, is forever slandering mankind." Like Carlyle a century later, Rousseau believed that history burns its brightest light in the intimacy of biography, and of all the writers in this department known to Jean-Jacques, he chose Plutarch as the most worthy of Emile's consideration.

If Rousseau once put his foot down on the pedagogic value of fables in the education of the young, now that Emile's reason has come to the right ripeness his teacher is willing to suppress his one-time grievance. Mature and more sensible, Emile is now immune to Aesop's hypnotic spell. In truth, his teacher is satisfied that fables, "by censuring the wrongdoer under an unknown mask . . . instruct without offending him." But a fable, to be of any worth, must be ably presented, so ably that a statement of a moral becomes supererogatory. "Nothing is so foolish and unwise," Rousseau allowed, "as the moral at the end of most fables. . . .The moral," he went on, ought "to be so clear in the fable itself that the reader cannot fail to per-

ceive it." The time for reading fables is also the period for pondering literature, the most universal of the arts, and for the study of art itself. It is the
occasion also to give some thought to what nowadays goes under the appellation of "social science," and in this domain nothing can serve Emile
better than his tutor's *Social Contract*. Finally, this is also the time for an
exploration of ethics, metaphysics, and religion.

Introducing Emile to God is no easy matter—in fact, it harassed Rousseau. It is said, he remarked, that "a child must be brought up in the
religion of his father; and that he must be taught that it alone is true, and
that all others are absurd." But, he proceeded, "if the power of this instruction depends only on authority, for which Emile has been brought up to
have no regard, what then? In what religion shall we educate him?" The
answer to that conundrum is "in none," to the woe and scandal, needless to
say, of the reverend pastors of every known persuasion. What Rousseau
sought was to put his pupil "in a condition to choose for himself that to
which the best use of his own reason may bring him." To put him in this
exalted state, his mentor resorted once more to the "book of nature," the
source of his own epiphany. "There is no excuse," so far as he could see,
"for not reading this book." If Emile "must have any other religion," his
teacher insisted that he had "no right to be his guide; he must choose for
himself."

After twenty years Émile's education eased to its end. Five years later
he has been appointed by his maker to assume the bonds of matrimony.
During these five years of waiting he will have been assaulted by powerful
carnal desires, but in the name of the Author of Nature, Rousseau prayed
him to safeguard his virginal rectitude. To this end he offered enlightenment to Emile along the lines of the laborious righteousness our forebears
used to absorb from the pages of such an educational classic as *What Every
Young Man Should Know*. The thing to do, Rousseau urged, is to show
Emile "the laws of nature in all their truth." Let him be apprised of the
"physical and moral evils which overtake those who neglect them." Annex
to this the idea of marriage "not only as the sweetest form of society, but
also as the most sacred and inviolable of contracts," and "of the horrors of
debauchery . . . of the downward road by which a first act of misconduct
. . . drags the sinner to his ruin." As has already been noted, Rousseau
discovered all this too late to do himself any good—even so, he entertained
the conviction that through his counsel "chastity will be so desirable in
Emile's eyes that his mind will be ready to receive our teaching as to the
way to preserve it."

SOPHIE, A GIRL

Meanwhile, Rousseau directed his talents to excogitating an educational
program for Sophie, Emile's spouse-to-be. The result of his pondering he
stored in the fifth and final part of *Emile*. What he actually discoursed

upon, however, was not merely the education of Sophie, but his theories on the education of girls in general. Girls, he contended with the sagacious Aristotle, are so constituted that unfailingly they are inferior to men, and so they are condemned to live in a state of subservience. Consequently, their education must at all times be relative to that of men. Are men, for example, strong and active? Then it follows that women "should be weak and passive." Do men seek to serve? Then it is women's lot to seek to please. The female's elemental function is "to gain man's respect and love, to train him in his childhood, to tend him in manhood, to counsel and console, to make his life pleasant and happy"—in sum, to service and comfort him. Whatever education is vouchsafed to such a being must be maintained within these bounds.

Let the business be launched by training the young girl to be obedient and industrious. Cultivate her figure. Irradiate her with loveliness. Invigorate her with health and stamina so that she may flatter her better half with a swarm of lusty children. Perfect her in the delicate points of needlecraft. And to be certain that she will be "sweet and agreeable" to her man, teach her to sing and dance. By the same score, lest she harass and irk him, stay her from the study of philosophy and science and suchlike unsettling disciplines, for as Rousseau's researches had clearly told him, "the quest for abstract and speculative truths, for principles and axioms in science . . . is beyond a woman's grasp." Let her specialize instead in the study of men. She should make it her duty "to learn to penetrate their feelings through their conversation, their looks, their gestures. . . ."

As for her traffic in divine matters, if she is espoused, then she is to worship in the church of her husband. If she is still unmarried, then she is to send up her prayers to the God of her mother. Under the circumstances, her religious upbringing must needs differ from that of Emile. In lieu of tarrying until her fifteenth birthday to learn that the Heavenly Father has honored her with the presence of a soul, she is to be introduced to the mysteries of some respectable rite while she is still a little girl, for, as Rousseau takes pains to tell us, if we wait until she is ready for a serious discussion of these deep subjects "we should be in danger of never speaking of religion at all." Indeed, since by nature she cannot be expected to master the rational processes, our wait might well endure until we die of old age.

THE CONTROVERSY

Historians have duly recorded that when Rousseau died, in 1778, he was mentally unhinged—a prosy detail perhaps, but not without its tragic obbligato. For, as with Henrik Ibsen and Friedrich Nietzsche, to name but two, Rousseau's antagonists lost no time in turning his derangement to their

JEAN-JACQUES ROUSSEAU   **213**

profit. If the man left this vale *non compos mentis,* they argued, then the seeds of his madness must have been germinating within him even before his death—who can tell for how long? In any case, whatever views he entertained must be looked at with suspicion. To tear Rousseau's work apart is easy enough, for inconsistencies in his thinking rear up like the Matterhorn, and flaws in his reasoning tower no less. Thus considered, *The Social Contract* descends into the abyss of decrepit logic; *Emile* is a chowder of sentimental pishposh; and the *Confessions*—well, who would place his credulity in that tale of fantasy, forgetfulness, and dereliction of truth by one already in the grip of a malignant paranoia?

On the other side range those who, less in thrall to the exigencies of schoolmastering, burrow far below the surface to discern not the Genevan's discourtesies to right thinking, or even the dead cats he heaved at the conventions of established morality, but rather the seeker, wandering in the endless alleys of a scarred and aching world, groping uncertainly, but hopefully, for the Open Sesame to enduring human happiness—the answer, in sum, to the vastest of all human riddles.

The fact seems to be pretty much forgotten that Rousseau was neither a scientist nor a logician but a mingling of ardent advocate and lyric bard, and so, privileged by the license of his ancient art, he engaged in frequent holidays from everyday sense. His ideas welled from the fountain of his heart to the little gray cells in his head, and in his art, as in love, instinct was a sufficient guide. In truth, his brain was not always able to robe his thoughts with a lucid precision. His writings—at least those of consequence—concern themselves not with facts, but with ideas, and his significance rests not in the formulation of categorical pronouncements, but in the questions that he raised. His era, like our own, was one of scientific and philosophical advance, but its illumination, he felt, was no more than a halfway lantern on the long road to human happiness. The life we lead, he mourned, fails to satisfy because at bottom it is unnatural. What sense does it make, he wanted to know, to live such a false and tormented life? What was needed was a renunciation of the boons of a so-called "progress" which, in the name of civilization, only serves to enslave us. The Genevan called for us to put the individual above convention, and the dignity of his soul higher than the penetrations of his mind. Thus conceived, Rousseau's was a spiritual defiance, a fact which can be confounding to those who would gauge their man with a footstick.

More than once Rousseau complained that *Emile* did not fetch the attention it deserved, but his lament, it must be said, had no warrant in fact. The book was only two days in the stalls when it was reportedly causing a stir. A few days more, and volleys of admiration and fault-finding began to let loose. Deep thinkers like d'Alembert, Diderot, and Duclos breathed scented words upon it. But the more cynical Voltaire saw in it nothing more than a "hodgepodge of silly wet nurse in four parts." The specialists in moral theology at the Sorbonne beat their breasts and denounced the work as that of the Antichrist. The English on the other hand acclaimed the volume with loud huzzahs and twice they translated it into their vernacular, a distinction they had never vouchsafed to a Frenchman.

Meanwhile, the Archbishop of Paris damned the whole business as libelous and recommended Rousseau for appropriate treatment. Even before the episcopal recommendation, the civil authorities had banned the book and ordered it for formal incineration, besides issuing a writ for its author's detention. But when Rousseau, who by now was scared half to death, ventured to seek cover in Protestant Geneva, the tidings reached him in Switzerland that *Emile* had been burned by the common executioner, and that the Free City's directors of public safety were preparing to welcome their native son with a warrant for his arrest.

Reduced to ashes in most right-thinking lands, but also diligently smuggled, *Emile* snared readers in packs. Although Rousseau felt confusedly, he nevertheless felt with a fierce and powerful obsession. Surely, it is no cause for wonder to witness the commoners of France acclaiming him to the tune of fifes and drums as their redeemer when the old order was crushed by the Revolution, which, rather curiously, he had foreseen as inevitable some thirty years before its outbreak. Nor is it any wonder to watch them placing what was left of him in his marmoreal tomb in the Pantheon. Nor, finally, is it beyond understanding to behold his memory being celebrated even in these days in some of the very places he had once incited to rage and hatred.

No other work on pedagogy has ever caused such an uproar as did *Emile,* and none has ever obtained a more thoroughly controverted appraisal. "Rousseau," said Madame de Staël, "invented nothing. He set everything on fire." But the sage Immanuel Kant acknowledged it to have held him so tightly in its thrall that he forgot to take his daily walk, a promenade he took so regularly, it has been said, that his neighbors set their clocks when he passed by. Even the ranking literary arbiters of the time were far apart in their critical pronouncements, as their successors still are today. Laserre, for one, rejected *Emile* as "not worth a shrug of the shoulders," while Lanson knocked it clean over the fence as "the most beautiful, the most thorough, and the most suggestive educational treatise ever written." The truth, as nearly always in such instances, falls somewhere in between. When all the ballots are in and examined, we find *Emile* charged with being individualistic, impracticable, negative, and even on occasion of a saccharine sentimentality.

On the other side we find a healthy stress on reason and a decent respect for the rights and dignity of the child. "Begin," Rousseau counseled, "by studying your pupil thoroughly, for it is certain that you do not know him"—a morsel of wisdom that is as perceptive today as when it was first expressed. Against the judgment of an almost solid phalanx of classroom impressarios, Rousseau urged that nothing should be taught a child that he was not ready to understand; that physical activity and health were of prime importance; that a child's natural needs, such as the urge to play and the satisfaction of his almost simian curiosity, should be put to use in his education; that he should learn from the senses and firsthand experience rather than vicariously from books.

"Our first teachers," he wrote, "are our feet, our hands, and our eyes. To substitute books for all these is to use the reason of others." Like Erasmus, Comenius, and other memorable sowers of light, Rousseau spoke with asperity against the fearsome burden put on the child's memory; and finally he cried up the idea that to be truly worthwhile education should be broad and diversified—the student is "to work like a peasant and think like a philosopher." "I demurred a long time over publishing this book," its author confessed, "but after vain efforts to make it better I believe I ought to print it as it is . . . and though my notions may be erroneous, I shall not have lost my time if I inspire better ones in others." And this is exactly what came to pass.

Chapter 19

Johann Heinrich Pestalozzi

THE START

Though several schoolmen presently elected to put some of Rousseau's naturalism into their classroom practice, the first of any consequence was a Swiss by the name of Johann Heinrich Pestalozzi (1746–1827). He was born in Zurich, the son of Susanna and Johann Pestalozzi, a licensed medico but free of any degrees. He was a diligent and hard-working man, yet for all his effort his practice netted him far more leisure than revenue—indeed, so lean were his professional pickings that he sometimes found it necessary to add to them by clerking in a city job. Life in the Pestalozzi household was thus never abundant and when, during young Johann's sixth year, his father died, it was only by dint of a resolute and adroit economy that his mother was able to keep her family on its feet. But the worldly goods the Fates had so miserly meted out, Frau Pestalozzi more than offset by her overflowing heart. Hers was a devotion which, in her relationship to her youngest, knew no bounds, but which, unluckily, did not work altogether to his advantage, for she not only pampered and coddled him, but to shield him from the harassments of the roughhouse world of boyhood she held him closely at her side, even keeping him out of school until he was nine. The result was that the boy grew up shy and unassertive, innocent of the reality of the everyday world—"everybody's plaything," as he was to mourn on some distant tomorrow.

As happens not infrequently, this Pestalozzi whom destiny had picked to work wonders as an educational reformer was no shining light at school. Indeed, to his very end his spelling remained anarchistic, his syntax a waste of decomposed grammar, and his handwriting so baffling that at times it required the services of a special commission of archeologists to make sense of it. Despite these lamentable deficiencies, Pestalozzi gained entrée to the sessions of the Collegium Humanitatis which, true to its venerable roots, featured instruction in the classical humanities. Two years following we see the youth taking his first lessons in the clergyman's craft at the Collegium Carolinum.

If, in the lower school, Pestalozzi neglected his duties and thereby fumbled his chance to master the elemental R's, on the higher level he profited handsomely from the infectious ideas of some of his dons, in particular the Herren Breitinger and Bodmer. The one taught Greek and Hebrew, and knew how to make his students take a fancy to these fearsome subjects. The other specialized in history and politics and, like Socrates, preferred to engage his students in discourse rather than set them to snoring with a learned lecture. Both men were of a poetic and dashing manner, and both exercised a powerful influence upon their students. So hypnotic, in fact, was their spell that for a time young Pestalozzi refused to eat meat, and despite his physical frailty he endeavored to sleep like a Spartan without clothes or coverlet on the bare floor.

While Pestalozzi's spirit went adventuring in his cloudborne better world, his interest in good works was fetched to an even greater degree by his grandfather Andreas, a country shepherd of the Lord, whose ministry often brought him into intimate contact with humanity at its ugliest. On occasion the pastor invited his grandson to join him on his ministerial rounds. So overcome was the lad by what he observed that before long he found himself panting "to stop at its source the wretchedness into which . . . these people have sunk." To such an exalted purpose he made ready to embrace the sacerdotal calling, but the shipwreck of a trial sermon threw him into such a panic that he changed his mind.

Still ridden by visions of social sanitation, however, he turned to the study of law, hoping to be able to help and counsel the swarms of half-slaves whom life had so shabbily misused. But again a skittish fortune paid him ill, and his plans jounced to an abrupt halt. Still not daunted, he bought a farm, called Neuhof, where, after committing matrimony, he undertook to demonstrate to a plodding and impoverished peasantry how their promiseless toil could be vastly bettered by the use of the most up-to-date methods known to agronomical science. Once more his hopes were spiked. A friendly man, affable and high-minded, but almost unbelievably gullible, Pestalozzi proved an easy mark for fraudulent and nefarious sharpers who spilled upon Neuhof from every side, and in 1774, after five years of sweat and anxiety and not a little misreckoning, he saw his dream break to pieces in the churning sea of insolvency.

"FIFTY LITTLE BEGGARS" AND NEUHOF

Meanwhile, Pestalozzi had occasion to read *Emile,* and after wading through its 800 pages, like scores of others he suffered a stroke of pedagogicomania. Its telltale symptoms showed themselves plainly enough when he insisted not only on teaching his firstborn, Jakob, but also on carefully observing his development and then depositing multitudinous notes thereon in a journal which, in later years, he was to present to the world as a modest little volume weighted down with a twelve-word title. The practice, though scarcely common—nor, for that matter, rigorously objective—was nevertheless to become well regarded in years ahead by some of the world's first more or less scientific probers into the nature of early childhood. As might be expected, Pestalozzi's venture into pedagogy bore a palpable suffusion of Rousseau's naturalism, with the important distinction, perhaps, that, unlike the Genevan, the man from Neuhof tested most of his doctrines in actual practice. Childish though Johann Heinrich may often have been in mundane matters, as a teacher he was apparently sufficiently realistic to sense that vast slices of Rousseau's pedagogy were unfeasible, and sometimes even nonsensical. "Let us make use of what is wise in his principles," he reflected, and of this he had satisfied himself there was a great deal.

Pestalozzi's next step on his way to pedagogic eminence came with the failure of his Neuhof experimental station. As he watched it sink into nothingness, the thought invaded his mind that although he had come to grief in his attempt to divert the peasantry from its set and antiquated ways, perhaps the younger generation might be more amenable to his good intentions. Accordingly, he transformed part of his home into a school and peopled it with a score of peasant boys and girls. He hoped not only to make them literate, virtuous, and high-minded, but also to train them in the knacks and skills of spinning, weaving, gardening, farming, dairying, and other useful arts and crafts. By making his venture as self-supporting as possible, and with contributions from persons of means, Pestalozzi was able to hold his own, and for the first time in his life his prospects looked promising.

But again his unbridled optimism, which at times amounted almost to insanity, would not be stayed. Not content to limit his boons to twenty beneficiaries, he increased their number to fifty, thereby putting an intolerable strain on his all-too-slender resources. For two years he did his utmost to keep going, living, as he wrote later, "in the midst of fifty little beggars, sharing in my poverty my bread with them, living like a beggar myself, in order to teach beggars to live like men." When those two years were done, his creditors, who had been generously patient, refused to be put off any longer, and the Neuhof experiment became one more entry in Pestalozzi's catalog of blasted hopes.

AUTHOR!

With Neuhof's collapse, its creator allowed himself a respite from his strivings for social reclamation in order to earn a living as an author. In 1780 he put out his *Evening Hours of a Hermit,* a confection of aphorisms that set down, some savants say, the pith of Pestalozzi's pedagogy. Even so, his literary endeavor got only scant notice, and it was not until their author had won fame for other attainments that they began to get the attention they deserved.

A year later, in 1781, when his novel *Leonard and Gertrude* appeared, his fortune abruptly turned about. Attuned to the romantic literary mood, then all the rage, it depicted how Gertrude, a simple hausfrau, spurred by the high potency of her faith, trust, and belief, not only restored Leonard, her spouse—who entertained a weakness for the grape—to the straight and narrow, but with the help of the village schoolmaster succeeded in elevating her sinful community of Bonnal from the mire of its corruption to a plane so lofty that it was second only to Eden. The story massaged the feelings with sentimental ointments, and in no time at all it assumed the proportion of a best seller.

More significant was that, apart from the story itself, the work advanced a number of proposals for political, social, and educational betterment. Though these were largely glided over by the general reading public, they did not escape some of the cerebrals of the day. Indeed, as a result of *Leonard and Gertrude,* Pestalozzi became an object of cardinal interest to enlightened liberals all over Europe. Presently even flint-headed practitioners of statecraft became impressed by his ideas, and high political dignitaries from Austria, Germany, and Italy made tracks to his door not only to observe this famous literatus in person, but to ask his help and advice on all sorts of baffling social perplexities. With so much appreciation buzzing in his ears, Pestalozzi undertook to unload a few sequels. But in the main his output constituted a mere réchauffé of what he had said before and added very little to his purse. And so, instead of settling into a life of ease and plenty, he had to satisfy himself with eulogies. The great German philosopher Fichte shook his hand in high esteem, and time saw the two develop an affectionate friendship. Republican France made him one of her honorary citizens, along with Schiller, Kosciusko, George Washington, Benjamin Franklin, and other notabilities. Not to be outdone, in 1814, Czar Alexander of Russia elevated him to knighthood. Yet for all these ovations, Pestalozzi regarded himself essentially as a failure, disappointed, frustrated, and rejected in nearly every one of his major aspirations.

FAILURE AND SUCCESS

Ever since he had tried to teach his fifty little beggars to live like men, the Neuhofer had yearned to be a schoolmaster. To such a purpose he had accosted some of his friends in the government, but aside from some compliments and unctuous evasions he got nothing. Then, in 1798, fortune plucked him by the sleeve. Those were the days when the French, having liberated themselves from the despotism of the Old Regime, believed it to be their manifest destiny to propagate their revolutionary blessings in other lands. Switzerland, ever hospitable to constructive idealism, cooperated by refashioning some of its governance in accordance with the latest Parisian mode. But this made some Swiss very unhappy, and some even objected fiercely. The Catholic cantons were openly scornful of the Gallic importation, especially its active hostility to Holy Church, and they would have no truck with it. In the canton of Unterwalden, heated up by Capuchin monks, the opposition presently erupted in riot.

Meanwhile, the French, having, so to speak, served as midwife at the delivery of the new regime, were determined to conserve it. To this end they deployed some of their military, who worked with a mean, masculine thoroughness. The little town of Stanz they scorched to cinders; they killed most of its residents; and when, finally, they marched off to other conquests, they left in their wake a horde of orphans. These the Swiss government, after the usual verbal shilly-shallying, offered to the care and tutelage of Pestalozzi, who rushed to Stanz "happy," as he said, "to offer these innocent little ones some compensation for the loss they had sustained."

Not in his wildest speculation could Pestalozzi have foreseen the troubles he was wooing. Not only did the town's surviving adults abominate him as one supposed to be in league with the hated French, and one who was a misbeliever to boot, but even the children eyed him with defiance. For months they had prowled as beggars and thieves. In the process their health and morals had heavily deteriorated—any attempt to resuscitate them seemed headed for certain disaster. To make matters worse—if possible—Pestalozzi confronted an almost unbelievable shortage of supplies.

The French, it is true, had donated the orphans, and the Swiss government, for its part, had provided a convent to give them lodging. But beyond that, the cupboard was bare.

But it did not take Pestalozzi long to make a virtue of his necessity. Books being unavailable, he hit upon what he called the "object method," by which a pupil studied things rather than words about things, and what his senses detected he reported in speech rather than with pen and ink. At bottom, the theory underlying Pestalozzi's method cannot, of course, claim any originality. It juts from the pages of *Emile;* and even before Rousseau had laid his curse on a child's precipitated use of books, Comenius was tossing bouquets at the principle of learning through the senses; and before the mighty Czech there had been several others proclaiming more or less the same idea.

As one might expect, at Stanz one discerns visible remainders of Neuhof, for here as there Pestalozzi started, as he said, "with the idea of connecting [the pupils'] learning with their manual work." But at Neuhof the reason behind this stress was to provide revenue for the school's survival, whereas at Stanz it was pedagogic rather than economic. When Pestalozzi plunged into his mission at Stanz, he was buoyed up by the conviction "that as soon as we have educational establishments combined with workshops and conducted on a truly psychological basis, a generation will necessarily be formed which will show us . . . that our present studies do not require one-tenth the time we now give them." Well, there have been madder ideas in the world than that! In any case, whether right or wrong, because of Stanz's poverty of equipment Pestalozzi never got a chance to put his reasoning to the actual test.

But the man's toughest task was not pedagogical but psychological. How to smuggle himself into the hearts of his band of juvenile scofflaws was his foremost problem, and it was one which even the most powerful pedagogy on earth could not resolve. With other advanced educationai thinkers Pestalozzi had convinced himself that discipline was not a matter of clouting the young into compliance. It was rather—to put it in his own felicitous phrase—"a thinking love," by which he meant that its natural prerequisite is the teacher's understanding and forbearance, but one that must be grounded on good sense. Indeed, whether one likes it or not, there will be times when a judicious recourse to the stick will be more effective than peaceful negotiation.

Pestalozzi's procedure, though derided by the teaching rank and file, was nevertheless a success. The man's patience and kindliness were apparently catching, and as his orphans gained in trust and self-assurance they opened and unfolded as never before.

Unluckily, this happy turn of circumstance proved only transient. After a half a year or so, the French, now dashing madly from the gunfire of the pursuing Austrians, suddenly reentered Stanz, where they summarily turned the orphanage to their own use. Thus, in their own peculiar manner these Gallic liberators, though to posterity they must be forever nameless, found their way into the folios of educational history. Not only did they serve to launch the Stanzian venture; they also brought it to a close. For Pestalozzi the unexpected cancellation of his assignment was very likely a stroke of good luck. He had been working much too hard and, when the end came, he was in fact teetering on the brink of a complete breakdown. Yet no sooner had he turned his wearied back on Stanz to regain his health in the highlands than malicious tongues began to wag. At two years past fifty, it was widely bruited about, the preposterous old man had credited himself with yet another failure. There is in this not a little truth, and hence also a shade of sadness, for the future—which his detractors would never see—was to recognize that at Stanz, Pestalozzi had fathered the modern elementary school.

Soon after Stanz, Pestalozzi returned to schoolmastering. He taught for a while in the village school at Burgdorf as an assistant to a man named Dysli, who, during the more earnest moments of his life, engaged his time as the town's shoemaker. That the two men did not see eye to eye on pedagogical matters is hardly necessary to state—in fact, the friction between the assistant and his chief presently became so fulsome that the town fathers, alarmed not only by the threat to Burgdorf's bucolic quietude but even more by Pestalozzi's newfangled ideas, decided to return Johann Heinrich to private life.

But the blow was softened when some of his friends prevailed upon the government to let him use part of an ancient castle and its garden as a school. Here in the century's closing year Pestalozzi set himself to work out his pedagogy. Time saw the number of his pupils increase impressively, and to instruct them effectively Pestalozzi hired a number of first-rate aides, who, needless to say, were partisan to his theories. As the work gathered force, he devoted part of his time to giving preparation to prospective teachers. Betweenwhiles—though how he ever found the time must forever remain a mystery—he completed a couple of books, the *Mother's Book* and *How Gertrude Teaches Her Children.* Unlike the author's celebrated *Leonard and Gertrude,* the latter was composed not as a novel, but as a series of letters to one Gessner, a bookhawker in Bern—in fact, save for the name of its leading character, and that it concerns itself with the art of teaching, the work bears no relation to *Leonard and Gertrude.* Despite the mask of its epistolary form, it was recognized for what it really was, namely, a declaration of Pestalozzi's educational doctrine.

As his school grew, so did its income. Money poured in from every side, not only from the hands of benevolent civilians, but from the government, which, though it had hitherto been anything but financially friendly, now found it possible to grant Pestalozzi a slight subvention. Meanwhile, the news of what he was up to was spreading, and by and by people were streaming to Burgdorf—even, indeed, from the new lands across the sea. Then, as more than once before, the exigencies of politics ran head-on into the visions of pedagogy, and in 1804 the Swiss government, having undergone a change of political heart, expropriated the Burgdorf castle and notified Pestalozzi of his dispossession. By way of atonement, however, the rulers tendered him other quarters, this time in a convent in a little town, a Swiss Podunk, as it were, anointing its aching ego with the splendiferous name of München buchsee. But Pestalozzi's stay was short-lived, and he collected no laurels. For a spell he joined forces with Phillip Emmanuel von Fellenberg, one of his admirers, and in some respects even a disciple, who ran a large and successful institute at Hofwyl. Then, unhappily, the joint enterprise blew up.

YVERDON

In 1805 Pestalozzi packed his bags and made for Yverdon, where he was to remain for the next twenty years, continuing what he had done so meritoriously at Burgdorf, but on a grander scale. His new school, like his old one, reserved its advantages for the manly sex, housing and feeding its members, besides Pestalozzi, his amiable wife, and sundry members of the staff. The passing years again witnessed the number of its pupils rise, cresting at an enrollment of some 200 head. They varied in their years from six to eighteen, and although most of them were Swiss, there were some outlanders too, from Britain, France, Germany, Italy—even from the remote reaches of Poland.

Although for its time Yverdon was of the exalted progressive order, this is not to suggest that its pupils were salved in any butter-soft indulgence. Out of their cots at cockcrow, they were expected to get into their clothes, winter and summer, in less than thirty minutes flat. From 6 to 7 A.M. they invoked the Heavenly Father to spread his blessing over the day's proceedings, whereupon followed the first secular instruction. Once this was over, there was a general scrubbing of hands and faces, and then an exigent stomach was allowed to play host to a light breakfast. Classes reconvened from 8 to 10 A.M., with a five- to seven-minute break for a second breakfast of a slice of bread and a slab of cheese or other delicatessen—a pleasant practice which still obtains in many unprogressive Old World spots. With the repast safely down the assembled esophagi, classes resumed until the stroke of noon—when all hands made for dinner, which was fol-

lowed by a bit of rest and recreation. At 1:30 P.M., the war against ignorance was renewed. It ran full tilt until 5 P.M., when a brief truce prevailed
for refreshment and relaxation, followed by further skirmishing until 8 P.M.
The ensuing sixty minutes were reserved for spiritual devotions, which came
to an end with a nightcap of prayer, after which the boys made for bed to
replenish their store of energy for the morrow.

Though all this may give an impression of a deadening formality, the
facts, nevertheless, drive it astray. The truth is the routine was not rigorously maintained, and when the occasion so demanded it was unceremoni-
ously ignored. Nor did Pestalozzi ever falter in his confidence that for
education there is no better place than home. "Our educational machin-
ery," he commented, "has only value insofar as it approaches the character
of a well-ordered household in all its details." Consequently, in all his maturer educational endeavors, Pestalozzi invested his first interest in bridging
the gap between the child's life at home and at school. Although the man
was a stranger to what German psychologists were to call "the economy
and hygiene of learning," which actually was not to be revealed for yet
another several generations, rather curiously he had the good sense to ar-
range his pupils' activities in accordance with some of the tenets of that still
unheard-of science. Thus, the first thing in the morning, when his pupils'
minds were still fresh and quick, Pestalozzi put them on the more taxing
subjects, such as arithmetic; whereas later in the day, when presumably
they had spent some of their earlier élan, he turned them loose on such
lighter matters as music, drawing, fencing, and assorted handicrafts.

On Wednesday and Saturday afternoons there were no sessions, a custom which is still favored in various continental schools, but which at Yverdon frequently became the occasion for some social undertaking, say, a
school picnic or a hike into the countryside. Also at Yverdon, as at Burgdorf, Pestalozzi made the training of teachers one of his prime preoccupa-
tions. So new was this practice at the time that presently a number of
forward-looking nations, eager to stock their schools with teachers of Pestalozzian overtones, began to grant scholarships to their most promising
schoolmasters to enable them to attend sessions at Yverdon. As time saw its
fame trumpeted to the four winds, it, like Burgdorf before it, became a
pedagogic Mecca, attracting spectators, lay and professional, including
even such whales as Napoleon and Talleyrand.

At Yverdon, Pestalozzi reached the summit of his glory, especially
during its first five years. Thereafter a pale cast of doubts and disputes
weakened his staff, and Pestalozzi's light began to dim. In 1825 the melancholy of night descended upon the school. Now in the childhood of senility,
he returned to his old haunt, where so long ago in the green and sunlit

period of his youth he had tasted the first rapture of his vision. Two years later, at the age of 81, he died at Brugg.

THE BASIC THEORY

Thus the man and his work. Let us now inspect his basic theory and note how he sought to infuse it with life. Although Pestalozzi was a God-loving Christian, like Rousseau he rejected religion as the necessary beginning and end of education, a stress which had given the primary school its paramount reason for being until the end of the eighteenth century. For Pestalozzi—again in tune with Rousseau—education was a natural, organic process. It was, to use his own words, "the natural, progressive, and harmonious development of all the child's powers and capacities." It addressed itself to the head, the hand, and the heart, developing them in concert. "To consider any one capacity exclusively," he insisted, "is to undermine and destroy man's native equilibrium." Yet this is not to say that the three share equal importance, and that as man journeys from the cradle to the grave, his head, hand, and heart are peers. Though the absence or misfiring of any one of them would cause dire consequences, still, of the three, it is the heart—man's ethical life—to which Pestalozzi awards the palm, for it primarily makes it possible for man to live in tranquility not only with others but with himself.

If Pestalozzi's proposition that education is a natural function holds water, then it follows that it cannot be regarded as the prerogative of those born to rank and wealth, but, like the breath of life itself, it is the birthright of every human being. Nor was education's concern confined simply to the improvement of the individual child; it embraced all children, and thereby it bore inevitably on the great neighborhood of human beings, which is to say society and the general social condition.

Like many an educator with reform gurgling in his veins, Pestalozzi turned a cold shoulder to the schoolmaster's hankering to clutter the child's memory with useless knowledge. Learning by rote, he declared, is so much "empty chattering of mere words." The teacher, he added, "should aim rather at increasing the power of his pupil than at increasing his knowledge." Like Rousseau, he had grave misgivings about the premature use of books, and like the Genevan he insisted that our first learning comes through our eyes, ears, hands, even our nose and tongue.

Looking back over the years, he concluded that what he had achieved "for the very being of education" was to fix "the highest . . . principles of instruction in the recognition of sense perception as the absolute foundation of all knowledge." Unlike the seventeenth-century Comenius, the arch-pleader for the study of things, or pictures of things, rather than words about things, Pestalozzi discerned in the method not just a means to pile up knowledge but also a way to exercise the powers of the mind. But his rocklike belief that the senses are the one and only source of everything we know, whether now or later, disabled him from understanding that for a small proportion of men the intellect too can be a source of knowledge.

Observation became the substructure of the Pestalozzian lesson. Led by the master's questions, the pupil, examining an object, was drawn out to note its salient characteristics and then, when his inspecting had exhausted whatever was observable, to frame the details his senses had detected into a coordinated generalization. Under Pestalozzi's sensitive touch the object lesson took on the aspect of a creative performance, and, through vivid insight, the lesson bounced with a sprightliness it had never known. It was in this sense a work of art, and one wherein its creator outclassed not a few of his numerous imitators, who, though they wrapped themselves in the cloak of learning and correctness, lacked his virtuosity and, even more, his exuberance of spirit, and thus much too often they degraded the object lesson into a transparent artificiality. The painful truth is that, as the years flicked by, the object lesson deteriorated into just another way to pour a flood of facts into the pates of children as if they were so many jugs.

PROBLEMS AND MISCALCULATIONS

Pestalozzi wanted, as he remarked rather indefinitely, "to psychologize education," by which he had in mind that whenever a young one is put upon learning he should be started off with what is simple, then, as he becomes its master, he should continue with the more complex. Nowadays the idea is of course a first lesson in the first reader of pedagogy, but when Pestalozzi expounded it, psychology as we know it still lay beyond the horizon. Hence, when he undertook to translate his theory into practice, his defective understanding of the workings of the human mind trapped him into some whopping, though quite understandable, miscalculations. What misled him was his supposition that what to him was as simple as a brass ring must, therefore, be equally simple to a child. Consequently, as Pestalozzi essayed to reduce what the pupil was to learn to its starkest simplicity, he sometimes in all innocence did exactly the opposite. Take reading as an instance. To distill the mystery to its barest essence, he refined words to their fewest components, namely, a vowel and a consonant: ab, eb, ib, ob, and so on from a to z. These couples, which he assembled in a collection he called "syllabaries," and which assumed a fearsome bulk, the pupil had to recognize before he was permitted the grace of confronting actual words, then sentences and passages, and then books.

Although Pestalozzi declared with great fervor for the principle of learning through observation, yet unlike Rousseau, he did not allow his pupils to sketch freely the things that caught their eyes. Like reading, drawing was first subjected to a rigorous dissection in order to determine its constituent elements, and so in place of putting on paper a sketch of a spreading linden tree with, maybe, a dog sniffing inquisitively at its base, the child was set upon day after day to perfect himself in drawing arcs, circles, angles, and lines, vertical, horizonal, slanting, and so on. Similarly, handwriting was begun as a subdivision of drawing. Letters were stripped to their unfleshed bones and were found to be composed of elements sometimes curved, sometimes straight, sometimes upward bound, and sometimes the other way. These the budding penmaster was made to rehearse and bring under control before he was trusted to try his skill on actual letters, followed in due course with bona fide words and sentences.

Despite such palpable absurdities, Pestalozzi's insistence that "everything which a child has to learn must be proportioned to his strength, getting more difficult in the same degree as his powers of attention, judgment, and thought increase," was solidly grounded. It was nature's way, as Rousseau had argued, and as Comenius had sought to translate into his schoolbooks and his teaching, and into his system of graded, articulated schools from the nursery to the higher learning.

THE PRACTICAL MAN—TRIAL AND ERROR

That Pestalozzi was no mental giant is scarcely news. His basic psychology, the so-called "faculty psychology" which sprang from the head of Aristotle, has been declared fallacious. Even in Pestalozzi's day critical sharpshooters were beginning to direct their fire upon it. Even so, for all his shortcomings, Pestalozzi went to great lengths to test his theories in actual schoolroom operation, and of those he found wanting or unworkable, he made short shrift. For this one must give the man his due, as, working when he did, he had to get along without the benefit of science, neither the natural ones nor the social ones having as yet penetrated into pedagogy. As a result, he had to conduct his searching with neither scale nor metric stick to give him guidance in appraising the validity of his findings, or even a way of knowing whether what succeeded in his hands would pluck a similar success in general.

Although circumstance had imposed upon Pestalozzi the haphazard procedure of trial and error, the superior vigor of his common sense guided him often enough to sound conclusions. As far back as his Neuhof days he had come to understand there is a vast difference between teaching and cramming facts into reluctant heads. It was at Burgdorf where, in seeking to perfect his teaching method, he had come to understand that the most ingenious method in the world is no better than a teacher's competence to put it into effective use—in sum, that teachers, like any other masters worthy of their title, may benefit by training.

Such a notion was, of course, no longer entirely fresh. The Jesuits and several other orders, whether of the Roman rite or the reformed, were not only its adherents but its executors as well. But in the vast ocean of educational practice they were mere fingerlings, and the generality of schoolmasters continued to be, as they had been for centuries, a pack of second-rate men, whose vital concerns, like those of Dysli, the Burgdorf bootmaker, lay far afield from teaching the young, not to say inspiring and elevating them.

By way of contrast, when Pestalozzi instructed his protégés, there reigned a passion in him which seldom stilled. He had the happy faculty for conveying a warmth and understanding to his pupils that invariably tended to break down the familiar classroom barriers. His school, some opinionators have said, was not a school at all, but a well-adjusted family, which was, of course, precisely the sort of earthly paradise on which Pestalozzi had set his hopes. "Let the child be a human being," he exhorted the candidates for teaching under his tutelage, and "let the teacher be his trusted friend." He had pledged when he was young to help his fellowman, and this pledge he had kept. It was a success, however, faintly touched by failure, for he had not been able to stop man's despairing wretchedness "at the source"—not because he had not tried, but because what he had set out to do was beyond the human capacity, as it still is today. Whatever Pestalozzi's faults and errors, they fade in the contemplation of his work as a whole.

FAME AND INFLUENCE

As Pestalozzi's fame increased, his methods too began to be adopted on an ever-increasing scale—except in his native land. There, to the run of his countrymen, Pestalozzi's liberal outlook, which his methods, of course, reflected, seemed forebodingly uncanonical, a clear and dreadful challenge to the established powers, whether spiritual or temporal. Not till 1830, after a revolution had booted out the old order, did the Swiss begin to draw on the lavish legacy this humble man had left them. Since then he has occupied a very special sanctuary for veneration in the Helvetian heart. For the Swiss to refer to a teacher as a Pestalozzi is to talk of him in the highest terms.

In some other lands, however, Pestalozzian pedagogy ignited an almost instantaneous interest. The Germans Herbart and Froebel, each destined to become a grandmaster of pedagogy in his own right, paid their respects to Pestalozzi at Yverdon, and the latter even studied and taught there from

1808 to 1810. When in the springtime of the century Napoleon made a shambles of the proud and powerful Prussians, their leaders turned to education, among other things, to get their shattered fatherland back on its feet. They renovated their school system with unsparing thoroughness, and in 1808, to man it with the most skillful teachers to be found, they dispatched seventeen of their most accomplished schoolmasters to Yverdon, squaring their bills for three years while they studied the new pedagogy. Returned to their Teutonic habitat, they were converted into provincial superintendents, heads of training schools, or other educational prominenti. In addition, the astute Prussians persuaded the Reverend Karl August Zeller, a devout Pestalozzian, to leave his native Württemberg to organize a school to train Prussia's Pestalozzis of tomorrow. Thus the work went on with a colossal zeal, and from Prussia, as happened so frequently in German history, it presently spread to other states.

Nor did Pestalozzi and his wonders confine their influence to the Germanic lands. The Swiss educator had his votaries in France and Britain, and across the water in Canada, and, as the years moved on, in our own republic. Various Americans had seen him and his work at Burgdorf and Yverdon, and some of them had been sufficiently impressed to report on him in divers journals of opinion. But such notices were few and far apart, and their general effect on American education caused not even a ripple. The honor of planting Pestalozzianism in American soil goes to Edward Austin Sheldon, a school superintendent at Oswego, New York.

In the summer of 1859, while taking life easy in Canada, Sheldon chanced to run into an exhibit of Pestalozzian object materials. True, they were of English provenance and represented a degenerated form of what Pestalozzi had conjured up as a living and breathing endeavor, yet so aroused was the American by his discovery that he straightaway decided to introduce the Pestalozzi revelation at Oswego. There ensued the usual cat-and-dog vendettas between the old-time standpatters and Sheldon and his partisans. After a couple of years, however, the innovators undid their antagonists when the city founded a normal school to tailor its prospective masters in accord with the new Pestalozzian fashion. In 1862, three years after the importing of the new system to Oswego, the National Teachers Association—now the NEA—gave object teaching its official blessing.

Meanwhile, the State of New York tendered the school a slight subsidy, and in 1866 Oswego Normal became its second normal school. There is no need to embroider on the successive course of events. It is sufficient to point out that the new school achieved a booming success. Before long, in fact, like Pestalozzi's own groves in Switzerland, Oswego Normal became the object of an almost unbelievable interest, not only among professionals but among the laity as well. Acclaimed as the most up-to-date purveyor of teacher training, it sent its graduates far and wide as teachers, principals, and directors of normal schools. For at least a generation it set the fashion of the nation's teacher training, and thereby inevitably it left its mark on American education. Then the power of its light began to diminish, and by the eighties Pestalozzianism as a living force in American education was spent.

Chapter 20

Johann Friedrich Herbart

THE HAND THAT ROCKED THE CRADLE

Though the years saw Pestalozzianism fall from favor, yet some of its revelations, whether original or distillations of the venerable juices of Rousseau,
Comenius, and a handful of others, have endured to the present day—for
example, its use of objects to aid and reinforce the learning process, its
more humane treatment of children, and its insistence on the necessity of
training teachers. But besides these and other boons, there existed a number
of debilitating deficiencies, such as its wobbly psychological foundations,
its mistaken notions about how to simplify learning, its exaggerated appraisal of the worth of sensory experience, and its failure to frame its principles into a unified system.

The man who was to settle pedagogy on a firm and solid base was
Johann Friedrich Herbart (1776–1841), a German. Sprung from the
Vaterland's upper bourgeoisie, he was born in the northwestern city of
Oldenburg in the politically fateful year of 1776, and he died some sixty-

five years following in the university town of Göttingen. Unlike his celebrated predecessors, the Messrs. Rousseau and Pestalozzi, Herbart came from a family known for its high intellectual candlepower. For almost forty years his father's father had directed the affairs of a classical secondary school, an office which in those paleolithic days made brains in its incumbents a primary prerequisite. The boy's father, though addicted to a severe punctilio, had nevertheless advanced himself into a successful legal practice—in fact, he rose to the rank of a state attorney, a *Regierungsrat.* But his wife must be scored even higher. Where her spouse had all the glow of an ice bag, she radiated warmth like a stove. Dynamic and ambitious, at a time and place which expected its women, like its children, to be seen but not heard, she inclined nonetheless to work her will. In her we come upon that rare and extraordinary amalgam of beauty and a dumfounding intelligence.

A devotee of the Lutheran truth, she broke her son to the rudimentary articles of domestic discipline and decorum. When, at the age of five, he well-nigh killed himself by falling into a tub of boiling water, she resolved that from that time on she would keep an eye cocked on his doings no matter where or when. She put herself in charge of his first ventures into learning, engaging the tutorial services of the Reverend Pastor Ulzen whose expressed pedagogic purpose he summed up in a half-dozen words: clearness, definiteness, and coherence of thought. To keep herself abreast of Johann Friedrich's intellectual and moral progress, the Frau Regierungsrat made it her business to attend the tutorial sessions herself, brushing up on her Greek, mathematics, and logic. She thus qualified as a sort of subtutor, able to assist her son over the rough spots with his homework and, more important, to shield him against the ever-lurking menace of false ideas and unseemly influences. Although young Herbart was not totally fenced off from boys of his own years, his associations were for the far greater part with grownups. As a consequence, instead of engaging in some of the wilder pranks of boyhood, he settled into a flaccid prematurity.

ON TO JENA

The boy was twelve years old when his mother relaxed her guard somewhat and allowed him to mix with others as a student in the Oldenburg Gymnasium. So relentlessly had Parson Ulzen drilled his pupil in clearness, definiteness, and unity of thinking, that this freshman gymnasiast was presently tapping a flood of unrestrained encomiums from his bedazzled professors. In fact, his intellectual exhibition was of such an unqualified superiority that before long he found himself in classes with boys three to fours years his senior. To achieve his extraordinary success, Herbart was tremendously aided not only by a fine and independent intelligence, but by a memory that retained nearly everything he had ever read or heard.

But it was in the department of the intellect that he performed his grandest feats. He hobnobbed intimately with Latin and Greek, and his liaison with logic, metaphysics, and mathematics was no less cordial. He was all of thirteen, a time in life when most boys are concentrating on horseplay, when he compounded an essay seeking to prove "the existence of an eternal God," which he followed a year later with a discourse "On the Doctrine of Human Freedom." Another twelvemonth, and we see him speculating "On the Commonest Causes that Affect the Growth of Morality in the Various States." When, as class valedictorian—he was still two years short of twenty—he addressed the assembled populace, he performed the oratorical obsequies in Latin with a treatise on the ideas of the greatest good as expressed by Cicero and Kant. When he was not actively sparring with ideas, he often disported in the tonal art. Not content to find surcease as a mere listener, he played the violin, the cello, the harp, and the piano, and he even composed a sonata. Characteristically, before long he descanted learnedly on harmony.

Squired by his mother, Johann Friedrich arrived at the University of Jena in 1794, where at the behest of his juridic father he dutifully placed himself in the hands of the faculty of law. In those times Jena was by long odds the brightest star in the German cultural firmament. Scan the register of its illuminati and you will find a parcel of vastly learned men, including such poets, novelists, and dramatists as Goethe, Schiller, Wieland, and Herder—to throw our spotlight on just a few.

Herbart's affection for jurisprudence was less than lukewarm, and with his deep interest in philosophy it was doubtless inevitable that from time to time his feet should steer him into the lecture halls of Jena's philosophers. Meanwhile, his mother resumed her familiar role of safeguarding him from the coarseness of beer halls and dueling fraternities, seeking out in their place those lofty souls who, like her Johann, were adorers of the higher thinking. It was through her that he came to know Schiller, then enjoying the agony of composing his *Letters on the Aesthetic Education of Man.* Time was to see their encounter take on the gleam of a cordial affinity. In fact, after a score of years or so Herbart, now himself robed in the professorial shroud, was to portray his own views on the beautiful under the title of "The Aesthetic Presentation of the World as the Chief Business of Education," a designation which would scarcely qualify its maker as being sensitive to the finer nuances involving artistic loveliness.

The time came, as it was bound to, when Herbart's allergy to law became unbearable, and he turned his back on Jena's Blackstones to anchor himself instead in the more congenial sessions of its metaphysicians. Among them he bestowed his preference upon Johann Gottlieb Fichte, an idealist who stressed the importance of the individual ego but who was also known as one of the most powerful orators the philosophic brethren had ever hatched. Yet despite the esteem in which Herbart held his professor, he was not long in sniffing certain imperfections in his thinking. In truth, soon he dismissed it altogether. "Fichte," he said some years later, "taught me mainly through his errors." The philosopher Schelling, second at Jena only to Fichte, performed a similar service.

TUTOR AND STUDENT

After three years of Jena, Herbart was ready for a change of scene, and in 1797 he headed for Switzerland where, after consultation with his mother, he accepted an offer to instruct the three sons of Herr von Steiger, the Governor of Interlaken. For two years Herbart executed his tutorial duties, cautiously treading his way over the strange highways and sideways of the learning and teaching processes, and though subsequently he was to become an insistent advocate of putting every prospective teacher through a stiff course of professional training, the two years he shone the lamp of guidance under the von Steiger roof constitute the sum total of his own preparation in the art of teaching the young.

Put upon by his astute employer to submit a bimonthly accounting of what he and the von Steiger fry were up to, which is to say, what they were studying, how he was teaching, and how the boys were making out, Herbart hit upon the idea of presenting his say in a series of letters, wherein, as is to be expected from a man so precise and methodical, he went into meticulous and almost microscopic particulars. All in all, twenty-four letters flowed from his pen, but time has fingered all but five. Yet even this scanty remnant reveals snatches of what was to become dominant in the Herbartian pedagogy. Thus, for the formulation of his method he leaned on psychology. Like Rousseau, he perceived in his learners so many individuals, each demanding special pedagogical consideration. Bearing heavily on all his educational endeavor were his two big goals, namely, morality and what he referred to as a "many-sided interest."

It was during the von Steiger intermezzo that Herbart made acquaintance with the ideas of Pestalozzi. When the chance offered itself, in 1799, he dropped in on him at Burgdorf. The bushy-maned Swiss gave him to think, as the French say, and young Herbart accorded him the respect befitting a celebrity, In due course, Herbart published a monograph on the Pestalozzian pedagogy.

The year 1800 saw Herbart settle in the home of a friend at Bremen, close by the sea in the dampness of northern Germany. He had gone there to put the final touches on his doctoral studies, imbibing for this purpose large drafts of philosophy and psychology. Meanwhile he found time to pen a couple of pieces on the work of Pestalozzi, to wit, *How Gertrude Taught*

Her Children and *Pestalozzi's ABC of Sense Perception,* which, though somewhat critical of Pestalozzi's widowed psychology, nonetheless drew a fair
and rather friendly portrait. In 1802, upon his doctoral transfiguration at
Göttingen, the university accepted his services as one of its lecturers. He
was now safely past his nonage, his mother having meanwhile arranged a
divorce from the Regierungsrat and gone to live and be happy in Napo-
leonic Paris.

THE RISE AND FALL

For seven years the young doctor worked steadfastly at an instructor's
appointed tasks. The vast learning he had under his bonnet stood him well,
and his lectures, illuminated by the pronouncement of an occasional wise
saw, enjoyed a respectable attendance. At the same time he maintained his
own studies, and in accordance with immemorial academic custom he issued some of his ponderings in print—such tidbits, for example, as *The
Moral and Ethical Revelations of the World.* One of his more important
effusions during this period, and also the statement of his final position on
Pestalozzi, he brought out under the title *On the Standpoint of Judging the
Pestalozzian Method of Instruction.* With its appearance Herbart bade adieu
to the Pestalozzian gospel. Not indifferent to Herbart's hard and high-grade
work, after having borne witness to it for six continuous years, in 1808 the
university converted its author into a professor. To express his gratification,
the professor consummated another book, his *General Pedagogics.*

But the crown and climax of his career were yet to come when, in 1809,
the University of Königsberg proffered him its chair in philosophy. Bediz-
ened not so long ago by the redoubtable Immanuel Kant, the chair was the
unbelievable crystalization of Herbart's castle in the air. It was, he confided
in a rare moment of outspoken ecstasy, "the place which, as a boy, I longed
for in reverential dreams as I studied the works of the sage of Königsberg."
Although nobody expected Herbart to conquer the dizzy heights scaled by
Kant, yet his admirer bore the test supremely well. For twenty-four years—
until 1833—he labored diligently, expounding his specialty, directing seminars, attending faculty meetings, counseling embryonic doctors of philosophy, besides presiding over a pedagogical seminary and practice-teaching
school, the first of the sort to make an appearance in the groves of the
higher learning. Meanwhile, he somehow managed to find the time to keep
on writing weighty, though scarcely exhilarating, books. The massiveness of
his creation, when due account is taken of all his other activities, was truly
amazing, and comprised the ensemble of his more important writings, as
witness, among others, his *Manual of Psychology* (1813), an *Introduction to
Philosophy* (1813), *Psychology as a Science Founded According to a New*

Method on Experience, Metaphysics, and Mathematics (1824), and *General Metaphysics* (1828).

For all the glamor of his Kantian chair, it cannot be said that Königsberg brought Herbart contentment. The dank chill of its climate was unfriendly to his arthritic bones, and the distance that separated him from his old haunts in Germany's west was far too vast for more than a rare excursion. No less oppressive to his peace of mind was the crochety conservatism of the Prussian bureaucracy. Its truculence dogged him at every turn, impinging on his academic freedom, undermining his seminary, and even prying into his personal affairs to assure itself of his political impeccability. By 1833, as matters threatened to become even worse, Herbart's crop ran over, and he made a one-way trip to Göttingen. It was a grave step, but it had not been taken lightly. There, unhobbled by devious government snufflers, he continued to work in his quiet way until 1841, when, a few hours after rendering a lecture, he died of a stroke.

PRINCIPLES AND METHODS

No irresistible impulse to teach and improve the lowborn overcame Herbart as it did Pestalozzi. Nor did he, like Rousseau in his mad and overflowing way, pine to promote the precepts of the Author of Nature. Unlike these and other seers and hopers of the world, the professor put a curb on wishful and romantic thinking, preferring to be guided by what had been demonstrated by plausible and impartial evidence. If he cherished any hopes to invent a better world, he kept them to himself. Instead, he took the world as he found it, and in his deliberate and reflective way he tried to make it acceptable and perhaps, for better or worse, intelligible. Not given to emotional demonstration, he nevertheless evinced a scholarly zeal in dissecting human emotions in order to ascertain their nature. He was above all a trained and disciplined thinker who passed most of the days and nights of his mature life in the hermitage of the academic community. In his dealings with education he had neither Pestalozzi's tenderness for his fellow creatures nor Rousseau's sweep of intuitive vision. In their place, however, he brought to his work the confidence which issues from the possession of an enormous fund of knowledge and the intellectual acuity to put it to effective use.

True to the universal watchword of pedagogic masters through the ages, Herbart relied heartily on the assumption that education's primary purpose is to make men good and thereby happy. But the principles which bottomed right and wrong, he was fond of telling us, were determined by the society they are designed to keep in peace and happiness. By this token it becomes education's primary mission to instill in the young the values held dear by the custodians of the established social order, to believe, in short, in all things that law-abiding citizens of Christendom believe in, from truth and justice to service, duty, good works, and a healthy body and mind. Not knowledge, but character and social morality, should be the end of education. "The term *virtue*," Herbart observed, "expresses the whole purpose of education," a pithy pronouncement admirably put, but one which, sad to say, the academician's predilection for prolixity caused him to enlarge with another load of several hundred words.

To get at the roots of good and evil, Herbart trained a searching eye on man's interests and activities. The first, which, after some little study, he found to be manifold, bred like so many bacilli in man himself, his environs, and his relations with people. The second resulted mainly from the responsibilities placed upon him by the society of which he is a part. Pestalozzi undertook to make the child privy to his world by the study of its objects, and to enable the learner to form satisfactory contacts with others, the Swiss educator encouraged him to engage in colloquy. To these Herbart annexed a third, to wit, an exposure to the panorama of our cultural legacy, especially in its literary and historical incarnations. But the professor's purpose was not to implant the seed of passion for the loveliness of humane letters, nor to pump the learner's memory full of information about the long ago, but rather to inflame him with moral zeal—the old refrain that the reason for pondering literature is primarily to make men better.

With Pestalozzi's notion that good teaching and learning could proceed only when they rested on a psychological foundation, Herbart was in hearty accord. But Pestalozzi's blithe acceptance of the existence of mental faculties, each one an entity performing its function apart from the others, Herbart could not take. More perceptive than his predecessor, Herbart undertook to rid psychology of its rickety assumptions. For a quarter of a century or so, he reminded us in his autumnal years, he used metaphysics and mathematics, and with them self-observation, experience, and experiment, "to find the foundations of true psychological insight." As a result, he conceived a psychology which, in at least one respect, is closer to our own, namely in its view that, save under unusual circumstances, mental behavior is a fairly integrated process.

But this is by no means saying that the professor was a modern psychologist. Innocent of the laboratory with its array of esthesiometers, dynamometers, polygraphs, computers, and other scientific contraptions, Herbart conducted his explorations of the psyche much along the line of an empirical philosopher, say a Locke, starting with what seemed to be a credible assumption, filtering it through the fine gauze of reason, and then proceeding by careful and, if possible, objective observation to a conclusion.

For all his handicaps, Herbart came up with several important theories on the then still fog-wrapped processes of teaching and learning, in illustration, his doctrines of interest and apperception, which he later stitched into his method of teaching, the so-called "Formal Steps." To the theme intoned now and then by some indiscreet educational forward-looker that a child learns most readily when he is interested in what he is learning, Herbart gave resonant approval. After thinking things out, the professor was able to differentiate between two major types of interest. One is the natural, self-begotten sort which a child entertains unbidden, and which needs no magisterial hocus-pocus to induct into operation. The other is a contrived interest, induced in the pupil by his teacher to make him want to learn something to which at the outset he was indifferent or even antagonistic. The doctrine in general currency in that day, that effective learning is basically a matter of overcoming obstacles, evoked no cheers from the Göttingen sage. He not only held interest to be indispensable to learning—the tinder, so to say, which ignites the fire—he also laid down the mandate that in its absence it is the teacher's bounden duty to employ all the necromancy at his command to create it—a tactic which nowadays is spoken of as "motivation," and which, needless to say, is in general good standing.

Pestalozzi, following in the track of Rousseau, Comenius, and a few other visionaries in education, committed himself to the doctrine of guiding the pupil to what he does not know by tying the material to be learned, insofar as common sense permits, to what he does know—or of going from the known to the unknown. This principle Herbart pronounced fundamentally correct. He not only amended and broadened the doctrine's scope, he also daubed it with psychological tints. Designated "apperception," the theory—stripped to its bare skin—asserts that any new idea or experience is interpreted by means of those already known.

Interest and apperception became the pedestal whereon Herbart erected his method of teaching. Denominated the Formal Steps, these at first were four: clearness, association, system, and method, but with the passing years, somewhat reworked, the quartet metamorphosed into a quintet, each step neatly and appropriately labeled, as follows:

1 *Preparation* Putting the Herbartian theories of interest and apperception to work, this endeavored to put the learner into a receptive mood and mind. The lesson's purpose was made clear, and such antecedent knowledge as might cast light on the new was brought to notice.

2 *Presentation* The new material was unveiled and explained.

3 *Association* The new material was examined in the light of the old, and apposite similarities and differences were noted.

4 *Generalization* The particulars brought out in the foregoing were embodied in a general statement or principle or rule.

5 *Application* True to the maxim that nothing is ever fully understood until it is tried out in practice, the learner's mastery of the generalization was put to the test with suitable problems and exercises.

Nothing like Herbart's Formal Steps had ever been dreamed of before, and so their very novelty brought them to notice. Entering upon the pedagogic scene when Pestalozzi's object lesson was beginning to gray around the edges, the Herbartian steps presently replaced their predecessor not only in Europe but in America as well. They attained their highest vogue during the century's final quarter, when it became their lot to fall to the challenges of a newer, more vital and valid psychology.

Besides the theories aforementioned, Herbart concocted several others. He was, indeed, one of the most fecund generators of pedagogic theorems in the teaching world. He was the first to arrive at the view that subjects should not be treated as so many isolated entities but, whenever possible, should be judiciously brought together. The mathematical studies, for example, "from elementary arithmetic to higher mathematics," Herbart asserted, "are to be linked to the pupil's knowledge of nature, and so to his experience. . . ." So taught, mathematical ideas would flow into the student's general stream of thought and thereby be of some personal worth. Contrariwise, "when the ideas generated form an isolated group . . . they are usually soon forgotten." This interweaving of subject matter the professor called "correlation," a name which is still used, though in its current form it is executed on a far vaster and more sophisticated scale.

Though Herbart merely sketched the broad outline of what he had in mind, his successors, on the other hand, putting his statement into practice, were not loath at times to push it to the edge of folly. They not only changed its name to "concentration," but they also paid no heed to the warning of its inceptor that "it would be an error to argue that one who is being initiated in one subject ought to combine it with a second, third, or fourth on the ground that they are essentially integrated." Instead, they worked themselves blue in the face to find correlation in everything, whether it was there or not. As a consequence, under the concentration principle, all instruction was to bear on a "core of study" for the purpose of revealing—in some inscrutable manner—"the moral universe." In the second grade, for example, the learner was set to "concentrating" on *Robinson Crusoe*. Defoe's classic served him not only as an exercise in reading, but it was also, so to speak, the hub of the wheel from which radiated instruction in ciphering and composition—even in the science of right and wrong.

Another doctrine in which Herbart showed some favorable interest was the so-called "culture epochs theory," which held that in his personal cultural evolution an individual recapitulated the cultural development of the race as it made its way from the primeval ooze to its present ethereal heights. The theory, though it is today a relic on the philosophic junk pile, nevertheless enjoyed more than a fair esteem among eighteenth-century traders in ideas. Although he never called the theory by its name (for the obvious reason that in his time it had none), Rousseau nevertheless embraced it. In fact, some are in favor of nominating him as its sponsor. The German poet and historian Schiller acclaimed it and even recommended it as a basic cultural principle. Whether the theory held water or not, Herbart believed that, in the name of a natural and orderly teaching procedure, it would be desirable to launch the beginner in the elemental epics of the race, for instance, the *Iliad* and the *Odyssey,* and thereafter to direct his studies to the more recent representatives of the belletristic art.

What Herbart had cast in a modest mold, his disciples saw fit to elaborate on a grandiose scale. So completely did some master pedagogues succumb to the culture epochs evangel that, for a starter, they steeped their beginners for a year or so in savage culture—within the limits, naturally, of civilized decency—after which, for a brace of years, they were made familiar with barbarian culture, followed, as their school years ebbed, with a chaser of modern civilization.

It is easy enough in retrospect to scoff at such doings. But even after the theory's logical quicksand had been plainly charted, the culture epochs gospel continued to exert a seductive attraction. In truth, although it defaulted on those high qualities demanded by logical criticism, yet even such mighty-minded worthies as Herbert Spencer and G. Stanley Hall flung forth broadsides in its behalf. Despite their superior scientific knowledge and their vaunted mental luxuriance, theirs was apparently a case, as Bacon once reminded us, of what a man "would rather have true, he believes." Today the theory is recognized as a doctrine more notable for its nonsense than its profoundness, with no more scientific justification than democracy or witchcraft.

Like Plato and Aristotle, Herbart devoted most of his years to philosophic reflection. Like the one, he was also a celebrity in mathematics, and like the other, he was a partisan of the natural sciences. Pedagogue though he was, whose overriding concern lay in the realm of educational theory, it was Herbart, nevertheless, who conceived the hope of studying education as a science. To him must go the credit for winning a reputable place for it in the groves of the higher learning, where he strove laboriously to transform his hope into a fact.

What went for education as a whole also went for its omnipresent handmaid, psychology. At a time when the study of the human psyche was largely a matter of guesswork, especially of those master guessers, the metaphysicians and divine scientists, Herbart tried to inject a measure of exactness into the subject by putting it on a mathematical basis. Though this turned out to be too baffling for even his prodigious mind, yet in the long run it proved to be a vision of things to come.

Finally, it was Herbart who, in his quest for a sound educational theory as scientific as time and circumstance would let him make it, instituted a model school which served him and his associates as a laboratory in which they could put their doctrines to the trial of classroom practice, and in which they could direct and observe the progress of their panting student teachers.

THE NEW RISE AND INFLUENCE

Despite Herbart's genuine stature, when he died in 1841 his countrymen hardly knew him. It used to be modish to account for his slump into oblivion on the ground of his aloof and cloistered intellectuality. This may be so, but only up to a point. True, compared to the romantic, warm-hearted, compassionate Pestalozzi, Herbart appeared as something of a frosty aristocrat, with all the mien and manner of a Hamilton. But it should not be overlooked that, for all his intellectual incandescence, when Herbart was alive there was no lack of cerebral luminosity from others, notably Fichte and Hegel. The result was that the Herbartian light was sometimes dimmed, and maybe even obscured, as German thinkers absorbed themselves in the syllogisms of these other two. "My poor pedagogy," the disconsolate Herbart moaned, "has not been able to lift up its voice."

Had Herbart lived for another generation, he would have seen his reputation rise again to assume an honorable place in educational chronicles. The balance began the slow process of redressment in 1856 when an Austrian by the name of Volksmann published an exhaustive analysis of the Herbartian pedagogy. Two years later came Gustav Linder's *Empirical Psychology.* A textbook, it reflected much of its light from Herbart's basic tenets, and since it was the only one of its kind it enjoyed a very satisfactory trade—in fact, in 1889 it was turned into English by Charles De Garmo, a worker in the Herbartian vineyard in the American republic.

What probably did more than anything else to fetch Herbart out of the enveloping darkness was Tuiskon Ziller's *The Basis of the Doctrine of Educative Instruction,* which, appearing in 1865, let in some daylight on Herbart's views on education as a moral force. Ziller, who was a professor at the University of Leipzig, not only burned away the haze which had enshrouded the German acquaintance with Herbart; he also stirred up a vast, if somewhat tardy, interest in his teachings. Presently the professor's adherents found themselves sufficiently numerous to organize their common interest in the Association for the Scientific Study of Education. Although in the beginning the run of Herbartians restricted themselves to propagating their idol's canon, some of them presently worked up their zeal to such a pitch that their early purpose no longer sufficed. By dint of their efforts there gradually appeared a Herbart who never was, a Herbart who, could he have returned to earth, would have been hard-put in certain instances to recognize some of the things that were being bandied about in his name. It was these neo-Herbartians who renamed and augmented the Formal Steps. It was they who converted "correlation" into "concentration" and, against the master's expressed caveat, proceeded to apply it on a sometimes preposterous scale. It was they who let themselves be carried away by the culture epochs theory. Finally, it was they who pushed the literary and historical studies at the expense of the natural sciences in a world where science was bidding powerfully to establish itself more and more in our everyday living.

More durable in its effect, and more in tune with the original orchestration of Herbart's pedagogy, was the performance of Professor Karl Volkmar Stoy. True, he granted a dispensation to several of the newer deviations, and he even adopted some of them, but by and large his chief concern was to stick as closely to Herbart's doctrine as prudence and the strength of his own conviction demanded. It was in this vein that Stoy established a pedagogical seminary and practice school at Jena. His success there was of the purest ray; soon, indeed, Jena was doing for the Herbartian pedagogy what Yverdon had done for that of Pestalozzi. At Jena, Herbart's doctrines were put under a sharp and perceptive eye. Lesson plans were laid and executed in classroom practice and, under the relentless coaching of their professors, young men were given preparation to enable them some day to wear the German teacher's cutaway coat with dignity and distinction. Stoy's success at Jena was, of course, not long in making itself heard. Educators flocked to the Herbartian Mecca from all directions, some merely to see it, and maybe carry home their impressions, and others for the graver business of perfecting themselves in the most advanced pedagogy known to the world's civilized West.

In due course the new pedagogy arrived in the United States. It was brought here by Americans who, having observed it at close range in its Teutonic home, made it their mission to plant it in their own soil. Through their unremitting zeal, and especially through the persuasive rhetoric of their leading apostles—Charles and Frank McMurry and Charles De Garmo—the Herbartian revelation was set securely on its legs. By 1882 its devotees had grown sufficiently copious to induce a small wedge of them to ally themselves under the flag of the National Herbartian Society. Summoned into being to promote the new education throughout the United States, the organization flourished for about a decade. Then, as commonly happens in this land of high-speed change, Herbartianism, like its Pestalozzian predecessor, began to suffer from the buffetings of time and fortune. In 1902, the defunctive Herbartian brotherhood purged itself of its once-re-spected title to become the National Society for the Scientific Study of Education. A decade or so following saw the discreet removal of the word "scientific" from its shingle.

Imported to these shores at about the time the Pestalozzian vogue was turning musty, the Herbartian pedagogy had the attraction at least of fresh-ness. Like its predecessor in its palmier days, the newcomer wooed and won the American normal school whence it presently made its way into the nation's schools. Thus, where less than a generation or so before, the mak-ers of American teachers were apprising their apprentices of the latest phar-macopia out of Yverdon—sense perception, oral language, and the object lesson—they now plied them avidly with instruction in such magic potions as interest, apperception, correlation, and the Formal Steps.

No more immune than the Pestalozzians to the pressures imposed upon their thinking by man's steadily expanding knowledge, the American Herbartians attained their peak in the 1890s, whereupon they began to slip. When, in 1902, they altered the name of their official fellowship, straws were plainly showing in the wind. Another decade, and whatever life the movement still possessed would be sapped as the forces of a new philoso-phy, psychology, and sociology converged upon it. Today, of course, the Herbartians have turned to dust, and so has their stock in trade. Even their enraptured gabble has passed into the dimness of the half-remembered, and save for historians and philologians, and suchlike diggers and shovelers in the past, their words often carry no meaning.

But this is not to imply even remotely that the Herbartian pedagogy has left no abiding mark. With us as with Herbart, the all-important prob-lem of moral conduct, whether personal or collective, remains a primary educational consideration. With us as with Herbart, it is an undeniable fact that without the powerful motivation of interest, teaching goes for naught, or at best, for very little. The Formal Steps, it is true, have suffered excom-munication, but in one guise or another lesson plans are still at large in the pedagogic world. Even the principle of correlation persists, as witness, the so-called "core curriculum," the social studies, general science, and the like. Finally, the scientific study of education, a hope Herbart cherished all his life but never realized, has now become a reality. The fact that so many of Herbart's principles have come to roost in modern education does not mean, of course, that their present fanciers are Herbartians; it simply means that in some of its aspects the professor's pedagogy was basically sound.

Needless to say, Herbartianism was not untarnished. Its votaries, for example, urged the conservation of the cultural heritage, yet for all their laudable purpose, their apéritifs of interest and apperception, they addressed themselves to their task like so many professors of anatomy, forgetting in their zeal the prodigal hunger of human feelings. The profoundly moving thunder and song which reverberate through great literary art they misprized completely. As a result, they turned what should have been a vital experience into the academician's chronic absorption with names and dates, rhetorical and syntactical phenomena, and above all moral rectitude. Herbart declared for the cultivation of a many-sided interest, but his followers inclined rather heavily toward intellectualism. By the same mark, they fell far below Pestalozzi, whose psychology may have been a shining example of triumphant error, but who had the good sense to appreciate that some of the most pressing needs of God's children are nonintellectual.

Despite the Herbartians' multiloquence on the theme of man's manifold interests, and despite their master's insistence that Homo sapiens is a variegated creature, his disciples were anesthetic to man's many-sided personality. To them it was not granted, as it was to Rousseau, to perceive even for a fleeting moment the inner man, and the complex nonintellectual forces which engage so relentlessly, and at times with an overwhelming sweep, within us all.

Chapter 21

Friedrich Wilhelm August Froebel

THE UPS AND DOWNS

Amidst the spruce-cloaked slopes of Germany's Thuringia, there was born another boy for whom destiny had reserved a place in the shrine of pedagogic fame. His name was Froebel, which the baptismal sprinkling enhanced with Friedrich Wilhelm August (1782–1852). Like Rousseau, the Thuringian was still bundled in his swaddling wraps when his mother died, and as in the case of the Genevan, this deprivation bore heavily upon him during his early years. His father was a country pastor, an acerbic man, given to self-righteousness, and lamentably overworked. To lessen his burden, at least in the domestic sector, the widower presently took himself a new wife. Neither the father nor the stepmother shed much affection on young Friedrich, the one concentrating on serving the Savior, and the other on bestowing her attention on her evangelical spouse and on her own infant, to whom in due and proper time she gave birth.

The pity is that the boy was quite beyond their understanding. Thus, although he was undoubtedly of a more than ordinary intelligence, his elders considered him dense and mulish, and when their strictures to break him to their rules and regulations failed, they accepted their plight as ordained by God and proceeded to minister to his most elemental wants as frugally as possible.

The situation grew steadily worse until, when the boy was ten, the Frau Pastor refused to have him on the premises any longer and he was deported to an uncle who was also engaged in the sacerdotal service. The uncle was, however, of a sunny mood, easy-mannered, and sympathetic, and the lad, given the understanding he so badly needed, quickly repaired his shaken self-confidence. In fact, the four-odd years he spent with his uncle he was later to describe as the most untroubled of his life. But when they were over and he returned to the family hearth the old boils soon festered anew. Froebel took refuge in reticence and tried to find peace in the quiet of the countryside, exploring its fields and forests, and in the endless cosmic ceiling overhead. A sensitive youth, he found himself pondering the mysterious riddle of the earth, from its minutest manifestation to the very purpose of life itself. Needless to say, his young and untrained mind found no answer. But, save for passing interruptions, his search went on until maturity was well upon him, when, as will be noted later, he came upon his answer.

At the age of fifteen Froebel was apprenticed to a forester. He had no say in the matter, and when he left his home harsh words heated the air. "Never come back to me with any complaint," his father admonished. "I shall not listen, but shall consider you wrong beforehand." Apart from its autocratic nature, the parson's vocational decision was actually prudent. A venerable and respectable calling in a country which prized its woodlands, the successful practice of forestry yielded a very comfortable living; at the same time it enabled the youth to continue studying the world of nature which he enjoyed so much. Yet there was also a serious detriment. His way of life was still too solitary, and though by now he might have become used to being alone, what he needed was the stimulus and reassurance which issue from a normal association with others. In a limited measure he found this in the company of a local medico who lent him books on natural science which he devoured with a hungry wonder. After two years Froebel's apprenticeship blew up and he returned home, where his father promptly put into execution the sinister warning he had delivered earlier.

It was a dismaying scene, to say the least, and one which, given the youth's hypersensitivity, might well have ended in disaster. Fortunately, however, for an incautious moment the youth's father relaxed his backward-looking leadership to commission his son to take some money to his older brother, then enjoying himself at the University of Jena. So powerful was the impact of its enlightened air that Froebel, after being treated to the usual parental snorts, was nevertheless allowed to stay there for a spell. He listened to lectures, tasting now this, now that, but never submitting to the serious intellectual enterprise of systematic study. Perhaps his deficiency in the fundamentals stood in his way, or perhaps as a chronic voluptuary of visions he was content to subordinate hard thinking to mere feeling.

In any case, before long, and through no fault of his, except possibly the overflowing kindness that led him to believe the best of everyone, he fell into debt, and the university confined him to its jail. His father bailed him out, roasting him to a turn while he was about it, and exacting the pledge from him that he would renounce all further discreditable deportment and go to work. For the next few years the young man drifted from one vocation to another. He worked as a bookkeeper, secretary, surveyor—he even attempted to manage a country estate. But none of them offered him a life which fundamentally fulfilled him.

In 1805 Froebel headed for Frankfurt to study architecture, but this too failed to rouse him. Happenstance led him to a Pestalozzian model school whose owner and director, a Dr. Grüner, warmed to him, and when opportunity unexpectedly chimed her gong, he offered this wooden-faced young man a place on his staff. Though Froebel had not a whit of teaching experience, he acquitted himself handily. Indeed, so laudable was his performance that his employer was convinced that he was face to face with that mysterious amalgam of what, in a less exacting age, used to be called a "born teacher." As for Froebel, green though he was, he had neither doubt nor misgiving. From the first he gloried in his work. He had discovered his "native element." "You cannot believe," he confided, "how the hours glide away. I love children from the bottom of my heart, and when I am out of class, I long to get back to their instruction."

For all his lyrical ecstasying, however, he soon realized that even a born teacher might profit from watching the performance of some accredited masters of the pedagogic art. To such an end he visited Pestalozzi, then at Yverdon. What Froebel saw compelled his respect and admiration; at the same time the thought that something was missing kept nagging at his mind. After his return to his own school, his dissatisfaction mounted. What irked him was the inevitable routine and the tethering authority of his superiors. His psyche was at war with the established way, and in his tormented state he succumbed to his old frustrations, and he resigned.

For a while he turned to the study of French, but he was felled by its syntax. So things passed for several months when, out of the blue, he was offered the tutorship of three boys. It was the release he had been yearning for, and the end of all his miseries. Needless to say he seized the opportunity with alacrity. The unexpected deliverance perked up his spirit, and to remove himself even farther from the repressions and prohibitions he despised so heartily he conducted himself and his clients to a backwoods retreat where he aspired to educate them in accordance with the principles of Rousseau's naturalism. Unhappily, the Genevan's sovereign cure for all our woes proved unworkable, and when at length this became plain even to Froebel, he installed his charges in Pestalozzi's school at Yverdon, where, for the next two years, he himself studied and taught under its headmaster.

On his return to his fatherland, Froebel resumed his search in furious earnest for that shifty principle of unity which had eluded him these many years. He enrolled at the University of Göttingen where, unmindful of how the grammar of the French had failed to filter through his intelligence, he applied himself to the study of Arabic and Hebrew in the belief that in these venerable tongues lurked the secret that would lead him to his quarry. After a year, in 1812, he migrated to Berlin to specialize in the study of mineralogy, and it was there, curiously, that he finally found his law of unity. Through his scientific studies he had convinced himself of the "demonstrable connection in all cosmic development." Or, as he was to say at another time, "thereafter my rocks and crystals served me as a mirror wherein I might discern mankind and man's development and history."

Meanwhile, however, his preoccupation with rocks and crystals was interrupted by Napoleon, who, had rampaged over Germany and made a mock of her vaunted might. It was a time of inflammatory patriotism when Germans were laying plans to bid this peace-disturber and his alien hordes a detonating and permanent farewell. And so, at the age of thirty-one, the discoverer of the principle of cosmic unity slipped on the soldier's uniform to engage in combat for his country.

In the year of 1814, his military task over—though he saw no carnage—he returned to contemplate his rocks and crystals. Two years more and he was making history by opening a private school in the town of Keilhau in Thuringia. He named it the Universal German Institute of Education, a name which was more impressive than the school's enrollment of five boys, each of them a nephew of the founder. Coutured along casual Pestalozzian lines, but with less to-do over sense perception, the school featured play, music, and self-activity besides, of course, the common elementary branches.

Froebel was presently joined by two friends and fellow believers, so that the little school was able to cater to the needs of its five pupils with a faculty of three, a ratio so rare in educational annals that it comes close to being unique. Time saw the Institute's custom increase, but troubles beset it almost from its inception. Dark looks were exchanged by its backers, who in one way or another were the founder's kinfolk, for there was a constant lack of cash; and there was open talk that the school was subversive of the mandates of God and king.

For much of this the blame falls squarely on Froebel. A mere babe—to let loose a cliché—in the wilderness of economic reality, he shrugged off its perils by asserting their nonexistence. Like so many forward-lookers, moreover, he was not only inflated wth certainty, but contemptuous of those who, however well meaning, attempted to set him straight. Although as a pedagogic experiment the Institute is generally counted as a fair success, nevertheless, after a decade of struggle, Froebel's high hopes for it ebbed to nothingness. During those ten years, however, Keilhau's director devoted whatever spare time he could to assembling his pedagogic doctrines on paper. They appeared in print in 1826 as *The Education of Man (Die Menschenerziehung)*. It is a solemn book of graceless prose, freighted with esoteric allusions and a transcendental symbolism, and extremely discomfiting to get through. Yet it is also an important work. The only full and systematic exposition of his pedagogy that Froebel ever put together, it is the fountainhead of his theory.

From Keilhau, Froebel repaired to Frankfurt, where he made the acquaintance of a high-minded Swiss who supported his idealism in the best way possible, namely, with a substantial income. Inspired by Froebel's theories, he established their author in Switzerland, but Froebel's curt dismissal of any views oppugnant to his own soon soured his altruistic admirer, and their venture came to naught. In 1835 the Swiss government, then on one of its progressive sprees, counted Froebel as the heir-apparent of Pestalozzi and invited him to exercise his art at Burgdorf in the very castle once illuminated by their beloved Heinrich. There Froebel convinced himself that the most fundamental reforms in education fall in the period of early childhood. "All school education," he stated, "is yet without proper initial foundation." Furthermore, "until the education of the nursery is reformed, nothing solid and worthy can be attained." To get such an improvement under way, Froebel recommended special training for mothers, a suggestion which although it was assuredly no novelty, was nevertheless at such unseemly odds with the communal mores as to be shrugged off as being somewhat noodled.

In 1837—Froebel was now five years under sixty—he returned to his Thuringian hills to make his home at Blankenburg, where, in a disused powder mill, he founded a school for young children. He named it the *Kleinkinderbeschäftigungsanstalt*——an institute *(anstalt)* for the occupation *(beschäftigung)* of little children *(kleine kinder)*. For all its surgical precision, the name was too horrendous even for Germans, and rather than persuading them to commit their tots to its delights, it aroused their suspicion and they kept their children at home. Time saw its inventor rechristen it as the *kindergarten,* a name which is as smooth as its predecessor had been abrasive, and kindergarten it has remained—not only in the land of its origin, but in the whole world around. The kindergarten, as Froebel first perceived it, was the child's own world, a place where he might develop naturally "in harmony, peace, and joy within himself and those about him." It was to be a world where he could function freely and agreeably with his mates, without being put upon by drill and imposition, a land, in short, of song and story and play.

To make this come true, Froebel and his coworkers kept themselves busy confecting games, tunes, and a host of activities worthy of the juvenile taste, and instructive as well. Although now and then Froebel reached the heady heights of imagination, he could not altogether avoid the academician's gully. Thus, we see him meticulously sorting and labeling his materials into "gifts" and "occupations." The former, in illustration, are cubes, spheres, cylinders, and circles, of an inalterable form, and each charged with symbolic meaning. The latter are things that can be transformed when put to use—such common stuff as clay, cardboard, paper, and sand.

Meanwhile, Herr Froebel occupied himself with his pen. To bring the kindergarten into the public ken, he edited the *Sonntagsblatt,* a weekly organ of letters and opinion. Much more important was his *Mutter- und Koselieder,* which appeared in 1843, and which later made its way into English under the title of *Mother and Play Songs.* Despite its didactic purpose, which was to assist a mother to launch her child's education correctly, the songs turned out to be Froebel's most captivating work. In fact they are still soughed and cooed by German mothers who elect to remain under the family roof to raise their young themselves.

Although the notion that play can be put to worthwhile educational use runs way back to Quintilian and had even come to be regarded by a few salient pedagogues as a platitude, yet it remained for the Thuringian to give play a leading part in the education of the young child. "Play," he once reflected, "is the purest, most spiritual activity of man at this stage, and at the same time, typical of human life as a whole—of the inner hidden natural life in man and all things." And again: "It gives . . . joy, freedom, contentment, inner and outer rest, peace with the world. It holds the sources of all that is good."

But once more Froebel's talent for getting into financial straits confronted his school with hard times. Presently, indeed, the wolf was at the door, and in 1844, after only seven years, the Blankenburg experiment was done for. To drum up a better public understanding of the kindergarten, its creator resorted to the lecture podium. Although he wielded no powerful rhetoric, yet he worked with a will, explaining the kindergarten's merits at great length, especially to women, and after a dozen years he achieved at least a fair success. When the kindergarten had been still only a faint gleam in its future father's eye he had held the opinion that mothers make the best teachers of the very young. But with the materialization of his dream his belief underwent some modification. Thus, when Froebel first ventured to train specialists in kindergarten teaching, he had an audience of three young men. The following year three women came to listen. It did not take the master long to discern that the female sex was better equipped to teach young children than was the general run of the male. Froebel's feminine trio not only took to the teacher's doctrines with surprising readiness, but they became his lifelong champions. The day would even come when one of them, Luise Levin, a childhood friend of one of his nieces, a kitchen-helper at Keilhau, and Froebel's junior by several decades, would so impress him that he would find himself leading her to the altar.

Froebel was much nearer seventy than sixty when he converted an aged peasant house into a practice school at Bad Liebenstein, a watering spot where Europe's *haut monde* gathered to drink and cleanse away their malaises. To assure the school of an adequate attendance, Froebel marshaled some of the local peasant tots for instruction, enchanting them with his art and prancing and laughing with them as if he himself were a child again. Needless to say, such an offense against the moral prejudices of his time brought him under public opprobrium. He was, some said, an "old fool"; others likened him to an ass; and not a few made so bold as to say that he was mentally unhinged.

Undeniably, such allegations could have worked heavy damage, and except that the Fates seem to have been in a felicitous mood, Froebel's endeavor, like its predecessors, would doubtless have come to grief. As it was, when the canards of the doings of this strange old man reached the ears of Bertha Maria von Marenholtz-Bülow, a baroness with a purse as sumptuous as her name, she made a point of subjecting him to a personal appraisal. What she found, of course, was not an imbecilic dotard, but a man of gentle spirit, a dreamer, perhaps, but one whose dreams pointed convincingly to the possibility of something better. Persuaded that this so-called "fool" was actually a man of tremendous vision—maybe even a genius—and that in essence his ideas were sound, she nominated herself to become, as it were, his public relations manager.

To meet the demands which this role imposed upon her, the baroness was well equipped. She was a woman of means who moved in high circles and who had influential friends. Add to this a messianic zeal, a persuasive tongue, and an unlimited vitality, and you have a well-nigh unbeatable combination. To acquaint herself with the kindergarten to its last jot and tittle, she became one of Froebel's pupils. She then successfully exercised her salesmanship to persuade the Duke of Weimar to grant Froebel the use of one of his country lodges for a training school, where, besides enlighten-

ing young women in the kindergarten lore, he also undertook to advance its
fortune as author, editor, and publisher of a weekly pedagogical review. It
was probably the baroness who got him an invitation to establish himself at
Hamburg at a salary that was of more than ordinary heft. And it was very
likely the good Bertha who, unbeknownst to Froebel, footed the bill. To the
end of her life this woman worked for the kindergarten, lavishing upon it
her devotion, both in print and speech, upholding it against its belittlers,
and traveling from one end of Europe to the other to spread her panegyrics
in its behalf.

In 1870, nineteen years after Froebel's death, his tireless apostle, now
herself crossing the frontier of sixty, founded the Froebel Seminar to train
the kindergarten teachers of tomorrow. Twenty-three years more on earth
were vouchsafed her, and during these years she had the satisfaction of
seeing the kindergarten achieve a tremendous success not only in its native
haunt, but in the rest of the civilized world as well.

PRINCIPLES AND DISAPPOINTMENT

A man of deep religious sensitivity, Froebel felt the divine presence in
everything, always. "God," he wrote in *The Education of Man,* "is the sole
source of all things." These, he went on, "live and have taken their being in
and through God." And finally, "all things are only through the divine
effluence that lives in them." This is "the essence of everything." Is God
present in all things? Then the entire universe must be a unity, and
education's paramount concern is to make it possible for the child to hear a
melodious echo of that unity within himself. "The essential purpose of education," Froebel tells us, "is not so much to teach and communicate a
variety and multiplicity of things as it is to give prominence to the ever-
living unity that is in all things."

So conceived, education undertakes to help bring the child's latent
personality to its full and finest flower, and the kindergarten was designed
to accommodate this growth. Basically, such education is self-development,
as Rousseau would have it. For, contended the author of the kindergarten,
"the purpose of education is to bring more *out* of man than to put more *into*
him." Thus, hearkening to nature's cue, the kindergarten has put a substantial store in the child's disposition to be active by confronting him with
carefully chosen materials and situations which unfailingly induce him to
satisfy his natural bent. "To learn a thing in life through doing," Froebel
asserted, "is much more developing, cultivating, and strengthening than
through the verbal communication of ideas." Not only was the child to be
kept active, but at all times his performance was to derive from his own
interests.

It was in this connection that Froebel palpably outdid even his most perceptive foregoers, and not a few of his after-comers as well, for among practicing pedagogues he was the first to catch more than a glimmer of the colossal educational value of the child's own world. Although Froebel had partaken heartily of some of Rousseau's ideas, in particular his stress on an education which is in harmony with the requirements of the child's nature, as well as one which recognizes the child's need to develop his personality without imposition, the kindergartener could not take the Genevan's lopsided individualism. Like his teacher, Pestalozzi, and his fellow cultivator of the pedagogical garden, Herbart, Froebel put great stock in education as a social force. "Man," he wrote in one of his letters, "should develop in harmony, peace, and joy within himself and those around him in accordance with human nature and destiny." And he added, "this should continue through all stages of development, and in all the various circumstances of life, in the family and school, in domestic and public life."

All these principles are given substance in the Froebelian kindergarten. Action, play, games, stories, and a miscellany of human doings constitute the heart of the kindergarten, which, as the observant Baroness Bertha remarked, was akin to "a miniature state for children, wherein the young citizen can learn to move freely, but with consideration for his little fellows." As has already been said, in its practice the kindergarten made use of three kinds of specially selected materials—gifts, occupations, and the *Mother and Play Songs*. It was Froebel's hope that somehow, by the use of gifts and occupations, the child's creative and esthetic powers would be enhanced. But the most dazzling gem in the kindergarten's possession was the story. Related by the teacher, it sparkled everywhere; it irradiated the child's talk, his play, and his music making, and it even showed itself in the things he made.

Much of Froebel's pondering transported him into the clouds of mysticism. His utterances, therefore, whether spoken or written, and even some of his kindergarten features, are frequently shrouded in a mist of symbolism, allegory, and vague allusion. The father of the kindergarten placed great weight on his symbols—without them, indeed, he would have been at an irreparable loss. Alas, to most of his contemporaries his symbols were so much bosh, and not infrequently they were cruelly dismissed. Nowadays, of course, they have been ostracized entirely. If the kindergarten still enjoys a huge approval, the reason lies in the solidness of its social and psychological grounding rather than in its creator's sprees of symbolic fancy.

Froebel's life drifted toward its end, as it had begun, on a doleful note. The kindergarten had made progress, it is true, but its antagonists were far more abundant and more vociferous than its advocates. Still worse, Froebel's progressivism had aroused the distrust and dislike of the Prussian government—then embarked on a policy of implacable reaction—and in 1851, loath to perceive the difference between Froebel and an unsavory radical nephew, the bureaucracy, bowing to the findings of its specialists in anarchic doctrine, proscribed the kindergarten for the reason that it was adverse to law and order and that it was "calculated to train the youth of the country in atheism," a charge which must have evoked a smile of recognition from the spectral Socrates. Despite a vigorous campaign on the part of Froebel's friends, the reigning bureaucrats stuck to their guns, and for not quite a decade no kindergartens were suffered to exist. Meanwhile, Froebel had gone to the world hereafter.

THE KINDERGARTEN TODAY

Had Froebel lived a little longer, he would have seen kindergartens spring up in every civilized land. The greatest development on the Continent was probably in Switzerland, in whose Germanic cantons it is sometimes affectionately spoken of as a *Haefelischuel,* which is to say a "school for the users of little chamber pots." No people, however, have given the kindergarten a heartier salute than the Americans. The first kindergarteners to open shop in the republic were Germans who, despondent over their broken hopes of being able to live in liberty in their own land after the shattering of the revolution of 1848, migrated to the United States, "the land," as Goethe expressed it, "of unlimited possibilities." Here, in 1855, at Watertown, Wisconsin, Mrs. Carl Schurz, a former pupil of Froebel, opened what may have been the first kindergarten in the nation. Like several other such enterprises which presently came into being, it was primitive, privately operated, and conducted in German.

Five years following, the kindergarten came to Boston. Owned and commanded by Elizabeth Palmer Peabody, it was the first of its kind to be conducted in English. Finally, in 1873, St. Louis established the first tax-supported kindergarten. However, in this hemisphere it was not Uncle Sam but his northern neighbor, Canadian Ontario, which in 1885 gained the honor of being the first to incorporate the kindergarten as a regular part of its public school system. Since those days, although modified to keep it abreast of progress, educational and otherwise, the kindergarten, aside from occasional setbacks during hard times, has enjoyed a steady growth. Currently, about half the nation's five-year-olds are kindergarteners.

As the years passed, Froebel's pedagogy began to get the serious attention of America's leading educators which it deserved, notably from Colonel Francis Parker and John Dewey, both staunchly dedicated to the reform and renewal of the American schooling of the young, as well as from James L. Hughes in Toronto, Ontario's capital. As the kindergarten gained in acceptance, not a few of its principles lodged themselves in the elementary learning, slowly, to be sure, but steadily. The idea, for example, that the child is an active being, and that to coerce it into stillness and immobility is in contravention of nature's law, is certainly no longer confined to the kindergarten. Nor is the doctrine that play has educational value. And so also with self-expression, learning by doing, creative education, education for social cooperation, and various other pedagogical ideas. In good time, indeed, even the secondary learning began to show a liberal soupçon of the progressivism which has its roots in the Froebelian revelation.

By making needlecraft, paper folding, weaving, and the use of sand, clay, paint, and glue, respectable school activities, Froebel unwittingly gave a potent boost to manual training. Unlike Rousseau, however, he made no plea for training the hand for economic and social ends. And unlike Pestalozzi he cherished no illusions that the adept use of the hands would somehow help a child to enlarge his supply of knowledge. Froebel saw the use of the hands simply as an aid to self-expression.

The Thuringian, of course, was not the first modern educator to take a strong stand for manual activities. But the far-reaching triumph of the kindergarten, together with Froebel's sound reasoning in his defense of manual activities, presently brought forth a development of manual training that was vaster and more ambitious than anything the father of the kindergarten could have anticipated. Without going into detail, let it just be noted that the movement to put courses in wood carving, basket weaving, metalworking, and the like, into the public schools was initiated in 1858 in Finland by Uno Cygnaeus, a Froebelian devotee. Thence it radiated to other lands to the east and west, making its way to our shore in the last quarter of the nineteenth century, where it presently became a smashing success.

As it prospered, things eventually got to such a state that some schools began to extend their benefits on equal terms to their female pupils as well as to their males. Nowadays, though courses in manual training are still in evidence, the movement has faded. What did it in was the change from the simple hand tools which served our fathers to the mechanized goliaths that now stamp and snort in almost every farm and factory. Nevertheless, despite its decline, and possibly its complete extinction on some tomorrow, the seeds of its possibilities have sprouted in newer acres, as witness, industrial education and the arts and crafts, both of which are currently basking in expansive approval.

After more than a century and a quarter, the kindergarten is enjoying a lush vitality. It is still, as Froebel conceived it, the child's own world, a wonderland where he may live and grow as nature meant him to, amidst warmth and understanding, in the good cheer of play and song. It is not the kindergarten of Keilhau or Blankenburg, to be sure, but could the shade of

Froebel be conjured up to gaze upon it, doubtless he would discern much of the original essence. There would be the sand and clay, the paint and paper, the cubes and cylinders, the play circle, and a good deal more.

But if the ghostly inventor spoke of gifts and occupations, the words would be wasted, for almost nobody would be privy to their meaning. As for the symbolism wherein he had laid so much trust, and which he had come to regard as everlasting and immutable, it, like the dodo, has vanished beyond recall. But for that loss Froebel should find ample consolation in our so-called "nursery school." Designed to serve the special educational needs of the very young—of an age of, say, three and up—the nursery school comes very close to Froebel's dictum that "until the education of the nursery is reformed, nothing solid and worthy can be attained."

Chapter 22

Ralph Waldo Emerson

THE YOUNG EMERSON

Ralph Waldo Emerson (1803–1882) was born in Boston on the twenty-fifth of May, and he died in Concord on the eve of his seventy-ninth birthday. His time on earth thus spans some of the most fascinating years in the republic's coming of age—its struggle, for example, with Britain in 1812, the so-called "Second War of Independence"; the inexorable onward push of its frontier; the rise of a commercial and industrial materialism; the outrage over the issues of slavery and abolition; the resulting blowup of the Union and its consequent carnage; and finally the gratuitous and unpopular aggression against our neighbor across the Rio Grande. The scion of an ancient family tree, planted in New England in the seventeenth century by the Puritan Peter Bulkeley, the founder and christener of Concord, Emerson had religion in his blood—indeed, the greater number of his male forebears, including his father and grandfather, had been men of the cloth.

Emerson's father, who died when his son was eight, was an adroit and

257

ingratiating man with a passion for books and music, who liked to entertain himself by playing solos on his bass viol. He was also a fancier of learning who fathered not only four sons but several libraries, athenaeums, and organs of letters and public opinion. A sightly fellow, he cut an impressive figure among Bostonians when he exposed himself to public view on the streets no less than in the pulpit. As was no more than right, the passing years saw him ennobled to the chaplaincy of the Massachusetts Senate and to membership on Harvard's Board of Overseers. Yet, despite the senior Emerson's blithe spirit and his demonstrated talents, his monetary reward from Boston's First Congregational Church was meager—so spare that Emerson's boyhood home lay forever under the pall of austerity, with only self-denial, faith, prayer, and hard work to buck it up.

Nevertheless, through abnegation, penny saving, and the assistance of friends and relatives, at the age of fourteen Emerson managed to enter Harvard, where he worked his way through college. He performed chores for the president and thereby got his lodging free; he waited on table; he tutored; and for 50 cents apiece he even ghostwrote papers for less gifted students or those too preoccupied with other than scholarly affairs. During vacations Emerson added to his purse by teaching boys in his uncle's school at Waltham, but he found no joy in his work "in the hot, steaming, stoved, stinking, dirty A-B spelling room." All in all, though, the result of Emerson's industry was that he not only paid his way toward his baccalaureate; he was even able to stash some of his gleanings in his sock. As a scholar, however, he was no cum laude, and finished thirtieth in a field of fifty-nine.

On the heels of Harvard—Emerson was then over the line of eighteen—there followed an engagement of instructing girls in a boarding school kept by his brother, but the job, even though he stayed in it for several years, did not especially quicken him. His good looks and eloquence incited feminine hearts to palpitating, but his glacial reserve kept them at a distance. Although even then his head may have been in the clouds, his feet were set on solid Yankee ground.

IN AND OUT OF THE CLERGY, OR FROM BOSTON TO CONCORD

In 1825 Emerson laid his chalk aside to declare himself for the clerical calling, and to make the necessary preparation he returned to Harvard to advance his knowledge of the divine and moral sciences. The year following, with the approval and best wishes of the Unitarian Synod, he obtained his license to preach, and before long he was braving his first sermon. But it was not until 1829, after a long and indecisive battle against consumption—the mouse in his chest, he called it—that he was appointed to preach at the Second Church of Boston, Meanwhile, he took himself a bride, only to have his bliss shattered by her early death.

Like his father, Emerson was a man of powerful eloquence, a word-smith of the first order, with a voice that vibrated with the resonance of a cello—in strange contrast to his almost blushful timidity. In consequence, he soon gained a following, among the women in particular, and had it not been for his disrelish of the general run of theologians, their sacraments and ceremonials, he would doubtless have achieved a good success. But theology, especially the Calvinistic sort, distempered him; and so did its corre-lated dogmas, which he dismissed as the "measles and mumps of the soul."

Compared to other sects of any standing of the time—forgetting for the moment the Quakers—the Unitarians, or as New Englanders commonly alluded to them, "the Boston Church," entertained a most advanced and liberal outlook. In fact, having rid their faith of the Son and the Holy Ghost, they sent up their prayers exclusively to the Father, a deed so pre-sumptuous that it made them suspect and even dangerous in the minds of the much more numerous trinitarians. Even so, in Emerson's eyes the Uni-tarians had not gone far enough. "Form remains," he reminded himself in his diary, "but the soul is well-nigh gone. . . .Calvinism stands," he contin-ued, "by pride and ignorance, and Unitarianism, as a sect, stands by oppo-sition to Calvinism. It is cold and cheerless." The result was that as year ran after year, the relationship between the parson and his congregation began to sour. The climax came in 1832 when, after having shepherded his flock for some three years, their pastor balked at celebrating Holy Communion. Instead, he presented his resignation, an act which terminated his aposto-late then and there.

Although Emerson's refusal to administer the holy sacrament was the immediate cause of his fall from grace, the motive behind it smoldered deep within him: he had reached the point—the tragic point of no return for an earnest ambassador of God—when he could no longer in good conscience tolerate organized religion. But even though he took a dank view of theolo-gians, he still went to church on Sundays, until, in the winter of that same year of 1832, he set sail for Malta and Sicily and points beyond, not only to lick his wounds and to seek counsel within himself, but to discover, if possible, a new revelation.

In the course of about a year the widower found the answer to his groping in the inspiration of the metaphysical Kant, in the poetic Words-worth and Coleridge, and especially in the intellectual Carlyle, the animator and seer of grander days and a demigod among the youth not only in Britain but in our own republic as well. Set adrift from the secure harbor of professional ministry, Emerson also found his natural vocation: henceforward he would set up his pulpit as a lecturer and writer—even, indeed, as a poet. He would make himself, so to say, a laic preacher.

From these and other European taps, Emerson drew his idealism, adulterating it, however, with a vague and muggy mysticism. Out of it the enraptured gospeler conceived the Over-Soul, the blue-sky instrument, as it were, of God's own spirit. "Once inhale the upper air, being admitted to behold the absolute natures of justice and truth," exulted Emerson, "and we learn that man has access to the entire mind of the Creator in the infinite." The divine spirit, in sum, flowed in man as it did in all God's creations, from the sweetest rose to the deadly fer-de-lance. Thus as the world spins round, man is able to surmount his mundane prison walls to commune with the Infinite.

A gallimaufry of individualism and idealism, Emerson's transcendentalism issued from his belief in a divine guidance relayed to Homo sapiens by way of his intuition, which is come by not by chance, but by deliberation and self-application. By the same route, the essence of truth is spirit, and not John Locke's empiricism which, Emerson was at pains to relate, was nothing more than "a solid, cold, and calculated apology for discursive reason." Scientists, conceded this contemporary of Darwin and Huxley, can uncover many natural laws, but when it comes to understanding man's relation to the universe, their laboratories avail them nothing, for this can be attained only through intuition, or as Emerson unblinkingly set it down in *Nature*, "a dream may let us deeper into the secrets of nature than a hundred concerted experiments." Thus the unfleshed bones of the Emersonian New Thought. As its author was to advise his countrymen in later years to follow his example, he had "hitched his wagon to a star," but to the run of Bostonians that star shone but dimly.

In 1835 the father of the Over-Soul moved to Concord, where, save when he was absent on vacation or, more likely, making tracks on the lecture trail, he was on view until his death. In Concord Emerson found a congenial intellectual climate. There he entered colloquy with such worthies as Henry Thoreau and Bronson Alcott; the bold and unconventional Theodore Parker, a Unitarian divine; George Ripley, an uplifter and social reformer; and Margaret Fuller, one of the first female shouters for women's rights to sprout in the United States. A garrulous crew, they found themselves engaging in heated conferences in what became known outside their esoteric circle as the Transcendental Club. Together, with Fuller mounted on the editorial stool, they put forth *The Dial,* an extraordinary periodical in the history of the American magazine, devoted to lovely letters and deep thinking, among which the offerings of Emerson and his comrades, needless to say, found a sumptuous welcome.

WRITINGS AND LECTURES

Emerson opened the door to letters with *Nature,* his first book, a slim volume which appeared in 1836. Therein, although its author did not know it at the time, he crafted the essence of ideas which were to become as characteristic of him as his sideburns and his vast, peninsular nose. The next year, on August thirty-first, Emerson delivered an oration on "The American Scholar" before a sitting of Harvard Phi Beta Kappans. The recital was calculated to unfetter the country from its bondage to the Old World culture. "Let the passion for America cast out the passion for Europe," Emerson exhorted his listeners. Soon, he told them, our free and enlightened nation will make an end of its "dependence and long apprenticeship to the learning of other lands." Though he himself had traveled far, journeying abroad, he assured the assembled savants, "added nothing to our true inner experience and self-revelation." Finally, let them remember that "the soul is no traveler. . . .Traveling is a fool's paradise."

The speech brought its maker almost instantaneously into the bright light of public approbation, both as a patriot and as a displayer of rich rhetoric, but even more as a man of prophetic inspiration. It was, said Oliver Wendell Holmes, "our intellectual declaration of independence"—getting his adjective out of kilter, as guardians of syntactical decorum have been at pains to tell us ever since. Yet for all of Emerson's plea for free and forthright thinking, the word open and frankly spoken, the Concord Plato knew how to be wary of Walt Whitman, his admirer.

In 1841 Emerson published *Self-Reliance.* An exaltation of man, it sings the praise of his self-assertion. "Whoso would be a man," the discoverer of the Over-Soul declaimed, "must be a non-conformist." The great man "is he who in the midst of a crowd keeps with perfect sweetness the independence of solitude." Naturally, such a prodigy is bound "to be misunderstood." By the same hackneyed token, let him remember that nothing is so sacred "as the integrity of his mind." With so many hardships and harassments, do you still wish to be seen as a man of greatness? Then "speak what you think today in words as hard as cannon balls, and tomorrow speak what tomorrow thinks in hard words again, though it may contradict everything you said today." Does this have the ring of an apology for intellectual inconstancy? Then let the "great soul" bear in mind that "a foolish consistency is the hobgoblin of little minds." But if the preacher clamored for the sacred rights of the individual and his kinship with the lonely soul, he drew the line at Thoreau's corollary that one has the right to refuse to pay taxes. The truth remains that despite his flights into oratorical space, at bottom Emerson was a Yankee, moonstruck on occasion, perhaps, but careful to keep himself within the bounds of a pragmatic respectability.

Other works followed, a book of essays in 1841, another two years after, and a volume of verse in 1847. Of lesser depth, and hence more agreeable to the public, was Emerson's later output, *Representative Men,* published in 1850, and *Conduct of Life,* which appeared a decade later. His *Journals,* wherein he deposited some of his pet thoughts and inner secrets, and which he maintained manfully for over half a century, were not offered to the public eye until long after their author had gone aloft to join the Infinite Mind.

Despite his unflagging industry as a writer, Emerson also made numerous appearances as a lecturer. After launching himself cautiously in the intellectual casinos of Boston and its outlying fringes, the sage of Concord discerned that he could make more money as a talker than as a writer. His literary industry, in fact, had never provided him with more than pocket money, and it was not until he celebrated his early seventies that his publisher vouchsafed him a yearly stipend of $1,500, a sum which must be considered in the light of the dollar's buying power in those days when a room cost a few dollars a week and a meal a few cents or which, if you bought a 5-cent glass of beer, was sometimes even free.

The former cleric found the spoken word to be an extraordinarily vendible commodity. His usual fee for a lecture ran from $50 to $75 per performance, or, in translation, a few hundred steaks, but for a series of presentations he could command $1,000, and with a little bargaining sometimes even more. The upshot was that as the years moved on Emerson enlarged his speaking itinerary as well as his bank account, confronting packed halls not only in the city on the Charles, but far away on the Mississippi's banks at St. Louis, and at Chicago and Milwaukee. In the Slavery Belt, however, Mr. Emerson with his Over-Soul and his support for abolition was taboo.

In time he cast his spell across the ocean. In 1847, and again in 1848, he lectured on the Continent as well as in the motherland, beseeching his hearers to tap the depths of happiness, optimism, confidence, courage, enthusiasm, enterprise, and self-revelation, besides making certain to cultivate their intuition. Concurrently, Marx and Engel were brewing their socialistic cure for all our troubles, the *Communist Manifesto.* If, as an American whose corpuscles ran red, white, and blue, and one who was a pantheist as well, Emerson had once permitted himself to state that "traveling is a fool's paradise," then one is tempted to suppose that he had no trouble squaring his Yankee conscience with the rationalization that his sorties to the Old World, after all, were a manifest cultural mandate, that in truth he was an exporter of American idealism, that his mission was earning him an honest and respectable emolument, and that he was thereby contributing to the maintenance of the republic's balance of trade.

Emerson has gone into American schoolbooks as a philosopher, which is not to say that he was on a footing with an Aristotle or a Bergson, or even, for that matter, a Victor Cousin, but rather that to the multitude of his countrymen his advanced thinking was incomprehensible and hence profound. Emerson himself rejected the philosopher's title. Except for his persistent harping on the pantheistic string he was not a deep, systematic thinker, but a rhetorician, skillful and effective. His impact on the main current of American thought was nil. He had admirers but no disciples. There is in actuality no Emersonian school of American thinkers. The philosophy which prevails today in America is not one which is consecrated to some Over-Soul beyond the reach of sense perception, but rather a way of thought which takes its stand at almost the opposite ₊ole—the pragmatism, that is, of William James, and, more recently, John Dewey. Its basic teaching is that there are no immutable absolutes, that what works is substantially true, and that whatever meets the senses, making due allowances, is the only reality worth consideration. It is a philosophic view far closer in its kinship to Locke's empiricism, his "solid, cold, and calculated apology for discursive reason," as Emerson had mourned, than it is to the latter's "revelation of a warm intuition."

IDEAS ON EDUCATION

Emerson was a man of large and delicate talents, a man of rumination rather than a trafficker in the pedagogic art and science. He conjured up no new and daring schools, as did Pestalozzi and Froebel, his contemporaries for a while, and he ventured no anatomy of pedagogy, as did Herbart— indeed, except for his thumbnail essay *Education,* his pedagogical pen stayed dry. His teaching confined itself largely to his brother's seminary for girls and a few other miscellaneous assignments, none of which infected him with the *cacoëthes docendi*, and he was relieved, when the time came, to wipe his hands of schoolmastering once and forever. Yet, as a propounder of ideas, he portrayed his thoughts on a spacious canvas, and some of them evoked pedagogical implications, In truth, some savants profess that in the broad sense nearly all his prose—books, essays, or lectures—is at bottom of an educational nature. Precisely the same, of course, could be said for the collected works of Prince Otto von Bismarck or Judge Alton B. Parker, or even a Sears Roebuck catalogue.

What are this faith dispenser's salient ideas that bear on education? There is, for one example, his high confidence in the power of education, a phenomenon which is as native to America as is Yankee Doodle. "When a man stupid becomes a man inspired," Emerson remarked in an early passage in *Education,* "when one and the same man passes out of the torpid

into the perceiving state . . . , all limits disappear. No horizon shuts down."
"Who," he wondered, "can set the bounds and possibilities of man?"

Second, there is Emerson's belief in the sanctity of the individual, his
right to be himself—within the limits, of course, of propriety. Like Rousseau, he plumped down his warning to parents who would spike their
offspring's individuality. Theirs is a "low self-love." "I suffer," he confessed, "whenever I see that common sight of a parent or senior imposing
his opinion and way of thinking on a young soul to which they are totally
unfit. . . .You," he upbraided the parent, "are trying to make that man
another *you*. One's enough!" With Rousseau, though doubtless unwittingly,
he insisted that before we undertake to teach a youngster we had better
make certain that we understand his nature, which in all likelihood we do
not. We treat our children, said the Concord sage, sniffing the currently
much bruited generation gap, like so many aliens. "We cannot understand
their speech, or the mode of life, and so our education is remote and acci-
dental and not closely applied to fact." In short, "we sacrifice the genius of
the pupil, the unknown possibilities of his nature, to a neat and safe con-
formity."

Third, by way of derivation, stands Emerson's distrust of organizations, whether religious, pedagogic, or otherwise, since all too often they
standardize and homogenize and hence, like a too tight pair of pants, bind
free movement. "Let us have men," he pleaded, "whose manhood is only
the continuation of their boyhood, natural characters still. . . .I believe,"
he went on, "that our own experience instructs us that the secret of education lies in respecting the child. Be not too much his parent. Trespass not on
his solitude." With Froebel, the father of the kindergarten, he held that we
should let children be children. "Don't let them eat their seed corn," he
warned. "Don't . . . let them be young men before they have finished their
boyhood. . . .Let them have the fields and woods," he went on, "and learn
their secret, and base- and football, and wrestling, and brickbats as such."

Again, there was nothing new in this imperative. It had been given
voice no less rapturously by Rousseau in the preceding century, and it had
even been put to the test by those dazzling champions of a child's inherent
and natural rights, the crusading Pestalozzi and Froebel and their followers.
In later years it was to be embraced much more sumptuously by Ellen Key
in her historic *The Century of the Child* and by the pioneer progressives,
both here and over there, in the so-called "child-centered school."

That the child is to make his own world does not mean, Emerson
hastened to explain, that he is to be left entirely to his own devices, that his
education tolerates neither form nor discipline. "The one element of life,
which is power or energy," asserted the Concord master in his essay on
"Experience," "needs the other, which is form." Therefore, he continued,

"every child must have inculcated in him 'habits' and 'discipline' with which to master himself and the tasks of life." Let the teacher "be the companion" of his pupil's thought, but let the latter soon find out that his preceptor is also the "irreconcilable hater of his vice and the imperturbable slighter of his trifling." But for Emerson, discipline did not tolerate the usual impositions upon the child, whether with words or with a shillelagh, but rather it undertook to "stop off his uproar, fooling, and horseplay," all of which, of course, came to him naturally, but which nevertheless must be curbed in order to forward his deeper natural being and "arm it with knowledge in the very direction in which it points."

Let the child develop a decent respect for exactness. "Teach him the difference between the similar and the same. . . .Pardon him no blunder. Then he will give you solid satisfaction as long as he lives." To fan into flame this affinity for exactitude, Emerson would fuel the growing mind with arithmetic and Latin grammar, both of which put a premium on exactness and, he believed, were much more effective than rhetoric and moral philosophy, which have enjoyed a perpetual immunity from intellectual precision. Although this process must inevitably be fortified by drill, such rehearsal is not to be trusted to "any mechanical skill or military method; it is not to be trusted to any skill less large than nature itself." In short, it must serve to clinch the essentials, joysomely when possible, but never, in any case, at the price of the child's psychological well-being.

Like Pestalozzi and Froebel, with whose views he entertained a close rapport, and even the seventeenth-century Comenius, about whom apparently he knew little, if anything, Emerson believed that a child's education should start during infancy—not, however, à la Robert Owen, in a special institution for tots, but in the home, the "school of the mother's knee," as Comenius had so neatly phrased it, proceeding thence to the family, the community, and the world space all about.

Like Froebel, himself a common frequenter of cloud nine, the Concord transcendentalist put a great store in the symbolic. "We learn nothing rightly," he announced, "until we learn the symbolic character of life. . . .Day creeps after day," he wrote, "each full of facts, dull, strange, despised things . . . .The time we seek to kill; the attention it is elegant to divert from things around us." Then bingo! he ecstasied, "the aroused intellect finds gold and gems in one of these scorned facts; then finds that the day of facts is a rock of diamonds; that a fact is an Epiphany of God." The moral for the teacher is not to pour facts into his pupil and then have him pour them forth again as if he were a human jug. Instead, let the master play sparingly upon them and stop trying to incarcerate them forever in the pupil's memory; let him treat facts as instruments to forge ideas. Let him resort to facts, in brief, to excite curiosity and interest in the "deeper meaning of life."

CRITICISM OF SCHOOLS

In Emerson's America such a pedagogic thought, though of foreign prove-nance, was no longer a novelty. Through the centuries reformers in the Old World—only a handful, it is true—had been vigorous cheerleaders thereof, but on both coasts of the Atlantic the common retailers of knowledge had scorned the idea as so much sentimental junk. Our education, Emerson lamented, "is not manworthy." There will be rogues and dunces in every school, he conceded, and unfortunately there will also be dullards robed in the schoolman's frock. All things can educate, and not a little of the under-lying process this detractor of organization found taking place outside the conventional chambers of learning. "I like boys," he jubilated, "the masters of the playground and the street—boys who have the same liberal ticket of admission to all shops, factories, armories, town meetings, caucuses, mobs, target-shooting, as flies have. . . .They are there only for fun," he added, "and not knowing that they are at school in the courthouse or the cattle show, quite as much and more than they were an hour ago in the arithmetic class." They are learning not by loading their memories with ever-mounting piles of hand-me-down material, but, as the schoolman's patois currently puts it, they are learning by living.

So far as the schools of his era went, Emerson found their quality on the exigent side. "The things which are taught children," he permitted him-self to rail in his *Journal,* "are not education, but the means of education." Grammar, geography, and writing—to cite only three examples—"do not train up the child in the way it should go, but may be used in the service of the Devil." To prevent such a miscarriage of the pedagogical art, the first thing the primary teacher must undertake is an assay of his catechumen in order to gain insight into his strengths and weaknesses, his innate propensi-ties, and his special needs. Give the lad a free chance to be himself; observe him at play; then show him what to do with what he has learned. Under such circumstances the master, instead of fitting the child to prefabricated precepts, now takes him as God made him, and whatever principles he may resort to are inherent in the nature of the individual, whom it now becomes his task to bring to full flower.

Does the Concord thinker grieve over what passes for education in the grade schools of the primary learning? Then he is no less disturbed by what goes on in the secondary and higher spheres. "How sad a spectacle," he deplored, "to see a young man after . . . years of college education, come out ready for his voyage of life, and to see that the entire ship is made of rotten timber!" Perhaps, he mused, "one of the benefits of a college educa-tion is to show the boy its little avail." What ails our so-called "learning," he concluded, is that "we are students of words," a familiar wail among pedagogical reformers. "We are shut up," he elaborated, "in schools and colleges and recitation rooms for ten to fifteen years, and come out at last with a bag of wind, a memory of words, and we do not know a thing." Who—to illustrate—in the course of warming the classroom bench, has been taught to use his hands, legs, eyes, or ears? "We do not know," said Emerson, echoing Rousseau, "an edible root in the woods; we cannot tell our course by the stars; nor the hour of the day by the sun." We are, in a word, nothing more than so many walking books.

What is the cause of this lamentable state? The answer, asserted Mr. Emerson, lies in our sterile curriculum, concocted more than a thousand years ago, but to which we still adhere—especially in its devotion to the classical languages. These tongues, Emerson granted, possess "beauty and structure, remains of genius, and sure appeal to like-minded men." But when it came to making their charms mandatory for everyone, the man from Concord pulled a hard brake. Like Jefferson and Franklin, Emerson put his confidence in the living languages—especially French—studied, however, for actual use and not for the intellectual wonders ascribed to the alchemy of their grammar. What held for the study of the corroded classics held also for mathematics, a subject Emerson saluted for its purported power to discipline the mind, but which as a student he had found to be "odious and unhealthy."

If the former divine failed to be inspirited by the traditional college offerings, then what did he propose as a replacement? Again his response is suggestive of the pioneering Messrs. Jefferson and Franklin. Let this New Englander have his way, and he would convert his curricular garden into a land of prodigal offerings with language, rhetoric, logic, ethics, philosophy, poetry, natural history, civil history, political economy, technology, chemistry, agriculture, literary history from Homer to Goethe, besides mathematics, but none of them to consume "a disproportionate amount of time." None of these subjects was to be required; the student was to make his own selection. He himself, and not another, "must judge what is good for him."

The divide between Emerson's pedagogic ideals and the reality of everyday classroom practice was, of course, immense. During his time on earth, no doubt, it was unspannable. "I confess myself utterly at a loss," he bemoaned toward the close of his essay on education, "in suggesting particular reforms in our teaching." From a realistic standpoint there was nothing to be gained by volunteering recommendations to the high and mighty who ran the schools. They inclined to turn a deaf ear to any proposals for change.

Educationally, then, the Concord thinker had long since concluded that nothing could be bettered until "we leave institutions and address individuals." Directing his words to teachers, he entreated them "to cherish mother wit. . . .I assume," he proceeded, "that you will keep the grammar, reading, writing, and arithmetic in order. . . .But smuggle in a little contraband wit, fancy, imagination, and thought." Let teachers insist on order and obedience, if they must, and particularly on a proper respect for the dignity of their office, "but if a boy stops you in your speech and cries out that you are wrong and sets you right, hug him!"

It is easy enough to laugh off such rhetorical Roman candles on the ground that they are against reason, and, maybe, even a threat to the established order. But if one should run the roll of progressive-minded pedagogues, whether past or present, one would discern more and more the sort of educator Emerson had envisioned. Some, like Colonel Francis Parker, acclaimed by not a few as the true father of progressive education in America, have been honorably niched in the shrine of pedagogic fame. But for one Parker there are herds of others, destined for historic oblivion, who ply their art from the republic's sea to sea, striving, as Emerson had urged, to make their schoolroom like the world. The sage's Over-Soul they have long since ignored, but his stress on the dignity of the child, his right to be himself, and his claim on the respect of his elders—to this much of the Emersonian doctrine they heartily subscribe. On the other hand, in our democratic commonwealth, where social-mindedness is a necessity, the lush prodigality with which Emerson endowed individualism has gone out of tune.

Although the Concord pantheist has been cataloged in cultural encyclopedias as an upholder, like Plato, of absolutes, perfect and everlasting, and hence is a man who would be blackballed by any right-minded pragmatist were he to seek membership in a guild restricted to the simon-pure disciples of James and Dewey, yet now and then this transcendentalist's pronouncements strike a veritable pragmatic chord. It was Emerson's contention, for example, that ideas have no value unless they are put to work. "Good thoughts," he observed, "are no better than good dreams unless they are executed," a sentiment shared by no less a pragmatic eminentissimo than James himself. It was Ralph Waldo Emerson, the begetter of the phantasmic Over-Soul, who said, "Only so much do I know as I have lived." And it was William Heard Kilpatrick, a pragmatist but lately departed, who delivered himself of an almost identical apothegm, namely, "We learn what we live."

Chapter 23

Francis Wayland Parker

THE COMMON SCHOOL

The nineteenth century saw the rise and triumph of America's common school, or as we call it now, the public school. Free, secular, tax-supported, and publicly controlled, after a long and arduous struggle it insinuated itself into the American heart. Once the principles on which it was grounded were beyond the peril of a public repudiation, its leaders were free to address themselves to the betterment of its practice. To such an end some of them took a hard look at the theory and practice of Europe's foremost educators, extracting therefrom whatever they regarded as useful and importing it to these shores. Thus the common school fell under the ameliorating influence, first of Pestalozzi, then of Herbart, and finally, in a lesser measure, of Froebel.

The common school attained more than an ordinary success. Unfortunately, its very prospering was to confront it with unexpected troubles, and in time it had to pay the penalty of its virtues. In the years following Appomattox, as the public school swept more and more children into its embrace, it found itself with more pupils than its limited resources could effectively sustain. The result was that, in order to attend its enormous flock, the public school took recourse in a cut-and-dried routine and uniformity. Its curricular provender it organized into graded subjects, serving them one by one in "periods," and designating special years for ingesting certain facts. Thus, for all the shining light of Europe's great educational reformers, the pedagogic enterprise of the late-nineteenth-century republic fell to a low state. Conceived in the main as an intellectual undertaking executed in school from 9 A.M. to 3 P.M., five days a week, except for holidays and vacations, education concentrated on stuffing children with book learning and on holding itself at a wary distance from the communal and national life from which it issued.

Although the common school had been designed to meet the needs of all children—which, of course, are as varied as the weather—it continued, as of old, to stress the elemental R's, a thin and watery geography and history, and, of course, the inevitable grammar. Here and there, usually in cities, some schools had conceded a place to such noncerebral "frills" as cooking and needlework, manual work, gymnastics, music, and drawing. Even so, in the nineteenth century's last decade, the American school was an emporium of hand-me-down knowledge, destitute of esthetic feeling, and devoid of any commanding philosophy of moral and ethical behavior.

Peculiarly enough, although the original common school had trickled from the fountainhead of democracy, as it embarked on its program of mass production the stream which had helped to give it life was diverted. The school may have been the heralded vessel wherein tomorrow's democratic American was to be compounded, yet within the school that democracy had become a mirage. The establishment of which the school was a part was an autocracy, a hierarchy from the board of education at the summit to the superintendent, principal, and teachers, in descending order and with diminishing rights, below. Lower still, and with no rights at all, was the pupil.

FRANCIS WAYLAND PARKER

A number of eminent and liberal-minded men, both lay and professional, had risen to plead and argue to have done with such un-American didoes, but the most striking, not only for the towering impressiveness of his achievement, but for the vivid previsional approbation he bestowed upon principles we still admire and use today, was Francis Wayland Parker (1837–1902). Born in rural New Hampshire, he descended from a long procession of Calvinistic pastors. He was of an age of three—so at least the tale is told—when he was articled for instruction in the village school. Three years later his father died and soon after the boy was apprenticed to a farmer. Between his endless tasks in husbandry he attended sessions in the local district school, where he presently became sufficiently proficient to direct himself through Holy Writ and *Pilgrim's Progress,* the beginning and end of his employer's library. Such spare time as he could round up he devoted, like Froebel, to exploring the hills and dales of the gorgeous New Hampshire landscape.

When he was thirteen he renounced the farmer's uncertain lot, bade good-bye to his beasts and birds, and set out to gain a fuller knowledge of life. Three years following, when he was sixteen, he was employed as head-master, faculty, and janitor of a one-room country school of seventy-five pupils ranging in years from tenderfoot beginners to hardened old-timers. As with Froebel, teaching moved and enchanted Parker. His affection for its magic was perhaps a jot less effervescent than the German's, but it was fervent enough to cause him to dedicate the rest of his life to the instruction of the young.

He was just out of his teens when he became principal of the schools of Carrolton, Illinois. But the outbreak of the Civil War made short shrift of his new career. For the next few years he fought as a private with the Union forces. He was wounded and taken prisoner; but when the bloodletting finally yielded to the aching chaos of peace, he shed his uniform—by now that of a colonel—and before long he was back in pedagogic circulation.

He picked up and repaired the torn thread of his previous activity, first as a principal in his native New Hampshire, and then of a normal school at Dayton, Ohio. He was already past the midpoint of his life when, in 1872, thanks to a small legacy from one of his aunts, he shipped for Germany to ponder philosophy under some of the Reich's most estimable metaphysicians—and, when the chance beckoned, to observe at close range the newer educational practices which had their wellspring in the work and thought of Pestalozzi, Herbart, and Froebel. Some of these he flooded with approval, and when he returned to the republic he ventured to give them a trial at Quincy, Massachusetts, where in 1875 he was installed as superintendent of schools, and again eight years after, when he was elevated to the principal's stool in the Cook County Normal School at Chicago.

The mark of New England is plainly visible on this man. Into his richly filigreed idealism he had spun the reinforcing fiber of Yankee common sense; democratic to his inmost recesses, he was also an unremitting individualist; a liberal in his relationship to the All Highest, he renounced the grisly dogmas of his forebears for the mellowed tolerance of the nonconformist. Under the sway of Emerson, whom he admired vastly, Parker dreamed almost as rapturously of perpetual human improvement and of progress without limit. Like the moonstruck Waldo, he glowed at times with transcendental flushes, even summoning forth epigrams which might have emanated from the Concord Magus himself. Yet often enough what the colonel found therein was not a reflection of that seeker of divine absolutes, but rather of the down-to-earth gainsayer of eternal unchangeables, William James. Like the Harvard professor and the latter-day pragmatists, Parker was suspicious of anything that radiated an odor of certainty or finality. "O Lord," he prayed, "preserve thou me from the foregone conclusion."

How did this incarnation of lofty dreams and common sense seek to inject reform into the ailing American school? He began by flinging open its shuttered windows to let in the fresh air that would resuscitate the child's benumbed spirit. At a time when the mass of schoolmen subscribed to the view that the school's primary reason for being was to weigh down its young with rules and facts, Parker declared with Froebel for the child's natural fondness for making things, and hence the necessity to release him forthwith from his handcuffs.

What was of paramount importance, as the colonel often said and wrote, was not history or geography or science, or any other school subject, but the child himself. "The child," Parker insisted, "must be the center of the educational experience, and everything he is taught must have meaning for him." In the child's nature lies the promise of his manhood, and to enable him to attain a complete fulfillment, we must grant his expression the utmost leeway.

Creative self-expression thus became the tutelary saint of Parker and his brethren. Does little Lafcadio crave to paint the fragrance of a skunk? Then let him try, and if what he produces turns out to be what others see as nonsense, it makes no difference. The important thing is that the creation is his own, and thus, for bolstering his self-confidence, it carries more worth than if he had perfectly reproduced a hundred masterpieces from a copy book. "The spontaneous tendencies of the child," commented Parker somewhat in the vein of one of Emerson's richer flights, "are the records of inborn divinity," a statement a cynic might incline to enrich with the words "or deviltry."

Although Parker's great stress on the natural right of every child to be himself doubtless reflects the colonel's own individualism, even more important was what Quincy's superintendent called the school's "social factor." This, he declared, stands "higher than the subjects of learning, than the methods of teaching, than the teacher himself." Above all else, he went on, it can "make the public school a tremendous power for the upbuilding of democracy."

Parker, who had gained much of his knowledge from direct personal experience, permitted himself a salty grain of skepticism when it came to the schoolman's common adulation of book learning. "The best school run in a densely populated city, " he avowed, "can never equal in educative value the life on a good farm, intelligently managed"—a declaration which doubtless brought him more invitations to assist at bucolic spreads of fried chicken than it did good wishes from the nation's book drummers.

It was no accident that Parker, who had started to earn his keep before he was in his teens, should sing the praises of hard work. Not only does Holy Writ command it, but, as Voltaire allowed, "it is the only way to make life endurable." With these sentiments Parker was in full accord. "The entire purpose of education," he said, "consists of training a child for work, to work systematically, to love work, and to put his brains and heart into his work. . . ." It is a golden fleece which, it needs no saying, has lost much of its lure not only among the contemporary young, but among some of their elders as well.

QUINCY, CHICAGO, AND COOK COUNTY NORMAL

It was at Quincy, Massachusetts, that Parker won his spurs. He had been fetched there in 1875 by John Quincy Adams and Charles Francis Adams, Jr., both lineal descendants of the sixth American president. Both were privy to Parker's doctrines which they admired and approved, and which, as members of the town's board of education, they were convinced were just what the schools of Quincy needed. Parker fell to work in his best shirt-sleeved manner, beginning, as he has recounted, by sweeping out "the old, stiff and unnatural order," which by ordering a child to sit completely still with nothing to do demanded something of him which was unnatural.

Accordingly, under the colonel such comportment was brushed aside, and in its place came an order of "work with all the whispering and noise compatible with the best results." In consequence, Parker observed, "the child began to feel that he had something to do for himself, that he was a member of society, with the responsibilities that accompany such an important position." Parker pressed his heaviest assault on the conventional methods, which, though they were the national rule, he regarded as out of date. Consequently, when he got his chance, he dumped them for some of the newer practices he had come upon in Europe. Geography, for example, ceased to be "the memorization of a conglomeration of unrelated facts" and was turned into a study of man in the physical world—or, as certain specialists have called it, anthropogeography. Hand in hand with it went sociology, which put its enlarging glass on Homo sapiens and his surroundings, whether natural or man-made. History went the same route. It, said Parker, "must grow out of the study of contemporary institutions," for this rather than the performances of dead men "prepares children for a history of the great industrial developments."

Although the colonel granted that in the study of numbers the knowledge of "certain facts should be absolutely automatic," he nevertheless went to great lengths to hold the "certain facts" to a comfortable modicum. Learned in the main through the child's everyday hand-to-hand transactions, arithmetic stressed actual use. The Quincy pupil was thus spared from grappling with such hair-raising conundrums as, say, the number of inches in 1,500 kilometers, or how much of an annual profit of $1,413 accrued to each of the partners A, B, and C, where the first had invested $1,000, the second $1 \frac{1}{2}$ times as much, and the third $\frac{1}{11}$ less than A and B in combination.

What held for numbers held equally for language. Thus, in lieu of sweating over the class system of nouns, the moods of verbs, the independence and subordination of clauses, and suchlike grammatical charades, youngsters were set upon developing their linguistic powers by presenting in writing or in speech an undissembling view of themselves and their doings.

At Quincy, Parker also ushered in the arts and crafts; the study of nature he supplemented with probings in the laboratory; and to enliven the study with reality and meaning, as Comenius had urged so long ago, the colonel fortified it with expeditions into the fields and woodlands, the caves and grottoes, bogs and dunes, streams and waterbanks—all for the purpose of coming to grips with nature at first hand. Later, while the pupil's impressions were still warm, he translated them to paper with brush and crayon.

Though Parker declared against the school's traditional stress on the mastery of subject matter, and even hazarded the view that all learning, whether practical or ornamental, must take its cue from the child, it would be erroneous to say that he discounted the importance of knowledge. What mattered, however, was not knowledge for its own sake, but rather the knowledge a child needed "for its present life," or as today's professional argot puts it, "knowledge for effective living."

Wiseacres have duly noted that as a begetter of educational theory the colonel was sterile, that he was a mere looter of other men's ideas. It was an arraignment he did not dispute. "The thing I commend in that charge," he responded, "is that it is solid truth. I did steal—stole it all from Cleveland, Cincinnati, Aristotle, Pestalozzi, Spencer, and anybody else I could find in possession of anything worth stealing." But what he burgled he also offered as a gift to anyone else who could use it, in hopes of bettering the nation's schools.

Behind his reforms at Quincy looms the spirit of the benign Froebel, for never before in America had the schoolchild been accorded such warm and respectful care. Viewed with the eyes of the heart as well as with those of the mind, at Quincy he was, indeed, the center of the school. Here he was free to develop naturally, true to his own being. Unfettered and unhindered, he could cultivate his inner self. But since at bottom nature is apparently opposed to democracy, through his experience he was also to be made privy to his ties and responsibilities to his fellows. "Every school in the land," asserted the Quincy superintendent with a palpable Pestalozzian accent, "should be a home and a haven for children." With the light of Froebel and Pestalozzi so refulgent, it is easy to overlook that Parker was not unappreciative of Herbart, though his feelings for this architect of system can scarcely be described as a passion. From this German issued the principle of correlation, whereby subjects are not taught in isolated compartments, but, wherever pertinent, are welded into a common unity around such central subjects as history, geography, and nature study.

For five years Colonel Parker employed his art at Quincy, spending no end of effort and devotion. But instead of winning the plaudits of a grateful citizenry, Parker became the target of its derisive snorts. He was—so ran the indictment of the town's directors of public safety—an undeniable charlatan, and his methods a portentous intellectual calamity. The Quincy board of education, led by Charles Francis Adams, its president, gave Parker its brave support, but the hurricane of abuse would not still.

At length, in 1879, the public's mounting furor persuaded the Massachusetts Board of Education to abandon its mood of detached ennui by ordering Quincy's pupils to undergo a special inquest. But to the consternation of Parker's would-be pallbearers, the commonwealth found that not only could Quincy's pupils read, write, spell, and calculate with ease, but they also gave an excellent display of their talents in history and geography; indeed, except in mental arithmetic, they clearly outshone the general run of the Bay State boys and girls. And so Parker enjoyed the unparalleled pleasure not only of walking off the field with the scalps of his detractors, but of having become an international notability as well.

As in the case of Oswego in its golden Pestalozzian heyday, visitors by the thousands, alien and domestic, made their way to Quincy to observe the first public progressive child-centered schools in the United States. "Under Colonel Parker's new system," commented *The New York Times* (July 5, 1883), "the schools of Quincy were lifted out of the old rut and they now lead all the other schools of the state."

In 1883 the colonel hoisted his flag at Chicago, where, as head of the Cook County Normal School, he continued to hatch his heretical schemes to the anguish and harassment of conservatives. There, abetted by one of the ablest bodies of teachers ever gathered under the same roof, Parker directed his offensive against the decrepit practices of the conventional school. As at Quincy, though on a much grander scale, he struck at its mechanized, assembly-line tactics which made children all appear indifferently alike. In their stead the colonel demanded "quality teaching," by which he had in mind the enterprise of men and women who reached into the heavens of imagination and feeling to ply their craft as artists rather than as so many technicians.

The training of such teachers became the mission of Cook County Normal. In its practice, which was as child-centered as the ingenuity of the colonel and his staff could make it, activity, play, exercise, excursions, and study were still the way of life. Nor did Parker waver in his conviction that to live as Omnipotence had willed, the child should study things before he read about them in books. Let him gratify his craving to be up and doing, to explore the environment, to express himself in art and music, to leap and run and shout—in short, to let himself loose. Not only did Parker put great stock in such nonintellectual delicatessen, but to teach music and art, manual training, science, and physical training, he went so far as to engage trained specialists in hopes that their virtuosity and enthusiasm would stimulate the development of such activities.

Although Parker had agreed with his critics that his pedagogy was a stranger to originality—that he had "stolen" the bulk of his educational theory from others—his admission, for all its frankness, cannot be accepted at face value. The fact is that the confidence in the democratic process which permeated his being proved to be a tonic leaven which clearly set him apart from the Europeans. When, for example, during his early stage in office, some of his teachers were gnawed by doubt and perplexity, Parker convened them in a weekly conference with his staff and himself to thresh out their problems and give them light and reassurance. When Parker's deviation from the conventional practice discomposed parents he organized them into a parent-teacher group, the first in the Windy City and one of the first in the republic. At its meetings, he went to great lengths to discuss his views. He not only smoothed ruffled parental feathers, but in time he was able to convert most of their owners into his staunch supporters.

But where Parker was able to influence and make friends of parents, when it came to politicians he stubbed his toe. They balked him on every side, putting their ax on essential appropriations, dismissing his work as worthless, and even passing sentence on his good intentions. The upshot was that when, in 1899, he received an offer to direct the affairs of the new and handsomely endowed Chicago Institute Academic and Pedagogic he accepted it at once. Yet even before the proposed school's cornerstone had been laid, it, and three others with it, were amalgamated with the University of Chicago to become its School of Education. Parker picked up the reins in 1901, but a year later he was dead.

In the same year, on Chicago's northern flank, the Francis W. Parker

School opened its doors. With Flora J. Cooke, one of Parker's former associates, in charge, and a staff of sixteen men and women, of whom the greater number had been trained at Cook County Normal, the school was consecrated to honor the great man whose name it bore. For more than thirty years it carried the Parker torch, bringing forth, as the years rode on, a new generation of pedagogical ground breakers. Many erudite words have been written and spoken to explain the Parker idea, but its essence is simple enough: "Freedom with a balancing responsibility is the best condition of moral and intellectual growth . . . real experience with actual material is essential to learning . . . opportunity for varied expression is necessary . . . for purposes of development children must be treated as individuals." Finally, "one of the most effective and wholesome motives of work is the social motive."

John Dewey

EVOLUTION OF A YOUNG MAN

Parker's successor as director of Chicago's new school of education was his forty-three-year-old colleague John Dewey (1859–1952). A New Englander like the colonel, Dewey was born in Burlington, Vermont, the habitat in those times of some ten thousand residents. His boyhood was happily free of adversity. A stranger to malaise and maladjustment, he grew up a normal lad, pursuing the familiar engagements of the growing male. When he had the time, and the inclination overcame him to enhance his fiscal standing, he performed odd jobs, and on the Day of Rest, appropriately scrubbed and groomed, he gave an earnest ear to the exhortations of his pastor. Dewey's record at school was magnificently unimpressive. In fact, when the years brought him to freshmanhood at the University of Vermont, aside from aspiring to snare his academic letters some four years following, no laudable ambitions inflamed him.

So things moved languidly until his junior year, when in a course in physiology he fell afoul of the writings of Thomas Henry Huxley, a partisan in the ranks of Darwin, and a materialist and agnostic to boot. As a punctilious churchgoer Dewey had no cause to question his parson's insistence that man's life is determined by moral will—indeed, the youth had long since contented himself to hold the pastoral pronouncement as something of an axiom. But now in artful words this Anglo-Saxon saucebox had unloaded the stunning proposition that life was shaped overwhelmingly by material forces, a view which was clearly and diametrically at odds with anything the student had ever heard of.

The cleavage between these views was not only stupendous; for Dewey it was also disturbing to his equanimity. The consequence was that to restore at least a semblance of his former calm, the young man set himself to serious and painstaking work, reading and reflecting far into the lonely watches of the night, hoping in some way to unriddle the vast and dismaying discrepancy. For all his efforts, his question proved unanswerable, but to conclude therefrom that his searching had been fruitless would be to make a bad mistake, for as he made his way through his final collegiate year his scholarship attained a verve it had never known, propelling him to the very pinnacle of his class with the highest marks in philosophy then on the university's records. Overweighing even this achievement was the fact that at the age of nineteen John Dewey had shown the unmistakable markings of a philosopher.

Out of college and on his own, he taught for two years in Oil City, Pennsylvania, where his cousin was the high school principal. But his thirst for philosophy refused to be quenched, and when he got the chance he headed for Baltimore to enroll at the Johns Hopkins University, a school but recently established and devoted strictly to the higher cerebration. There Dewey put himself under the counsel and tutelage of men who have since become greatly honored, Charles Peirce and G. Stanley Hall. But Dewey's favorite teacher, and the one who at the time served his purpose most usefully, was George Sylvester Morris. A votary of the philosophic idealism of Georg Wilhelm Friedrich Hegel, Morris directed his student to a system of thought which bore the agreeable advantage of disposing of the distinction between mind and matter by the simple assertion that matter was, after all, only a mirage. The universe and all its cargo, from the amoeba to the diplodocus, is in essence "spirit," and life is the eternal uphill struggle toward the universal mind of God. It was a dogma which, though in later years rejected by Dewey, went far to dispel the Huxley bogle and to moor Dewey in the contented harbor of certainty.

DIOGENES AND HIS LANTERN

When, in 1894, Dewey became *frater in facultate* at the University of Chicago, he was no stranger to college teaching. He had mounted the academic podium a decade or so before as instructor of philosophy at Michigan, proceeding thence as the years moved on to Minnesota, only to return for a while to Michigan before accepting the summons from Chicago which—so spake its stationery as late as 1915—had been founded in 1893 by John D. Rockefeller the Elder.

Dewey entered his academic novitiate in the Middle West a staunch Hegelian, and it was as a Hegelian that he made his advent at Chicago. He still believed, as he had at Hopkins, that reality was not matter but spirit, absolute, unalterable, and everlasting. But in the Middle West of the 1890s, and especially at Chicago, "the universe," as William James so trimly put it, "was wide open." A vast vitality gripped Midwestern life to make it a dynamo of political, economic, and social change. It was a world of unlimited possibility, of knockdown individualism, of hair-pulling and arm-biting competition, where a striving and not-too-finicky man might store up quick and gigantic riches. But it was also a world which took its toll, and for every well-stuffed magnifico it wrought, there were hordes of losers in life's battle, the host of gaunt and despairing poor, buffeted molecules in the dreadful struggle for existence.

A world where things metamorphosed at such a dizzy pace, at times for weal, but much more often for woe, gave a social-hearted man like Dewey a painful pause, and it became ever harder for him to find comfort in the felicity of that glorious land of Hegelian certitude. As a consequence, Dewey's concern tacked increasingly to the hand-to-hand antagonisms of life which seethed all around. Time, indeed, saw his thinking bear increasingly on the unsolved problems of human life, and especially those which ensued from conflicts when the forces of democracy, industry, and science collided head-on. Approached by this route, the philosopher's task, Dewey felt, is "to clarify man's ideas as to the social and moral strifes of our day." "Better it is," he added, "for philosophy to err in the active principle of its own age and times than to maintain a monastic impeccability." In such a philosophy there was obviously no place for Hegel's confidence in the singular and exclusive reality of the nonmaterial.

FIVE ARTICLES

It was at Chicago that Dewey tuned his harp in the key of the so-called "new education." For one thing, he committed his children, Fred and Evelyn, to the Cook County Normal School to study in the grades taught by Flora Cooke, a teacher, as was stated, of a vigorous progressive temper. For another thing, in 1896 Dewey founded what has gone into the official annals of Mr. Rockefeller's University as the Laboratory School, but which in the professional vulgate is commonly spoken of as the Dewey School. Finally, a year later, he set forth his educational faith in "My Pedagogical Creed." Cast into five articles, it runs as follows:

Article one holds that education proceeds at all times and everywhere through a person's participation in the social awareness of the race. The business begins soon after he leaves the womb, and it goes on to the brink of the tomb, shaping his powers, saturating his consciousness, working on his habits, and even his emotions, his rages and sorrows, his joys and gratifications.

Article two projects Dewey's concept of the school. It is that form of communal life wherein everything is brought to bear upon the child to enable him to share in the race's inherited resources, and also to help him to use his own powers for social ends.

Article three is a refinement and amplification of the foregoing in that the child's training and growth are to issue from his social life. By this score, subject matter becomes subordinated—to quote Dewey—"to the child's own social activities."

Article four puts its eye on educational method. The cue comes from Froebel out of Rousseau, both of whom contended—to the horror of right-thinking pre-Darwinians—that the child is "an active animal." Method, hence, is imbedded in the child's own nature, which is active rather than passive.

Article five asserts that "education is the fundamental method of social reform." This view was a startling novelty in the days of eighteenth-century revolutionary France when the Marquis de Condorcet, writing in the shadow of the guillotine, swathed it in approbation. Echoed some years later by Switzerland's Pestalozzi, it made its way into nineteenth-century American humanitarianism, and thence into our educational theory, where in one form or another its essence has prospered ever since.

THE LABORATORY SCHOOL

Like Franklin and Jefferson, and even somewhat the transcendental Emerson, Dewey held the conviction that unless our ideas stand the test of workability, they are no more than so many vain phantoms. Such, among other things, was the reasoning which brought the Laboratory School into being. Founded, as has been said, in 1896, with Dewey and his wife Alice at the helm, it embarked upon a voyage that was to endure for seven years, during which it was often badly battered by the heavy sea of public criticism. The venture had started with 16 children and 2 teachers, but when it ended, it could run off the names of 140 pupils, aged from four to fourteen, 23 instructors, and 10 assistants, all graduate scholars at the university.

The idea of an experimental school, which is to say a school given to testing new or untried pedagogical principles, was scarcely singular in the middle nineties. Parker, of course, had instituted one at Quincy and another at Chicago, and so in other places had Pestalozzi, Froebel, Herbart, and several other pedagogic messiahs. All the same, such trail blazing challenges to the established pedagogical order were still rare enough to be dismissed by the teaching generality as something of an aberration, and in this respect the Laboratory School was vouchsafed the deference of equality. Indeed, its very name bred misgivings.

Its rooms had no conventional rows of benched and muffled children, hands clasped behind their backs while they bided their turn to be examined and graded. Gone too was the familiar trafficking in the three R's, their handmaids of spelling, grammar, and chirography. In place of such schematized lessons there were scattered groups of children engaged in divers affairs. Some might be collected over books or pictures, or even a conch or a frog. Others might be making things. Still others might just be talking.

As for Miss Birch, she has become a person of amiability, imagination, and humor, and instead of drilling and policing her wards from behind her redoubtable desk, she has taken to her feet, making her rounds to mingle with the learners, assisting here, counseling there, and giving a genial heed to the ceaseless buzzing of their questions and observations. There is, of course, also the sort of learning in which the entire class takes part, but even then the artificial decorum of the traditional school is conspicuous by its absence. All in all, what would meet a visitor's eye is activity heartily executed, with talk in plenty, and now and then even an intrusive dash of laughter—a spectacle, in short, of children enjoying what they are doing.

Such a scene, needless to say, did not often evoke the viewer's critical encomium. Not understanding what it was all about, he observed it down a superior nose, predicting with great assurance that such innovations would never last, but if by some unintelligible vagary of the will of God, they nevertheless should, the republic would, as the vernacular has it, go to pot.

. . . CONTINUED

What Dewey essayed in the Laboratory School was, as he said, "to carry into effect certain principles which Froebel was perhaps the first consciously to put forth." To such an end he strove "to train children in cooperative and useful living." Like some of his discerning predecessors who had dug deep enough into the nature of the child, the Chicago professor had observed that a youngster's natural educative activity is primed with his "instinctive impulsive attitudes." Beyond the academic confines the child is forever learning; for him not to learn is well-nigh impossible. He learns, moreover, not because he is driven by his teacher, but because of his own self-generated interest. Such, in Mother Nature's scheme of things, is particularly true when Johnny is at play. Does he want to fly a kite? Or sail a boat? Or build a tree house? Then the chances are that he will apply himself unsparingly to mastering the necessary know-how. As in life, contended Dewey, so be it in school. The school should perform its art in the light of life's typical conditions.

Hence the formalized operation, then still the admired hub of a great circle of devotees, a method which, to put it in Dewey's own language, "stressed the presentation of external material," was quietly shouldered aside. It was replaced by what in the professional patter of pedagogy is spoken of as the "activity program," which in its broadest sweep seeks to squeeze forth every worthwhile element constituting the child's personal life. Then, all subjects—even the old and groggy three R's—become fitted to the child's "life activities." Thus there is educative activity all along the way, not only in the schoolroom, but in whatever the child engages. Given the boost of this adrenalin, "the entire spirit of the school," observed Dewey, "is renewed. . . .[Having] become the child's habitat," he went on, where he is elevated and enlightened "through directed living," it has ceased to hamper him with "lessons having an abstract and remote reference to some possible living to be done in the future." Like Froebel's kindergarten, it had a great chance "to be a miniature community, an embryonic society."

Although the Laboratory School gave the old-style recitation a permanent holiday from its classrooms, its founder also insisted that its role was preeminently social, and that if it were ever to be, as he hoped, an embryonic society, then its work must be grounded on the fundamental principle that education is a social process. Not only was the child to be active rather than complaisant, a doer instead of a mere listener, he was also to become socially efficient. To bring this about, the child's personal attributes were to be "organized and directed through uses made of them in keeping up the cooperative living," or to put it plainly, the school was to be a small society where, among other things, children learn to live and work together in peace and harmony. The idolization of the individual, to the tune of his unlimited self-expression, which was then the high vogue in certain ultra-progressive schools, got no quarter from the social-minded Dewey. "Deplorable egotism, cockiness, impertinence, and disregard for others" was his candid assessment of the business. Permissiveness, in short, he flatly disesteemed.

When the Laboratory School hove into view, the idea of a school especially designed to replace the old educational ways with new and presumably better ones was no longer a novelty. If Dewey's school was at odds with a worn-out pedagogy, then so had been the schools of several others, in America notably those of the estimable Colonel Parker. But in one respect Dewey made his way into a domain which none of his pioneering forerunners had penetrated. Thus, while Parker performed his feats, as had Pestalozzi and Froebel, in the mood of a romantic, even going so far as to convince himself that a child's spontaneous tendencies were the manifestation of his "inborn divinity," Dewey, deficient in his knowledge of such ghostly matters, performed his operations as a pragmatic experimentalist. What he was attempting was to probe in school practice certain hypotheses of culture, philosophy, and psychology, which were then germinating in his mind. He had set his hopes, among other things, upon integrating and reconciling what at first glance appeared to be separate and oppugnant entities, as, for example, interest and effort, school and society, individualism and collectivism, the child and the curriculum, and so on.

Such antithetical disjunctions, the professor suspected, were rooted in the intellectual and cultural clefts which had come to eminence as the nation swept from a simple agrarian, homespun economy to a commercial and industrial one, which for good or ill is currently upon us. For the school, Dewey perceived, this cultural alteration was not without significance. It was his conviction, for one thing, that the school was "the only place in which a comprehensive theory of knowledge can receive an active test . . . in the processes of education." Furthermore, when it comes right down to pedagogical tacks, the modifications in method and curriculum which Dewey was testing in his pedagogical clinic were, as he explained, "as much an effort to meet the needs of the new society that is forming as are changes in the modes of industry and commerce."

It was a bizarre jest of the gods to pit the Laboratory School against the prevailing established educational practice. Although through the years several thousand spectators came to see what Dewey and his crew were up to, what they saw was so utterly at odds with what they were used to that it aroused their distress and often their indignation. It was not only the visiting John Does who were shocked; even the mass of practicing teachers who, like most people, believed very positively in their own ideas, found Dewey's endless defiances of their sacred axioms objectionable. The professor's methods coddled the young; they failed to teach them the elementals; and they made them disdainful of authority. Nor was it long before hints began to drop that the professor bore an aversion to true American idealism—that he was even against God.

To recuperate from such murmurs, some men resort to the jug, and some to religion. Dewey resorted to his pen. He elected to parry the thrusts of his accusers in a slender book, *The School and Society,* which came out in 1899. He might as well have saved his ink and paper. A dealer primarily in ideas, Dewey lacked the power to craft his thoughts into a strong and agreeable prose, so that in large part his apologia, like the Lab School whose enterprise it undertook to explain and defend, made few converts. But as the years ticked on, Dewey's advanced thinking began to come closer to the nerve of the changing culture. In 1915 the book was tendered a second printing, and this time it received the consideration which was its rightful due.

THE PRAGMATIST

As has been said, Dewey began his philosophical cogitations in the ranks of Hegel, an idealist; then he made camp with the pragmatists, with whom, cast as an instrumentalist or an experimentalist, he identified himself for the rest of his life. Philosophically, he was of the timber of William James, the king oak, so to speak, of the pragmatic forest, and of Charles Peirce, the inventor of the word "pragmatism" and cerebrally one of the most powerful philosophers to come to growth in America.

Philosophy's concern, contended the pragmatic Dewey, is not to ascertain how we know the world, but what needs to be done to improve and control it. "Philosophy," he declared, "is a study of social conflicts," particularly those engendered by the interaction of the forces of democracy, industry, and science. Thus construed, philosophy should try "to clarify men's ideas as to the social and moral strifes of their own day," a view which was not only held, but was put into execution by no less a light than Socrates.

Unlike the older and more conventional philosophies—especially those which conduct their reflections by the artificial light of a priori assumptions—Dewey's experimentalism, both as a method and as a system of thought, abstains from the metaphysician's inquiries into questions concerning matters beyond the pale of observable human experience. Thus, instead of expending their virtuosity upon God and the universe, for example, pragmatists concentrate their intellectual pressure on the problems which consume us here below. For the pragmatist nothing on this mad and twirling globe is fixed and eternal. The universe itself is in a state of flux, and to disgorge dicta about absolute verities is not only fatuous, it is also delusive. For truth is not immutable. It is as alterable as man himself because it is, as it were, the looking glass which reflects his own slow but steady evolution.

Rejecting a supernatural world, the experimentalist argues that man must strike out on his own. To such a purpose let the philosopher, in the scientist's experimental vein, put a sharp eye and ear to the problems of man. Let him put every belief, tradition, and institution, no matter how old and hallowed, to the experimental test, with its conclusions subject at all times to verification. When philosophy thus becomes concerned in throwing light on the social plagues which currently devour the world, it does not mean, Dewey reassured his philosophical brethren, "the lowering in dignity of philosophy from a lofty plane to one of gross utilitarianism." On the contrary, it is an indication that "the prime function of philosophy is that of rationalizing the possibilities of experience, especially collective human experience."

All this, needless to say, puts a large dependence on thinking. But for Dewey thinking is not simply a high-powered cerebral activity as, say, in the case of the transported Hegel. For Dewey, to be of any tangible worth, thinking becomes significant only when it bears upon actual life situations. Thinking, said the professor, is "an instrumentality used by man in adjusting himself to the practical situations of life." Or, to say it simply, human beings think in order to live. Because of this impetus, which has its source in our biological and social makeup, it is impossible—even ridiculous—to try to interpret life in any abstract and detatched way. And since Dewey held life to be in perpetual flux, it becomes an impossibility to solve man's problems with any assurance of attaining a definitive finality, for tomorrow's problems will unquestionably vary from today's.

Addressing himself to the nature of knowledge, as has been the philosopher's wont, it seems, almost since before the time of man, Dewey believed that what we know is imbedded in what we experience, and that to be of any realistic benefit, experience must be "functional." Accordingly, the question is not so much "What is a certain thing?" as "What is it for?" Is a mine of coal a mere depository of a black or brownish-black substance? Or does it serve a purpose? And if it does, then what is it? Such queries can be answered only in the light of previous action. Action is, so to say, the mother of knowledge. The knowledge we possess, whether singly or in concert with others, is the consequence of our activities—our sweat and ache to survive. Only that which has been transfused into our being so as to enable us to grapple successfully with the demands imposed upon us by our surroundings, and by its presence to help us adapt to our wants and longings to the situation wherein we find ourselves, is really knowledge.

Like the Hellenic Sophists of long ago, the pragmatist cherishes an aversion for philosophic absolutes. All things, he says, even the good and the true, are relative. What is morally right, say, in Tomato, Arkansas, may be reprehensible in Bean City, Virginia; and what is true in our own era may be absurdly false in the sharp glare of a more sophisticated tomorrow. The pragmatic test of truth is: "Does it work in the best interests of the individual and society?" "Pragmatic," wrote Dewey in *Essays in Experimental Logic,* means "only the rule of referring all thinking, all reflective considerations, to consequences for final meaning and test." By processes which run from the searcher's groping of trial and error to the guarded procedure of the scientific method, man, interacting with the observable world, manages to achieve a hypothesis which works. So long as it continues to with-stand the assault of contravening claims, which is to say, so long as it keeps on working to our satisfaction, it remains the truth. But even as kings and messiahs come to an end, so do pragmatic truths, ceasing to work, giving way to newer ones. To paraphrase William James: We have to live by what truth we can get today, and be ready tomorrow to call it a falsehood.

DEMOCRACY AND EDUCATION

In the spring of 1904 Dewey resigned from the Laboratory School, and in the summer he entrained for New York to teach philosophy at Columbia University. For the next few years he concentrated almost solely on the reconstruction of his philosophy, with only rare divagations into education. Then, in 1916, with the appearance of *Democracy and Education,* he reen-tered the pedagogical arena. Although he had composed the volume some-what reluctantly—more, it has been said, to still his colleagues than to gratify himself—its publication brought him instantaneous critical acclaim.

For all its involved and lusterless prose, *Democracy and Education* has gone into intellectual chronicles as the profoundest and most recondite treatise on education to issue from the mind of an American. Some critics, penetrating its thicket of words and its layers of abstruseness, offered the opinion that Dewey's work was indubitably without rival, that it stood above *Emile,* and even the *Republic.* There were, of course, a number of dissenters, such as Dewey's one-time teacher, the redoubtable G. Stanley Hall, who expressed a sardonic peradventure or two. But for each such blind disdainer, there were dozens of believers.

The years have seen *Democracy and Education* become an educational classic, or semiclassic—the first and only one from this republic. In the process it has been translated into the languages of the whole civilized world, into patriarchal tongues like Chinese, Japanese, and Arabic, besides, of course, the common Western ones—a distinction which, not counting such imperishable glories of the race as *Emile* and the *Republic,* has befallen but one other educational work, namely, Jan Amos Comenius's *Orbis Pic-tus,* which made its way from its author's seventeenth-century Czech ver-nacular into some forty other languages. Whatever may be the merits of such recognition in the critical assessment of a work on pedagogy, the fact remains that in the days of its grandeur, which, speaking generally, fall between the two world wars, Dewey's book inspirited the remaking of American education.

EDUCATION IS . . . ?

In *Democracy and Education* Dewey displayed the substance of his philo-sophic convictions and the educational principles which spring therefrom.

The two, he believed, entertain a mutual relationship: the one makes us privy to desirable social values, while the other undertakes to forward them. Thus regarded, education becomes the laboratory of philosophy, which was precisely the role assigned to the Laboratory School.

True to his philosophic doctrine that eternal verities and absolutes as well as fixed and ultimate ends are purely imaginary, Dewey held that education proceeds to no final end. It is instead a continuous, endless experience, "a reconstruction," the learned professor described it, "of human experience." Its aim is welded into its process, which in its fullest exercise takes on a social coloration. Accordingly, the good school is one where the child learns by doing, especially in cooperation with others. Here, to use the speech of Dewey's devotees, the child's education is life itself. It is, as they like to say, "a cumulative growth," each state of attainment being the starting place for the one to follow. Thus viewed, the educational process is one of continuous adjustment and readjustment.

In this finespun fabric two strands show themselves. One is the psychological, which derives from the nervous system and which commands an infinite repertory of behavioral displays from, say, a simple cough to the most carefully calculated human activity ever heard of. The other is the sociological, with its array of impinging mores, traditions, institutions, and the like.

Although what a child is made to learn may be fraught with the wisdom of his elders, yet, as Parker and several others had declared, every child must be thought of as singular, a creature having his own special attributes, his own life to live, and facing a future overflowing with strange and formidable problems. With this view Dewey stood in hearty concurrence—hence his stress on the importance of arming ourselves with an understanding of the child's not-always-visible psychology. To educate him effectively, we must gain insight into his powers and capacities, his habits and interests.

Of the latter, Dewey singled out four of particular concern: the child's interest in conversation; his interest in finding out things; his interest in making things; and his interest in expressing himself artistically. Since man's stay on earth is steeped in these activities, to ignore them in a school curriculum would be highly malapropos not to say stupid. As the mainspring of the entire educational process, the youngster must learn to put a judicious eye on his cultural legacy, amending and renovating it as time flows by to accommodate his unfolding needs in a changing world. To facilitate the fulfillment of his needs, the child's creative activity must be allowed free play—not, however, Dewey cautioned, to express itself haphazardly, but under guidance. Nor should such endeavor be strictly individual; at its finest it often radiates the glow of adventure and discovery shared with one's fellows.

If historical observation is correct, the first lesson in the primer of pedagogic liberalism, be it according to Quintilian or to later reformers during succeeding centuries, is that the door to vital and effective learning swings on the hinges of interest. Without interest, learning, though possible, is full of pain and is doomed in all likelihood to early disintegration. Although the Columbia sage endorsed the proposition that interest is the indubitable prerequisite to dynamic learning, he did not hold, like some of its espousers, that interest and effort are opposing entities. Instead he regarded them as complementary, since all authentic effort issues from a deep-seated interest in something which calls for mastery or resolution—a "purposeful activity." In such instances, like true love, the interest becomes pervasive.

Summarizing the main points set forth in the last few pages, we observe that for Dewey education is actual living in the here and now, and not just making ready for living in some time to come. Education, furthermore, is the process of growing, and so long as growth continues, so unavoidably does education. Next, education is the unceasing stocktaking and reassembling of previous experience. Finally, it is a social process, and to enable it to thrive the school must be a democratic society.

THOUGHTS ON FROEBEL AND HERBART

It was wholly natural that in his contemplations on education, John Dewey should draw on the store of some of the master pedagogues who had preceded him, especially the work and thought of such figures as Froebel and Herbart. With the former, for example, Dewey agreed that the heart of education is growth, but he could find no sense in the Froebelian assertion that human growth is the inevitable unfoldment of "latent principles." Nor could the mundane Dewey endure the kindergartener's gropings in the mists of metaphysics. The German's proclivity for the mystical and symbolical, Dewey politely ignored. Froebel's "gifts," his spheres and cubes and the like, the Columbia savant sheered of their transcendental hocus-pocus, and if, in his school, some children used them nonetheless, then it was for their entertainment.

Froebel, it may be recalled, had not been insensible to life's vocations. He even celebrated them lyrically in songs about bakers, cobblers, joiners, farmers, and similar indispensable folk. Although Dewey was not averse to such activity, his concern centered in what the modern child himself might do. Accordingly, he put his stress on "social occupations of real meaning," especially those which bore on man's eternal endeavor to obtain food, shelter, and clothing. An unswerving idealist, Froebel was conscious of God's inscrutable presence in all things, and life for him represented man's slow but steady inching toward the Infinite and Eternal. For Dewey, the disavower of absolutes, such a proposition was worth no straw—indeed, neither was any other planned development toward a faraway and indiscernible end.

On several matters the two displayed a measure of accord. Both favored "creative activity," but in different ways and for different reasons; both declared for learning by doing; and both envisioned the school as a bustling community where children learn from participation in the common enterprise.

Herbart, as has been noted, was of a different kidney from his starry-eyed compatriot. The vastness of Herbart's mental bulk could not fail to impress even a man of Dewey's cerebral stature. But the Herbartian pedagogy for the most part chilled him. He found the German's method of instruction, with its finical step-by-step prearrangement of the lesson to be taught, too stiff and overly managed. The heavy-handed emphasis on formalized instruction and the concentration on imparting subject matter, Dewey gave a wide berth. On the whole, the Herbartian revelation contained more than a delicate soupçon of the very things to which Dewey objected, and the Columbia master cried down its general temper as being teacher-dominated, authoritarian, and hence undemocratic. In sum, Herbartian pedagogy, though brightened with the veneer of a new psychology and a passionate will to make it as scientific as man could make it, still left something to be desired.

On a very few principles the two professors were in agreement. Both recognized the desirability of paying heed to the role of individual differences in the furtherance of the educational process, and, with a deferential tip of the hat to Rousseau, both agreed that before undertaking to teach a child a teacher should understand his essential nature. Finally, both men invested heavily in the doctrine that for learning to function well it should be accompanied by interest. With Herbart, however, interest was simply a means to stimulate the learner's effort and once that interest had been aroused and had performed its function, it left the scene to remain in the background until it was called forth again for another lesson. For Dewey, by contrast, interest and effort were not discrete and autonomous entities; they were yoked, and without their sustained and concurrent presence, learning could not flourish.

As for their methods of teaching, Herbart and Dewey were miles apart. While the German deposited his hopes in the magic recipe of the Formal Steps, the American relied on his so-called "Act of Thought." The former places the teacher in the position of a competent bandmaster, directing the members of his troupe with a knowing hand to produce planned responses. The latter, focusing on the child as an active learner, deprives the teacher of his baton and thereby allows the learner considerable leeway for improvisation.

The essence of Dewey's method is akin to that of orderly reflection. The process is set in motion when the pupil finds himself face to face with "a genuine situation of experience." From this, if it is powerful enough to arouse his curiosity, there appears a "genuine problem." To find the answer he makes observations and collects information. From these gleanings, given time, patience, and a little luck, he will presently extract some suggestive leads and, maybe, even tenable explanations. These, declared Dewey, "he shall be responsible for developing in an orderly way." Thus armed with potential evidence, he is to put it to the trial of application in actual practice "to discover [its] validity"—or, as has been known to happen, its falsity. Disrobed of all expository particulars, the Dewey Act of Thought displays five identifying hallmarks: (1) activity, (2) problem, (3) data, (4) hypothesis, (5) testing.

No matter how wide the range of their respective usefulness, the two methods render their best service in different fields. The Herbartian procedure lends itself most suitably to the teaching of language, literature, and history, while Dewey's method is superior in the sciences and the industrial arts—wherever the approach to learning is not primarily contingent upon mastering the contents of books, but on the solution of problems.

Although it may be an observation of no importance, the fact remains that in teaching his own classes the Columbia professor did not employ the method he had so diligently wrought; instead, he lectured.

FINALE

Despite the robust critical acceptance of *Democracy and Education,* the book's initial impact on America's schools was almost zero. Dewey's train of thought baffled most Americans, and his fogbound and tortuous diction left them stranded. What the professor obviously needed was someone to make his thinking intelligible to others, and, if possible, someone to demonstrate its virtues in actual practice. As things turned out, both appeared. By 1918, William Kilpatrick was unriddling the Dewey arcanum before his gigantic classes at Columbia's Teachers College, animating it in the process with an exuberance of spirit it had never known, and as a result, like an irresistible John the Baptist, he made converts by the hundreds. At Ohio State, meanwhile, Boyd Bode was rendering a somewhat similar service. From the lecture halls of these wizards, and others not unlike them, flowed an ever-lengthening stream of teachers who were not only on an intimate footing with the Dewey canon, but who were also prepared to translate it into practice, especially in the lower branches of learning.

Meanwhile, here and there some of the progressives had begun to season their pedagogy with some of Dewey's recommended extracts. In the twenties, when the Progressive Education Association made its advent, the names of Charles Eliot, a former Harvard president, and John Dewey were blazoned on its official propaganda as the society's honorary grand archons. During the years that followed, the Dewey seedling grew, and though the philosopher had never intended his views to root deep and firm, time saw them do just that.

The progressives framed no particular philosophy of their own, and though they honored and admired the Columbia scholar, in practice they sometimes did violence to his thinking. From its beginnings, progressive education, which in the general opinion was all too often synonymous with Dewey, was under the heel of criticism, not only from such thinkers as William Randolph Hearst and the departed Senator Joseph McCarthy, but from such high-minded teachers of teachers as Isaac Leon Kandel, Herman Harrell Horne, and William Chandler Bagley and his banner-carriers, the essentialists, who inveighed against what they designated the "debilitating" effects of the "new education."

For all his critical frowns, however, Bagley entertained a high regard for Dewey, and in the essentialist's manifesto he cited several educational issues in which the two men saw eye to eye. So well disposed, in fact, was Bagley toward his Columbia *frater in facultate,* that he insisted on calling Dewey "the present educational leader" on the pedagogical landscape—to the dismay of some of the less tolerant essentialists. What Bagley was gunning for was not Dewey, but the progressive extremists—or as some of their critics called them, the "lunatic fringe." Supplementing the aforesaid were the scholastic sharpshooters of Mother Church and the neoscholastics, led by Robert Maynard Hutchins, at that time the head of the University of Chicago.

The attack on the progressives is not without a tinge of humor. Surely it seems not a little ironic that when the tide against progressivism raged at flood height some of its best friends became its most eager denouncers. They exercised themselves especially on John Dewey, that bemuser of honest and well-meaning Americans. Although more than once the professor had declared against some of the more unseemly grotesqueries of progressive education, particularly in 1938 in his *Experience and Education,* the scapegoat hunters paid no heed. Dewey, in a word, was a progressive, the father of America's new education, and that education had become so sadly enfeebled that it enabled the Russians to get the jump on us in the space race.

Since those early post-Sputnik years, many earnest Americans have been disturbed by sober second thoughts. Was progressive education totally bad? Were its assumptions and aspirations so many clouds of perfumed mist? And were its prime intellectual movers, its Bode, Kilpatrick, and especially Dewey, so many spinners of gossamer utopias? The judgment is not yet in, but unquestionably the critical balance is in the process of being redressed. Directly, through his own reflection and the straining of his findings through the pragmatic filter of workability, and indirectly through the devoted labor of countless educators who did him honor, John Dewey, say what one will, did more than any other American to give the native education a new meaning and direction. Embracing Parker's contention that the school should be a live and active community, Dewey fondled the notion in its beginnings and guided it, as it took on form and strength, to a rich maturity. He not only supported the principle of growth; he also penetrated its nature better than any of his predecessors and was therefore able to offer the world a better understanding of the conditions essential to its highest realization.

A connoisseur of the deed, like Rousseau, Pestalozzi, and Froebel— and let us not pass Parker by—Dewey was the first to set school life and its program in the operational psychology of action. The harnessing of "problem-solving thinking," though grantedly beset by serious shortcomings even in the eyes of some of its most spirited admirers, has nevertheless withstood the bombs and grenades of its most hostile critics. In the same way, the Fates visited their felicity on Dewey when he made man's occupations the basis for determining what is to be studied, a principle which has been granted recognition in numerous seminaries of learning here and across the sea. Nor has Dewey's method of teaching been immune to critical hospitality. Its hand is visible not only in the decline and fall of the atrophic formal recitation (which had served time enough to be paroled long ago, Dewey or no Dewey), but in its replacement here and there with methods more in key with the Dewey orchestration, as—to submit but one example—the project method.

Dewey's pedagogy has come down the road of time as the "democratic philosophy of education." Underscoring that philosophy was its author's belief that democracy is not merely a political contrivance, but a way of living in which man's intelligence and imagination are made to serve in the furtherance of human freedom.

BIBLIOGRAPHICAL NOTE

The most useful works on the ideas explored in the foregoing pages are, of course, the writings of their holders. They are the fountainheads and therefore the primary authorities. Copious reference to them has been made in the body of this volume, and there is not much to be gained by putting them on parade as a grand finale. Such books should be read when they will best serve the student, which is to say when their contents come under scrutiny in the text itself.

Not a few of these writings are now classics, and most libraries of any size have made it a point to store at least a representative number of them in their stacks. As classics, they have also undergone translation aplenty, and over the years some have gone through many editions, appearing both in hard cover and in paperback. For the student who is bent on making a firsthand acquaintance with the grandmasters themselves, there is thus every chance of success.

When times in our republic were flush, and there was an endless supply of almost everything, the literati and their publishers were not bedeviled, as they are now, by shortages and ballooning costs. In consequence, there was always space in a work such as this for an extended, annotated bibliography. Historians and jurisconsults were its special devotees, and it became their manner to bring their learned compositions to a close with a vast bibliographic flourish. At their best, such splurges strove to bring to students, especially those with an eye on the doctoral robe, an array of scholarly aid and counsel. Not infrequently, of course, they were also a powerful tonic to their inaugurator's ego.

Thus the established academic practice. It is a meritorious practice, though if the truth be told it was sometimes overdone. Nevertheless, I have tendered it my fealty, and on occasion I have even openly engaged in it. Witness for example, the bibliographic commentary in my *An Educational History of the Western World,* pages 522–530, published in its second edition in 1972 by the McGraw-Hill Book Company, and the expansive spread of fifty-seven pages in *An Educational History of the American People,* issued in its second incarnation by the same house in 1967.

Through the bibliographic convention is laudable, the exigencies of ecology, economics, and patriotism forbid me at this time to give it the usual heed. Therefore, for supplementary rumination, I politely direct the reader to the above-mentioned compilations. Numerous libraries have been hospitable to their presence, and they are not difficult to come by. The only additions I would make at this time are three, which, for some errant reason, eluded me earlier. They are: Henri-Irénée Marrou's *A History of Education in Antiquity* (translated from French by George Lamb, and put out by Sheed and Ward, New York, 1956); Micheline and Marie Sauvage's *Socrates and the Conscience of Man* (translated from French by Patrick Hepburne-Scott, and published by Harper and Brothers in 1960); and the *New Catholic Encyclopedia* (issued in 1967 by the McGraw-Hill Book Company).

Index